The Cooper Hill Stylebook

A guide to writing and revision

Gregory Heyworth

Rosette Liberman

Cooper Hill Press
American Language Sourcebooks
New Haven

Cover design: Gregory Heyworth, Christine Narain
Technical supervision: Michael Muzzie, Princeton University
Typesetting: Ivor Humphreys, Good Imprint, East Grinstead, Sussex, UK

Manufactured in the United States of America.
Library of Congress Control Number: 2001091157

First edition, 2000
Published under the title *The Writing and Revision Stylebook*

Second edition, 2005
Published under the title *The Cooper Hill Stylebook, a guide to writing and revision*

ISBN 0–9701113–1–2

Address inquiries to
Cooper Hill Press
1440 Whalley Avenue, #232
New Haven, CT 06515-1144

Tel./fax (203) 387–7236
Internet address *www.cooperhill.com*

ACKNOWLEDGMENTS
To our students and colleagues we owe a debt of gratitude for
their expertise and advice on various matters of language. Special
thanks to David Owens for his insights on dangling adverbs.

Permissions and copyrights are on page 444.

How to use this book

To the writer

Taking time to scrutinize and revise your writing is an essential part of learning to write well. Use *The Stylebook* either as a writing tutorial or as a reference book to develop habits of clear expression, clear reasoning, faultless grammar, and to produce correctly documented research papers.

As a guide to proofreading your own work

Before submitting an essay, leave ample time to go over your essay in hard copy. First, proofread for errors using the shorthand symbols and methods in *Proofreading*. Next, edit for structure and content using the *Checklist for Evaluating the Essay*. Rewrite as necessary.

As a guide to rewriting a corrected essay

Upon receiving a corrected essay from your instructor, you will find two types of comments: *marginal comments* dealing with the details or mechanics of your writing and *final comments* at the end of the essay dealing with the content, structure, and cogency of your argument.

If the instructor is using the *Stylebook* as a correction instrument, you will find algebraic notes (e.g., *22b*) in your margins next to the problem sentence. Proceed to the appropriate section in the *Stylebook* and use the explanations, examples and exercises to correct the sentence next to which you find the algebraic note. Compare your answers to those at the end of each chapter. Remember, each answer in the book has a reasonable explanation.

If the instructor is not using the *Stylebook*'s algebraic notes, he or she will make marginal notes — often abbreviations — that describe a type of error. First, go to the *Quick Key to Marginal Comments* inside the front cover to locate the appropriate marginal comment or abbreviation. Next, the *Quick Key* menu will direct you to a general explanation in the *Marginal Abbreviations and Comments* section. Each of these explanations has a cross-reference to more specific, in-depth information.

Often, marginal notes or final comments will mention specific types of problems. You can easily find these problems either by using the *Correction Key* at the front of the book, or the *Index* at the back.

As a reference guide or writing tutorial
While writing a first or second draft, you may have a question of grammar, punctuation, spelling, or documentation. Consult the *Index* for the specific problem, or the *Grammar, Punctuation; Spelling, Capitalization and Abbreviation*; or *Quotations and Documentation* sections as appropriate and use the exercises and explained answers.

Frequently, writers find themselves in a rut in the argument. Either it is too complex and confusing, or the ideas seem unclear or awkward on paper. For problems of clarity, complexity, and heaviness of language, consult the *Structure and Sense* section of the *Stylebook*. For problems with the effectiveness of the argument, look at *Rhetorical Fallacies* or *Rhetorical Figures*.

To the instructor

The Stylebook is a time-saving tool for experienced teachers, and an effective professional guide for new teachers and for teaching assistants. In addition to being a textbook in its own right, it serves as an effective supplement to any English course.

To reduce correcting time
Most correction time is taken up in the repetitive task of writing the same comments for the same types of mistakes over and over. Instead, indicate the problem by using the algebraic number corresponding to the problem found in the *Stylebook's Correction Key*. This shorthand cuts correction time in half. After correcting several sets of class essays, most people find that they have memorized the numbers to which they habitually refer. To that end, the *Correction Key* is conveniently placed at the front of the book for easy reference. Those who like to use abbreviations as their comments can refer to the *Quick Key to Marginal Comments* on the inside of the front cover in addition to using the *Correction Key*.

To direct students' attention to specific errors
The benefit of using the *Quick Key* and the *Correction Key* to refer to errors is that the topics listed target the most frequent errors made by students in specific terms, not as general categories. By jotting down a number or an abbreviation, teachers can direct their students to the exact problem that needs revision, not to a vague approximation. Students directed to the *Marginal Abbreviations and Comments* section will find cross-references to in-depth entries in the numbered body of the text.

To use The Stylebook as a programmed tutor
A teacher can confidently assign an independent rewrite of an essay knowing that each error and its remedies are explained in clear, succinct, classroom-tested language that avoids technical terms as far as possible. Extensive exercises for practice are available at the end of each section. Answers to the exercises and explanations of the answers are located at the end of each chapter. The detailed *Index* is another aid to students offering them a menu of the specific aspects of each entry instead of just a general page reference. These resources eliminate the need for conferences to explain the written comments, and turn students into self-teachers.

To structure group and peer correcting in class
The *Stylebook* is a useful instrument for independent group work in class where students who need practice on the same types of errors can work together on the relevant explanations and exercises, then check the answers and study the reasons behind them. Students tend to find this exercise enjoyable and profitable. Equally useful for peer correcting is the *Checklist for Evaluating the Essay.*

To service various student levels
The *Stylebook* is a flexible tool. Teachers at the university and secondary school levels can use as much or as little of it as they wish in their classroom teaching. They can address simple problems in agreement or sophisticated problems in the uses of the subjunctive. The extensive chapter on *Rhetorical fallacies* can serve as a coursebook in itself on persuasion, propaganda, and misleading reasoning by public personalities and by the media.

To provide understanding and mastery of documentation
Teachers can assign research papers confident that the documentation section is self-explanatory. Preceding the specific examples is a basic model and an explanation of the reasonable variations. The

presentation de-mythologizes documentation and provides students with the confidence to adapt citation forms to their needs. This chapter also includes the latest documentation styles for electronic sources that show the print model and its electronic variation.

Grammar

Correction Key

Correction Key

Correction Key

Correction Key

Usage

Structure and Sense

Correction Key

Rhetorical Fallacies

Correction Key

Rhetorical Figures

Spelling, Capitalization, Abbreviations

Correction Key

Correction Key

Correction Key

Correction Key

74 Works Cited / bibliography 391

Glossary 407

Index 417

Proofreading

Proofreading marks

What is the purpose of proofreading marks?

Proofreading marks are a shorthand language editors use to suggest simple changes in the content, formatting, structure, spelling and punctuation of a piece of writing. Rather than clutter the margins with explanations, it is clearer to mark the text itself with symbols leaving the margins free for other comments. Professional proof-readers use a wide variety of technical marks, often specialized by subject. The ones given here are the most common. Knowing them will enable you both to decipher someone else's revisions of your writing and to revise your own work more efficiently.

Why use proofreading marks on hard copy rather than making changes directly on the computer?

Most writing today is done on computers and aided by the latest *spell-* and grammarchecks. Revisions, however, should always be made *first on hardcopy*. There are several reasons for editing on hardcopy. First, errors show up more clearly on paper than on the screen where the text moves and words are more jagged and difficult to read. Second, proofing hardcopy allows the editor to sug-gest changes and the reader the chance to consider them and how they affect the essay *before* they are made.

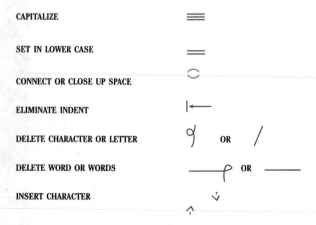

CAPITALIZE	≡
SET IN LOWER CASE	=
CONNECT OR CLOSE UP SPACE	⌒
ELIMINATE INDENT	⊢—
DELETE CHARACTER OR LETTER	℘ OR /
DELETE WORD OR WORDS	—℘ OR ——
INSERT CHARACTER	⌄ / ∧

INSERT LETTER, WORD, OR PHRASE	∧
INSERT BLOCK OF TEXT (ON BACK OF PAGE)	[A] ∧
MOVE	⌒⌐
PARAGRAPH OR INDENT	¶
TRANSPOSE LETTER	∿
TRANSPOSE WORD	⎣⎤
RESTORE DELETED WORD OR FORMAT	*Stet.*

LINCOLN'S Gettysburg Address

Four score and seven years ago our fathers brought

fourth on this Continent of North America a new nation

conceived in liberty and dedicated to the proposition
stet.

that all men are created equal. We are now engaged in

a great Civil War testing whether that nation can long
[A]

endure.

A: , or any nation so conceived and so dedicated,

We have met on a great battlefield of that
are

war; we have come to dedicate a portion of it as a
that field

final resting place for those who here have given their
stet. *gave*

lives that that nation might live. It is altogether

fitting and proper that we should do this. But in a

larger sense, we cannot dedicate — we cannot -

consecrate — we can◯not hallow — this ground. The [B]

world will little note/

> B: The brave men, living and dead, who struggled here, have consecrated it far beyond our poor power to add or detract.

~~nor long remember~~, what we say here, but it can never

forget what has been done here. It is for us, the liv-

ing, rather, to be work dedicated here to the great [C]

> C: the unfinished work which they who fought here have thus far so nobly advanced. It is rather for us to be here dedicated to

task
~~talk~~ remaining before us — that from these honoured
dead
~~bones~~ we take increased devotion to that cause (which)

they gave the last full measure of devotion (for)— that

we now highly resolve that these dead men shall not

have died in vain — that this nation‸under god, shall

have a new birth of freedom — and *that* government of the

people, by the people, for the people, shall not per-

ish from the earth.

LINCOLN'S GETTYSBURG ADDRESS

Fourscore and seven years ago our fathers brought
forth on this continent a new nation conceived in
liberty and dedicated to the proposition that all men
are created equal. Now we are engaged in a great civil
war testing whether that nation, or any nation so
conceived and so dedicated, can long endure. We are
met on a great battlefield of that war. We have come
to dedicate a portion of that field as a final resting place for those who here gave their lives that
that nation might live. It is altogether fitting and
proper that we should do this. But, in a larger sense,
we cannot dedicate — we cannot consecrate — we cannot
hallow — this ground. The brave men, living and dead,

who struggled here, have consecrated it far above our poor power to add or detract. The world will little note what we say here, but it can never forget what they did here. It is for us the living, rather, to be dedicated here to the unfinished work which they who fought here have thus far so nobly advanced. It is rather for us to be here dedicated to the great task remaining before us, — that from these honored dead we take increased devotion to that cause for which they gave the last full measure of devotion — that this nation, under God, shall have a new birth of freedom — and that government of the people, by the people, for the people, shall not perish from the earth.

Checklist for evaluating an essay

What makes an essay good?

A good essay accomplishes two tasks: it takes original and insightful ideas and delivers them in a clear, well-organized package. While the quality of insight cannot be easily quantified, the quality of expression can. The following checklist is designed to question how effectively an essay communicates its ideas by evaluating how it is structured.

Is there a title, and is it specific enough?

A title is a contract with the reader. It makes a promise to explain some aspect of a topic which it must fulfill. Too large or vague a scope, and the essay will fall short of its promised goal and be judged accordingly. The title first identifies a topic, then addresses a specific problem related to it.

TOPIC   Genetically modified food

ISSUE   Coverage in the media

The two propositions can be combined in several ways:

BY *AND/OR*   *Genetically Modified Food and the Objectivity of the Press*

BY A COLON   *'Frankenstein' Food: Media Metaphors in the Service of Hard Science*

Finally, the title may be phrased as either a declarative statement as above or as a question.

QUESTION   *Genetically Modified Food: Feeding the Frenzy or Informing the Public?*

Does the introduction frame a problem and does it organize a response?

An introduction has two objectives. First, it must frame the topic stated in the title in terms of a problem. Second, it must indicate the perspectives from which the writer will approach the problem. That is to say, it breaks the topic up into categories to be developed in subsequent paragraphs. The example below omits the first and the last sentences of the introduction.

PROBLEM   Admittedly, the press is faced with the dilemma of presenting a story that is both highly compelling and deeply complex. Its readership deserves to be informed but, for the most part, does not possess the scientific background to appreciate the issue's finer details. Newspapers have adopted several strategies

CATEGORIES   for covering this and similar stories. Some have chosen to discuss genetically modified food by analogy to popular science

DEVELOPED   fiction, making the subject more accessible but neglecting science

IN THE BODY   fact. Others have treated the story primarily as a political issue, discussing its repercussions in a forum of politicians, lobbyists and other interested non-scientists. The minority has attempted to explain the problem scientifically in a series of articles enlisting the expert scientists on both sides of the issue.

Do the body paragraphs explain and support the categories?

Not all paragraphs serve the same function. Some redirect the argument or provide transitions from one point to the next. Analytical paragraphs, however, perform four tasks. (1) They *state* a category to be discussed; (2) they *define* and *explain* the particular problems or questions it raises; (3) they *support* the writer's claims with facts, quotations, and reasoning; (4) they *relate* their support to the larger problem of the essay.

STATE   *The Daily Mirror* is among those newspapers that chose to present the story by analogy to science fiction. In an article entitled "Frankenstein Food At Large in the Supermarket" (April 12, 1999),

EXPLAIN   *The Daily Mirror* focuses not on the subject itself but on the perception of the subject, not on substance but on image. "The danger of Frankenstein food," writes the journalist, "is that scientists

SUPPORT   cannot predict all its consequences. Once created, it is like an unchained monster with a will of its own." Notice how the "danger" is defined not by what we do know but what do not know.

RELATE   Genetically modified food is a "monster" not because it is unhealthful but because it has "a will of its own," whatever that may mean.

Does the conclusion return to the problem raised in the introduction?

A conclusion usually comments on or responds to the problem raised in the introduction in light of the argument and evidence developed over the course of the essay. A good conclusion always conveys the impression that the original idea has evolved in the hands of the writer into something new and noteworthy.

> Thus, the consequence of diverting attention from the subject to the public perception of that subject (or rather to the media's projection of what the public perception might be) is the loss of the reader's confidence in all authority, including that of the press. Genetically modified food has mutated from a health question into a media question; the original controversy has been all but forgotten.

Marginal Comments

Marginal comments

What are marginal comments?

Marginal comments are the corrections that instructors write on essays. The list below explains and illustrates the typical, generic comments that appear on most papers. Each comment is cross-referenced to other relevant sections of the *Stylebook* that treat individual problems in greater depth.

The examples that illustrate each of the comments below are taken from the *Model essay with revisions* that appears in full at the end of this section. The essay and its extracts come from a real student essay selected for its range of errors *not* for its views. Its use here should not be considered as a political endorsement. A revised version of the essay immediately follows the draft.

arg. (argument), false conc. (false conclusion)

Arguments cannot persuade if they don't make sense. Their conclusions must be based on reason and deduction rather than on mere opinion. Arguments must proceed step-by-step toward a conclusion, without unspoken assumptions or logical jumps. In general, see §40–45 *Rhetorical fallacies*.

Consider the example below in which the writer argues that embarrassing the United States is grounds for impeaching a president.

UNPERSUASIVE   Kenneth Starr argued that the President should be impeached because he has been an embarrassment to the United States.

The argument is unconvincing because it disregards the constitutional grounds for impeaching the President of the United States: *high crimes and misdemeanors*, not *embarrassment.*

REVISED   Kenneth Starr argued that the President should be impeached because *he committed high crimes and misdemeanors.*

(See specifically §40c *Argument to shame*, §42b *Non sequitur.*)

awk. (awkward)

Awkward is a common editorial comment on the way an idea is expressed. When writers attempt to use elevated vocabulary or complicated diction, they may lack the necessary knowledge to apply it correctly. Awkwardness is a frequent result of *heavy language*. In general, see §34 *Rewriting heavy language* and §33 *Wordiness and word order.*

In the example below, the writer uses too many words, and needless repetition to express a relatively simple thought.

WORDY/
REDUNDANT
When they wrote the Constitution for us to live by, they wrote it in such a way that interpretations were possible based on the given time and situation.

REVISED
The language of the Constitution provides a degree of flexibility that allows it to be interpreted in accordance with previously unforeseen attitudes and circumstances.

(See specifically §36a *Redundancy.*)

cliché

Strive for original ideas expressed in an original way. Clichés do the opposite. They are timeworn expressions that have lost their meaning from overuse. In general see §22 *Non-standard speech.*

CLICHE
In his campaign speeches, the politician has lied time and time again

REVISED
In his campaign speeches, the politician has lied *repeatedly.*

(See specifically §22b *Clichés.*)

colloq. (colloquialism)

Colloquial speech is informal. It uses language in non-standard ways. Unlike clichés, colloquialisms may be lively and colorful. They are unreliable vehicles for serious ideas, however, because their meanings are imprecise and inconsistent. In general see §22 *Non-standard speech.*

COLLOQUIAL
The House Republican leadership played hardball and drove directly for impeachment.

REVISED The House Republican leadership *refused to compromise, guiding the proceedings toward impeachment.*

(See specifically §22a *Slang and colloquialisms.*)

cont. (contradiction)

An internal contradiction is a rhetorical problem. Here, the claims of two statements or paragraphs clash with each other. The contradictions may also occur between a claim and its explanation, or between a claim and its supporting facts or quotations. Always reread your essay critically to be sure that you are not contradicting yourself. The contradiction in the example below occurs because there is no definition of *a good president.* See in general §37 *Contradictions in terms.*

CONTRADICTORY Peruvians have called President Fujimori a corrupt and dictatorial person but a good president.

REVISED Peruvians have criticized President Fujimori's actions as corrupt and dictatorial. *However, even his harshest critics admit that he guided Peru to relative economic prosperity.*

This revision also avoids *argument against the person* (*ad hominem*) by criticizing the behavior instead of the person.

(See specifically §19b *Specific instead of general terms,* §35 *Assertions and illustrations.*)

def. (define)

Abstract concepts and terms must be defined to avoid miscommunication between writers and their readers. These cannot be definitions simply copied from a dictionary. Definitions must make words and ideas clear and meaningful *within the sense of the essay.* They must be specifically relevant to the writer's topic and viewpoint. See in general §20 *Definitions and examples.*

NON-DEFINING Impeachment is a legal way for America to overthrow its leaders.

This statement does *not* tell us what impeachment *is.* It tells us what impeachment *does,* in a vague, general way which not informative.

REVISED　　　　The U.S. Constitution defines impeachment as the accusation brought against civil servants for high crimes and
misdemeanors.[1]

(See specifically §41b *Argument by definition.*)

exag. (exaggeration), hyp. (hyperbole), overstatement

Overstatement or exaggeration is a *logical fallacy*. It makes an
assertion that lacks adequate evidence. An overstatement is
incorrect not because its premise is false, but because it goes too far
in its claims. In general, see §45g *Overstatement* and §47a *Hyperbole.*

EXAGGERATED　　　By announcing that the U.S. will do whatever is
necessary to defend Taiwan, President Bush destroyed
America's relationship with mainland China.

REVISED　　　　By announcing that the U.S. will do whatever is
necessary to defend Taiwan, President Bush *antagonized
mainland China and undermined America's policy of constructive ambiguity.*

(See specifically §42a *If...then,* §44b *Loaded terminology,* §45e
Generalization, §35 *Assertions and illustrations,* §40a *Ad hominem.*)

exp? (explain), inc. (incomplete thought), why?

To be comprehensible, terms must be defined, and ideas must be
clearly explained and supported with reasoning, evidence,
examples. Editorial comments such as *explain, define, incomplete
thought, why* are asking for elaboration and for a more complete
definition of terms. See in general §28 *Incomplete and self-evident
thoughts.*

A useful technique for elaborating is to ask yourself three
important questions about your idea:

1. *How* does my idea work?
2. *Why* does it work in this way?
3. *So what* if it works in this way? What are its implications and
   ramifications?

In the example below, *excuse* must defined or clarified by
completing the thought: otherwise the reader is left wondering,
"What kind of excuse? Excuse for what?"

INCOMPLETE   For many witch hunters in the Massachusetts Bay colony, accusing a neighbor of witchcraft was just an excuse.

REVISED   For many witch hunters in the Massachusetts Bay colony, accusing a neighbor of witchcraft was *merely a pretext for acquiring his property.*

(See specifically §20 *Definitions and examples,* §27 *Correct and complete comparisons.*)

fact? (factual error), wrong, no!

Factual errors are mistakes in information: names, dates, places, titles, plot or character details, quotations, and the like. Factual errors rob your work of credibility and authority. In the example below, the writer incorrectly states that the courts, rather than the House of Representatives, impeach the President. For using supporting material effectively see in general §65 *Plagiarizing and documenting)*

FACTUAL
ERROR   The Founders of the Constitution left it up to the courts whether one is to be impeached.

REVISED   The writers of the Constitution *accorded the power of impeachment to the House of Representatives.*

(See specifically §66 *Using quotations effectively.*)

frag. (fragment)

A fragment is an incomplete thought masquerading as a sentence. Sometimes it is a phrase, at other times a subordinate clause. A fragment is caused by an error in punctuation. Correct fragments by absorbing them into adjacent sentences. In general, see §29 *Fragments.*

FRAGMENT   Cigarette manufacturers claim the right to advertise on billboards near schools. Because of their right to free expression.

REVISED   Cigarette manufacturers claim the right to advertise on billboards near schools because of their right to free expression.

(See specifically §24a *Eliminate* being that, seeing that.)

gen. (generalization)

A generalization is a way to give your opinion the appearance of fact. Think of a generalization as a type of exaggeration. Whether it insults or praises, it is often inaccurate. Statistics, for example, are common generalizations.

The danger in a generalization is that what is true in *most* cases may not hold true in *all* cases. Often generalizations use a single example to prove a universal rule, but fail to account for conflicting examples. In order to be valid, generalizations need, at the very least, to be defended or substantiated by evidence cited in the text. See in general §35 *Assertions and illustrations*, §45e *Generalization*, and §45f *Oversimplification*.

UNSUBSTANTIATED   Top grades in high schools make any college accessible to an applicant, and later ensure an enjoyable and highly paid job.

This statement generalizes about admission to college without citing any authoritative support: no facts, no quotations. Its claims are optimistic without any reservations. It fails to mention the role played by standardized test scores and recommendations, for example. It fails to impress its readers.

REVISED   Top grades in high school make many colleges accessible to an applicant, and later can help her land an enjoyable and highly paid job. *According to a recent Gallup Poll, an overwhelming 73% of 3600 employers preferred to hire managers who had maintained an excellent academic record throughout high school and college.*

(See specifically §44b *Loaded terminology*.)

good, nice, ok, √, !

These comments show approval of a strong point, vivid image, apt observation etc. Often good ideas that also show rhetorical balance earn the most enthusiastic of these comments.

➤ He magnified *a personal dilemma* into *a national catastrophe*.

jarg. (jargon)

Jargon is the technical vocabulary of particular professions or disciplines. Even when it filters into the general vocabulary, it is often not comprehensible. Frequently jargon turns a noun into an adjective by adding to it the suffix -*wise*. Clear writing avoids jargon because, like colloquialisms, its definitions are inconsistent. The example below contains jargon in addition to colloquialisms. See §22c *Jargon.*

JARGON   Crimewise, the student who brought a loaded gun to school put his foot in it when he took the plunge, and now he must face the music.

REVISED   When the student *decided to bring a loaded gun to school, he chose to risk suffering his current hardships.* Now he must *accept the consequences of his illegal act.*

(See specifically §39a *Mixed metaphors that confuse meaning.*)

mod. (modifier problem), misp. mod. (misplaced modifier), dang. mod. (dangling modifier)

A misplaced modifier is too far from the word or words it describes, and seems to describe the wrong expression. A dangling modifier describes something that is not actually in the sentence. Other modifier problems can occur as well. The example below contains a *dangling modifier.* The phrase *neglecting his presidential duties in combination with his commission of perjury* describes a person who is missing from the sentence.

DANGLING
MODIFIER   Neglecting his presidential duties in combination with his commission of perjury, Congress had no choice other than impeachment.

REVISED   By neglecting his presidential duties and committing perjury, *President Clinton* left Congress no choice but impeachment.

(See §9 *Placement of modifiers.*)

pron. ref. (pronoun reference)

A pronoun that refers to a preceding word (*antecedent*) must be in the same *number* (*singular,* or *plural*) and the same *person* as the antecedent. A pronoun like *this*, or *it* is too general to refer to a preceding idea. Use it as an adjective instead — e.g., *this concept, this procedure* etc. See in general §3 *Ambiguous or doubtful references*.

PRONOUN REF. (*THIS*)	In some families, when a person reaches his thirties, insulin plugs can start to metabolize the glucose in the body. The reason for *this* is that the cells have ceased to function normally.
REVISED	In some families, when a person reaches his thirties, insulin plugs can start to metabolize the glucose in the body. The reason for *this change* is that the cells have ceased to function normally.
PRONOUN REF. (*THEY*)	Their message is that if an important person breaks the law, they don't have to pay any penalty.
REVISED	Their message is that if an important person breaks the law, *he* doesn't have to pay any penalty.

(See specifically §3b *Errors with they,* and §3c *Errors with* this *and* it.)

punct. (punctuation)

Writing with incorrect punctuation is like driving without road signs or traffic lights, or, worse still, with the wrong signs and lights. Mispunctuated writing is disorienting and misleading. Correct punctuation divides a sentence into groups of words that fit together logically. It signals when a person is speaking and for how long, when a sentence begins and ends, whether the sentence is a question or a statement. Below is a brief checklist of four commonly misused punctuation marks.

COMMAS
◆ Separate complete thoughts (independent clauses) in a sentence to prevent a run-on sentence
◆ Set apart introductory material
◆ Set apart incidental information
◆ Indicate the person being addressed
◆ Introduce dialogue informally
◆ Separate items in a list
◆ Separate repeated or similar words that may create confusion

(See specifically §53 *Commas* for examples and detailed explanations.)

SEMICOLONS AND COLONS separate *complete thoughts* and are used in certain lists. Colons also introduce quotations and salutations, and are used in citations.

(See specifically §54 *Semicolons* and §55 *Colons* for examples and detailed explanations.)

APOSTROPHES indicate possession, contraction, and sometimes pluralization of words used as words, abbreviations, letters, numbers, and signs.

(See specifically §56 *Apostrophes* for examples and detailed explanations. See also §57 *Parentheses*, §58 *Brackets*, §59 *Dashes*, §60 *Hyphens*, §61 *Italics*, §62 *Quotation Marks*.)

ref. (reference), cit. (citation)

References and citations indicate the *source* of ideas and quotations. They credit the words and ideas of others. They avoid plagiarism. In the sentence fragment below, the writer fails to cite the source of his quotation. In general, see §65 *Plagiarizing and documenting*.

NO CITATION   Nightmares are fairly common among *two* and three-year olds because "this is the age when children begin to suffer separation anxiety."

This statement may be valid, but it is unpersuasive without supporting citations.

REVISED   Nightmares are fairly common among *two* and three-year olds. According to psychologist Emma Brodsky: "This is the age when children begin to suffer separation anxiety."[5]

(See §62 *Quotation marks*, §63 *Punctuating and capitalizing with quotations*, §64 *Punctuating a quotation-within-a-quotation*, §65 *Plagiarizing and documenting*, §66 *Using quotations effectively*, §68 *Quoting prose*.)

rel. (relevance)

Irrelevancy is a problem in the logic of your argument. Your reader feels that the example or discussion does not develop the main idea of your essay adequately, or diverts attention from important issues to trivial ones.

To identify irrelevancies, reread the topic sentence of your paragraph and review your title and introduction. This review will refocus you on the paragraph's or essay's claims and objectives. Compare these claims and objectives with the passage in question. Often, adding an explanatory transition makes an apparently irrelevant statement, relevant to the context. In the example below, the irrelevancy is italicized.

IRRELEVANT Immigrants from the former Soviet Union were astonished by the American right to privacy. *For example, a person who works as a custodian in a high school may purchase a large and expensive house.*

The example seems irrelevant because an explanatory transition is missing.

REVISED Immigrants from the former Soviet Union were astonished by the American right to privacy. In their native land, personal expenditures were subject to government scrutiny. By contrast in America, a family's expenditures are a private matter. For example, a person who works as a custodian in a high school may purchase a large and expensive house without asking anyone for permission.

(See specifically §42b *Non sequitur*, §43c *Irrelevancy*, §43d *Red herring*, §30 *Transitions*.)

r-o (run-on)

A run-on happens when two or more independent clauses do not have adequate punctuation between them. Each independent clause is a complete idea and should be separated by punctuation from other complete ideas. The type of punctuation depends on how closely these complete ideas are related to each other.

- ◆ The closest connection requires a comma and conjunction.
- ◆ A more distant connection requires either a semicolon (;) or a colon (:).
- ◆ The most distant connection calls for a period, or even a new paragraph.

The example below requires a comma before the conjunction *and*.

RUN-ON
Teenage girls who become bulemic see an endless parade of beautiful models and they feel that they too are expected to look like a Hollywood creation.

REVISED
Teenage girls who become bulemic see an endless parade of beautiful models, and they feel that they too are expected to look like a Hollywood creation.

(See specifically §53a *Avoid run-on sentences and comma splices*, §54 *Semicolon*, and §55 *Colon*.)

self–evid. (self–evident), truism, obv. (obvious)

Self-evident statements, or truisms, are arguments so obviously true that they don't need proving or often even mentioning. Some statements are so obvious that they sound absurd when they are said. See in general §28b *Eliminate self-evident statements*.

- ◆ Comedies are comic because they make us laugh.
- ◆ People are people.
- ◆ Every religion has its beliefs.

In the example below, the authorship of the Warren Commission's report is self-evident.

SELF-EVIDENT
In the Warren Commission's report on the assassination of President Kennedy, written by Earl Warren, ...

REVISED
In his commission's report on the assassination of President Kennedy, Earl Warren wrote ....

(See specifically §36a *Redundancy*.)

sp. (spelling)

Spelling errors damage a writer's credibility by casting doubt on her thoroughness. Always proofread carefully to eliminate errors. Use dictionaries and spellchecks. In the example below, the errors are italicized. In general, see §50g *Commonly misspelled words*.

MISSPELLED
When the leader of a country *committs* an act not *permissable* by law, he should *except* the consequences.

REVISED   When the leader of a country *commits* an act not *permissible* by law, he should *accept* the consequences.

(See specifically §50h *Homophones.*)

supp. (support), e.g., quot. (quotation), proof?

Strengthen your argument and illustrate your ideas by providing facts and by quoting authorities. Be sure to have support for your allegations. Unsupported statements serve only to create doubt about your thesis. Also, be sure that your support is from serious sources and contains substantive information.

UNSUPPORTED ASSERTION   Living a comfortable life in the suburbs is very expensive especially when one has children. Thus money necessarily becomes the priority in suburban values.

                    This statement may be valid, but it is unpersuasive without supporting citations.

REVISED   Living a comfortable life in the suburbs is very expensive especially when one has children. In her April 2002 study on the cost of living in suburban America, Ignatius University economist Janet Barnes notes that "on average, the cost of raising a family in the suburbs is more than double the cost for the same family in a rural area."[3] Thus money necessarily becomes the priority in suburban values.

UNSUPPORTED CONJECTURE   He thought this would delay any punishment.

REVISED   He *may have* thought this would delay any punishment.

INSUBSTANTIAL SUPPORT   What is impeachment? "Impeachment is a legal way for America, to overthrow its leaders."[1]

REVISED   What is impeachment? *The U.S. Constitution defines impeachment as the accusation brought against civil servants for high crimes and misdemeanors.*[1]

(See also §35 *Assertions and illustrations,* §62 *Quotation marks,* §63 *Punctuating and capitalizing with quotations,* §64 *Punctuating a quotation-within-a-quotation,* §65 *Plagiarizing and documenting,* §66 *Using quotations effectively.*)

synt. (syntax)

Syntax is the placement of words in a sentence in relation to one another. *Syntax* or *synt.* is the marginal comment instructors use for a particular kind of *awkwardness* of expression (see *awk.* above) in which a word, phrase, or clause is placed in an odd or confusing position in the sentence.

SYNTAX PROBLEM	Joseph Stalin, who was extremely ambitious, from the moment of Lenin's final illness plotted to wrest control of the Party from Trotsky.
	The sentence is confusing because the subject (*Joseph Stalin*) is too far from the verb (*plotted*).
REVISED	From the moment of Lenin's final illness, the ambitious Joseph Stalin plotted to wrest control of the Party from Trotsky.

(See §33 *Wordiness and word order.*)

title

A title identifies both the topic of the essay and the writer's approach to this topic. A title limited to a single word or two is usually not very useful because it can almost never adequately convey all the necessary information. The title of the *Model essay* fails to convey the situation in which President Clinton finds himself; neither does it suggest the writer's perspective on this situation. See *Is the title specific enough?* in *Proofreading.*

INADEQUATE	President Clinton
REVISED	Presidential Impeachment: Private Sins and Public Penalties

und. (understatement)

An understatement minimizes the value, impact, or importance of a fact or event. Understatements can be useful if you intend to be ironic. However, avoid unintentional or faulty understatements that diminish the significance of your topic. For example, a dangerous illness or environment cannot be called an *inconvenience.* A war or another cataclysmic event in which many lives are lost cannot be called an *unpleasantry*. In the same way, the killing of schoolchildren cannot be called an *incident*.

UNDERSTATED   The killings at Columbine High School were a shocking incident that illustrated the danger of guns in the hands of children and teenagers.

REVISED   The killings at Columbine High School provided shocking *proof* of the danger of guns in the hands of children and teenagers.

(See specifically §47c *Understatement.*)

vague, ?, meaning, huh?

The reader is confused by one or all of the following:

♦ Word choice – words are too general (*emotion, negative behavior*)
♦ Word order (syntax) – see *synt.* above
♦ Sequence of ideas – see *arg.* above
♦ Use of the conditional – *would*
♦ Redundancy – *they wrote*

See in general §3 *Ambiguous or doubtful references,* §33 *Wordiness and word order,* §34 *Rewriting heavy language,* and §11 *Simple verbs instead of progressive and conditional.*

MEANING   When they wrote the Constitution ... they wrote it in
UNCLEAR   such a way that interpretations were possible based on the given time and situations.

REVISED   The Founding Fathers incorporated a measure of flexibility into the Constitution to allow for current interpretation of its mandates by future generations.

(See specifically §19b *Specific instead of general terms,* and §36a *Redundancy.*)

vary sents. (vary sentence length/construction)

To maintain the interest of your reader, vary the length, construction, and rhythmic pattern of your sentences.

- Follow long compound or complex sentences with short simple ones.
- Organize some sentences in the standard order of subject-verb-complement, but balance these with others in which this order is altered, or which begin with a phrase or a subordinate clause.
- Avoid *stringy sentences* in which phrases or clauses are connected by repeated conjunctions such as *and, but, or* etc. Repair stringy sentences by subordinating one to another, or by dividing a single sentence into two.
- Vary the arrangement of ideas in your sentences by placing the main idea in different locations within the sentence.

UNVARIED The exact cause of stomach cancer is unknown. It has often been associated with gastritis. This is an inflamation of the stomach. It may be attributable to alcohol intake.

The "choppy" quality of the writing is caused by a lack of variety in the sentence structure.

REVISED The exact cause of stomach cancer is unknown, although it has often been associated with gastritis. This inflamation of the stomach may be attributable to alcohol intake.

(See specifically §32 *Sentence length, order, and type.* Other problems in the passage are addressed elsewhere.)

wc (word choice), ww (wrong word)

Look up words in the dictionary to be certain you are using them correctly. When using a new or unfamiliar word from the dictionary, consult the dictionary's example showing how the word is used in context.

When using a thesaurus, be aware that the suggested synonyms are only approximately the same in meaning. Often incorrect words or expressions slip into essays when writers use unfamiliar synonyms or antonyms from a thesaurus. By all means use a thesaurus, but look up the definitions of the suggested synonyms in the dictionary. Note the subtle and less subtle misuse of words in the examples below.

MISUSED The *Founders* of the Constitution …

REVISED The *Founders* of the American nation …

OR

The *authors* of the Constitution ...

MISUSED   The prosecutor *entailed* all of the details of the incident.

(*Entailed* means resulted in or contained certain consequences.)

REVISED   The incident *entailed* severe penalties.

MISUSED   The burning of the White House in 1814 *instilled* a great deal of stress upon our nation.

(To *instill* means *to implant gradually and persistently*.)

REVISED   The burning of the White House in 1814 *subjected our nation to* a great deal of stress.

(See §19 *Word choice*, and §25 *Frequently misused words*.)

1   Subject-verb agreement

What does subject-verb agreement mean?

The subject of a sentence indicates who is acting: the first person (I, we), the second person (you), the third person (he, she, it, they). The third person includes all people, objects, or abstractions to which we give names — The Empire State Building, game shows, J. Edgar Hoover, world hunger. Each person has a number (singular, plural) showing how many are acting.

The verb indicates what the action is, when it is occurring, and how many people or things are acting in the sentence: one or many, singular or plural. The verb indicates person and number by changing the way it is written or conjugated.

Subject-verb agreement means that the person and number of the subject must match the person and number of the verb. Below is a chart of matching persons and numbers using the verb *to be*.

	SINGULAR	PLURAL
FIRST PERSON	I am	we are
SECOND PERSON	you are	you are
THIRD PERSON	he/she/it is	they are

Most people have learned to recognize basic mistakes in person and number by ear.

➤He doesn't NOT He don't.

➤It was NOT It were.

➤We have NOT We has.

When subjects and verbs are side by side as above, agreement in person and number is straightforward. Mistakes occur when verbs are separated from their subjects by intervening phrases, or when the number or person of the subject is difficult to distinguish as with compound subjects and indefinite pronouns. Remember that verbs agree with *subjects* not with *complements*.

➤The people's rioting ~~cause~~ *causes* disruptions in the country.

Both the subject (*rioting*) and the verb (*causes*) are in the third person singular.

Verb agreement with pronouns ending in *-one,* *1a*
-body, -thing

Indefinite pronouns ending in *-one, -body,* or *-thing* (as well as several others) are always *singular.*

one	anybody	anything	each
anyone	everybody	everything	every
someone	somebody	something	either
everyone	nobody	nothing	neither
no one			none

➤We can easily distinguish the team members because *each has* her name written on her uniform.

➤*None* of the team, however, *is* required to bring her own bat.

➤*Is everyone* ready?

☛ All these pronouns are in the 3rd person.

Collective nouns as singular or plural subjects *1b*

Collective nouns are words that designate a group of people or things acting as a single unit such as *police, team, United States, audience.* When individual members within the collective act in concert, treat them as a *single subject.*

➤The Los Angeles police *is* the largest law enforcement body in the world.

➤The United States *hasn't* won an Olympic medal in fencing since 1984.

➤The club *is* holding elections for officers.

However when members of the collective are acting as individuals or against each other, treat them as a *plural subject.*

➤The Mafia *were* killing each other in a bloody power struggle.

➤The jury *were* hopelessly divided in their opinion.

➤The committee *were* in disagreement over the agenda.

In all other instances, allow the sense of the sentence to determine whether a subject is singular or plural. The expression *the number of,* for example, is singular because it refers to a specific number, but *a number of* is plural because it refers to a general group.

➤ *The number of* people who insist on stringent airport inspections *is* growing.

➤ *A number of* people *have* expressed their support of stringent airport inspections (.n all flights.

(See also §1e *Distinguish the subject of a sentence from the object of a prepositional phrase.*)

If the subject has several parts, which number and person of verb are used?

Subjects with more than one noun or pronoun are called *compound subjects.* Depending on how they are combined, *compound subjects* may take a *singular* or *plural* verb. Here are the most common situations.

1c	**Compound subjects joined by** *and*

Compound subjects joined by *and* take a *plural* verb.

➤ Ultramarine and cerulean *are* both shades of blue.

➤ The Jukes and the Kallikaks *were* famous feuding families studied by sociologists.

If, however, the two items form a single unit, they take a *singular* verb.

➤ *Kind Hearts and Coronets is* my favorite classic movie.

➤ Peanut butter and jelly *makes* a better sandwich than ham and cheese does.

Notice from the example above that titles of *movies, books, plays, articles, music,* and *artwork* are always treated as singular even when they are joined by *and.* The same holds true for official titles of *organizations, courses, time periods* etc. that seem to be plural but indicate a single unit.

➤ The United Nations *is* committed to maintaining world peace.

➤ Physics *is* my most interesting subject.

➤ An additional six months *is* a long time to wait for an overdue bonus.

1d	**Compound subjects joined by** *either...or, neither...nor*

If both parts of the compound subject are singular, the verb must be singular.

➤Neither Albert nor Niels *has* a sense of humor.

➤Either flavor of ice cream *is* fine for me.

If one part of a subject joined by *either ... or, neither ... nor* is singular while the other part is plural, the verb will agree in number and person with the closer part.

➤Either the weather or the squirrels *are* to blame for the holes in the roof.

➤Either the squirrels or the weather *is* to blame for the holes in the roof.

➤Neither I nor my friends *are* on vacation.

➤Neither my friends nor I *am* on vacation.

Distinguish the subject of a sentence from the object of a prepositional phrase 1e

The subject of a sentence *can never be in a prepositional phrase.* Often prepositional phrases come between the subject and the verb. They may contain nouns that seem to be the subject, confusing the choice between a singular or plural verb. In the examples below, the prepositional phrases are italicized.

➤A high level *of toxins in local lakes and waterways* ~~are~~ *is* polluting our water supply.

➤The number *of jobs for PhDs in English* ~~have~~ *has* fallen dramatically.

➤The horseshoe crab *along with its fellow arachnid the spider* ~~have~~ *has* eight legs.

Test for subject-verb agreement by rereading the sentence without the prepositional phrases

☛ Don't be fooled by prepositional phrases that mean *and* such as *as well as, in addition to, along with.* Unlike *and*, they *don't* make a compound subject, and nouns contained in them *do not* agree with the verb.

Are here or there *ever subjects?*

Here are and *there are* at the beginning of sentences are known as *expletives* — words empty of grammatical function in the sentence other than to mark a beginning, as in the sentence *There are many fish in the sea. Here* and *there* are never subjects except in a sentence like this one which discusses them as terms. (For other expletives see §33b *Eliminate the indirect constructions* there are, it is, one of the... *etc.*)

Exercise

Correct any errors in subject-verb agreement. Answers on p.95.

GROUP A
1. I am also supposed to attend the play, aren't I?
2. Either his presentation or his facts are at fault.
3. Do each of the members have an e-mail address?
4. Neither Hans nor Igor like snowless winters when the skiing is bad.
5. Both the prosecution and the defense has rested their case.
6. Neither Kevin nor I is in the mood for pizza.
7. Both the jacket and the skirt is too long.
8. A number of studies show that slender women think they are overweight.
9. Every one of Seattle's coffee houses are connected to the Internet.
10. Neither the passengers nor the driver have any idea where the stadium is.

GROUP B
1. Do either of you remember the last time we swam in Lake George?
2. The investment club is in disagreement about whether or not to buy Japanese securities.
3. Everything in the cabinets were moldy.
4. Three weeks is not long enough to relocate a household across the country.
5. The entire group of applicants were outstanding.
6. There are a grand total of six fireplaces in the house.
7. Spaghetti and meatballs is my favorite meal.
8. Any one of these symptoms have a great impact on the victim.
9. For peace between warring countries to be concluded, there has to be treaties signed.
10. Their skills and information makes it possible for them to get good jobs.

2 Pronoun–antecedent agreement

What is pronoun–antecedent agreement?

Pronouns often refer to a preceding word in a sentence or to a concept earlier in a paragraph called an antecedent. An antecedent is a noun or pronoun that is replaced by another noun or pronoun further on in the sentence or paragraph. Just as subjects agree with verbs in number and person, so must pronouns and their antecedents.

➤ Imelda Marcos explained her reason for not going shopping yesterday.

Imelda Marcos is the antecedent to which the pronoun *her* refers.

➤ The dog wagged its tail.

Dog is the antecedent of the pronoun *its*.

➤ All of us helped raise our flag.

All is the antecedent of the pronoun *our*.

What does agreement in number and person mean?

If an antecedent is *singular*, the pronoun to which it refers must also be *singular*. A *plural antecedent* must be followed by a *plural pronoun*. Likewise, if the antecedent is, say, in the first person, the pronoun must be in the first person, and so on. Below is a chart of personal pronouns.

	SINGULAR	PLURAL
FIRST PERSON	I/my	we/our
	myself	ourselves
SECOND PERSON	you/ your	you/ your
	yourself	yourselves
THIRD PERSON	he/she/it	they/their
	his/her/its	themselves
	himself/herself	
	itself/oneself	

☛ *Hisself, ourself, theirself, themself, oneselves,* and *theirselves* do *not* exist.

2a   Agreement with pronouns ending in *-one*, *-body*, *-thing*

The most common agreement problem for writers concerns antecedents ending in *-one, -body,* or *-thing*. Below is a list of common, singular, indefinite pronouns.

one	anybody	anything	each
anyone	everybody	everything	every
someone	somebody	something	either
everyone	nobody	nothing	neither
no one			none

Because these words are singular, any pronoun that refers to them must also be singular. That's why *they, their* or *themselves* cannot refer to a singular antecedent. Instead, use the singular *him, himself, her, herself,* and do so interchangeably without bias toward either the masculine or the feminine. Or, change the pronoun to an article: *a, an, the.*

> ➤Everyone was proud of ~~themself.~~ *himself*

> ➤I hope someone brought ~~their~~ *a* flashlight.

(To avoid awkwardness in creating gender balance see §18e *Using non-sexist controlling pronouns*.)

2b   Pronoun agreement with *person* and *individual* etc.

Person and *individual* are the most common singular antecedents mistaken for plural. Using plural pronouns with singular antecedents causes shifts in subject like those below.

> ➤The person responsible for breaking the Ming vase will have to pay for it ~~themselves.~~ *himself*

> ➤In America, when a person so much as stubs his toe ~~we sue.~~ *he sues*

2c   Agreement with relative pronouns *who, which, that* etc.

Relative pronouns have no person or number of their own. They take on the person and number of their antecedents.

►The hecklers *who were* in the balcony kept interrupting the speaker.

Who refers to *hecklers* and, therefore, takes the plural verb *were*.

►The coats, *which were* in the shop window last winter, are now out of style.

Which is plural because its antecedent, *coats*, is plural.

►The food *that is* on the table is making me ill.

That is singular because it refers to a singular antecedent *food*, and therefore takes the singular verb *is*.

Sometimes antecedents are collective nouns (see §1b *Collective nouns as singular and plural subjects*). When group members in a collective noun act in concert, they are singular, and the relative pronoun that refers to them is also singular. If the members of the collective are in disagreement or act as separate individuals, the noun is plural, and the relative pronoun that refers to it is also plural.

►The hockey *team who was* enjoying a winning season returned home in triumph.

The pronoun *who* is singular because its antecedent (*team*) is a collective noun whose members are acting in concert.

►The hockey *team who were arguing* over competing strategies left the locker room thoroughly dissatisfied.

Here the pronoun *who* is plural because the members of the collective are acting as separate individuals.

📖 Exercise

Correct any errors in pronoun-antecedent agreement. Answers on p.96.

1. A hundred years ago, upper class women used to spend her day visiting or shopping.
2. The way one feels often affects the way they perceive their environment.
3. The more money a person stands to gain from a business deal, the less likely they are to behave morally.
4. This decision shows that a person might reject someone else's solution to a problem in order to retain their pride.
5. "Sour grapes" refers to how anyone reacts to something they cannot have.
6. When an individual believes their own lies, they do not change the

actual situation except in their minds.

7. The more anybody tries to deny a risk, the more convincing their false sense of security becomes.

8. A younger applicant may be chosen over an older one because they are considered more agile and energetic.

9. No one likes to betray their friends, but they have to when other people may be in danger.

10. Anybody who wants dessert should raise their hand before it's too late.

3 Ambiguous or doubtful pronoun references

What is an ambiguous or doubtful reference?

An ambiguous or doubtful reference is one in which the reader must guess what a noun's or pronoun's antecedent could be.

Common ambiguous reference errors occur with the pronouns: *he, she, it, they, this* (*these*), *that* (*those*).

3a   Errors with *he* and *she*

➤ Ernest Hemingway didn't want to go rollerblading with Wallace Stevens because he was a clumsy skater.

What is the antecedent of *he*? Is it *Ernest Hemingway* or *Wallace Stevens*? Which man was clumsy?

Clarify the pronoun reference by separating the two key nouns from each other in the sentence.

➤ Because Ernest Hemingway was a clumsy skater, he didn't want to go rollerblading with Wallace Stevens.

OR

➤ Ernest Hemingway didn't want to go rollerblading with Wallace Stevens who was a clumsy skater.

3b   Errors with *they*

Informally, speakers may refer to authorities such as the government, big business, or even parents with the generic *they*. Sometimes this practice of generalizing can lead to confusion.

➤Gas prices keep going up and up. *They* really know how to hit you where it hurts!

Who are *they*? Major gas companies? Foreign oil producing countries? The government who puts a tax on gas? The local gas station?

Avoid ambiguous references to an authoritative *they* simply by naming the authority.

➤Gas prices keep going up and up. The state's gas tax really hits where it hurts!

Errors with *this* and *it*   **3c**

Frequently an ambiguous pronoun reference occurs when the writer uses *this*, *these*, *that*, *those* to stand in for a complex idea explained in a previous sentence or paragraph.

➤Faith in others is a virtue; misplaced, however, it may lead people into vice. *This* is a problem particular to those who are naive about human nature.

Does *this* refer to *faith*, *it*, *being misled*, *vice*? The antecedent is the *misplacement of faith*, an idea that is implied but not stated explicitly..

Complex notions like *misplaced faith* develop their meaning over several sentences. Replacing them with a blanket *this* or *it* abbreviates their meaning and creates a misleading reference. Restore clarity and precision by using *this* as an adjective that describes the antecedent.

➤Faith in others is a virtue; misplaced, however, it may lead people into vice. *This misplacement of faith* is a problem particular to those who are naive about human nature.

In order to use *this* as an adjective, you must supply the implied antecedent to which *this* refers, namely *misplacement of faith*. Where do we get this implied antecedent? We simply change the verbal from the first sentence into a noun in the second sentence.

➤The CEO *planned* to cut manufacturing costs. This *plan* involved moving factories abroad where labor is cheaper.

The verb *planned* in the first sentence becomes the noun *plan* in the second sentence.

Or, you may choose to replace *this* by *such* or by *the*.

➤Faith in others is a virtue; misplaced, however, it may lead people into vice. *Such misplacement of faith* is a problem particular to those who are naive about human nature.

➤The CEO *planned* to cut manufacturing costs. *The plan* involved moving factories abroad where labor is cheaper.

3d   Errors with adjectives as antecedents

Another common reference error uses an adjective instead of a noun for the antecedent, as in the example below:

➤In *Aesop's* fable, he illustrates how people deceive themselves.

He does not refer to *Aesop's* which is merely an adjective describing *fable*. There is no noun or pronoun that acts as the antecedent to *he*.

Instead, eliminate the pronoun altogether, and place the subject of the sentence directly in front of the verb.

➤In this fable, Aesop illustrates how people deceive themselves.

📖   Exercise

Correct any errors in pronoun references. Answers on p.97.

1. The long friendship between Queen Victoria and her maid was over the day that she stole the gold bracelet.
2. Janet is constantly talking about her money problems. It is her primary topic of conversation.
3. Mikhail Baryshnikov's dance partner stepped on his foot, leaped into the arms of other men, and forgot his name. This seriously annoyed Mikhail.
4. Is it acceptable etiquette to eat fried chicken with your fingers? Well, they say it is.
5. In McCarthy's book, she tends to romanticize socialist ideals.
6. Because people's control of their environment is often uncertain, they tend to feel insecure.
7. He knew that getting an education was very important for success in his career. But when he saw that he would have to work a night shift and pinch pennies, he realized that this was not what he wanted.
8. When a few people behave badly, it gives the entire group a bad reputation.
9. Charlton Heston campaigned against gun control saying that all Americans are guaranteed the right to own one.
10. The woman next to my mother in the theater was biting her nails.

4 Pronoun errors in subjects and complements

What are subjects and complements?

Sentences consist of three basic parts: subjects, verbs, complements. Subjects tell us *who* is acting, thinking, or feeling in a sentence. Verbs tell us *what* the action or condition is and *how many* are acting. Complements tell us who or what is *receiving* the action.

The pronouns that may be used as subjects or as complements are not interchangeable. Pronouns are grouped by *cases*, and each case has its specific uses. The two pronoun cases that are most frequently confused are the *nominative case* and the *objective case*.

	NOMINATIVE		OBJECTIVE
		SINGULAR	
FIRST PERSON	I		me
SECOND PERSON	you		you
THIRD PERSON	he/she/it		him/her/it
		PLURAL	
FIRST PERSON	we		us
SECOND PERSON	you		you
THIRD PERSON	they		them

Nominative pronouns as subjects   *4a*

When pronouns are the subjects of sentences, they are always nominative.

➤ *I* gave my roommate the keys to the Corvette.

The person doing the giving and the *subject* of the sentence is *I* (nominative case).

In this instance, we know by ear which case to use for each pronoun. For example, we would never say:

➤ *Me* gave her the keys to the Corvette.

Compound subjects joined by *and, both, either, neither*   *4b*

Choosing correct pronouns becomes more complicated when two or more pronouns are joined by *both...and*, *either...or*, and *neither...nor.* Intervening words and punctuation tend to confuse us. A quick glance at the chart of nominative case pronouns above shows us how to correct the pronoun errors in the subjects of the following sentences:

➤"~~Him~~ and his hundred knights are too expensive," said Goneril to
    He
Regan.

➤Neither Mac and his band *The Lounge Lizards* nor ~~us~~ and our band
             we
Stairs to Nowhere will be able to play at the concert tonight.

➤Either ~~me~~ or you will have to go first.
    I

Another way to eliminate confusion is to read a sentence aloud cutting out all subjects but the pronoun. With this method, the examples above show themselves to be obviously incorrect.

➤*Him* is too expensive...

➤*Us* won't be able to play...

➤*Me* will have to go first...

4c   Nominative pronouns as complements with the verb *to be*

Complements that use nominative pronouns are called predicate nominatives. They appear in sentences with linking verbs. Linking verbs show condition instead of action. They are usually *to be* verbs: *am, is, are, was, were,* and any verb phrase ending in *be, been* or *being.* Or, they can be replaced by a *to be* verb without altering the sense of the sentence. Find predicate nominatives using the formula below.

PREDICATE NOMINATIVE (P.N.) SUBJECT + *TO BE* VERB + *WHO* OR *WHAT*?

   S. V. P.N.
➤It was *she* on the telephone.

        S.   V.   P.N.
➤The driver of the getaway car could have been *he.*

Some typical verbs that can sometimes be replaced by a *to be* verb are *to appear, to become, to feel, to look, to seem, to smell, to sound, to taste* etc. Usually the complements of these verbs are adjectives. When these complements are pronouns, however, they must be nominative.

S.　　V.　　　P.N.
➤It appeared to be *she* who was driving too fast.

S.　V.　　　P.N.
➤It seems to be *they* who are mistaken.

Objective pronouns as direct and indirect objects　**4d**

A pronoun is in the objective case when it is the direct or indirect object of an action verb, and when it is the object of a preposition.

| **DIRECT OBJECT** | SUBJECT + ACTION VERB + *WHOM* OR *WHAT*? |

S.　　V.　　　D.O.
➤The whale swallowed *him*.

| **INDIRECT OBJECT** | SUBJECT + ACTION VERB + DIRECT OBJECT + *TO/FOR WHOM TO/FOR WHAT*? |

S　V.　I.O.　　D.O.
➤She gave *them* the book.

| **OBJECT OF A PREPOSITION** | Any noun or pronoun that ends a prepositional phrase. |

PREP.　OBJ.　　OBJ.
➤The dog ran between *him* and *me*

> ☞ An indirect object is always located between the action verb and the direct object in a sentence, and is never inside a prepositional phrase.

Objective pronouns as objects of prepositions　**4e**

Always use objective pronouns — *me, you, him, her, us, you, them* — in a phrase that begins with a preposition. Prepositions, however, can be difficult to recognize. Below is a list of some common prepositions.

about	as well as	concerning	near	throughout
above	at	down	next to	till
according to	because of	during	of	to
across	before	except for	off	toward
after	behind	for	on	under
against	below	from	onto	underneath
alongside	beneath	in	out of	until
along with	beside	in addition to	over	unto
among	between	in front of	past	upon

as	but (except)	instead of	prior to	with
aside from	by	into	since	without
as of	by means of	like	through	within

➤What I'm telling you is just *between you and me.*

➤*Except for us and them,* no one enjoyed the movie.

4f Compound objects joined by *and, or, either, neither*

Sentences with two or more objects that include pronouns can create confusion about which type of pronoun to use as *direct object, indirect object,* and *object of the preposition.*

DIRECT OBJECT

➤They will choose either my friend or ~~I~~ *me* for the job job.

➤The consulate furnished ~~she~~ *her* and her husband with temporary visas.

INDIRECT OBJECT

➤The raffle organizers gave both Ralph Nader and ~~she~~ *her* a second chance.

➤You can ask the professor, the lab assistant, or even ~~I~~ *me* the answer to this question.

OBJECT OF A PREPOSITION

➤People like you and ~~he~~ *him* have the power to change the world.

➤Everyone knows how to ski except for her and ~~they.~~ *them.*

Just as with compound subjects, read the sentence with one object at a time to unconfuse the ear.

4g Meaning as a guide to choosing the correct pronoun case

Ultimately, the choice of pronoun case depends on your intended meaning. Consider the following sentence. In the first example, it uses the nominative pronoun *he.* In the second example, it uses the objective pronoun *him.* Both, however, are correct.

➤We have never known a better butler than he.

The intended meaning of the sentence is "We have never known a better butler than *he is.*" The nominative case is grammatically correct because *he* is the subject of the implied verb *is,* and subjects are always nominative.

➤We have never known a better butler than him.

The meaning of the sentence remains the same, but the objective pronoun is correct because *him* refers to the direct object (*butler*). A pronoun that takes the place of a *direct object* is *objective.*

Subjects and objects in apposition   *4h*

Apposition means that a word or phrase is explained by another word or phrase that follows it immediately. The appositive consists primarily of nouns, or pronouns and is set off by commas or dashes.

When *pronouns* in apposition describe the *subject* of the sentence, they must be in the *nominative* case; when they describe the *objects* of the sentence, they must be in the *objective* case.

➤Two members of the gang, you and ~~her,~~ *she* are responsible for all the graffiti.

You and *she* are appositives describing the subject *members.* Therefore, *you* and *she* are in the *nominative* case.

➤We are giving two puppies in the litter — ~~he,~~ *him* the spotted one, and ~~she,~~ *her* the one with the black tail — to our neighbors.

Him and *her* are appositives describing the direct object *puppies.* Therefore, *him* and *her* must be in the *objective* case.

Errors with pronouns in apposition can be difficult to recognize even for the most adept stylist. Consider the beginning of T. S. Eliot's famous poem, "The Love Song of J. Alfred Prufrock":

➤Let us go then, *you* and *I,*

When the evening is spread out against the sky

Like a patient etherised upon a table[...].

You and I replace the objective pronoun *us,* and, therefore, should be in the objective case. Granted, changing the case may alter the rhyme scheme of the poem.

➤Let us go then, *you* and *me,*

When the evening is spread out against the sea

Like a poet bowdlerized posthumously[...].

📖 Exercise

Correct any pronoun errors in subjects and complements. Answers on p.98.

1. Everyone except he and I received a door prize.
2. Could that be they at the door right now?
3. Leonard Nimoy showed she and I his favorite *Star Trek* episode.
4. Both Mickey Mouse and me are in the picture we took at Disneyworld.
5. It sounds like she on the phone.
6. The watchdog growled when he saw Charlene and I in our Halloween costumes.
7. We watched them, my neighbor and he, as they swam out to save our stranded cat.
8. In the end, we did not invite either they or their friend.
9. Both our cousins and us liked swimming in the lake after dark.
10. Only the leading actors, Laurence Olivier and her, took a second bow.

5 Reflexive pronouns

What are reflexive pronouns?

Reflexive pronouns all end in *-self* or *-selves*.

myself	ourselves
yourself	yourselves
himself, herself	themselves
oneself, itself	

Reflexive pronouns have two functions. First, they show that an action is performed upon oneself.

➤ Romeo killed *himself* when he thought Juliet had died.

Second, they make statements more emphatic in response to doubt.

➤ What do you mean I'm mistaken? I heard him say so *myself*!

Do not use reflexive pronouns interchangeably with personal pronouns.

Errors in case with reflexive pronouns   **5a**

Reflexive pronouns are immune to changes in case: they always stay the same. Their constancy is the reason some people use them instead of personal pronouns when they are unsure if a pronoun should be nominative or objective. Reflexive and personal pronouns, however, do not mix-and-match. Avoid the mistake of using reflexive pronouns arbitrarily in place of nominative or objective pronouns.

➤ Your husband and ~~yourself~~ *you* may board the plane through the first class gate.

➤ Except for the Newmans, the Douglases and ~~ourselves~~ *us*, every Hollywood couple is divorced.

➤ That is a private matter between Gertrude and ~~myself~~ *me*.

Exercise

Correct any errors in reflexive pronouns. Answers on p.99.

1. Abused children tend to become abusers themselves.
2. A bully thinks that anyone physically weaker than himself has no rights.
3. The nobles may have had less authority than the king; nonetheless, they themselves enjoyed a lot of power.
4. Our grandparents gave our cousins and ourselves a graduation party.
5. He had two sons, Jonathan and myself.
6. Darth Vader is outranked only by the Emperor himself.
7. During the interview I told the reporter all about me.
8. They marketed the computer programs developed by themselves.
9. The flowers were sent to her roommates and herself.
10. She sent herself those flowers.

6 *Who/whoever* versus *whom/whomever*

How do you know whether to use who *or* whom*?*

Who and *whom* are relative pronouns that refer to people. The difference between them lies in how they are used in the sentence, and therefore what case — nominative or objective — they take (see §4 *Pronoun errors in subjects and complements*).

Who and *whoever* act as subjects and predicate nominatives and belong to the *nominative case*. *Whom* and *whomever* act as objects and belong to the *objective* case.

6a   *Who* and *whoever* as subjects

Who and *whoever* belong to the nominative case: *I, you, he, she, it, we, they*. They act as *subjects* just as other nominative pronouns do.

In the example below, *who* is the subject of a simple sentence that consists of just one main clause. It has a subject and a verb, and makes sense without any additional information.

    s.   v.
➤Who ate all the brownies?

Some sentences, however, have subordinate clauses that have subjects and verbs just as the main clauses do, but do not make sense by themselves. While *who* can be the subject of any clause, as a rule, *whoever* can be the subject only of a subordinate clause.

In the examples below, *whoever* is the subject of each underlined subordinate clause.

         s.   v.
➤Whoever breaks the piñata first will get a special prize.

                            s.   v.
➤The winner of the special prize is whoever breaks the piñata first.

                            s.   v.
➤The special prize will be won by whoever breaks the piñata first.

No matter where a clause is located in the sentence, its subject is always nominative. In the preceding example, the entire clause is the object of the preposition *by*, but within this clause, the subject must be nominative which is why *whoever* is the correct choice. (1) In a choice between *who* and *whom* for the subject of *any* clause, always choose *who*. (2) In a choice between *whoever* and *whomever* for the subject of a *subordinate* clause, always choose *whoever*.

Who and *whoever* as predicate nominatives   *6b*

Who and *whoever* act as predicate nominatives. Remember that a predicate nominative is the complement of a *linking* verb (see §4a *Nominative pronouns as subjects*, and §4c *Nominative pronouns as complements with the verb* to be). In the examples below the subordinate clauses are underlined.

Who is the predicate nominative of both main and subordinate clauses.

P.N. V.   S.
➤Who was that masked man?

                P.N.   S. V.
➤Do you know who that masked man is?

Whoever is the predicate nominative of subordinate clauses only.

        P.N.   S. V.
➤Whoever that masked man is, I am more interested in his faithful Indian companion.

                P.N. S. V.
➤That masked man, whoever he is, nearly ran me over.

In a choice between *who* and *whom* for the predicate nominative of any clause, always choose *who*. In a choice between *whoever* and *whomever* for the predicate nominative of a subordinate clause, always choose *whoever*.

Whom and *whomever* as objects   *6c*

Whom and *whomever* are related to *objective* pronouns: *me, you, him, her, it, us, them* (see §4d *Objective pronouns as direct and indirect objects*, and §4e *Objective pronouns as objects of prepositions*).

Whom acts as the object of both main clauses and subordinate clauses. *Whomever* acts as the object of subordinate clauses only.

Like other objective pronouns, they act as *direct objects* (D.O.), and *objects of a preposition* (O.P.), and very rarely as *indirect objects* (I.O.).

DIRECT OBJECTS

➤ *Whom* do you love?
(D.O. V. S. V.)

➤ She had to choose between *whom she loves* and
(D.O. S. V.)

whom she respects.
(D.O. S. V.)

Both *whoms* are direct objects of subordinate clauses. Each entire clause is the object of the preposition *between*.

➤ The President can nominate *whomever he wants* to the cabinet.
(D.O. S. V)

OBJECTS OF PREPOSITIONS

➤ To *whom* did she leave all her money?

Whom is the object of the preposition *to*.

➤ She left all her money to *whomever*.

Whomever is the object of the preposition *to*.

BUT

➤ She left all her money to *whomever she wanted.*

The object of the preposition to is the entire underlined clause. Within this clause, *whomever* is a direct object, not the object of the preposition.

INDIRECT OBJECTS

➤ She left whom all her money?
(S. V. I.O. D.O.)

➤ She left whomever all her money, because she had no close relatives and didn't care who got it.
(S. V. I.O. D.O.)

6d   *Who* in the same person and number as the word it replaces

When *who* stands in place of someone mentioned earlier, it takes on the person and number of this antecedent. For example, if the antecedent is in the first person singular, *who* becomes first person singular, and its verb must be in the first person singular(see §1 *Subject-verb agreement,*§7d *Which and that*).

➤It is I *who am* the real Count of Monte Cristo.

> *Who* replaces the subject *I.* Because *I* takes the verb *am,who* must also take the verb *am.*This is how we get the construction *who am.*

The same agreement holds true for both singular and plural pronouns. In the first example below,*who* replaces *they* to produce the construction *who have accused.* In the second example, *who* replaces *he* to produce the construction *who is.*

➤It is they *who have* accused the wrong man.

➤It is he *who is* the real villain.

Who and *whom* used for people instead of *which* and *that*　　6e

Use *who* or *whom* when referring to people. Although *that* has been used to refer to people on and off throughout the history of the English language and is currently accepted by some stylists, *who* and *whom* are still preferable.

➤Was Alan Shepard the American astronaut ~~that~~ *who* first orbited the earth?

Above all, never use *which* to refer to people, although you may use the adjectival variation *whichever.*

➤She was the teacher ~~which~~ *whom* I remembered with the greatest affection.

➤*Whichever* friend he decides to bring will be welcome in our home.

Which and *that,* however, should be used to refer to inanimate objects, animals, emotions, and ideas (see §7 *Which and* that).

➤The house *that* overlooks the bay was owned by Katharine Hepburn.

➤The timber wolf, *which* used to roam widely in the Rocky Mountains, was hunted nearly to extinction.

(See §7a *Use* that *for essential and* which *for incidental information.*)

6f   *One of the...who/that/which* used with a plural verb

The expression "one of the ... who/that/which" always takes a plural verb. The pronouns *who, which, that* seem to refer to the singular *one*. In fact they refer to the plural group of which *one* is the example.

➤She is *one* of the Marines *who have been cited* for bravery.

Who refers to *Marines* not to *one*. Because *Marines* is third person plural, *who* is now also third person plural.

➤Mt. St. Helens is *one* of the volcanoes in North America *that have erupted* in recent years.

Even though *one* is a singular antecedent, it belongs to a plural group (volcanoes) with which the verb *have* agrees in number.

Do not be confused, however, by variations on the "one of the..." formula. For example, the expression "the only one of the..." takes a singular verb.

➤She is the *only one* of the Marines *who has been cited* for bravery.

Because of the emphasis placed on *one* by the word *only*, the sentence now focuses not on *Marines* but on *one*. *Who* now refers to *one* and becomes third person singular. If it's *one has been*, then it's *who has been*.

➤Mt. St. Helens is the *only one* of the volcanoes in North America *that has erupted* violently.

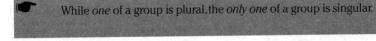

☛   While *one* of a group is plural, the *only one* of a group is singular.

📖   Exercise

Correct any errors in using *who/whoever* versus *whom/whomever*. Answers on p.100.

GROUP A

1. "Sigmund Freud," she said, "has always been one of those people who enjoys practical jokes."
2. It is not they but I who are out of luck this time.
3. A society is an organization of people that are united by common loyalties and lifestyles.
4. Some believe that a man can perform immoral acts and still be a "good guy" which made some mistakes.
5. The answer depends on who you ask.
6. Who did you give my phone number to?

7. I loved the characters which were like many people I know.
8. Give the flowers to whichever contestant you like the most.
9. Unless people think for themselves, our society will be run by a select few which speak for the rest of us.
10. I don't care who gets the prize. Give it to whoever you want.

GROUP B

1. On second thought, we want you to give the prize to whomever deserves it.
2. Am I one of the people who is responsible for this disaster?
3. The 1999 Mustang has the looks and control that dominates its competition.
4. Whom did you get the gift from?
5. Who do you know that lives in Muncie?
6. I will accept affectionately whoever my son marries.
7. Who do you think committed the crime?
8. There are many great guitarists which are similar in style.
9. This is the only one of all these fabrics that match my wallpaper.
10. On the first day of battle at Gettysburg, the Union army lost 4000 men, one of which was General Reynolds.

7   *Which* and *that*

How are *which* and that *alike, and how do they differ?*

Both *which* and *that* are relative pronouns. Both introduce additional information into a sentence about a thing, idea, or emotion, but *not* about people (see §6e Who *and* whom *used for people instead of* which *and* that).

Which and *that* are *not* interchangeable. *That* introduces essential information while *which* provides incidental detail. *Which* should be used to refer to locations. When both *which* and *that* appear in the same sentence, *that* usually comes first.

Use *that* for essential and *which* for incidental   **7a** information

Clauses beginning with *which* or *that* are of two types. They provide either incidental or essential information about an antecedent.

When the information is *incidental*, use *which* to begin the clause. Notice that *incidental* clauses — sometimes called *non-restrictive* — are usually set apart by commas, parentheses, or dashes.

➤The white jeans, *which I bought in New Jersey*, are too tight on me.

The clause begins with *which* because where the jeans are bought is largely irrelevant.

When the information adds significant or *essential* details either about its antecedent or about its speaker, use *that* although *which* is also acceptable. *Essential* clauses — sometimes called *restrictive* — are not set apart by punctuation.

➤The white jeans *that I bought only a week ago* are tight on me.

This time, the tightness of the jeans is a meaningful addition implying either that the jeans shrank or that the owner gained weight, hence *that*.

To test whether or not a clause is essential, remove it from the sentence. If the sentence retains the same implications that it had earlier, the clause is *incidental* (*non-restrictive*) and should start with *which*. If, however, the sentence loses significant details or implications, it is *essential* (*restrictive*) and should, when possible, begin with *that*.

7b   Using *that* and *which* sequentially in a sentence

For reasons of clarity, writers usually place the most important information at the beginning of a sentence. Therefore, when *which* and *that* appear in the same sentence, generally, *that* should precede *which*.

➤Where is the flashlight *that* is supposed to be in the kitchen, the one *which* we use in emergencies?

The *that* clause contains the essential information (location); the which clause adds incidental detail.

Exact usage, however, depends upon applying the *incidental/essential* rules above. Sometimes, however, the *incidental* detail can precede the *essential*.

➤The elephant, *which* was recently acquired by the zoo and *that* escaped in a Dallas suburb yesterday, has been sighted in Anne Richards' back yard.

Use *which* to show location 7c

Use *which* preceded by a preposition — in *which, through which* etc. — to show location. Although *that* is not grammatically incorrect for location, usage dictates that *that* may not be preceded by a preposition, while *which* may be. In using *that* to show location, we are forced into awkward constructions such as doubling a preposition or ending in one. (

➤The restaurant ~~that~~ *in which* we ate ~~at~~ in Greenwich Village was called The Cupping Place.

➤The ship ~~that~~ *on which* my mother immigrated to America ~~on~~ was called the S.S. Marine Carp.

Which and *that* in the same number as the words they replace 7d

When *which* or *that* stands in place of something mentioned earlier, it takes on the number of the antecedent. If the antecedent is singular, *which* or *that* becomes singular and takes a singular verb. If the antecedent is plural, *which* or *that* becomes plural and takes a plural verb. (See §6d *Who in the same person and number as the word it replaces*.)

➤Buddhist practices strive to calm the fear and desire *that cloud* people's minds.

That refers to *fear* and *desire*. Therefore, it is plural and takes the plural verb *cloud*.

➤His aptitude for mathematics, *which runs* in the family, has made him a brilliant astronomer.

Which is singular because it refers to a singular antecedent *aptitude*, and it takes a singular verb *runs*.

📖 Exercise

Correct any errors in using *which* and *that*. Answers on p.102.

1. I lost the ring which had been in my family for a hundred years.
2. The child brought home a frog that she had found and that she expected to become a prince.

3. The logic problem that gave me so much trouble was the one that compared apples to oranges.
4. She was expert in the strategy and marketing that characterizes an effective advertising campaign.
5. They liked the dining room that was located adjacent to the kitchen.
6. Their gardens were irrigated, which was innovative in those times.
7. This must be the tree that you carved our initials on.
8. One of nature's phenomena that are interesting to study is camouflage.
9. He described a series of events which are not part of normal life experience.
10. The technology that Americans are blessed with makes their lives unusually comfortable.

8 Gerunds and participles

What is a gerund?

A *gerund* looks like a verb but behaves like a noun, and always ends in *-ing*. In a sentence it acts as a *subject, complement,* and *object* of a *preposition.* Gerunds can be individual words or entire phrases and clauses.

➤*Being happy* is the most important thing in life.

The gerund phrase *being happy* is the subject of the sentence. Notice that *being happy* could be replaced by the noun *happiness* without changing the meaning of the sentence.

➤Enrico Caruso devoted his life to *singing*.

The gerund *singing* is the object of the preposition *to*.

☞ Gerunds are used frequently after certain prepositions such as: *despite, in spite of, in fear of, in danger of, prior to, in exchange for.*

8a Possessive nouns and pronouns in front of gerunds

Because gerunds behave exactly like nouns they can be possessed by someone just as one possesses a hat or a car. To show ownership we add -'s or -s' to nouns and use the possessive pronouns — *my, your, his, her, its, our, their.*

➤Scotty was deeply affected by the *captain's* leaving.

➤Scotty was deeply affected by *his* leaving.

Nouns or pronouns coming before a gerund *must* be possessive. Just as we cannot say "the captain departure" or "him departure," we cannot say "the captain leaving" or "him leaving." The same rule holds true for the gerund with a *not* in front of it.

➤*Ernest Hemingway's* attending a ballet was the first clear sign of his depression.

➤*His* not attending a bullfight was the second sign of his depression.

What is a participial phrase, and how does it differ from a gerund phrase?

Like a gerund, the *participle* in a *participial phrase* looks like a verb. Unlike a gerund, which behaves like a noun, the participle in a participial phrase behaves like an adjective.

➤*Reading the newspaper,* the man didn't see the UFO land in his front yard.

Reading the newspaper is a present participial phrase describing the man.

Like gerunds, present participles such as the one above, end with *-ing* and are easily confused with gerunds. Participles, however, *never* take a possessive noun or pronoun in front of them.

Confusing gerundial with participial phrases   **8b**

Because gerunds and present participles are both verbals that end in *-ing*, they can be easily confused. As a result, writers may incorrectly add an *-'s* to a noun that precedes a present participle. To distinguish between them, just keep in mind their functions. Think of *gerunds* as *nouns* or *pronouns.* Think of *participles* as *adjectives.*

PARTICIPIAL PHRASE	Benjamin Franklin, *having an unusually large head,* had to have his wigs custom-made.
	The participial phrase *having an unusually large head* is an adjective that describes Benjamin Franklin.
GERUND PHRASE	Benjamin Franklin's *having an unusually large head* caused problems for his wig-makers.
	Here *having an unusually large head* is a noun and the subject of the sentence. It therefore takes a possessive — *Benjamin Franklin's* — in front of it.

8c   Simplify language by avoiding gerunds and participles

Sometimes, using a possessive and a gerund yields unnecessarily complicated constructions. One such instance occurs regularly after verbs of *helping* or *hindering*.

➤The forest prevented *their seeing* the trees.

➤The fast current caused the *beach's eroding*.

A simpler and clearer construction is to use a preposition before the gerund, or to use an infinitive (*to* plus the verb) instead of the gerund.

➤The forest prevented them from seeing the trees.

➤The fast current caused the beach to erode.

Do not use gerunds where a simple noun would do.

➤The physiotherapist watched the old man's ~~walking~~ *walk* for signs of a limp.

Avoid participles when possible, especially after the verbs *to see*, *to watch*, and *to feel*. Instead, use simple verbs.

➤The proud mother watched her baby ~~walking~~ *walk* for the first time.

➤Coal miners can feel the earth ~~moving~~ *move* above them before a cave-in.

While not grammatically incorrect in the examples above, these participles are unnecessarily cumbersome.

📖   Exercise

Correct any errors in gerunds and participles. Answers on p.103.

1. Abelard was thrilled by Heloise confessing that she loved him.
2. The Red Queen, irritated by Alice's questions, began screaming uncontrollably.
3. Nixon lying on national television meant that I could never again trust a politician.
4. He watched the baby, while his wife's cooking dinner bustled about the kitchen.
5. As for Haldeman and Ehrlichman, I found them destroying evidence entirely predictable.
6. I helped my cousins' moving into their new apartment.

7. I forgot to tell him about us going to Hawaii.
8. My family was very excited about my brother having been admitted to U.C.L.A.
9. My brother's having been admitted to U.C.L.A. began packing immediately even though it was only April.
10. The Confederate troops' attacking Fort Sumter was the immediate cause of the Civil War.

9 Placement of modifiers

What is a modifier, and how should it be used in a sentence?

A modifier is an adjective or an adverb. It provides detail about a character, a thing, or an action. It can be a single word, a phrase, or a clause.

➤*By the age of five,* Mozart was already an adept pianist.

By the age of five is an adverb phrase because it modifies the verb *was*.

To use a modifier correctly, a writer must make sure of the following: (1) that it refers to the word or expression she intends to describe, (2) that the modified word or expression is named in the sentence, and (3) that the modifier is placed as close as possible to the expression it describes.

Three types of errors result when these rules are broken: *misplaced modifiers, dangling modifiers,* and *two-way modifiers.*

Misplaced modifiers   **9a**

The misplaced modifier is too far from the expression it describes. It confuses the reader by describing the wrong expression.

➤Standing behind the tree, the charging elephant was invisible to Safari Bob.

Charging elephants don't stand behind trees.

➤With a nuclear reactor in the tail, the captain of a Trident submarine never needs to surface to refuel.

Captains don't have nuclear reactors in their tails.

Correct misplaced modifiers either (1) by placing the modifier next to the word or expression it describes and adjusting the sentence, or (2) by moving the introductory modifier to a different part of the sentence.

➤Standing behind the tree, Safari Bob could not see the charging elephant.

Switching the positions of the *charging elephant* and *Safari Bob* clarifies the sentence.

➤With a nuclear reactor in the tail, a Trident submarine never needs to surface to refuel.

Placing a *Trident submarine* next to *in the tail* eliminates the confusion.

9b   Misplaced limiting words: *only, merely, either, just* etc.

Among the most common misplaced modifiers are *only, also, merely, simply, either...or, just, almost, not only...but also*. Misplacing them can give rise to a host of unintended implications.

➤Ernest Hemingway *only* gave $20.00 to Save the Whales.

Here, *only* modifies the act of giving and therefore emphasizes the method of the gift not the amount. He only *gave* it implies he didn't mail it, throw it, or send it by special messenger.

Placing *only* elsewhere in the sentence suggests other motives behind the gift.

➤Ernest Hemingway gave only $20.00 to Save the Whales. (*Not more.*)

➤*Only* Ernest Hemingway gave $20.00 to Save the Whales. (*No other writer did.*)

➤Ernest Hemingway gave $20.00 to Save the Whales only. (Not to any other charity.)

9c   Dangling adjectives

A dangling modifier is a word or phrase that refers to an *absent* or *hidden* subject. It is an action without an actor. A dangling modifier is often an adjective, usually a participle.

➤The books must be catalogued before placing them on the shelves.

Who is doing the placing? The agent is unnamed.

➤Falling asleep on the sofa, the TV stayed on all night.

TVs don't fall asleep on sofas. Who did fall asleep on the sofa?

Dangling modifiers are corrected by inserting the missing words as close as possible to the modifier and rewriting the rest of the sentence to fit.

➤The books must be catalogued before *you* place them on the shelves.

You is now the agent performing the action — *placing*.

➤Falling asleep on the sofa, *Uncle Harry* left the TV on all night.

Uncle Harry is the missing agent who fell asleep.

Dangling adverbs: *hopefully, unfortunately, happily* etc.   **9d**

Avoid beginning a sentence with an adverb that *evaluates* the emotion of a situation instead of describing it factually. Almost invariably the result is a *dangling adverb*. Typical dangling adverbs are expressions of hope, luck, pleasure, or misfortune:

fortunately	ironically	tragically
happily	luckily	unfortunately
hopefully	sadly	unhappily

It is impossible to know what these dangling adverbs modify, as in the example below.

➤Unhappily, the man lost his wallet.

Whom does *unhappily* describe? Is the reader *unhappy* that the man lost his wallet? Does *unhappily* describe the way the man lost his wallet? We can't even say, "The unhappy man lost his wallet," because we don't know if he is unhappy, or at what point he became unhappy. Was he unhappy even before the loss?

Other beginning adverbs that evaluate the emotional impact of situations are equally misleading and inconclusive.

➤Frankly, my dear, I don't give a damn!

➤Hopefully, I'll win the lottery.

➤Tragically, they lost their child in the flood.

Correct these dangling adverbs by changing them into adjectives, verbs, or nouns, and rewriting the sentences to fit.

➤The man was unhappy because he had lost his wallet.

➤Speaking frankly, my dear, I don't give a damn!

➤I hope I win the lottery.

➤Losing their child in the flood was a tragedy.

By contrast, adverbs that inform or describe a *specific action* instead of evaluating a general mood are meaningful, even when they deal with emotion.

➤Angrily, she slapped the table.

Angrily describes *slapped.*

➤Rapidly, the train approached the station.

Rapidly modifies *approached.*

➤Alternatively, you take the I-95 and get off at the Greenwich exit.

Alternatively modifies *take.*

9e Two-way modifiers

A two-way modifier — sometimes called a *squinting* modifier — refers ambiguously to either of two expressions in a sentence. It often occurs with reported or witnessed events especially when *that* or *which* are missing from the beginning of a subordinate clause.

➤I didn't recognize you without my glasses.

Is the problem that I am not wearing glasses, or that you are not wearing my glasses?

➤He told me during the party Miss Manners had insulted the hostess.

What happened during the party, the insult or the conversation about the insult?

A two-way modifier can be corrected in three ways. Move the modifier next to the word it describes.

➤Without my glasses, I was unable to recognize you.

Rewrite part of the sentence to provide an explanation.

➤I was unable to recognize you because you weren't wearing my glasses.

Insert the missing *that* or *which* at the beginning of the subordinate clause.

➤During the party, he told me *that* Miss Manners had insulted the hostess.

OR

➤He told me *that* Miss Manners had insulted the hostess during the party.

📖 Exercise

Correct any errors in the placement of modifiers. Answers on p.104.

GROUP A

1. If done correctly, your snowboard will turn you to the right.
2. Did he tell you when you were in camp I was traveling in Europe?
3. I just wanted to go to a movie, not to a big party.
4. Telling no one of his only catch that day, Ernest Hemingway threw back the baby bluefish thoroughly embarrassed.
5. Macbeth had greater will power than Lady Macbeth because he killed the king instead of his wife.
6. General Longstreet tried to assist Lee with reinforcements at Gettysburg. Later, he helped defend Richmond. Unfortunately, none of this mattered because soon thereafter the South surrendered.
7. As a child, Benito Mussolini's mother never fed her son spaghetti.
8. While in their cradles, Richard's and Esmeralda's parents decided that the children would be married to each other.
9. The principal discovered at lunchtime the boys were absent.
10. The South viewed hopefully Northern protests against the war.

GROUP B

1. After he had had a heart attack, Dr. Morris prescribed exercise and a fat-free diet for Mr. Keller.
2. Once licensed, the job opportunities in orthopedics are plentiful.
3. After reopening Madison Avenue just last week, a large portion of the street will have to be shut down again.
4. At Cemetery Hill, Pickett's men were told not to fire until they reached the Union line. Unluckily, too many men were killed in the charge, and the plan failed.
5. Anthropology and sociology have a lot in common especially when looking for a college department to apply to.
6. Later, on Cythera, when Odysseus's men ate the Lotus blossoms and lost their memory, Odysseus did not eat them.
7. With its three available suspensions, one can find just the right mixture of comfort and handling in a Corvette.
8. Lex Luthor gave a piece of kryptonite to Lois Lane covered with mud.
9. Playing for a dog can be tiring as well as fun.
10. Walking through the corridors of the stadium, baseball paraphernalia fill the walls.

10 Splitting infinitives and verb phrases

What is an infinitive, and what is a verb phrase?

An *infinitive* is the basic form of a verb usually preceded by *to* as in *to be, to go, to have* etc. A verb phrase is a verb and its helpers which convey action, emotion, condition, or thought in a sentence.

10a

Split infinitives

To "split" an infinitive means to insert another word or a phrase between *to* and the verb as in the famous phrase "to *boldly* go where no one has gone before." Elegant prose avoids split infinitives even though they do not seriously impair meaning, as in the examples below.

➤ Turbo charging is recommended *to greatly improve* acceleration.

➤ Once on stage, Joan Collins began *to deliberately and effectively upstage* the other actors.

Correct split infinitives by moving the inserted word or phrase. Because these insertions are adverbs, do *not* place them before the infinitive, or the result may be an awkward construction like the one below.

➤ Turbo charging is recommended *greatly* to improve acceleration.

Place the adverb after the infinitive. The insertion does not have to remain right next to the infinitive.

➤ Turbo charging is recommended to improve acceleration greatly.

➤ Once on stage, Joan Collins began to upstage the other actors deliberately and effectively.

By placing *deliberately and effectively* after *began* and before *to upstage*, you modify the verb *began*, not the infinitive *to upstage*.

 As a rule, adverbs follow the words they modify.

10b

Split verb phrases

A verb phrase consists of a main verb and its helpers — *can be, might have gone, would be selling*. Splitting verb phrases is *not* grammatically incorrect. As a rule, we split verb phrases by inserting *not* to make a verb negative, as in, "She did *not* eat all the chocolate truffles." However, long insertions into verb phrases muddy meaning and should be moved elsewhere in the sentence.

SPLIT   The governor should *with all deliberate speed* integrate the school system.

CORRECT   The governor should integrate the school system with all deliberate speed.

SPLIT   I will *if your work continues to improve* give you a raise.

CORRECT   I will give you a raise if your work continues to improve.

Exercise

Correct any errors in split infinitives or verb phrases. Answers on p. 106.

1. Spoiled children don't understand how it feels to not get what they want.
2. My dream is to someday own a design firm.
3. Every employer should while firing competent senior workers be aware that he can be charged with age discrimination.
4. To properly wash a car one must caress and massage it as if it were a baby.
5. He began to greatly enjoy the adventure after he had found the magic ring.
6. Internships might if described properly make a résumé sound more professional.
7. Often young people want to simply have a good time without thinking about the future.
8. An experienced salesman can at a moment's notice and with no warning whatsoever understand what his clients want, and can use this understanding to his advantage.
9. The widow seemed to not want any sympathy from us.
10. Marlon Brando decided to surgically lose weight by having his ego removed.

11 Simple verbs instead of progressive and conditional

How are simple tenses different from progressive and conditional tenses?

Simple tenses are what we commonly call the past, present, and future. They indicate habitual and completed actions. These actions are completed at the time of the statement, even if they persisted over a period of time in the past. Other fine stylistic and grammatical points also dictate the use of simple tenses.

Progressive tenses indicate an action or condition in *progress*, continuing over a period of time with no end in sight. The habitual — *every day* — cannot be added to a continuous action.

The conditional tense refers to events that do not exist at the time of the statement, but might, given certain circumstances. It always involves supposition.

11a Choosing between continuous, or habitual and completed actions

If you must show that an action is continuous, choose a progressive tense.

➤They are jogging.

The progressive is correct because the *jogging* is in progress with no end in sight.   BUT

➤They jogged every day OR They jog every day.

The simple tense shows habit and completion.

In all other instances, use the simple tense in preference to the progressive. The simple tense is stronger and more authoritative than the progressive tense. Consider the example below.

➤Peace is possible in a society only when the people and their rulers *are cooperating*.

The progressive *are cooperating* is tentative and unpersuasive. Far stronger and more definitive is the same sentence in the simple present tense.

➤Peace is possible in a society only when the people and their rulers *cooperate.*

Using the present tense to express a future action *11b*

The simple present expresses not only present events but also habitual future events when it is in a subordinate time clause that begins with such words as *when, after, before, as soon as, until,* and with verbs that indicate time: *open/close, begin/end, arrive/leave.*

➤Let us make him feel welcome when he ~~will come~~. [*comes*]

➤She should eat something before she ~~will leave~~. [*leaves*]

➤Do not tell that story until I ~~will~~ return.

The verb *to hope* in the present tense has a similar future aspect: it looks ahead to events to come. Do not use the future tense after to hope in the present.

➤I hope they ~~will~~ return soon.

Placing emphasis in the simple future and conditional *11c*

In the simple future, *will* is commonly used as the helping verb for all person. However, in formal usage, the first person — *I, we* — takes *shall.* To insert emphasis, use *will* for the first persons (I will, we will) and *shall* for all the other persons.

➤I shall major in French literature.

➤He will complete the requirements if he plans to graduate.

The speakers in the examples above are merely conveying a future intention. No emphasis is intended. By contrast, the reversal of *shall* and *will* in the examples below creates an emphatic tone.

➤I *will* major in French literature.

➤He *shall* complete the requirements if he plans to graduate.

Emphasis is created in the conditional in the same way as it is created in the future. While *would* is the standard conjugation for all persons, in formal usage, the first persons take *should* as a helping verb. These are reversed for emphasis.

NEUTRAL   He *would* major in French literature if he could.

EMPHATIC   He *should* major in French literature if he plans to study in Paris.

11d   Selecting conditional and simple tenses

If you are speculating about events or consequences that might happen under certain possible conditions, use the conditional.

➤What *would* people do without pets? Many *would* have no companions and *would* be lonely.

The conditional is correct in this example which considers the possible effects of circumstances that do not exist at the time of the statement.

Avoid the common error of using the conditional for actual events, especially those that occurred in the past. For existing facts, use the simple tense.

➤Baseball players like Ruth, Cobb, and Williams, ~~would spend~~ *spent* their summers at the parks, then ~~would go~~ *went* back to their normal jobs during the rest of the year.

➤In a duel, when Cyrano ~~would attack~~ *attacked*, he ~~would do~~ *did* so swiftly and accurately.

Here the conditional is incorrect. The events are facts, not suppositions, and require the simple tense.

📖   **Exercise**

Correct any errors in using simple verbs instead of progressive and conditional. Answers on p.107.

GROUP A

1. Victorian dresses would have long sleeves, high necklines, and hems that would reach the floor.
2. A driver's education course will have classroom time as well as driving time.

3. The other Cyclopes did not assist Polyphemus when he was calling for help.
4. Jerry Seinfeld is watching reruns of his shows.
5. The new Corvette is the kind of sportscar that will make any driver look like a professional.
6. As long as I pay the bills, you will do as I say.
7. The people who are being excluded from material advantages resent those in power.
8. Maria Calas is being temperamental again.
9. Under the Constitution, impeachment would be a responsibility of the House of Representatives.
10. Dodger fans are very loyal and will cheer for their team even during a losing streak.

GROUP B

1. The features that would distinguish a great team are fan support, individual player success, and overall team success.
2. Whereas cirrhosis takes years to develop, this condition will take only a few days.
3. Dr. Kevorkian was feeling ill last week.
4. A realist is simply accepting existing circumstances.
5. A bigger vehicle can take more of a pounding than a two-door sportscar that leaves its occupants wishing they had purchased a luxury sedan.
6. As in other organs of the body, dead liver cells will be replaced by tough scar tissue.
7. Throughout the Civil War, the shortage of cannons would be a disadvantage for the Confederate forces.
8. The judge ruled that the defendant will pay the fine immediately.
9. Free agency gives players the right to play for whichever team wants them after their contract will expire. In other words, whichever team will pay the most usually will get the desirable player.
10. It seems logical that legalizing narcotics would reduce the spread of disease.

12 Perfect tenses and the sequence of events

What do perfect tenses do, and when should they be used?

The "perfect" in *perfect tense* comes from the Latin meaning "completed" or "finished." Use the perfect tenses for actions completed at the time of speaking or at the specific time referred to by the speaker. By using the perfect tense with a *time word* such as *now, before, since, when* etc., you enable your audience (1) to gauge the duration of an action by signaling the precise moment it finishes, and (2) to recognize that one action has been completed before another and thus get a sense of the correct *sequence of events*.

Use the *perfect progressive tenses* for continuous actions that occur over a measurable period of time — *for a long time, since 1932.* By using the perfect progressive with time words such as *for* (an amount of time), *regularly, continuously* etc., you let your audience know (1) how long the action has been going on at that moment in time, and (2) that it may continue past that moment.

12a Forming the perfect and perfect progressive tenses

Perfect tenses take a form of the helping verb *to have* plus the *past participle* of the main verb. Perfect progressive tenses take a form of the verb phrase *to have been* plus the *present participle* of the main verb.

PRESENT PERFECT

| I, you, we, they | have gone |
| he/she/it | has gone |

PRESENT PERFECT PROGRESSIVE

| I, you, we, they | have been going |
| he/she/it | has been going |

PAST PERFECT

| I, you, he/she/it, we, they | had gone |

PAST PERFECT PROGRESSIVE

| I, you, he/she/it, we, they | had been going |

FUTURE PERFECT

| I, you, he/she/it, we, they | will have gone |

FUTURE PERFECT PROGRESSIVE

| I, you, he/she/it, we, they | will have been going |

CONDITIONAL PERFECT

| I, you, he/she/it, we, they | would have gone |

CONDITIONAL PERFECT PROGRESSIVE

| I, you, he/she/it, we, they | would have been going |

Be careful not to substitute the preposition *of* for the verb *have*. The verb phrase must be *should have* (NOT *should of*),*must have* (NOT *must of*) etc.

Using present perfect instead of simple present or past *12b*

Use the present perfect tense instead of the simple present or past for three types of events:

1. An activity or condition that occurs at an *unspecified* time in the recent past.

UNSPECIFIED	The remains of the Elizabethan theater *The Rose* ~~were~~ [*have been*] found recently north of the Thames.

Recently leaves the time of the event vague, therefore the present perfect *have been*. *Were* would be correct only if the sentence gave a precise date to the discovery — *yesterday, last week* etc.

UNSPECIFIED	Middle East leaders just signed a peace accord. [*have*]

Just is more immediate than *recently* but is still a non-specific time, therefore the present perfect *have signed*. Leaving *just signed* in the simple past changes the meaning of *just* from a time word to a limiting word, that is from meaning *in the last few moments* to *only*.

2. An activity or condition occurring *repeatedly* or at regular intervals in the recent past.

REPEATED	Since 1986, the United States ~~appoints~~ [*has appointed*] a new poet laureate every other year.

Both the simple present and the present perfect can be used for repeated actions. The present perfect, however, connects the past with the present. The time phrase *since 1986* indicates that the action started in the past and continues into the present, therefore the present perfect.

REPEATED	She ~~was~~ [*has been*] late to dinner before.

Using the present perfect *has been* shows her repeated lateness in the recent past and implies that she will repeat her past lateness in the present.

3. A state of being or mind that begins in the past and *continues* into the present.

CONTINUOUS

has been

King Tutankhamen ~~was~~ dead for over 3000 years.

Saying that Tutankhamen *was dead* (simple past) implies that he *is no longer* dead, which, as far as we know, is not the case. *Has been dead* assures the reader that the mummy's state of death is ongoing.

CONTINUOUS

have known

I ~~knew~~ her since I was twelve.

I knew her (simple past) implies that the speaker *no longer* knows her. The simple past would be correct if the time word *since* — which implies continuity over time — were changed to *when* which implies a one-time action.

12c   Using the past and future perfect for sequences of events

The past perfect and future perfect tenses place two events in sequence. If these two events occur in the past, the *earlier event* is in the *past perfect*, while the *later event* is in the *simple past*. If the two events occur in the future, the *earlier event* is in the *future perfect* and the *later event* in the *simple present*. The past and future perfect may sometimes imply that the conditions of the later action depend on the completion of the earlier action.

PAST
SEQUENCE

After Carl Sagan *had finished* his stellar map of the universe, he *rewarded* himself with an ice cream soda.

Notice that the earlier event — finishing the map — is in the past perfect. There is also the implication that the reward depends on his completing the task.

PAST
SEQUENCE

Einstein *had* just *solved* the problem of relativity when he *realized* that his checkbook wasn't balanced.

Again, both events happen in the past, with the earlier event — solving the problem of relativity — indicated by the past perfect. In this example, however, there is *no* causality between the events.

FUTURE
SEQUENCE

The burglar *will have gone* by the time the police *arrive*.

Both events are in the future. At the moment of this statement, the police have not yet arrived and the burglar has not yet gone. The word *arrive* seems to be in the present, but the phrase *by the time* shows that it is in the future (see §11b *Using the present tense to express a future action*). The future perfect *will have gone* is the earlier of the two events.

FUTURE SEQUENCE

By Monday, I *will have been* in the hospital for a week.

The earlier event — being in the hospital — is in the *future perfect*. The later event is implicit in the time phrase *by Monday*.

The sequence of two events in the present employs the future and the simple present as in the sentence, *I will use the telephone when you finish.*

Using perfect progressive tenses for continual and continuous actions   *12d*

The *perfect progressive* tenses share with the *simple present* and the *present perfect* the ability to convey *repeated* or *continual* actions, that is actions occurring at regular intervals over a period of time. Note the interchangeability of tenses in the examples below.

	PRES. PERF. PROG.
CONTINUAL	We *have been vacationing* here every year.
	PRES. PERF.
CONTINUAL	We *have vacationed* here every year.
	PRES.
CONTINUAL	We *vacation* here every year.

The *perfect progressive* tenses, however, are the only tenses to convey both *continual* and *continuous* actions. *Continuous* actions occur without a pause and are usually signaled by the time phrase *for + an amount of time*.

	PRES. PERF. PROG.
CONTINUOUS	They *have been feeling* uncomfortable in that environment for some time.

The discomfort is a condition beginning in the past and continuing into the present. It is also a condition that has been occurring continuously without pause.

PAST. PERF. PROG.

CONTINUOUS   Doris Day *had been sitting* at the window for an hour before Rock Hudson finally drove up.

Here, the event has been continuing for an hour without pause.

FUT. PERF. PROG.

CONTINUOUS   By two o'clock, I *will have been lying* in the dentist's chair *for an hour and a half.*

COND. PERF. PROG.

CONTINUOUS   I *would* still *have been struggling* in the coal mines if I had not won the lottery.

Here, the action is both continuous and continual as indicated by the word *still.*

12e   Using time words as shortcuts to the perfect tenses

The following common time words and expressions quickly signal the need for a perfect tense.

This is the first/second/third time that...

➤"This is the first time that I ~~was~~ on the moon," said John Glenn.
  have been

➤This is the fifth time I ~~am traveling~~ by plane.
  have traveled

Just/recently/lately

➤I just ~~got~~ back from the movies.
  have gotten

➤Lately I ~~suffer~~ from insomnia.
  have been suffering

Since/for + number/date

➤Robert Frost ~~wrote~~ poetry for seventy years when he died
  had been writing

➤Arbor day ~~was~~ a school holiday since 1872.
  has been

Up to now

    have been calling
➤Up to now I ~~called~~ him instead of the other way around.

As soon as

        have heard
➤Let me know as soon as you ~~hear~~ from the Admissions Office.

Often/frequently

   has
➤His picture often appeared in *The New York Times.*
    ^

 have
➤They frequently dropped in at dinner time.
  ^

Ever/never

 Have   *seen*
➤~~Did~~ you ever ~~see~~ this man before?

 have   *seen*
➤I never ~~saw~~ that man before in my whole life.
 ^

So far

   have
➤So far, I read twenty pages.
   ^

Yet/already

   have   *had*
➤They ~~did~~ not ~~have~~ dinner yet.

   had   *seen*
➤They already ~~saw~~ the Grand Canyon.
  ^

Just…when

    had fallen
➤James Brown just ~~fell~~ off his roof when he thought of the perfect song
lyric. ^

Before/after

    had been
➤Lincoln ~~was~~ shot a year before the Civil War ended.

          had
➤After Tropical Depression Juanita pounded Cuba's coast for a week, it
settled over Florida. ^

By the time

         have forgotten
➤By the time I return to Oklahoma, you will ~~forget~~ all about me.

12f   *If...then* constructions

If...then is a shorthand way of referring to a cause-and-effect relationship between actions or conditions in different tenses. The action of the cause (*protasis*), located in the *if clause*, logically occurs before the action of the effect (*apodosis*) located in the *then clause*. Consequently, the tense of the cause will always be earlier than the tense of the effect.

Be aware, however, that the cause need not begin with *if* — other words such as *because* and *when* also signal a cause — nor must the effect begin with *then* — often the *then* is implied. Finally, the *cause* may be mentioned in the sentence after the *effect*.

Most importantly, the relationship between the tenses in *if...then* clauses is fixed. The tenses are partners. When the *if clause* is in a given tense, the *then clause* must be in its partner tense.

PRESENT   ⮕   **FUTURE**

➤If you *leave* at 9:00, you *will arrive* by 10:00.

PRESENT PERFECT   ⮕   **FUTURE PERFECT**

➤If you *have left* at 9:00, you *will have arrived* by 10:00.

PAST   ⮕   **CONDITIONAL**

➤If you *left* at 9:00, you *would arrive* by 10:00.

PAST PERFECT   ⮕   **CONDITIONAL PERFECT**

➤If you *had left* at 9:00, you *would have arrived* by 10:00.

If...then constructions also set up relationships between tenses in the subjunctive mood, although the subjunctive affects only those causal sentences that begin specifically with the word *if* and use the verb *to be* (see §15 *Subjunctive mood*).

PAST SUBJUNCTIVE   ⮕   **CONDITIONAL**

➤If you *were* punctual, we *could have* time for lunch.

📖   **Exercise**

Correct any errors in using perfect tenses in sequences of events. Answers on p.108.

GROUP A

1. Penelope would have behaved differently if she knew that Odysseus was home.
2. Throughout history, technology creates inventions to facilitate daily tasks.
3. He would buy a house on the shore if he were rich.
4. If my brother would buy a house on the shore, I would spend my vacations there.
5. After the next presidential election, I will be voting for the fourth time.
6. Since the early 1900s in the American League and the National League, the Yankees and the Dodgers are always in the race for the pennant.
7. I left messages for my agent all week without any response.
8. After news of the murder, she refused to walk alone by the river.
9. Once again the Chevy people failed to impress the consumer who should be their main target.
10. On the morning of the battle he felt full of courage, although the night before he was terrified.

GROUP B

1. If you don't train your dog, he leaps up and covers your best outfit with mud.
2. If they were never abused as children, they would be leading healthy normal lives today.
3. That summer we frequently strolled on the Boardwalk in the evening.
4. If he had been exiled from his country, he would become a stateless person.
5. Shortly after the release of her first film, Marilyn realizes that strangers are staring at her.
6. By the year 2007, my neighbor will become one hundred years old.
7. I know that Darren would not have been such a difficult student if his parents did not spoil him.
8. This is our third year in Sarasota, and we enjoy it more than ever.
9. Any friendship that had been meaningful should be salvageable.
10. By the time she apologizes, it will be too late.

13 Past tense and past participles

What is a past participle, and what problems occur in using it?

The past participle is the final verb in a verb phrase such as "I have eaten" or "they had tried." While present participles always end in *-ing*, past participles have a variety of endings, most often *-ed* or *-d* as in *lived, called, told*; *-en* or *-n* as in *given, known, been*; and *-t* as in *bent, meant, went.*

Problems occur with verbs that have irregular past tenses and past participles. The simple past and participial forms of a verb can be confused.

13a   Use correct past tense and past participle forms

Three types of errors occur with irregular past tenses and past participles. The first and most common is confusing the simple past with the past participial form of the same verb.

➤ "Honey, I ~~shrunk~~ the kids."
  shrank
➤ I was so angry I could have ~~bit~~ that dog!
  bitten
➤ I'm sorry I ~~bursted~~ your balloon.
  burst

The second type of error is misconjugating the verb in the past tense — that is, using a form of the verb that doesn't exist.

➤ They ~~swimmed~~ in the salt water pool.
  swam
➤ You should have ~~brung~~ your brother.
  brought
➤ Having lost its engines, the plane ~~glid~~ down to a safe landing.
  glided

The final and rarest type of error is the confusion between the past tenses and past participles of verbs that look the same in the infinitive but have different meanings and conjugations.

➤ She ~~hanged~~ her head in shame.
  hung

Hanged is the past tense of the verb *to hang* meaning *to execute*. Using the wrong verb makes it sound as if she killed herself.

might
➤ The prisoner asked if he ~~could~~ be paroled early for good behavior.

Could is the past tense of the verb *to be able to* (can) meaning capable of. The prisoner means to ask if he *will be allowed to* (might) be paroled which is the other meaning of *to be able to.*

Irregular and problematic past tenses and past participles   *13b*

The only way to avoid these errors is to learn the correct conjugations. Below is a list of some common irregular past and past participial verbs.

INFINITIVE	PAST	PAST PARTICIPLE
to arrive	arrived	(have) arrived
to be	was, were	(have) been
to be able to (can)	could	(have) been able to
to be able to (may)	might	(have) been able/allowed to
to become	became	(have) become
to begin	began	(have) begun
to bend	bent	(have) bent
to bite	bit	(have) bitten
to bleed	bled	(have) bled
to blow	blew	(have) blown
to break	broke	(have) broken
to bring	brought	(have) brought
to build	built	(have) built
to burst	burst	(have) burst
to catch	caught	(have) caught
to choose	chose	(have) chosen
to cleave(stick together)	cleaved	(have) cleaved
to cleave (split apart)	cleaved/cleft/clove	(have) cleaved/cleft/cloven
to come	came	(have) come
to cost	cost	(have) cost
to do	did	(have) done
to drink	drank	(have) drunk
to eat	ate	(have) eaten
to freeze	froze	(have) frozen
to glide	glided	(have) glided
to grow	grew	(have) grown
to hang (a thing)	hung	(have) hung
to hang (a person)	hanged	(have) hanged
to heave	heaved/hove	(have) heaved/hoven

to lay (set down)	laid	(have) laid
to lend	lent	(have) lent
to lie (recline)	lay	(have) lain
to prove	proved	(have) proven
to ring	rang	(have) rung
to rise	rose	(have) risen
to run	ran	(have) run
to see	saw	(have) seen
to seek	sought	(have) sought
to shoe	shod	(have) shod
to show	showed	(have) shown
to shrink	shrank	(have) shrunk/shrunken
to swim	swam	(have) swum
to write	wrote	(have) written

Exercise

Correct any errors in using past tenses and past participles. Answers on p.111.

1. The Civil War costed the US six billion dollars and 620,000 lives.
2. Then I heard that James had ran away from his foster parents.
3. He loaned his sister $10,000 to help with the down payment on the house.
4. During the Reign of Terror, lynch mobs hung aristocrats in the streets of Paris.
5. She hung plants in every room of the new apartment.
6. He had to take a summer job instead of laying on the beach all day.
7. He was angry that she had went to movies without even calling him.
8. When the balloon bursted, the child begun crying.
9. No sooner had I laid down, that the doorbell rang.
10. The witness has proved that he is an unreliable observer.

14 *Did* and *had* as helping verbs

Why is did *sometimes used in place of* had*?*

Both *had* and *did* serve as verbs in their own right and as helpers to other verbs. The confusion between them occurs when they are helpers in a verb phrase in which the main verb is only implied and does not actually appear. This confusion occurs in the past perfect tense only.

Use *did* and *had* correctly 14a

As the main verb in its own right, *did* is the past tense of *to do*. Using it in this way is simple and straightforward.

➤Old MacDonald *did* his chores before dawn as usual.

As a helper in a verb phrase, *did* serves two functions. It is used for emphasis, and it is used to formulate a question.

EMPHASIS I certainly *did* deliver the package on time, and here is the proof.

QUESTION *Did* the messenger ask for a signature?

As the main verb in its own right, *had* is the past tense of *to have*. In this form its use is uncomplicated.

➤She *had* only $25 in her purse.

As a helper, *had* creates the past perfect tense (see §12c *Using the past and future perfect for sequences of events*).

➤Old MacDonald ate breakfast after he *had done* his chores.

Resolving the *did* and *had* confusion 14b

Confusion between the two verbs arises in the past perfect when the main verb is implied rather than stated, and the single helper stands alone for the entire verb phrase.

In the simple present tense and in past tenses, the single helping verb can stand alone for the whole verb phrase without any confusion as in the first two examples below. In the past perfect tense, however, *did* is often incorrectly used instead of *had*.

PRESENT   They travel more than I *do*.

Do is the helping verb that stands for the verb phrase *do travel*.

PAST   They traveled more than I ~~had~~ *did* last year.

Did is the helping verb that stands for the verb phrase *did travel*. Both traveled in the same time period. However neither is in the past perfect (*had traveled*) because there is no indication that one activity preceded the other.

PAST PERFECT

>   *had*
> They traveled more than I ~~did.~~

The sentence should read, "They traveled more than I *had traveled.*" The helping verb *had* stands alone for *had traveled*. The past perfect here shows that *I had traveled* earlier than they.

Test which helping verb is correct by adding the implied main verb. If there is a tense shift from past to past perfect, use *had* as the helper instead of *did*.

>   *had*
> ➤Jack Nicholson won an Oscar after Tom Hanks ~~did.~~

After signals a tense shift. Thus the sentence requires the past perfect and the form *had won*.

>   *had*
> ➤Jacques Cousteau knew more about scuba diving than I ~~did~~ at the time.

At the time signals a tense shift, and thus the past perfect *had known*.

📖   Exercise

Correct any errors in using *did* and *had* as helping verbs. Answers on p.111.

1. There are many reasons why the potato famine affected Irish society as strongly as it did.
2. Andrew Jackson intended to lead as firmly in the White House as he did on the battlefield.
3. Hitler had started out much as Milosevic did.
4. Parents want their children to have more than they did when they were growing up.
5. While she did not actually see the crime, she did hear the screams.
6. Tactful people have the ability to resolve many more conflicts than tactless people do.
7. Over the years, as women's lifestyles have changed so did their fashions.
8. Sherlock Holmes had more self-discipline and ingenuity than his adversaries did.
9. We would go to war over slavery today, just as we did in 1861.
10. Being grounded for a month made me realize that disobedience did have consequences.

15 Subjunctive mood

What is a mood?

Verbal moods express the writer's relationship with the reader; they indicate the degree of authority and certainty with which the writer speaks. There are three verbal moods in English: the indicative, the imperative, and the subjunctive.

In the *indicative mood*, the writer is objective and factual. The *indicative* is used for descriptions of events, thoughts, or emotions: *I went to the circus and loved the clowns, but was scared during the high wire act.*

In the *imperative mood*, the writer assumes greater authority and a superior, commanding tone. The *imperative* is used for commands or instructions: *Don't be afraid; they won't fall. Sit down and enjoy the show.*

In the *subjunctive mood*, the writer is the least certain or authoritative. The subjunctive is even more uncertain than the conditional tense. It describes hypothetical situations entertained in the mind not as facts or likelihoods but as desires, needs, or dreams. Use the subjunctive to show state of mind, *not* actual locations. Thus *If he was on the beach yesterday, he must have seen the accident,* but *I wish I were a clown.*

When should the subjunctive be used?

The subjunctive has become less a grammatical necessity than a grammatical refinement. With the exception of a few stock expressions, it can be replaced by the indicative without appreciable harm to meaning. Using the subjunctive accurately, however, adds a note of grace to one's prose, inflecting it with elegance. Overuse the subjunctive and you risk sounding old-fashioned. The rules for its use below, therefore, should be treated not as commandments but as stylistic guidelines.

Use the subjunctive to express *wishes* or *strong suggestions* (the *jussive* subjunctive), conditions of *uncertainty or conjecture, importance* or *urgency, divine appeals* (the *vocative* subjunctive), and with certain *concessions* (the *concessive* subjunctive). The subjunctive commonly appears after the words *if, that, as though, I wish,* and sometimes *whether.*

15a   Forming the subjunctive

PRESENT SUBJUNCTIVE

Take the infinitive of the verb and drop *to*. Use this basic form with all persons — *I, you, he, she, it, we, they.*

INFINITIVE	SUBJUNCTIVE
to be	be
to have	have
to use	use
to bring	bring

➤ The script requires that the father *run up* and *embrace* his little girl.

➤ It is vital that she *bring* her résumé.

Use the present subjunctive of the verb *to be* judiciously in order not to sound stuffy and outdated.

OUTDATED If he *be* a man, he will step outside and settle this matter right now.

CURRENT If need *be*, we can reschedule the class reunion.

PAST SUBJUNCTIVE

The past subjunctive is distinguished from verbs in other moods only in the verb *to be*. Its basic form for all persons is *were*.

➤ I would not marry him if he *were* the last man on earth.

15b   Wishes and strong suggestions (the jussive subjunctive)

The jussive subjunctive covers the gamut from wishes to hopes, desires to intentions, earnest exhortations to strong suggestions. Jussive subjunctives are triggered by verbs or nouns followed by *that* or by *is that/was that*. Below are some common examples.

VERBS THAT TRIGGER THE SUBJUNCTIVE

advise (that)	request (that)
ask (that)	require (that)
demand (that)	suggest (that)
insist (that)	urge (that)
plead (that)	wish (that)
recommend (that)	

➤ The mayor *requested* that they *be given* the key to the city.

➤ The attorney *advised* that he *plead* not guilty.

NOUNS THAT TRIGGER THE SUBJUNCTIVE
> his hope (is that)
> our desire (was that)
> my intention (is that)

➤ The mayor's *request* was that they *be given* the key to the city.

➤ My *hope* is that she *come* home safely.

Compare this last example to the indicative construction which lacks *that — I hope she comes home safely.*

Note also that all *wishes*, whether stated as verbs or as nouns, always take the *past subjunctive*, never the present subjunctive.

➤ I wish I *were* a movie star. NOT I wish I *be* a movie star.

Implied wishes that omit the actual word *wish* but retain its spirit also take the past subjunctive.

➤ Oh, that the situation *were* different!

Uncertainty or conjecture   *15c*

The subjunctive applies to situations that are contrary to fact or which have not yet come about. Contrary-to-fact situations are uncertain and require conjecture. They usually start with the conjunctions *if, as though,* and *whether.*

If

➤ I'll be rich *if* my horoscope ~~proves~~ ^{prove} true.
➤ *If* I ~~was~~ ^{were} you, I'd watch my step!

As though

➤ Allegra acted *as though* she ~~was~~ ^{were} the guest of honor.

Whether

➤ *Whether* the reward ~~is~~ ^{be} large or small is not the point; it's the principle that counts.

A few expressions seem to express uncertainty but do *not* take the subjunctive.

it is probable that

it is possible that

it is likely that

it is improbable that

it is impossible that

it is uncertain whether

In fact, they express *likelihood* and *unlikelihood* which is closer to the conditional than to the subjunctive.

15d Importance or urgency

A limited number of expressions of importance or urgency takes the subjunctive.

> *It is important*
> *It is necessary*
> *It is vital*
> *It is essential*
> *It is crucial*
> *It is imperative*

that this document *be* kept secret.

15e Divine appeals (the vocative subjunctive)

The standard prayer formula "May so and so come to pass," or "May God perform such and such" can be abbreviated using the subjunctive. Thus, "God help us," "God save the queen," "Lord have mercy!" "Damn it!" etc.

What distinguishes these vocative subjunctive expressions from the imperative is the absence of a comma separating the person addressed from the verb. In the imperative we write:

➤Jim, help me!

In the vocative subjunctive no comma is necessary.

➤God help me!

15f Concessions (the concessive subjunctive)

Idiomatic expressions that concede a point take the subjunctive.

truth be told

suffice it to say

be it

as it were

far be it for me to

so be it

be that as it may

come what may

➤Be it ever so humble, there's no place like home.

➤The "little woman," as it were, happens to be your boss.

📖 Exercise

Correct any errors in using the subjunctive mood. Answers on p.112.

GROUP A
1. If I was not his oldest friend, he would not have told me the truth.
2. If this information is correct, then she is clearly not guilty.
3. Although I am totally innocent, the legal system requires that I am punished.
4. I know that she wishes she was more agile because she has always wanted to be a gymnast.
5. He treated me as though I was his slave.
6. My personal tastes notwithstanding, far be it for me to disagree with an acknowledged authority on art.
7. Whether it is the sleek but rugged look of the F-150 or F-250, or the powerful appearance of the Super Duty, Ford's styling will delight any aficionado.
8. It is crucial that she is calm during the questioning.
9. Please, God, let this story prove false.
10. It is imperative that he has his skis in time for the competition.

GROUP B
1. If the truth is told, I am actually just as guilty as she is.
2. He wouldn't have dared to challenge the bully if he wasn't brave.
3. His father insisted that he does his homework before he goes to the dance.
4. I wish Andy Roddick was the number one tennis player in the world.
5. The contract requires that he sends out the manuscript by September 10.
6. One important consideration in choosing a gift is that it is easy on my wallet.
7. Whether the reward is large or small is not the point; it's justice that counts.
8. I must admit the truth, whether it is damaging or not.
9. She acted as though she was the guest of honor.
10. The diet demands that she sees her doctor once a month.

16 Shifts in subjects, verbs, and direction

What is a needless shift in subject?

For reasons of continuity, readers expect the same subject to control an entire sentence. They also expect the subject to remain in the same person. Likewise, for coherence, governing pronouns need to remain in the same person throughout a paragraph or even an entire essay.

Do not shift subjects needlessly. Or, if a shift of subject is necessary, be sure to signal the change. The most common errors with shifting subjects fall into three categories: *shifts in person and number, shifts between indefinite and definite pronouns,* and *misuse of change-of-direction words.*

16a
Shifts in the subject

Each sentence is about a particular subject and cannot switch subjects unless there is an intentional change of direction in thought (see below §16f). Likewise, sentences that begin with a subject in a particular person — first (*I/we*), second (*you*), or third (*he/she/it/they*) — and number (singular or plural) must stay in the same person and number. (See specifically §66c *Integrate quotations into text.*)

> When *people* are learning to drive, ~~you~~ *they* have the greatest problem with changing gears.

The subject shifts from *people* (meaning *they*, third person plural) to *you* (second person). (See §3 *Ambiguous or doubtful pronoun references*).

> Chaucer's Pardoner admits ~~that~~ "I preach for nothing but for greed of gain."

The shift is from the third person *Pardoner* to the first person *I.* Correct by deleting *that* and by adding a colon or a comma before the open-quotation mark.

16b
Shifts from *one* to other pronouns

The pronoun *one* requires careful treatment. In gender, *one* is *indefinite.* Therefore, any pronoun that refers to it must also be indefinite. It is a mistake to pair *one* with a *definite* masculine or feminine pronoun. Do not refer to *one* with the pronouns *he, she, him, her, his, himself, herself.*

➤One's behavior reflects ~~his~~ character. *(one's)*

➤One is as old as ~~she~~ feels. *(one)*

Likewise, because *one* is singular, any pronoun referring to it must also be singular. Do not refer to *one* with the plural pronouns *they, them, their, themselves.*

➤One's experiences often determine ~~their~~ decisions. *(one's)*

One may act as antecedent only to *one* or *oneself.*

➤Periodically, one should reward ~~themselves~~ with a small but luxurious gift. *(oneself)*

➤In planning for college, one must give ~~himself~~ as many academic and financial options as possible. *(oneself)*

What is a needless shift in verb?

Clear writing is consistent in its use of both subjects and verbs. Verbs convey information to the reader not only through their meaning but also through their grammatical structure. They communicate grammatically in three ways: tense, form, mood.

First, a verb's *tense* provides the reader with a point of reference in time. An essay that begins in the present tense should remain in the present tense. A sudden shift to the past tense may suggest that the action described is old and no longer relevant, while a shift to the future or conditional tense may imply that the action is uncertain or untrue in the present.

Second, a verb's *form* demonstrates the writer's engagement with her subject. The *active* form of the verb — *I decided* — demonstrates the writer's commitment to an idea or action. The *passive* form of the verb — *it was decided by me* — demonstrates the writer's emotional detachment, caution, or desire for objectivity.

Third, a verb's *mood* indicates the writer's attitude toward the reader. We normally write using verbs in the indicative mood which is used for communicating our experiences, feelings, or thoughts — *I am finishing my work.* On occasion we use the imperative mood to give orders, instructions and commands — *finish your work!* The

imperative mood is common in instructional manuals such as
this one — *do not needlessly shift a verb's mood from indicative to
imperative.* (See §15 *Subjunctive mood.*)

16c Shifts in verb tense

Shifts in verbs can occur among all the tenses, but most commonly
from the present tense to the past, future, or conditional.

PRESENT TO PAST	The suspect *admits* being at the scene of the crime but *claims* ~~claimed~~ he ~~wasn't~~ *isn't* involved.
PRESENT TO FUTURE	In *The Lord of the Flies,* a group of boys *is stranded* on a desert island and ~~will have~~ *has* to learn to survive.
PRESENT TO CONDITIONAL	So you're Sigmund Freud, and ~~would~~ *is* that hysterical young woman ~~be~~ Anna O?

Verb tense shifts often occur in responses to another person's
questions. Even though the answer is a new sentence spoken by a
different person, it is expected to be in the same tense as the question.

➤ "What is the name of that English sport similar to baseball?"

"That ~~would be~~ *is* cricket or perhaps rounders."

16d Active to passive shifts

Active verbs must never give way to passive verbs. The result is not
only a verb shift but a subject shift.

➤ After the mechanic *removed* the carburetor, the valves *were cleaned.*

The active form *removed* changes to the passive *were cleaned.*
Consequently *mechanic,* the subject of the first part of the sentence,
shifts to *valves* in the second part.

➤ Ernest Hemingway *raised* his rifle, and suddenly Jane Goodall *was
shot.*

The shift from the active *raised* to the passive *was shot* leaves in doubt
who shot Jane.

Indicative to imperative shifts

16e

Shifts in mood from the indicative to the imperative may occur when instructions are narrated indirectly or reported to a third party. The imperative is used for commands or instructions given directly to another person. But when these commands or instructions are reported to a third party as part of a story, they become descriptions of an event. Descriptions use the indicative mood.

> ➤ The park rangers said that to avoid bears we *should store* our food in the car and ~~don't~~ ^{not} eat in the tent.

> *Said that...* signals a description of events, and must be in the indicative mood. Originally the rangers' instructions were imperative, *Don't eat!* But once they are reported, they must be converted into the indicative, unless they are quoted directly.

When recounting reported instructions either place them in quotation marks or convert them to descriptions of events.

> ➤ The park rangers said, "To avoid bears, store your food in the car, and don't eat in the tent."

OR

> ➤ The park rangers said that to avoid bears we should store our food in the car and not eat in the tent.

Change of direction in thought

16f

A change of direction in thought occurs when a writer states a generality and then focuses on the exception, or when a writer shows two different consequences of, or reactions to, a particular event.

> Although the Mensheviks and the Bolsheviks were revolutionary allies, their attitudes toward pursuing World War I were diametrically opposed. The Mensheviks insisted on continuing Russia's military campaign, *while* the Bolsheviks called for an unconditional cease fire.

To signal such a change, the writer must use a transitional expression that indicates contradiction or disagreement. In the example above, that expression is *while*. Other useful expressions are listed below.

by contrast	instead
but	nevertheless

contrary to	nonetheless
despite	otherwise
even though	rather than
however	still
in spite of	though

Misleading changes in the direction of a thought may occur when the writer uses a word to signal agreement between ideas instead of indicating contradiction.

> *but*
> ➤Marriages are intended to last forever, ~~and~~ teenagers jump into them as if deciding which flavor of ice cream to choose.

The seriousness of marriages in the first part of the sentence contrasts with the frivolousness of the teenagers in the second. Rather than indicate a contrast, *and* implies continuity. *But* supplies the necessary change of direction.

Sometimes final punctuation — a period, for example — supplies a signal to the reader strong enough to indicate a shift. Often, though, punctuation alone is inadequate to signal a change in the direction of the thought.

INADEQUATE   Marriages are intended to last forever. Teenagers jump into them as if deciding which flavor of ice cream to choose.

IMPROVED   Marriages are intended to last forever. Teenagers, *however*, jump into them as if deciding which flavor of ice cream to choose.

Of course, the most powerful indication of a change of direction is a paragraph. It, too, may be introduced by a change of direction word as a way of smoothing the transition from one idea to the next.

📖   Exercise

Correct any shifts in subjects, verbs, or direction. Answers on p.113.

GROUP A
1. When pedestrians cross at traffic lights, you do not get into so many accidents.
2. The hero goes on an adventure to discover who he was.
3. The police investigated the company's financial records, but no irregularities were uncovered.
4. Because people are not perfect, you are likely to make mistakes.
5. The restaurant was already closing, and I went in.
6. Many displaced farmers were never trained for other jobs, and so it was impossible to gain employment.

7. When one refuses to ask for directions, they end up taking the wrong route.
8. According to the instructions, I must take the first exit and don't turn right until the gas station.
9. The Corvette goes from 0–60 in 4.7 seconds but has a top speed of 189 mph.
10. When Marco Polo arrived in China, he discovered to his surprise that no one spoke Italian, so that sign language becomes his method of communication.

GROUP B
1. In Ray Bradbury's novel, the protagonist thinks that if my wife dies I will never have a chance to restore our relationship.
2. We saw her cheat on the exam, and she said she didn't do it.
3. Some men think that they can be unfaithful, but as long as he pays the bills he will be forgiven.
4. Often parents didn't know where their children are at night, and they don't care.
5. They proofread the proposal twice, but no mistakes were discovered.
6. People can be drawn to one because he is very funny, or kind, or smart.
7. Gulliver was so frightened by the voices of the giants that "I [...] thought it was thunder."
8. The first rule of good management is to understand the desires of the consumers and don't take your employees for granted.
9. Whether one admits it or not, we cannot learn without making generalizations about our social experiences.
10. The emergency team arrived at the scene of the accident, and first aid was given promptly to the victim.

17 Referring to literary or historical time

What is literary or historical time?

Literary or historical time is time *as experienced by literary or historical characters within the frame of a text* as opposed to time *as experienced by the writer in the real world*. Many words and expressions such as *now, ago, soon,* take the time as experienced by the speaker as their point of reference. However, *now* spoken from the point of view of the literary or historical character is very different from the writer's and reader's *now*.

When reporting events in the past, make sure that your time words relate *to the time frame of the text*, not to your own time frame (unless you are writing about the present).

17a   Using literary or historical time words

When reporting past events, time words must be translated from real time to literary or historical time. This translation often becomes necessary when turning quoted speech into reported speech.

Ago, preceding, heretofore   ⇨   *earlier,   before,   preceding, thereotofore*

           earlier
➤Several years ~~ago,~~ Napoleon had married Josephine.

Ago gives the impression that he had married her a few years before the writer wrote this sentence. The marriage is in relation to the writer's time, not Napoleon's time.

Current   ⇨   *then current, contemporary*

                                           then
➤After the treaty of Tilsit, Napoleon had little respect for the current leader of Prussia.

Current means *happening now*. What is current for Napoleon is the past for the writer and reader.

Currently   ⇨   *during that time*

➤"Currently, I am trying to regain control over Haiti," said Napoleon.

Turning quoted speech into reported speech eliminates the quotation marks and requires the writer to change her time words.

➤Napoleon said that *during that time* he was trying to regain control over Haiti.

From now on   ⇨   *from then on, thenceforth*

                                       then
➤The Russian campaign of 1812-13 proved disastrous, and from ~~now~~ on Napoleon's fortunes were in decline.

Future ⇨ *later, subsequent*
Later
➤~~Future~~ rulers of France enjoyed markedly less success in war.

Hereafter ⇨ *thereafter*

➤"Up to now I have been France's first Roman Consul. Hereafter, I will be its Emperor," announced Napoleon.

In reported speech, two time words need changing.

➤Up to *then* Napoleon had been France's first Roman Consul. *Thereafter,* he was its Emperor.

Modern ⇨ *contemporary*

Contemporary
➤~~Modern~~ historians of Napoleon's time considered Napoleon an enlightened despot.

Modern means existing in the present age. Historians *of Napoleon's time* cannot, therefore, be modern. They can be *contemporary* which means *existing in the same time period as* the person in question.

Next ⇨ *the following, the subsequent*
following
➤Napoleon escaped from Elba in March, 1815 and in the ~~next~~ hundred days was defeated decisively at Waterloo.

Now ⇨ *then, at that moment*
At that moment
➤The news arrived that Nelson had won at Trafalgar. ~~Now,~~ without a navy, Napoleon realized he could never invade England.

Present ⇨ *erstwhile, former*
erstwhile
➤Napoleon replaced the ~~present~~ King of Spain by his brother Joseph Bonaparte.

Soon ⇨ *shortly thereafter*
Shortly thereafter
➤In March 1814, the Quadruple Alliance was formed. ~~Soon,~~ Napoleon abdicated.

Today, tomorrow, yesterday ⇨ *that day, the day after, the day before*

the day before
➤In 1799, Napoleon could rightly say that ~~yesterday~~ he had been a
that day   the day after
General, ~~today~~ he ruled France, and ~~tomorrow~~ the whole of Europe.

17b Use the present and present perfect to refer to authors' and critics' work

Treat all fictional events and characters, no matter how remote in the past, as if they belonged in the present. The *present tense* is used for discussing an author and his work, and for summarizing his opinions.

➤ In the Narcissus story, Ovid *explores* themes of self-knowledge.

Even though Ovid wrote two thousand years ago, his ideas are current. Hence *explores* is in the present tense.

Scholarly opinion in the majority should be expressed in the *present tense*. Dissenting opinions, however, should be phrased using the *present perfect*.

AUTHORITATIVE OPINION   Most scientists *agree* that Koko the gorilla's ability to use sign language *demonstrates* that humans are not the only animals capable of using symbols.

DISSENTING OPINION   Some linguists, however, *have disputed* the quality of Koko's verbal acts.

Exercise

Correct any errors in referring to literary or historical time. Answers on p.115.

1. In 1836, Arkansas entered the Union as a slave state. The next year, Michigan entered as a free state.
2. Now Romeo thought that he was in love with Rosaline.
3. Before, Robin Hood had been a respectable young nobleman.
4. Donne's poems revealed a passionate spirit.
5. General Johnson surrendered to General Sherman after the Civil War was officially over — Lee had surrendered to Grant two weeks before.
6. A year ago, Ernest Hemingway had vacationed in Florence.
7. Soon the competition between Eisenhower and Montgomery intensified.
8. Even the conservative American Medical Association argues that unionizing doctors will improve health care. However, insurance companies have been protesting that it will not affect the quality of care but will drastically increase the cost to the consumer.
9. In the future, Bilbo Baggins became the actual leader of the expedition to Lonely Mountain.
10. In *Watership Down*, the rabbits triumphed only because of the diversity of talent among the members of the group.

1–17 Answers to exercises

 ## 1 Subject–verb agreement

GROUP A

1. *Agreement in person.* Subject is first person singular (*I*). Verb (*are*) is not.
   Revision: I am also supposed to attend the play, am I not?

2. *No revision.* In *either...or* construction, verb agrees with the closer subject.

3. *Agreement in person and number.* Indefinite pronoun *each* is third person singular. Verb (*do/have*) is third person plural
   Revision: Does each of the members have his own e-mail address?

4. *Neither...nor construction.* Verb (*likes*) agrees with the closer subject (*Igor*).
   Revision: Neither Hans nor Igor *likes* snowless winters when the skiing is bad.

5. *Compound subject* joined with *and* must take plural subject. *Has* is singular.
   Revision: Both the prosecution and the defense *have* rested their case.

6. *Neither nor construction.* Verb (*is*) must agree with closer subject (*I*).
   Revision: Neither Kevin nor I *am* in the mood for pizza.

7. *Compound subjects* (*jacket/skirt*) joined by *and* must take plural verbs.
   Revision: Both the jacket and the skirt *are* too long.

8. *No revision. A number of* studies clearly indicates more than one. Therefore, the subject is plural and requires the plural verb, *show.*

9. *Agreement in number.* Singular, indefinite pronoun (*one*) is paired with plural verb (*are*).
   Revision: Every one of Seattle's coffee houses *is* connected to the Internet.

10. *Neither...nor construction.* Verb (*have*) must become singular to agree with closer subject (*driver*).
    Revision: Neither the passengers nor the driver *has* any idea where the stadium is.

GROUP B

1. *Agreement in number.* Subject (*either*) is singular. Verb (*do*) must also be singular.
   Revision: Does either of you remember the last time we swam in Lake George?

2. *Collective nouns* (*investment club*) are plural if their members act as separate individuals who disagree, instead of as a unit.
   Revision: The investment club are in disagreement about whether or not to buy Japanese securities.
3. *Agreement in number.* Subject (*everything*) is singular. Verb (*were*) must also be singular.
   Revision: Everything in the cabinets was moldy.
4. *No revision.* The time period *three weeks* may look plural, but is singular because it represents a single unit.
5. *Agreement in number.* Singular subject (*group*) must take singular verb (*was*).
   Revision: The entire group of applicants *was* outstanding.
6. *Agreement in number.* Singular subject (*total*) must take a singular verb.
   Revision: There is a grand total of six fireplaces in the house.
7. *No revision. Spaghetti* and *meatballs* is a single unit and takes a singular verb.
8. *Singular indefinite pronoun* (*one*) takes singular third person verb (*has*).
   Revision: Any one of these symptoms *has* a great impact on the victim.
9. *Agreement in number.* A plural subject (*treaties*) takes a plural verb (*have*).
   Revision: For peace between warring countries to be concluded, there *have* to be treaties signed.
10. *Compound subject* joined by *and* takes a plural verb (*make*).
    Revision: Their skills and information *make* it possible for them to get good jobs.

2 Pronoun–antecedent agreement

1. *Plural antecedent* (*women*) with singular pronoun (*her*).
   Revision: A hundred years ago, upper class women used to spend *their* day visiting or shopping.
2. *Singular antecedent* (*one*) with plural pronoun (*they, their*).
   Revision: The way one feels often affects the way *one* perceives *one's* environment.
3. *Singular antecedent* (*person*) with plural pronoun (*they*).
   Revision: The more money a person stands to gain from a business deal, the less likely *he* is to behave morally.
4. *Singular antecedent* (*someone*) with plural pronoun (*their*).
   Revision: This decision shows that a person might reject someone else's solution to a problem in order to retain *his* pride.
5. *Singular antecedent* (*anyone*) with plural pronoun (*they*).
   Revision: "Sour grapes" refers to how anyone reacts to something *she* cannot have.

6. *Singular antecedent (individual) with plural pronouns (their, they).*
   Revision: When an individual believes *his* own lies, *he* does not change the actual situation except in *his* mind.
7. *Singular antecedent (anybody) with plural pronoun (their).*
   Revision: The more anybody tries to deny a risk, the more convincing *his* false sense of security becomes.
8. *Singular antecedent (applicant) with plural pronoun (they).*
   Revision: A younger applicant may be chosen over an older one because *he* is considered more agile and energetic.
9. *Singular antecedent (no one) with plural pronouns (their, they).*
   Revision: No one likes to betray *his* friends, but *he has* to when other people may be in danger.
10. *Singular antecedent (anybody) with plural pronoun (their).*
   Revision: Anybody who wants dessert should raise *her* hand before it's too late.

3 Ambiguous or doubtful references

1. *Error with* she. Who stole the bracelet? To whom does *she* refer?
   Revision: The day that Queen Victoria stole the gold bracelet, the long friendship between her and her maid was over.
2. *Doubtful reference with* it *and agreement in number.* Does *it* refer to money problems? If it does, then a singular pronoun is referring to a plural antecedent.
   Revision: Janet is constantly talking about her money problems. *They are* her primary topic of conversation.
3. *Ambiguous reference with* this *and agreement in number* (as well as poor style). To what does *this* refer? If it refers to *stepped, leaped,* and *forgot,* then a singular pronoun refers to three antecedents. (Also, in this case, *this* should be used as an adjective — e.g., *this behavior.*)
   Revision: Mikhail Baryshnikov's dance partner stepped on his foot, leaped into the arms of other men, and forgot his name. *These actions* seriously annoyed Mikhail.
4. *Missing antecedent.* Who are *they?* There is no antecedent for this pronoun.
   Revision: Experts on etiquette say that you may eat fried chicken with your fingers.

   OR

   Ms. Manners says that you may eat fried chicken with your fingers.
5. *Missing antecedent. She* has no antecedent. *McCarthy's* is not a noun; it is an adjective describing *book.*
   Revision: In this book, McCarthy tends to romanticize socialist ideals.
6. *Missing antecedent. They* has no antecedent. *People's* is merely an adjective describing *control.*

Revision: People tend to feel insecure because their control of their environment is often uncertain.

7. *Ambiguous reference with* this. To what does *this* refer—Studying? Working nights? Pinching pennies? All of them together? *This* should be used as an adjective.
Revision: He knew that getting an education was very important for success in his career. But when he saw that he would have to work a night shift and pinch pennies, he realized that *this kind of sacrifice* was not what he wanted.

8. *Missing antecedent*. What is the antecedent of *it*? There is none.
Revision: The entire group gets a bad reputation when a few people behave badly.

9. *Missing antecedent*. What is the antecedent of *one*? It can't be gun control. It has no antecedent.
Revision: Charlton Heston campaigned against gun control saying that all Americans have the right to own a handgun.

10. *Ambiguous reference*. Whose nails was the woman biting—her own or my mother's?
Revision: In the theater, next to my mother, a woman was biting her nails.

✍ 4 Pronoun errors in subjects and complements

1. *Objects of preposition. Except* requires objective pronoun.
Revision: Everyone except *him* and *me* received a door prize.

2. *No revision.* Subject = *that.* Linking verb = *could be.* Predicate nominative = *they.*

3. *Incorrect use of nominative pronouns* she, I *for indirect objects.*
Revision: Leonard Nimoy showed *her* and *me* his favorite *Star Trek* episode.

4. *Incorrect use of objective pronouns.* Subjects take nominative pronouns. *Me* is objective.
Revision: Both Mickey Mouse and *I* are in the picture we took at Disneyworld.

5. *Object of the preposition (like)* takes an objective pronoun.
Revision: It sounds like *her* on the phone.

6. *Incorrect use of nominative pronouns.* Direct objects are in the objective case. Use *me* instead of *I.*
Revision: The watchdog growled when he saw Charlene and *me* in our Halloween costumes.

7. *Apposition. He* should be converted to *him* because it is in apposition to *them* which is objective.
Revision: We watched them, my neighbor and *him*, as they swam out to save our stranded cat.

8. *Incorrect use of nominative pronouns. They* should be *them* because it is the direct object.

Revision: In the end, we did not invite either *them* or their friend.

9. *Incorrect use of objective pronouns. Us* should be *we* because subjects are always nominative.
   Revision: Both our cousins and *we* liked swimming in the lake after dark.

10. *Incorrect use of objective pronouns. Her* should be *she* because it is in apposition to the subject *actors*.
    Revision: Only the leading actors, Laurence Olivier and *she*, took a second bow.

 5 Reflexive pronouns

1. *No revision.* Reflexive *themselves* correctly identifies action performed on oneself.

2. *Subjects must be nominative.* The comparison should be between anyone and *he* which is the subject of the implied clause *than he is.* Because the pronoun is the subject of this clause, it must be nominative (*he*) not reflexive (*himself*).
   Revision: A bully thinks that anyone physically weaker than *he is* has no rights.

3. *No revision. Themselves* is correctly used for emphasis.

4. *Objects must be objective. Ourselves* should be the objective *us* because it is the indirect object of the sentence. There is no reason to use the reflexive as it shows neither emphasis nor an action performed on oneself.
   Revision: Our grandparents gave our cousins and *us* a graduation party.

5. *Objects must be objective.* The sentence requires a direct object *me* in the objective case.
   Revision: He had two sons, Jonathan and *me*.

6. *No revision. Himself* emphasizes the importance of the emperor.

7. *Action performed on oneself is reflexive. Me* should be replaced by *myself.* Even though *me* is the object of the preposition *about*, it refers to an action performed on oneself and, therefore, should be reflexive rather than objective.
   Revision: During the interview I told the reporter all about *myself*.

8. *Emphasis uses reflexive. Themselves* is intended to be emphatic. If possible, avoid using a reflexive pronoun as the object of a preposition, and place it as close as possible to the pronoun it emphasizes.
   Revision: They marketed the computer programs that they *themselves* had developed.

9. *Objects must be objective. Herself* is the object of the preposition and should be objective (*her*), not reflexive unless it shows emphasis or an action performed on oneself.
   Revision: The flowers were sent to her roommates and *her*.

10. *No revision.* Even though *herself* is the indirect object, it shows an action performed on oneself and is properly reflexive.

✍ **6** *Who/whoever* versus *whom/whomever*

GROUP A

1. *Agreement in number and person.* Subject of subordinate clause (*who*) must be plural to agree with its plural antecedent (*people*). Verb (*enjoys*) must also be plural.
   Revision: "Sigmund Freud," she said, "has always been one of those people who *enjoy* practical jokes."

2. *Agreement in person and number.* Antecedent is *I*. Pronoun *who* stands in place of *I* and must use a verb (*am*) that agrees with *I*.
   Revision: It is not they but I *who am* out of luck this time.

3. *Who* refers to *people*. *That* should be *who*.
   Revision: A society is an organization of people *who* are united by common loyalties and lifestyles.

4. *Who* refers to *people*. *Which* refers to *guy* and, therefore, must be *who*.
   Revision: Some believe that a man can perform immoral acts and still be a "good guy" *who* made some mistakes.

5. *Objects are objective.* *Whom* should be used because it acts as a direct object (you ask *whom*).
   Revision: The answer depends on *whom* you ask.

6. *Objects are objective.* Object of the preposition (*to*) has to be objective.
   Revision: Whom did you give my phone number to?

   OR

   To whom did you give my phone number?

7. *Who* refers to *people*. *Who* replaces *which* because it refers to people (*characters*).
   Revision: I loved the characters *who* were like many people I know.

8. *No revision.* While *which* may not refer to people, *whichever* may do so.

9. *Who* refers to *people*. *Which* must be replaced by *who* because it refers to *few* and to *people*.
   Revision: Unless people think for themselves, our society will be run by a select few *who* speak for the rest of us.

10. *Objects are objective.* Direct object of the subordinate clause must be objective (*whomever*) not nominative (*whoever*).
    Revision: I don't care who gets the prize. Give it to *whomever* you want.

GROUP B

1. *Subjects are nominative.* Incorrect use of objective pronoun *whomever* for subject of a subordinate clause. The entire subordinate clause *whoever deserves it* is the object of the preposition *to*. However, subjects are always nominative regardless of where they are located.

Within this clause, preserve the subject-verb relationship between *whoever* and *deserves*.

Revision: On second thought, we want you to give the prize to *whoever* deserves it.

2. *Agreement in person and number. Who* is third person plural and takes the third person plural verb (*are*) because it refers to *people*.
Revision: Am I one of the people *who are* responsible for this disaster?

3. *Agreement in number. That* stands for the third person plural because it refers to two items *looks* and *control*. It must take the third person plural verb (*dominate*).
Revision: The 1999 Mustang has the looks and control *that dominate* its competition.

4. *No revision: Whom* is the object of the preposition *from*.

5. *Objects are objective. Who* should be *whom* because it is a direct object (you do know *whom*). *That* should be *who* because it refers to people.
Revision: Whom do you know *who* lives in Muncie?

6. *Objects are objective. Whoever* should be *whomever*. It is objective because it is the direct object of the subordinate clause *whoever my son marries* (subject=*son*, verb=*marries*, direct object=*whomever*).
Revision: I will accept affectionately *whomever* my son marries.

7. *No revision. Who* is correct. It is the subject of the subordinate clause *who committed the crime*. Subjects are nominative.

8. *Who refers to people. Which* should be *who* because it refers to people (*guitarists*).
Revision: There are many great guitarists *who* are similar in style.

9. *Agreement in person and number. That* is correct because it refers to an inanimate object. But, it refers to a third person singular antecedent (*one*) and, therefore, must take a third person singular verb (*matches*).
Revision: This is the only one of all these fabrics *that matches* my wallpaper.

10. *Whom refers to people. Which* should be *whom*. It refers to *men*, and is the object of the preposition *of*.
Revision: On the first day of battle at Gettysburg, the Union army lost 4000 men, one of *whom* was General Reynolds.

7 *Which* and *that*

1. *Essential clause.* The clause explains the strong emotional value of the ring. It adds significant information and, thus, should begin with *that*.
Revision: I lost the ring *that* had been in my family for a hundred years.

2. *Essential clause out of sequence.* Sequentially, the second *that* should be *which*. However, the first clause (*that she found*) is incidental and should begin with *which* and be enclosed in commas. The essential

clause is the one about the frog's turning into a prince, and should
begin with *that.*
Revision: The child brought home a frog, *which* she found, and *that*
she expected to become a prince.

3. That *and* which *in sequence.* Use *that* first and *which* next when the
two appear in the same sentence. However, for two essential clauses in
one sentence, using *that* and *that* is equally acceptable.
Revision: The logic problem *that* gave me so much trouble was the
one *which* compared apples to oranges.

4. Which *and* that *in the same number as the words they replace.*
That must be plural because it refers to two items (*strategy* and
marketing), so the verb *characterizes* must also be plural.
Revision: She was expert in the strategy and marketing that
characterize an effective advertising campaign.

5. *No revision. That* starts an essential clause even though it deals with
location. Also, with no ending preposition to eliminate, *which* is not a
consideration.

6. *No revision.* Comma and *which* are appropriate for an incidental
clause.

7. *Location.* Use *which* to show location and to avoid ending awkwardly
in a preposition (*on*).
Revision: This must be the tree *on which* you carved our initials.

8. *Incidental clause. That* should be replaced by *which* and should be
enclosed in commas because the information in the clause is
incidental to the meaning of the sentence.
Revision: One of nature's phenomena, *which* are interesting to study, is
camouflage.

9. *Essential clause. Which* should be replaced by *that* because the
clause (*which are not part of normal life experience*) is essential to
the meaning of the sentence.
Revision: He described a series of events *that* are not part of normal
life experience.

10. *Incidental clause.* Replace *that* with *which* because the clause is
incidental to the sentence, and enclose this clause in commas.
Revision: The technology, *with which* Americans are blessed, makes
their lives unusually comfortable.

8 Gerunds and participles

1. *Gerund* (*confessing*). Possessive nouns and pronouns precede gerunds.
Add -'s to *Heloise.* Better still, change the gerund *confessing* to a noun
confession.
Revision: Abelard was thrilled by *Heloise's confessing* that she loved him.
OR
Abelard was thrilled by *Heloise's confession* that she loved him.

2. *No revision. Irritated* is the past participle that acts as an adjective.
3. *Gerund (lying).* Use a possessive in front of the gerund.
   Revision: Nixon's lying on national television meant that I could never again trust a politician.
4. *Participle. Cooking dinner* is a participial phrase that describes *wife.* It is not a gerundial phrase. Eliminate the *-'s.*
   Revision: He watched the baby, while his wife, *cooking dinner,* bustled about the kitchen.
5. *Gerund (destroying).* Use possessive *(their)* in front of the gerund *(destroying).*
   Revision: As for Haldeman and Ehrlichman, I found *their destroying* evidence entirely predictable.
6. *Gerund (moving).* While the sentence is grammatically correct, it is unclear and clumsy. Simplify by eliminating the gerund. Notice that the possessive apostrophe is also eliminated.
   Revision: I helped my cousins *move* into their new apartment.
7. *Gerund (going).* Use the possessive *(our)* in front of the gerund.
   Revision: I forgot to tell him about *our going* to Hawaii.
8. *Gerund. Having been admitted to U.C.L.A.* is a gerundial phrase. Use the possessive *(brother's)* in front the gerund. Better yet, change *having been admitted* to *admission.*
   Revision: My family was very excited about my brother's admission to U.C.L.A.
9. *Participle. Having been admitted to U.C.L.A.,* is a participial phrase. It requires no possessives, but it should be set apart in commas.
   Revision: My brother, *having been admitted to U.C.L.A.,* began packing immediately even though it was only April.
   OR
   Having been admitted to U.C.L..A, my brother began packing immediately even though it was only April.
10. *Gerund (attacking).* The construction is grammatically correct but very awkward. Correct it by eliminating the gerund. Notice that *troops* is not necessary in this revision.
    Revision: The Confederate *attack* on Fort Sumter was the immediate cause of the Civil War.

9 Placement of modifiers

GROUP A

1. *Dangling adjective. If done correctly* cannot modify *snowboard.* It must modify a missing *maneuver.*
   Revision: If done correctly, *the maneuver* will turn your snowboard to the right.
2. *Two-way modifier.* What happened *when you were in camp,* the *telling,* or the *travelling?*

Revision: When you were in camp, did he tell you I was traveling in Europe?

OR

Did he tell you I was traveling in Europe when you were in camp?

3. *Limiting word misplaced.* *Just* is in the wrong place. It should modify *movie*, not *wanted*.
Revision: I wanted to go just to a movie, not to a big party.

4. *Misplaced modifier.* It was *Hemingway*, not the *bluefish* who was embarrassed. Move the modifier.
Revision: Telling no one of his only catch that day, Ernest Hemingway, *thoroughly embarrassed*, threw back the baby bluefish.

5. *Misplaced modifier.* Actually Macbeth loved his wife and had no intention of killing her.
Revision: Macbeth had greater will power than Lady Macbeth because he, *instead of his wife*, killed the king.

6. *Dangling adverb.* Here *unfortunately* modifies *mattered.* But who feels it's unfortunate that these efforts did not matter? It is not the reader, and it should not be the author. Eliminate the emotional *unfortunately*, and add a factual *Confederacy* for whom *none of this mattered.*
Revision: General Longstreet tried to assist Lee with reinforcements at Gettysburg. Later, he helped defend Richmond. *Finally however, for the Confederacy* none of this mattered because soon thereafter the South surrendered.

7. *Dangling adjective.* Benito Mussolini's mother was an adult, not a child, at the time that she fed her son.
Revision: Benito Mussolini's mother never fed her son spaghetti *when he was a child.*

8. *Dangling adjective.* Why were the parents sitting in cradles?
Revision: While Richard and Esmeralda were in their cradles, their parents decided that the children would be married to each other.

9. *Two-way modifier.* What happened *at lunchtime,* the absence or the discovery? Correct by moving *at lunchtime* to either the beginning or the end of the sentence.
Revision: At lunchtime, the principal discovered the boys were absent.

OR

The principal discovered the boys were absent *at lunchtime.*

10. *No revision.* Here the *hopefully* describes accurately how the South felt.

GROUP B

1. *Two-way modifier.* Who had the heart attack, Dr. Morris?
Revision: After Mr. Keller had had a heart attack, *Dr. Morris prescribed* him exercise and a fat-free diet.

2. *Dangling modifier.* Who is licensed? It should be the missing *applicants.*
Revision: Once licensed, *applicants* find that job opportunities in

orthopedics are plentiful.

3. *Dangling modifier.* Who is doing the reopening? It should be the missing *workers*.
   Revision: After reopening Madison Avenue just last week, *workers* discovered that a large portion of the street will have to be shut down again.

4. *Dangling adverb.* Here *unluckily* describes *were killed.* But who thought that this was unlucky? Certainly not the Union soldiers. The writer is being emotional and showing partiality in what should be an objective record of past events; therefore, what she says becomes less trustworthy. Eliminate *unluckily* and replace with a factual statement. Or, specify for whom this event was unlucky.
   Revision: At Cemetery Hill, Pickett's men were told not to fire until they reached the Union line. Unluckily for them, too many men were killed in the charge, and the plan failed.

5. *Dangling modifier.* Who is looking for a college department? It's the missing applicants.
   Revision: Applicants to college departments find that anthropology and sociology have a lot in common.

6. *Misplaced modifier.* Odysseus refrained from eating not his *men* but the *Lotus blossoms.*
   Revision: Later, on Cythera, Odysseus *did not eat the Lotus blossoms*, but saved his men who had eaten them and had lost their memory.

7. *Misplaced modifier.* It's the Corvette not the buyer that has the *three available suspensions.*
   Revision: One can find just the right mixture of comfort and handling in a Corvette *with its three available suspensions.*

8. *Misplaced modifier.* Move *covered with mud* so that it modifies the *kryptonite* not *Lois.*
   Revision: Lex Luthor gave a piece of kryptonite *covered with mud* to Lois Lane.

9. *Misplaced modifier. For a dog* is in the wrong location and gives the impression that the dog is the prize in a game. Move the phrase to the beginning of the sentence to clarify the meaning of the sentence.
   Revision: For a dog, playing can be tiring as well as fun.

10. *Dangling modifier.* This dangling modifier has the *paraphernalia* doing the walking. Insert the missing stroller.
    Revision: Walking through the corridors of the stadium, *fans can see* the baseball paraphernalia that fill the walls.

 10 Splitting infinitives and verb phrases

1. *Split infinitive (to not get).*
   Revision: Spoiled children don't understand how it feels *not to get* what they want.

2. *Split infinitive (to someday own).*
   Revision: My dream is *to own* a design firm *someday.*
3. *Split verb phrase (should...be aware).* Move *while firing competent senior workers* to either the beginning or end of the sentence.
   Revision: While firing competent senior workers, every employer should be aware that he can be charged with age discrimination.

OR

Every employer should be aware that he can be charged with age discrimination *for firing competent senior workers.*
4. *Split infinitive (to properly wash).*
   Revision: To wash a car *properly,* one must caress and massage it as if it were a baby.
5. *Split infinitive (to greatly enjoy).*
   Revision: He began *to enjoy* the adventure *greatly* after he had found the magic ring.
6. *Split verb phrase (might...make).* Modifier splits the verb phrase and should be moved.
   Revision: Described properly, internships might make a résumé sound more professional.

OR

Internships might make a résumé sound more professional *if they are described properly.*
7. *Split infinitive (to simply have).*
   Revision: Often young people want *simply to have* a good time without thinking about the future.
8. *Split verb phrase (can...understand).* Move *at a moment's notice and with no warning whatsoever* to eliminate the split verb phrase and to clarify the meaning of the sentence.
   Revision: At a moment's notice and with no warning whatsoever, an experienced salesman can understand what his clients want, and can use this understanding to his advantage.
9. *Split infinitive (to not want).*
   Revision: The widow seemed *not to want* any sympathy from us.
10. *Split infinitive (to surgically lose).*
    Revision: Marlon Brando decided *to lose* weight by having his ego removed *surgically.*

 ## 11 Simple verbs instead of progressive and conditional

GROUP A

1. *Choose simple tense not conditional to express a fact.* Eliminate *would.*
   Revision: Victorian dresses *had* long sleeves, high necklines, and hems that *reached* the floor.
2. *Future habitual action* uses the simple present.

Revision: A driver's education course *has* classroom time as well as driving time.

3. *Continuing action* should be replaced by a completed action for consistency and meaning.
   Revision: The other Cyclopes did not assist Polyphemus when he *called* for help.

4. *No revision.* Sentence shows continuing action at the time of the statement, and correctly uses the present progressive.

5. *Future habitual action* uses the simple present.
   Revision: The new Corvette is the kind of sportscar that *makes* any driver look like a professional.

6. *Emphasis* requires a reversal of *will* and *shall.*
   Revision: As long as I pay the bills, you *shall* do as I say.

7. *Continuing action* should be replaced by a completed action. *Being* is unnecessary.
   Revision: The people who *are excluded* from material advantages resent those in power.

8. *No revision.* Her temperament is a continuing condition.

9. *Use simple tense (is) instead of the conditional (would be).* This is an existing fact in the Constitution.
   Revision: Under the Constitution, impeachment *is* a responsibility of the House of Representatives.

10. *Future habitual action* requires the simple present. There is no *will* about it. They *do,* in fact, cheer at all times.
    Revision: Dodger fans are very loyal and *cheer* for their team even during a losing streak.

GROUP B

1. *Choose simple tense not conditional to express a fact.* Eliminate *would.*
   Revision: The features that distinguish a great team *are* fan support, individual player success, and overall team success.

2. *Future habitual action* requires the simple present.
   Revision: Whereas cirrhosis takes years to develop, this condition *takes* only a few days.

3. *No revision.* Sentence shows continuing action at the time of the statement, and correctly uses the past progressive.

4. *Continuing action* should be replaced by a completed action. The sentence shows a habitual attitude, not a continuing activity.
   Revision: A realist simply *accepts* existing circumstances.

5. *No Revision:* A bigger vehicle can take more of a pounding than a two-door sportscar that *leaves* its occupants wishing they had purchased a luxury sedan.

6. *Habitual action* in the present requires the use of the simple present.
   Revision: As in other organs of the body, dead liver cells *are replaced* by tough scar tissue.

7. *Use simple tense instead of conditional for actual circumstances.* There

is nothing speculative about the *shortage of cannons,* and this shortage *was* in fact a disadvantage.
Revision: Throughout the Civil War, the shortage of cannons *was* a disadvantage for the Confederate forces.

8. *Emphasis* requires a reversal of *will* and *shall.*
Revision: The judge ruled that the defendant *shall* pay the fine immediately.

9. *Future habitual action* requires the simple present.
Revision: Free agency gives players the right to play for whichever team wants them after their contract *expires.* In other words, whichever team *pays* the most usually *gets* the desirable player.

10. *No revision.* Conditional is correct for speculation about the results of an event that is *not* a fact at the time of the statement.

 12 Perfect tenses and the sequence of events

GROUP A

1. *Simple past* should be replaced by past perfect. Two actions occur in the past. The earlier of the two (*had known*) must be in the past perfect.
Revision: Penelope would have behaved differently if she *had known* that Odysseus was home.

2. *Simple present* should be replaced by present perfect progressive. The sentence shows a repeated action that is both continual and continuous. It occurs at repeated intervals over a period of time.
Revision: Throughout history, technology *has been creating* inventions to facilitate daily tasks.

3. *No revision.* Conditional (*would buy*) is paired with past subjunctive (*were*) in this *if...then* construction. The order of the clauses does not alter the sequence of tenses.

4. *Conditional* in the *if* clause must be replaced by the simple past. Never use a conditional in an *if* clause. The paired *if...then* tenses are simple past (*bought*) and conditional (*would spend*).
Revision: If my brother *bought* a house on the shore, I *would spend* my vacations there.

5. *Future progressive* (*will be voting*) must be changed to the future perfect (*will have voted*) because it is the earlier of two future events.
Revision: After the next presidential election, I *will have voted* for the fourth time.

6. *Time words* like *since* signal the need for a perfect tense. Change the simple present (*are*) to the present perfect (*have been*).
Revision: Since the early 1900s in the American League and the National League, the Yankees and the Dodgers *have* always *been* in the race for the pennant.

7. *Simple past (left)*should be changed to present perfect (*have left*) for an activity at an unspecified time in the recent past.
Revision: I *have left* messages for my agent all week without any response.

8. *Time words* like *after* signal the perfect tense(*has refused*) or the perfect progressive instead of the simple past (*refused*). Also this is an example of using the present perfect instead of the simple past for an activity at an unspecified time in the recent past.
Revision: After news of the murder, she *has refused* to walk alone by the river.
OR
After news of the murder, she *has been refusing* to walk alone by the river.

9. *Conditional (should be)* must be changed to conditional perfect (*should have been*) to show a continuous effort by the automaker, instead of a completed activity.
Revision: Once again the Chevy people failed to impress the consumer who *should have been* their main target.

10. *Simple past (was)* in the earlier of the two events (*the night before*) should be changed to the past perfect (*had been*)
Revision: On the morning of the battle he felt full of courage, although the night before he *had been* terrified.

GROUP B

1. *Simple present (leaps up, covers)* should be changed to simple future (*will leap up, will cover*) in the *then* portion of this *if...then* construction.
Revision: If you don't train your dog, he *will leap up* and *cover* your best outfit with mud.

2. *Simple past (were abused)* must be changed to past perfect (*had been abused*) because it is the earlier of two past events. The conditional progressive (*would be leading*) must be changed to the conditional perfect (*would have been leading*) because in an *if...then* construction, the two tenses are paired.
Revision: If they *had* never *been abused* as children, they *would have been leading* healthy normal lives today.

3. *Time word (frequently)* signals the need for a perfect tense (*had strolled*) for a continual past activity.
Revision: That summer we *had strolled* frequently on the Boardwalk in the evening.

4. *Conditional (would become)* must be replaced by the conditional perfect (*would have become*) as the partner to the past perfect (*had been exiled*).
Revision: If he had been exiled from his country, he *would have become* a stateless person.

5. *Present progressive (are staring)* should be replaced by present perfect progressive (*have been staring*) to indicate a repeated activity in the

recent past extending into the present.
Revision: Shortly after the release of her first film, Marilyn realizes that strangers *have been staring* at her.

6. *Simple future* (*will become*) must be changed to future perfect (*will have become*) to indicate the earlier of two future events.
Revision: By the year 2007, my neighbor *will have become* one hundred years old.

7. *Simple past* (*did spoil*) must be changed to the past perfect (*had spoiled*) as a partner to the conditional (*would have been*).
Revision: I know that Darren would not have been such a difficult student if his parents *had* not *spoiled* him.

8. *Simple present* (*enjoy*) must be changed to either the present perfect (*have enjoyed*) or the present perfect progressive (*have been enjoying*) to show a continuing condition extending into the present. The time words *this is our third year* signal the need for a perfect tense.
Revision: This is our third year in Sarasota, and we *have been enjoying* it more than ever.

9. *Conditional* (*should be*) must be replaced by conditional perfect (*should have been*) in order to partner the past perfect (*had been*) in the first part of the sentence.
Revision: Any friendship that had been meaningful *should have been* salvageable.

OR

   Past perfect (*had been*) should be replaced by simple present (*is*) to partner the conditional (*should be*).
Revision: Any friendship that *is* meaningful *should be* salvageable.

10. *Simple future* (*will be*) must be replaced by the future perfect (*will have been*) to indicate the earlier of two situations.
Revision: By the time she apologizes, it *will have been* too late.

13 Past tense and past participles

1. The Civil War *cost* the US six billion dollars and 620,000 lives.
2. Then I heard that James had *run* away from his foster parents.
3. He *lent* his sister $10,000 to help with the downpayment on the house.
4. During the Reign of Terror, lynch mobs *hanged* aristocrats in the streets of Paris.
5. *No revision*
6. He had to take a summer job instead of *lying* on the beach all day.
7. He was angry that she had *gone* to movies without even calling him.
8. When the balloon *burst*, the child *began* crying.
9. No sooner had I *lain* down, that the doorbell rang.
10. The witness has *proven* that he is an unreliable observer.

14 *Did* and *had* as helping verbs

1. *No revision.* Add the main verb to the helper, and the result (*did affect*) shows no need for the past perfect. Therefore, *did* is correct.
2. *Did* should be replaced by *had.* The past perfect is correct because both actions are in the past, and the battlefield activity precedes the White House activity. *Had* is actually an abbreviation of *had done.*
   Revision: Andrew Jackson intended to lead as firmly in the White House as he *had* on the battlefield.
3. *No revision.* Add the main verb to the helper, and the result (*did start out*) shows no need for the past perfect. Here *Hitler* is in the past perfect because his actions precede Milosevic's.
4. *Did* should be replaced by *had.* The verb is *to have,* not *to do. Had* is the correct past tense.
   Revision: Parents want their children to have more than they *had* when they were growing up.
5. *No revision.* In *she did see,* the *did* correctly serves as the helping verb to the present participle. In *she did hear,* the *did* provides the necessary emphasis.
6. *Have* should replace *do* because the verb is *to have* not *to do.*
   Revision: Tactful people have the ability to resolve many more conflicts than tactless people *have.*
7. *Did* should be replaced by *have.* Add the main verb to *have* and you see the need for the past participle (*have changed*).
   Revision: Over the years, as women's lifestyles *have changed,* so have their fashions.
8. *Did* should be replaced by *had* because the verb is *to have* not *to do.*
   Revision: Sherlock Holmes had more self-discipline and ingenuity than his adversaries *had.*
9. *Did* should be replaced by *had* because when you add the main verb to the helper, you get the construction *had done.*
   Revision: We would go to war over slavery today, just as we *had* in 1861.
10. *No revision. Did* acts to emphasize the verb *have.*

 15 Subjunctive mood

GROUP A

1. *Uncertainty or conjecture.* The *if* clause indicates supposition and requires the subjunctive (*were*).
   Revision: If I *were* not his oldest friend, he would not have told me the truth.
2. *Uncertainty or conjecture.* The *if* clause indicates uncertainty and requires the subjunctive (*be*).
   Revision: If this information *be* correct, then she is clearly not guilty.

3. *Importance or urgency.* The word *requires* is urgent and creates the need for the subjunctive (*be*) following *that.*
   Revision: Although I am totally innocent, the legal system requires that I *be* punished.
4. *Wish or strong suggestion.* The obvious *wishes* dictates the subjunctive (*were*).
   Revision: I know that she wishes she *were* more agile because she has always wanted to be a gymnast.
5. *Uncertainty or conjecture.* The *as though* indicates uncertainty and supposition, and requires the subjunctive (*were*).
   Revision: He treated me as though I *were* his slave.
6. *No revision for the concession.* The speaker concedes and bows to the art critic.
7. *Uncertainty or conjecture. Whether* signals uncertainty and requires the subjunctive (*be*).
   Revision: Whether it *be* the sleek but rugged look of the F-150 or F-250, or the powerful appearance of the Super Duty, Ford's styling will delight any aficionado.
8. *Importance or urgency. Crucial* signals the need for the subjunctive following *that.*
   Revision: It is crucial that she *be* calm during the questioning.
9. *No revision for the divine appeal.* which correctly uses the subjunctive *prove* instead of the indicative third person *proves.*
10. *Importance or urgency.* The word *imperative* creates a sense of importance and the need for the subjunctive (*have*) instead of the indicative (*has*).
    Revision: It is imperative that he *have* his skis before the competition.

GROUP B
1. *Concession* requires the subjunctive (*be*) in the *if* clause.
   Revision: If the truth *be* told, I am actually just as guilty as she is.
2. *Uncertainty or conjecture.* The *if* clause indicates supposition and requires the subjunctive (*were*).
   Revision: He wouldn't have dared to challenge the bully if he *weren't* brave.
3. *Importance or urgency.* The word *insisted* creates a sense of importance and the need for the subjunctive (*do* and *go*) instead of the indicative (*does* and *goes*).
   Revision: His father insisted that he *do* his homework before he *go* to the dance.
4. *Wish or strong suggestion.* The obvious *wish* dictates the subjunctive (*were*).
   Revision: I wish Andy Roddick *were* the number one tennis player in the world.
5. *Importance or urgency.* The word *insisted* creates a sense of importance and the need for the subjunctive *send* instead of

the indicative *sends*.
Revision: The contract requires that he *send* out the manuscript by
September 10.

6. *Importance or urgency.* The word *important* indicates the need for the
subjunctive *be* instead of the indicative *is*.
Revision: One important consideration in choosing a gift is that it *be*
easy on my wallet.

7. *Uncertainty or conjecture* requires the subjunctive *be* after *whether.*
Revision: Whether the reward *be* large or small is not the point; it's
justice that counts.

8. *Concession* requires the subjunctive (*be*).
Revision: I must admit the truth, *be* it damaging or not.
OR
I must admit the truth whether it *be* damaging or not.

9. *Uncertainty or conjecture* in a situation contrary to fact requires the
subjunctive (*were*).
Revision: She acted as though she *were* the guest of honor.

10. *Importance or urgency.* The word *demands* indicates the need for the
subjunctive *see* instead of the indicative *sees*.
Revision: The diet demands that she *see* her doctor once a month.

 16 Shifts in subjects, verbs, and direction

GROUP A

1. *Shift in the subject* from 3rd person (*pedestrians*) to 2nd person (*you*).
Revision: When pedestrians cross at traffic lights, *they* do not get into
so many accidents.

2. *Shift in verb tense* from present (*goes*) to past (*was*).
Revision: The hero goes on an adventure to discover who he *is*.

3. *Active/passive shift* from *investigated* to *were uncovered. Shift in
subject* from *police* to *irregularities*.
Revision: The police investigated the company's financial records but
uncovered no irregularities.

4. *Shift in the subject* from 3rd person (*people*) to 2nd person (*you*).
Revision: Because people are not perfect, *they* are likely to make
mistakes.

5. *Shift in direction. And* signals agreement between the ideas that
precede and follow it. Here, however, going into a restaurant which
is closing is a contradiction and requires a *but*.
Revision: The restaurant was already closing, *but* I went in.

6. *Shift in the subject* from *farmers* to *it*.
Revision: Many displaced farmers were never trained for other jobs,
and so *they* found it impossible to gain employment.

7. *Shift from* one *to* they. Choose the one form or the other, and stay
with it.

Revision: When one refuses to ask for directions, *one* ends up taking the wrong route.

OR

When *people* refuse to ask for directions, *they* end up taking the wrong route.

8. *Shift from imperative to indicative. Don't* in the imperative mood becomes *not* in the indicative.
   Revision: According to the instructions, I must take the first exit and *not* turn right until the gas station.
9. *Shift in direction.* There is nothing contradictory between the two parts of the sentence. *But* should be replaced by *and.*
   Revision: The Corvette goes from 0–60 in 4.7 seconds *and* has a top speed of 189 *mph.*
10. *Shift in verb tense* from past (*arrived, discovered, spoke*) to present (*becomes*). Change to one consistent tense.
    Revision: When Marco Polo arrived in China, he discovered to his surprise that no one spoke Italian, so that sign language *became* his method of communication.

GROUP B

1. *Shift in the subject* from the 3rd person (*protagonist*) to the 1st person (*I, my, our*).
   Revision: In Bradbury's novel, the protagonist thinks that if *his* wife dies *he* will never have a chance to restore *their* relationship.
2. *Shift in direction. And* shows agreement, while the meaning of the sentence requires contradiction (*but*).
   Revision: We saw her cheat on the exam, *but* she said she didn't do it.
3. *Shift in the subject* from the 3rd person (*men*) to 2nd person (*he*).
   Revision: Some men think that they can be unfaithful, but as long as *they* pay the bills *they* will be forgiven.
4. *Shift in verb tense* from past (*didn't*) to present (*are, don't*). Be consistent in either the one tense or in the other.
   Revision: Often parents didn't know where their children *were* at night, and they *didn't* care.
5. *Active/passive shift* from *proofread* to *were discovered. Shift in subject* from *proposal* to *mistakes.*
   Revision: They proofread the proposal twice, but *did not discover* any mistakes.
6. *Shift from* one *to* he. Stay with *he,* or you will have too many *ones* in a single sentence.
   Revision: People can be drawn to a man because he is very funny, or kind, or smart.
7. *Shift in the subject* from 3rd person (*Gulliver*) to 1st person (*I*). Correct by deleting *so* and *that* and adding a colon or a comma, or by deleting *I* from the quotation.
   Revision: Gulliver was frightened by the voices of the giants: "I [...] thought it was thunder."

OR

Gulliver was so frightened by the voices of the giants that he "thought it was thunder."

8. *Shift from imperative to indicative. Don't* in the imperative mood becomes *not* in the indicative.
Revision: The first rule of good management is to understand the desires of the consumers and *not* take employees for granted.

9. *Shift from* one *to* we. Stay with *we* to avoid awkwardness.
Revision: Whether *we* admit it or not, we cannot learn without making generalizations about our social experiences.

10. *Active/passive shift from* arrived *to* was given. *Shift in subject from* team *to* first aid.
Revision: The emergency team arrived at the scene of the accident, and promptly *gave* first aid to the victim.

 17 Referring to literary or historical time

1. *Change next* year to *following* year.
Revision: In 1836, Arkansas entered the Union as a slave state. The *following* year, Michigan entered as a free state.

2. *Change now* to *at the time.*
Revision: At the time, Romeo thought that he was in love with Rosaline.

3. *Change before* to *previously.*
Revision: Previously Robin Hood had been a respectable young nobleman.

4. Change *revealed* to the present *reveal.* The poems exist now as they had in his day.
Revision: Donne's poems *reveal* a passionate spirit.

5. *Change before* to *earlier.*
Revision: General Johnson surrendered to General Sherman after the Civil War was officially over — Lee had surrendered to Grant two weeks *earlier.*

6. *Change ago* to *preceding.*
Revision: The *preceding* year, Ernest Hemingway had vacationed in Florence.

7. *Change soon* to *shortly thereafter.*
Revision: Shortly thereafter the competition between Eisenhower and Montgomery intensified.

8. *No revision.* Use present for scholarly opinion; use present perfect for counter argument.

9. *Change* in the future *to* thenceforth.
Revision: Thenceforth, Bilbo Baggins became the actual leader of the expedition to Lonely Mountain.

10. *Change* the past (*triumphed*) to the present (*triumph*).
Revision: In *Watership Down*, the rabbits triumph only because of the diversity of talent among the members of the group.

Usage

18 Addressing the reader and choosing a voice

What is a voice, and which one is appropriate?

One of the first decisions that a writer must make is how to address the reader: that is what choosing a voice means. Many writers of formal essays use an impersonal voice avoiding any controlling pronoun. Others prefer to use a controlling pronoun such as *I, we, you, one*. The choice of pronoun establishes the writer's relationship to the reader; it can be formal and objective, or casual and personal depending on the subject of the essay. When considering which voice to use, follow the general rule that the more serious the topic, the more formal the tone of address.

Besides representing you to your reader, pronouns also represent your vision of your reader. Using the pronouns *he*, *she*, *one* and *they* in hypothetical examples implies what gender you expect your audience to be. Take care not to alienate your reader. Part of choosing an appropriate voice, then, is using nonsexist pronouns.

18a   Using *I*

In narrative and descriptive essays, writers frequently choose to speak from the first person singular perspective. The *I* voice produces a sense of intimacy. It draws the reader into the writer's state of mind, allowing him to view the circumstances in the essay from the writer's viewpoint. It fosters credibility by conveying sincerity.

> In the August dawn, the sun pauses momentarily on the horizon before resuming its ascent. I reach into the back seat of the old car to store the final and most important piece of baggage, my backpack filled with drawing pads, neatly banded brushes, pens, and charcoal sticks. Once behind the wheel, I glance again at my schedule of lectures and studios. My new jeans feel stiff and unfamiliar. I shift into gear, and, at the last minute, glance back at my home reflected in the rearview mirror. The shadows of the maple trees stir disapprovingly across its brick façade as if it had expected me to move down that driveway toward a different destination.

At one time, the *I* voice belonged strictly to the informal essay. However, writers of formal analytical essays are adopting this voice with greater frequency. The *I* voice is an effective way to engage in discourse of conflicting opinions on a subject.

> I shall not take up the case of Jean de Meun's social "naturalism" or "egalitarianism." To be sure, the myth of ages topos is articulated five times in the romance by different characters and, therefore, to different polemic and ironic ends. Rather, I need only point out the signs of a controversy in medieval romance regarding the legitimacy of violence in society, a controversy that is between the poetic perspective and the Stoic-Patristic one.

The *I* voice can also smoothly show the process of change in your own thinking or emphasis. It can lead the reader strongly and authoritatively toward your current position or area of research.

> In an earlier discussion of civil strife in Republican Rome, I attempted a rather general survey of the kinds of civil disruption that earned the name of strife, from the venial practice of political pluralism to faction, rebellion, and revolution. My intention now is to focus narrowly upon a single, defining incident — the Catiline conspiracy — and thence to draw political lessons from the writings of those closest to it, in particular Cicero and Sallust.

Using *we*   *18b*

Like the *I* voice, the *we* is a standard choice in narrative and descriptive essays. In formal writing, *we* has long been a favorite of writers who wish to exhort and persuade. In the example below, Thomas Jefferson's choice of the *we* voice creates a bond between himself and the reader. He establishes an instant communality of beliefs.

> ➤We hold these truths to be self-evident, that all men are created equal, that they are endowed by their Creator with certain unalienable Rights....

The *we* voice is a frequent tool of lecturers as well as essayists. It invites the reader to enter with the writer into a serious reasoning process, often one that requires consideration of various options.

> ➤At this juncture, we need to weigh the possible dangers of estrogen therapy against its advantages for post-menopausal women.

The *we* is also a useful voice for ironic commentary as in the segment below which touts the advantages of war.

> In fact, there are just too many of us! Once the rampant propagation of our species escapes our control, our planet is doomed. With humanity

multiplying exponentially, any technique for reducing the number of people in the world must be viewed as an environmental boon. While various strategies have been attempted over the ages, even skeptics among us must admit that the single most effective and time-honored method is war. Surely the solution to environmental disaster is a nice old-fashioned war with orderly rules of engagement that can claim maximum casualties at minimum expense. And, unlike contraception, war accomplishes its ends without injuring religious sensibilities.

18c   Using *you*

The second person — *you* — is the most informal address possible. As such, it is a standby for columnists who invite readers to partake in the minor frustrations and misadventures of their lives. It is also an acceptable voice for the informal narrative or descriptive essay, as long as it is used consistently throughout the essay.

In formal, serious writing, however, the explicit use of *you* is unacceptable. Its tone is too intimate, and the person to whom *you* refers is often ambiguous.

> Courage in adversity helps ~~you~~ *people* regain the dignity ~~you~~ *they* have lost.

> Einstein's theory of relativity explains what would happen to ~~you~~ *a person* if ~~you~~ *he/she* were to travel at the speed of light.

To avoid inaccuracy and inappropriate intimacy, writers use an implied *you*. They address their audiences in an imperative mode. Typically, such an address begins with a command such as *let us, take, assume, consider, imagine.*

> Assume, for a moment, that *Romeo and Juliet* is not about star-crossed lovers or feuding families.

> Imagine what the world must have been like before electricity.

> Take, for example, the common house fly.

18d   Objective and impersonal voices

The objective voice commonly used in the formal essay can be achieved in two ways: (1) by using the controlling pronoun *one* or (2) by dropping the controlling pronoun altogether and using the impersonal articles *a* or *the*.

The pronoun *one* requires careful treatment. If possible, use *one* only *once* in any sentence. Used too often, it produces stilted sentences like the one below.

STILTED
In considering a career as an English teacher, *one* must ask *oneself* if *one* is prepared to sacrifice *one's* evenings and weekends spent making comments on papers that *one's* students will read hastily if at all.

Compare the overuse of *one* here to the single *one* in the revision below

OBJECTIVE
In considering a career as an English teacher, *one* must take into account the sacrifice of weekends and evenings spent making comments on papers that students will read hastily if at all.

Compare the objective *one* to the impersonal *a* in the alternative revision below.

IMPERSONAL
A prospective English teacher must take into account the sacrifice of evenings and weekends spent making comments on papers that students will read hastily if at all.

Using non-sexist controlling pronouns 18e

Non-sexist terminology emphasizes the equality of men and women by injecting gender-neutral nouns and feminine pronouns into writing. While gender equality is socially commendable, its effect on writing style is often deplorable. In a short piece of writing, the hybrid pronoun *he/she* or its cousin *his or her* can be non-intrusive. Persistent use of this construction is distracting and awkward.

A dieter's first step is to eliminate the unnecessary fat in *his/her* diet. This is not to say that *he/she* should suddenly become a vegetarian or deny *himself/herself* all the delights of the dessert cart in a restaurant. Rather, *he/she* should practice moderation. Treating *himself/herself* to an occasional cookie prevents *his/her* feeling like a martyr and ensures the continuation of *his/her* regimen.

This example can be corrected in several ways. The controlling voice can be converted to the plural *they*, to the objective *one*, to the exclusive use of either the masculine or the feminine, or to alternating use of *he* and *she*.

THE PLURAL *THEY*

Dieters must first eliminate the unnecessary fat in *their* diets. This is not to say that *they* should suddenly become vegetarians or deny *themselves* all the delights of the dessert cart in a restaurant. Rather, *they* should practice moderation. Treating *themselves* to an occasional cookie prevents *their* feeling like martyrs and ensures the continuation of *their* regimen.

THE OBJECTIVE/IMPERSONAL VOICE

A dieter's first step is to eliminate unnecessary fat in the diet. This is not to say that *one* should suddenly become a vegetarian or deny *oneself* all the delights of the dessert cart in a restaurant. Rather, the dieter should practice moderation. Treating *oneself* to an occasional cookie prevents the feeling of martyrdom and ensures the continuation of the regimen.

When a single subject such as "a dieter" is discussed at length, the controlling pronoun should remain the same throughout. Often, though, writers treat a subject in a single sentence and move on to a new subject. Then the controlling pronoun can *alternate between female and male* from one example to the next.

ALTERNATING BETWEEN *HE* AND *SHE*

A dieter's first step is to eliminate unnecessary fat in *his* diet. An athlete, however, may be more concerned with *her* protein intake. An arctic explorer, meanwhile, is interested in calories: *he* may wolf down a pound of chocolate a day. Finally, the average person must choose a balanced diet to match *her* lifestyle.

📖   Exercise

Correct any errors in addressing the reader and choosing a voice. Answers on p.146.

1. It is essential to stretch yourself to the limit.
2. In planning for college, a student must give himself/herself as many academic and financial options as possible. He/she has to be aware of the competition for admissions that he/she will face and of the financial responsibility placed upon him/her by educational loans.
3. Einstein's theory of relativity explains what would happen to one if one were to find oneself hurtling through space at the speed of light.

4. You should not judge a potential employee strictly by the way she looks. If you were to judge her by appearance alone, you could easily overlook talents that could benefit your company.
5. Your emotions affect your perception of situations and mislead you into unrealistic decision.

19 Word choice

When are words used imprecisely?

The English language provides us with a wealth of near synonyms and expressions of roughly equivalent meaning. Very few similar words, however, have exactly the same meaning. To write well we must choose the most accurate among similar words.

Using words precisely is a matter of avoiding common mistakes in word choice. Some common mistakes include using words that pertain to people to describe objects, using general instead of specific terms, and using simple verbs instead of phrasal verbs.

Words that refer to people not to objects   19a

Some words refer to the actions of people exclusively. Below is list of words that should not be used with abstract or inanimate subjects.

accompany	demand	help
appreciate	demonstrate	intend
believe	describe	reveal
convince	explain	try
create	force	use
decide	give	validate

► The situation ~~decides~~ the way a person should react. *determines*

► The weakness of the Euro ~~explains why~~ the Frank' fell today. *is the reason that*

► What kind of gas does your car ~~use?~~ *run on*

Academic writers sometimes misuse su *consider* with abstract subjects in order to av person.

➤ This chapter will discuss...

➤ The argument must now consider...

Strictly speaking, the writer should have said *I will discuss* or *consider* an issue. Some leeway should be given to academic style, although writers must take care not to abuse their poetic license.

19b **Specific instead of general terms**

Avoid using vague adjectives and generic nouns. Instead of *good/bad, positive/negative,* use adjectives that describe the object or emotion more accurately.

➤ Saving the hedgehog from being run over in the road made me feel
virtuous
~~good.~~

➤ Slavery was a *shameful* ~~bad~~ chapter in American history, but one we must remember.

➤ Hatred is a *destructive* ~~negative~~ emotion that can make people ill.

➤ My colleague and I had a *productive* ~~positive~~ working relationship.

Avoid using *thing* and words that end in *-thing* such as *anything, something* in definitions.

➤ Love is *an emotion* ~~something~~ everyone experiences in life.

➤ The new location had many *advantages* ~~things~~ to offer.

Search for the precise term to express your meaning. Words that are *close enough* won't do.

➤ His great will power enabled him to *survive* ~~live~~ while others perished.

➤ Odysseus does not fully trust Athena's assurances and asks Zeus for two specific omens to *verify* ~~ensure~~ her prediction.

Eliminate the meaningless adjectives *such, so* when possible

The waves rose *mightily* ~~so mightily~~ and then crashed

...ything came together *harmoniously* ~~with such harmony~~

Simple verbs instead of phrasal verbs   *19c*

Phrasal verbs are verbs with one or more prepositions attached to them. The most common kind of idioms, phrasal verbs are appropriate for everyday speech but are imprecise and can be misleading in writing.

➤The president *swore in* his new cabinet today.

Did the president use inappropriate language, or did he *administer the oath of office?*

Verbs with fewer or no added prepositions can always be found to replace phrasal verbs. Below is a short list of common substitutions:

be enough – suffice
be up to – plan, plot, scheme
break up – divide, destroy
bring about – cause, induce
bring together – unite
bring up – mention, raise
come from – originate, derive
get around – trick, outwit, avoid
get away from – evade, escape
get together – meet, assemble
give in to – accede, yield, capitulate

hold back – desist, refrain, protect
hold off – delay, postpone
look for, go after – seek, pursue
make believe – pretend
make easier – simplify, facilitate
make up – invent
mount up – accumulate, collect
put on – don, assume (attitude)
stand for – represent
watch over – guard, defend, protect

📖   Exercise

Correct any errors in word choice. Answers on p. 146.

1. The address is located in a prestigious neighborhood of San Francisco.
2. A neutral perspective on the market situation allows a reasonable rather than an emotional career choice.
3. He was insulted by the negative criticism of his play.
4. Fan support is one of the most important factors in deciding whether or not a team can be called great.
5. When Don Juan meets together with a lady, he promptly c⌐ her.
6. The bad things her teacher said about her essay had a on her self-confidence.
7. Kinesiotherapy is a very involved area of study.
8. Even though she did not have much experience around on a golf course.
9. Such things as being good were more import anything else.
10. We all lead busy lives and do not always take t tial duties such as flossing and brushing our te

20 Definitions and examples

Are there particular ways of stating definitions and examples?

Definitions help to explain ideas; examples serve to illustrate them. While there are no prescribed ways of formulating definitions and examples, there are express ways in which they should *not* be formulated.

20a Using dictionary definitions

Dictionary definitions are useful in determining what a word actually means. However, they should not be simply copied into a piece of serious writing. Dictionary definitions make a writer look naive.

> At the start of the twenty-first century, we have at last learned to equate discrimination with prejudice. Yet, discrimination is not necessarily prejudice, which is "an adverse judgment or opinion formed beforehand or without knowledge or examination of the fact." According to the American Heritage Dictionary, discrimination also means "discernment, or the ability or power to make fine distinctions."

Instead, once you have ascertained the exact meaning of a word, translate the definition into your own words and adapt it to your specific piece of writing.

> At the start of the twenty-first century, we have at last learned to equate discrimination with prejudice. Yet discrimination is not limited to adverse prejudgments made in ignorance. Often it is the process of making tasteful and educated choices in lifestyle.

20b Avoid circular reasoning in definitions

A definition must explain the meaning of a word or idea without using the word itself. Using the word in its own definition is called circular reasoning and is illogical (see §43b *Circular reasoning*).

> **...AR** Racial discrimination means *to discriminate* against other people because of their *race*.
>
> If we do not know the meaning of *discrimination*, we certainly will not know the meaning of *to discriminate*. ... remain puzzled.

LOGICAL   Racial discrimination means rejecting people because of their color.

Another form of circular reasoning in definitions is to repeat a statement in different words without explaining it.

REPETITIVE   Some golf clubs exclude people whom, for various reasons, they do not want to allow into the membership.

To exclude means *not want to allow into the membership.* The explanation is circular: it repeats itself instead of explaining the idea of exclusion.

EXPLAINED   Some golf clubs deny membership to people whom they consider inferior, in various ways, to their members.

Give definitions before examples   **20c**

Definitions explain ideas in general terms; examples illustrate an explanation with specifics. An example that *defines* an idea, *becomes* the entire idea, not just one expression of it. The idea's range of meaning is limited to the details of that particular example, and all other possible examples are excluded. Logically, definitions or explanations must come before examples.

MISUSED   At the start of the twenty-first century, we have at last
EXAMPLE   IDEA
           ⌐learned to equate discrimination with prejudice⌐ For example,
                    EXAMPLE WITHOUT A DEFINITION
           ⌐not allowing an Asian person into a golf club⌐ is discrimination

by that club.

Because the explanation is missing from this example, we get the misleading impression that discrimination applies solely to *Asians* barred from *golf clubs*. How about other minority groups excluded from other organizations?

REVISED   At the start of the twenty-first century, we
                              IDEA
           ⌐learned to equate discrimination with prejudic
                    EXPLANATION
           of minority groups have been barred from

           organizations by people in power fear⌐

           Some golf clubs, for example, have⌐den

           applicants⌐ simply because of their etr

Here the definition explains the idea, while the example illustrates a single, specific case without excluding other similar cases.

20d   Avoid *when* and *where* in definitions and examples

When refers to time. *Where* refers to place. Definitions and examples do not answer either of these questions. They usually answer the questions *what* or *what kind.* Using *when* or *where* in definitions is inaccurate and clumsy.

INACCURATE	Being an optimist is *when* you feel that a glass is half full; being a pessimist is *where* you feel that a glass is half empty.
	Being an optimist or *a pessimist* is not a time or place, but a condition.
REVISED	An optimist is one who feels that a glass is half full; a pessimist is one who feels that a glass is half empty.

OR

REVISED	Being optimistic is feeling that a glass is half full; being pessimistic is feeling that a glass is half empty.
INACCURATE	According to experts, a typical example of dyslexia is *when* a person misspells a word by reversing the order of the letters.
REVISED	According to experts, a typical example of dyslexia is misspelling a word by reversing the order of the letters.

20e   Use examples accurately

Do not use *individuals* to exemplify *attitudes* or *behaviors.* People exemplify groups or types of people. Behavior exemplifies behavior.

➤ Some psychologists claim that Napoleon Bonaparte is an example
of ~~the need of short men~~ *short men who need* to compensate for their height.

Bonaparte is an example of *men* not of *need.*

OR

➤ Some psychologists claim that Napoleon Bonaparte's aggression is an example of the need of some short men to compensate for their height.

aggression is an example of *need.* Both deal with *attitude* or

> Never use the expression *perfect example* or *classic example.*Your reader should be able to recognize that your example is perfect or classic without any prompting.

 Exercise

Correct any errors in using definitions and examples. Answers on p.147.

1. An example of Marie Antoinette's indiscretion was when she said,"Let them eat cake,"within earshot of the media.
2. Stalin is an example of how a dictatorship can enslave their nations.
3. One of the greatest challenges of being a coach is dealing with players who do not want to work hard. For example, they will not do the required fitness training or skills work and yet expect to make the team.These are not athletes with special needs, but rather those who are simply lazy or undisciplined.
4. An experiment is where you actually try out the theories in textbooks.
5. Self-esteem is when people have a lot of self-respect.
6. The mob in *Julius Caesar* is a perfect example of mindless emotion.
7. Being *charismatic* means possessing the quality of charisma or magnetic charm.
8. True love is a unique experience. Examples of famous lovers in literature are Antony and Cleopatra, and Romeo and Juliet.True love is an overwhelming and lasting passion between two people.
9. *Sectionalism* is when people feel more loyalty to their local regions than to the country as a whole.
10. General Sherman in Georgia is a typical example of modern warfare in which the invading army lives off the land.

21 Expressing similarity and difference

What is the difference between like *and* as?

Like and *as* are both used to draw comparisons, but they *cannot* be used interchangeably. *Like* is only a preposition. *As*, however, is both a preposition and a conjunction and, therefore, has broader application than *like*.

21a   Using *like* and *as*

As can introduce both a *phrase* — a group of words without either a subject or a verb — and a *clause* — a group of words with both a subject and a verb.

PHRASE
➤*As such,* it was the an excellent example of pre-Columbian art.

PHRASE
➤He was as handsome *as a prince* in a fairy tale.

CLAUSE
➤*As I had noted earlier,* the old lady seemed both intelligent and dignified.

Notice the presence of a subject *I* and a verb *had noted* in the clause.

CLAUSE
➤They generously ignored my mistakes just *as they had always done.*

The clause's subject is *they,* and its verb is *had done.*

Like can introduce *only* a phrase. Do not use *like* to introduce a group of words containing a verb.

As
➤~~Like~~ I said, we had never been very close.

Use *like* to compare *people* or *things* and *as* to compare their *actions.*

as
➤She runs five miles a day ~~like~~ I do.

The comparison is between *actions* — running five miles — hence *as.*

like
➤Just ~~as~~ Mr. Hyde, my acupuncturist seems to suffer from multiple personalities.

Here, the comparison is between the Mr. Hyde and the acupuncturist, hence *like.*

What is the difference between different *and* various?

Both *different* and *various* are used to draw distinctions; both show contrast and unlikeness. The number of items being compared determines which one should be used: for *two* items use *different;* for *three* or more use *various.*

Using *different from*

Use *different* to contrast *two* individuals or categories of things — cats and dogs, Robert and James, right and wrong. In standard usage, the word *different* is followed by *from*.

➤New York and Paris are *different from* Honolulu.

➤Eggplant is a different color ~~than~~ *from* mauve.

The expression *different from one another* is often used with three or more items. In fact, the comparison is always between two categories — *one* and *another* — as in the example below.

➤New York, Paris, and Honolulu are all different from *one another*.

Sometimes *from* can be implied rather than stated explicitly.

➤Some words have similar sounds but different meanings.

> *Different than* cannot be substituted for *different from*. *Than* indicates a difference in preference (as in *rather than*), or a difference in degree (as in *more than, shorter than, hotter than*). *From* indicates a difference in kind. *Different than* is colloquial and substandard.

Using *various*

Use *various* to compare *three* or more kinds of things whose qualities are more unlike than alike — romaine, Boston, and iceberg lettuce; going to Hawaii, Japan, or France on vacation. Use *various* before such words as *times, kinds*, or *ways* to imply more than two options.

➤There are *various* ways to travel from Chicago to Los Angeles.

➤I have told him at *various* times to prune that plum tree.

Do not use *different* to mean *various*. *Various* applies when the number of items under comparison is multiple and unspecified.

➤I enjoy ~~different~~ *various* kinds of music.

The kinds of music are multiple and unspecified, therefore *various*.

➤~~Different~~ *Various* people have ~~different~~ *various* tastes.

People in general is a multiple group by definition, while *tastes* is plural and unspecified in number, therefore *various*.

📖   Exercise

Correct any errors in expressing similarity and difference. Answers on p.148.

1. Like I said, we're not growing any younger!
2. I like reading about the different inhabitants of the future Earth in H. G. Wells's *The Time Machine*.
3. To my surprise, she acted like an old friend.
4. Gulliver became a very different person than he had been at the beginning of his travels.
5. After slaughtering hundreds of prisoners, Genghis Khan realized that he was just like his father in many ways.
6. T.S. Eliot talked about literature like he had a Ph.D. in English.
7. I was fascinated by the different colors in an opal.
8. In today's global village, we have to learn to be knowledgeable about customs different than ours.
9. The Scottish have a different way of pronouncing words, which I find very attractive.
10. The air traffic controller gave instructions like she knew what she was doing.

22 Non-standard speech

What is standard speech?

Standard speech provides the clearest and most precise form of expression. It is mandatory for conveying serious and complex ideas especially in writing where meaning cannot be imparted by tone of voice, facial expression, or body language. Non-standard speech is not used universally in a country. Its application is limited. Its definitions are either too vague or too technical for general use. Non-standard speech consists of slang and colloquialisms, clichés, and jargon.

22a   Slang and colloquialisms

Slang and colloquialisms are expressions specific to particular groups of people or to particular regions of a country. Slang and colloquial expressions may be useful in lending local color to creative writing; in expository writing, however, they are imprecise, redundant, or too informal. Their meanings change frequently with the fashion. Below are some commonly used slang and colloquial phrases.

Be in over one's head – flounder, fail, lack competence
Be hyper – be nervous, be overactive
Change up – just *change* is enough
Check out – examine, peruse, authenticate
Dead and gone – simply *dead* is enough
Discuss about – the *about* is unnecessary
Disrespect (someone) – to treat someone with disrespect; to behave disrespectfully toward.
Expect for – the *for* is not needed
Fake out – trick, outwit
First off – *first* is all that is needed
Go and (*do, buy, see* etc.) – *go and* is unnecessary. The meaning is in the second verb.
Go south – fail
Hard and fast – immutable, firm, unchangeable
Have an attitude – be arrogant, argumentative, aggressive
Look to (*be, do, find*) – strive, seek, wish
Meet together – the *together* is redundant
Meet up with – just *meet* will serve
Off of – simply *off* is sufficient
Put to rest – allay, squelch
Suck up to – flatter, truckle, pander
Try and (*catch, reach, call, see* etc.) – the *and* implies an additional action and is incorrect when only one action is intended. Use *try to* instead of *try and*.
Up and (*leave, find, go* etc.) – to leave (find, go etc.) abruptly, suddenly, unexpectedly

➤The security guard ~~checked out~~ *examined* the credentials of each journalist.

➤The stock market ~~went south~~ *declined or lost points* as soon as interest rates rose.

➤For years Stalin tried to ~~put to rest~~ *squelch* the story that he had had Trotsky assassinated.

➤*Try* ~~and~~ *to* get some tickets.

➤In North Africa, Rommel, the Desert Fox, constantly ~~faked out~~ *outwitted* General Montgomery.

➤He just ~~up and left~~ *left abruptly* without saying a word.

22b   Clichés

Clichés are stale, worn out expressions made virtually meaningless from overuse. Avoid them in your writing; they annoy rather than inform. Here are a few typical clichés:

after all is said and done	last but not least
day in and day out	send shivers up one's spine
first and foremost	stick out like a sore thumb
have a nice day	take one day at a time
in any way, shape, or form	tender loving care
it isn't over until the fat lady sings	time will tell
in this day and age	tried and true

▶After their exile from Paradise, Milton's Adam and Eve realize how important it is for them to *be there for* each other.

Be there for is not only a cliché, it is too vague to be meaningful. Replace it by a more precise synonym such as *support*, or *sustain*.

22c   Jargon

Jargon is speech that uses technical terms familiar only to people within a given discipline or profession. To others these terms are confusing. Jargon can be abbreviations or acronyms with verbal or adjectival endings. Jargon often converts nouns into adjectives, adverbs, or verbs. A typical use of jargon is the addition *-ize* and *-wise* to nouns: *systematize, utilize, optimize, prioritize* etc. Worse still, jargon turns nouns into hybrid adverbs: *ideawise, personalitywise* etc.

JARGON	This student has not been IEPd for time-and-a-half.
TRANSLATION	This student does not have an Individual Education Program that allows her half again as much time as others are given to complete assignments and tests.
JARGON	You must prioritize your activities schedule-wise to maximize your opportunities of interfacing with interesting men.
TRANSLATION	You must organize the activities on your schedule to have more chances of meeting interesting men.
JARGON	He left Wall Street to start his own business in order to optimize his self-realization coefficient and to minimize his future regret risk factor.

TRANSLATION   He left Wall Street to start his own business, to fulfill his deepest aspirations, and to reduce the risk of future regrets.

Exercise

Correct any errors in non-standard speech. Answers on p.149.

GROUP A

1. The data for this project came off of the Internet; so I refuse to be responsible for them in any way, shape, or form.
2. People start talking and hype rumors out of proportion.
3. Telling her the truth would have blown James Bond's cover.
4. "Better safe than sorry," I always say.
5. The graphic design field has lots to offer location-wise. There are many job openings all around the U.S.
6. After my internship, I developed a real feel for the demands of the job.
7. A wise administrator is willing to compromise instead of relying only on hard and fast rules.
8. He decided to leave Wall Street and start his own business based on a regret minimization framework.
9. Free agents can up and leave their fans for a team that pays more.
10. Many people buy into the notion that seances allow them to communicate with people who are dead and gone.

GROUP B

1. Ricki Lake was angry at Jerry Springer because he disrespected her when she met up with him at the party.
2. Players look to be part of a winning team that pays high salaries and treats them with tender loving care.
3. A no-fault divorce is intended for couples who cannot commit to a lifetime together.
4. Last but not least, you have to improve your writing stylewise.
5. His psychological motivation profile revealed an authority-averse personality.
6. He simply didn't fit into a prep school. Day in and day out, he stuck out like a sore thumb.
7. After all is said and done the doctor puts me in the ICU and says he will have to pull my C-5 and C-6 back in place.
8. The noblemen in the antechamber suck up to Monseigneur in *A Tale of Two Cities*.
9. First off, she needs your input because she's totally out of it fashion-wise.
10. Time and time again, he wanted to try and get together to discuss about the best way to resolve their differences.

23 Ending in prepositions

Is ending in a preposition always wrong?

As a general rule, do not strand prepositions at the ends of sentences, phrases, or clauses unless it is the clearest way of stating your idea. Ending in a preposition usually creates a clumsy construction that may force the reader to pause or double back in the sentence to grasp its meaning.

Sometimes, however, insisting on *not* having a sentence end in a preposition tortures the natural syntax of the sentence or confuses its meaning. In these cases *do* end phrases, clauses, and sentences in a preposition, especially when the preposition is part of a phrasal verb.

23a   Ending sentences and clauses in a preposition unnecessarily

Prepositions often help show who performs or receives an action in a sentence and need, therefore, to be as close to the agent or recipient as possible. Sentences or clauses of *giving, getting, receiving, bringing,* and *taking* should not end in a preposition.

➤Equity is the union I received the acting scholarship ~~from.~~ *from which*

➤The man I gave my green leather suitcase with the gold monogram ~~to~~ left abruptly. *to whom*

➤Was Caracas the city I got that nasty stomach virus ~~in~~? *in which*

23b   Necessary ending in a preposition

Ending in a preposition can be desirable or unavoidable when the preposition is part of a phrasal verb and cannot be separated from the verb stem. Consider the following sentences with phrasal verbs which sound ludicrous without a preposition in the end.

➤This is the bandage ~~off~~ which the doctor said I should not take. *off*

The phrasal verb *to take off* should not be broken up.

➤Football is the one team ~~out for~~ which I would like to try. *out for*

The phrasal verb *to try out for* must be kept whole to remain idiomatically correct.

Phrasal verbs that combine common verbs such as *to be* and *to go* with prepositions can be more difficult to recognize. A good rule of thumb is that if you must end a sentence in either a preposition or a verb, choose to end in a preposition.

➤There is the umbrella ~~without~~ which I never am. *without*

The phrasal verb is *to be without* meaning *to lack*.

➤Because I am a diabetic, insulin is something ~~without~~ which I cannot *without* go for long.

Here, the phrasal verb is *to go without* meaning *to survive without*.

Exercise

Correct any errors in ending in prepositions. Answers on p.150.

1. One project is an environmental poster that I won second place for.
2. Qualifications depend on the type of job one is involved with.
3. In those days, people took pride in the teams they played for.
4. Audie Murphy showed his courage by overcoming the enemies that his friends had been captured by.
5. The airplane which the atomic bomb was loaded onto was called the *Enola Gay*.
6. As you research, be sure to include any relevant statistics that you come across.
7. The credit company I owe $5000 to has cut off my membership.
8. My computer is something I just can't get along without.
9. Now what sort of trouble did you get into?
10. Enjoying each day should be what life is about.

24 Showing cause

What words mean because*?*

Only *because* means *because.* Other expressions used to show causation such as *being that, seeing that, due to, owing to, for, since* are either inaccurate or old-fashioned. Use *because* to show cause.

24a   Eliminate *being that, seeing that*

Being that, or *seeing that* are not conjunctions as *because* is. They appear to be participles showing cause, but they do not describe anything. Avoid them without exception.

> *Because*
> ➤~~Being that~~ it was almost noon, he decided to get up.

> *because*
> ➤She decided to go to the prom with him ~~seeing that~~ he was the only one who had asked her.

24b   Use *due to, owing to* for debts not causes

Due to or *owing to* used to mean *because* may be more or less accepted in spoken English but not in serious writing. Both expressions refer to *debts* rather than to *causes.* In the examples below, notice that it is impossible to replace *due to* and *owing to* with *because.*

> ➤A refund is *due to* him for returning the empty bottles.

> ➤He admits *owing* his life *to* her.

Do not use *due to* and *owing to* in order to show cause.

> *because of*
> ➤The flight to Atlanta will be delayed ~~due to~~ bad weather.

> *Because of*
> ➤~~Owing to~~ a prior engagement, I will have to turn down your invitation.

24c   Avoiding *for*

For is an old-fashioned way of saying *because.* Employ it only if you want to sound quaint and faintly poetical as in the famous chorus, "For he's a jolly good fellow."

> *because*
> ➤She sent him back to the grocery store ~~for~~ he had forgotten to buy deodorant.

> *because*
> ➤The Ancient Mariner killed the albatross ~~for~~ he feared it was a bad omen.

The expression *for a reason,* however, does show cause and the *for* in it should not be replaced by *because.*

> ➤I have given up smoking *for reasons of* health.

Using *since* to indicate time not cause   *24d*

Since means *from the time that.* Use *since* as a time word.

> ➤*Since* I was three years old, I have adored steam locomotives.

> ➤Women's rights have come a long way *since* Susan B. Anthony was alive.

Use *because* to mean *because* in preference to *since.*
> *Because*
> ➤~~Since~~ I have a well-paying job, I will be able to afford a new car.

The speaker is showing *cause* not elapsed *time: why* he is able to afford a new car not *for how long* he has be able to afford a new car.
> *because*
> ➤Sarah joined Greenpeace ~~since~~ she felt strongly about ecology
> *because*
> and ~~since~~ they advocate direct action against polluters.

📖 Exercise

Correct any errors in showing cause. Answers on p.151.

1. He thinks he can give us orders being that he's the oldest.
2. Due to the storm, the shuttle blasted off later than NASA had expected.
3. I carried extra cash since they did not accept credit cards.
4. The gangsters decided to murder the witnesses due to the fact that they were going to testify.
5. Since she loved me, she left me all her money.
6. The secret agent didn't tell the stranger his name for he was afraid of being betrayed.
7. A meeting at Yalta was necessary seeing that Churchill, Roosevelt, and Stalin had many problems to work out.

8. He owes much of the credit for his success to his grandparents who raised him.
9. She might as well take the time to change her clothes, being that she's late to the party anyway.
10. They corresponded for many years for they had many interests in common.

25   Frequently misused words

Which words are most likely to be misused?

Words can be easily misused if they sound alike but have quite different meanings. The way to avoid embarrassing mistakes is to read widely and to become aware of differences in spelling. Below are some frequently misused words that can mislead readers and destroy the meaning of otherwise thoughtful passages. (See also §50g *Commonly misspelled words*, and §50h *Homophones*.)

accept *v.* – to receive willingly, to admit, to regard as true, to consent to, to respond affirmatively.

> ➤ I *accept* this responsibility willingly.

except *prep.* – other than, excluding.

> ➤ I invited everyone *except* Monica.

except *v.* – to leave out.

> ➤ He *excepted* Monica from the guest list.

affect *v.* – (most common usage) to influence or control.

> ➤ Too little sunlight *affects* most people by making them feel depressed.

effect *v.* – to cause to happen.

> ➤ The governor *effected* important changes in the welfare policy.

effect *n.* – result, consequence, outcome.

> ➤ My depression is the *effect* of too little sunlight this February.

impact *n.* – a collision, the effect of one thing upon another.

> ➤ The *impact* of the blow gave me a concussion.

> Never use *impact* as a verb to mean *affect*.

➤The news ~~impacted~~ *affected* me badly.

aggravate *v.* – to make worse or more serious.

➤Please do not *aggravate* the situation by continuing to argue with your boss.

irritate *v.* – to annoy.

➤The constant whining of the child began to *irritate* everyone on the bus.

anxious *adj.* – worried, uneasy.

➤It was ten o'clock, and I felt *anxious* because I didn't know where my children were.

eager *adj.* – intensely desirous, impatiently expectant.

➤I was *eager* to receive confirmation that I had won the Nobel Prize.

assure *v.* – remove doubt, create a feeling of certainty.

➤The troop leader *assured* me that my son was safe.

assure *v.* – to indemnify a person against loss.

➤It is wise to *assure* property against flood damage.

ensure *v.* – to make certain.

➤I sent a limousine to pick him up at the airport, to *ensure* his safe and prompt arrival.

insure *v.* – to indemnify against loss (like *assure*). (Sometimes a synonym for *ensure*, but no longer in common usage.)

➤It is wise to *insure* property against flood damage.

between *prep.* – indicates a relationship of two.

➤This secret is to be kept just *between* the two of us.

among *prep.* – indicates a relationship of three or more.

➤This secret is to be kept just *among* the four of us.

bring *v.* – to carry something *to* the speaker.

➤*Bring* me my diamond tiara.

take *v.* – to carry something *away from* the speaker.

➤*Take* this diamond tiara to Her Majesty.

commit *v.* – always *commit* (*someone* or *something*), as in *commit crime*, or *commit oneself to a cause*. As a transitive verb, *commit* takes a *direct object*.

➤Men can never *commit themselves* to relationships.

continual *adj.* – an action that occurs regularly with gaps of time in between.

➤This film is shown *continually* at one, four, seven, and ten p.m.

continuous *adj.* – an action that progresses without a moment's interruption.

➤The fire alarm rang *continuously* throughout the film.

disinterested *adj.* – having no stake in, neutral, having nothing to gain.

➤Judges should always be *disinterested* parties.

uninterested *adj.* – bored by, not caring about.

➤Judges should never be *uninterested* in the cases they hear.

each other *pron.* – indicates a connection between members of a pair.

➤Romeo and Juliet loved *each other* deeply.

one another *pron.* – indicates a connection between members of pairs within an entire group, or among the various members of a group in general.

➤Ideally *husbands and wives* love *one another*.

➤Ideally *family members* love *one another*.

eminent *adj.* – prominent, outstanding, famous.

➤The *eminent* scientist was about to enter the convention hall.

imminent *adj.* – about to happen, impending.

➤His arrival was *imminent*.

enormity *n.* – excessive wickedness, monstrous evil.

➤The *enormity* of child abuse is beyond forgiveness.

enormousness *n.* – largeness in size, extent, number, or degree

➤The *enormousness* of the stage made me feel small and insignificant.

good *adj.* – desirable, suitable, usable, high quality, in fine working condition, virtuous. Describes a noun or pronoun. Acts as a predicate nominative.

> ➤He is a *good* person.

> ➤The massage is very pleasant. It feels *good*.

well *adv.* – satisfactorily, properly, reasonably, prudently, intimately, extremely. Describes verbs, adjectives, other adverbs.

> ➤She feels *well*. She is in good health.

> ➤She is an intelligent person who reasons *well*.

healthy *adj.* – in good health, feeling well.

> ➤I am a *healthy* person who seldom becomes sick.

healthful *adj.* – good for you, beneficial.

> ➤I eat *healthful* food. *Healthful* choices keep me from becoming ill.

historic *adj.* – momentous, having great influence on history.

> ➤The Teheran Conference attended by all three Allied leaders was an *historic* occasion.

historical *adj.* – occurring in the past, occurring in history.

> ➤Well-educated people easily recall many *historical* characters and events.

infer *v.* – to draw a conclusion from what someone else has said or done. Readers or listeners *infer*.

> ➤From the expression on his face, I *inferred* that he was angry.

imply *v.* – to suggest a conclusion. Writers or speakers *imply*.

> ➤Her comment seemed complimentary, but in fact it *implied* that I had said something unusually stupid.

suggest *v.* – to imply with reference to *evidence* as opposed to *people*. Evidence only *suggests*; people both suggest and *imply*.

> ➤These photos *suggest* that intelligent life exists in other galaxies.

less *adj., adv.* – deals with amount.

> ➤The *less* work he has to do, the happier he is.

> ➤This problem is *less* difficult to solve than the earlier one.

fewer *adj.* – deals with number.

> ➤ The *fewer* jobs he has to perform, the happier he is.

liable *adj.* – answerable or legally responsible for.

> ➤ The airline is *liable* for any lost luggage.

likely *adj., adv.* – probable, apt to occur.

> ➤ It is not *likely* that they will lose your luggage, but if they do, you can hold them *liable*.

lie *v.* – place *oneself* down in a reclining position.

> **PRESENT** I *lie* down every afternoon for a nap.

> **PAST** Yesterday I *lay* down and slept for an hour.

> **PRESENT PERFECT** I *have lain* down every afternoon as far as I can remember.

lay *v.* – place something or someone else down.

> **PRESENT** I *lay* the baby down for a nap every afternoon.

> **PAST** Yesterday I *laid* the baby down, and she slept for an hour.

> **PRESENT PERFECT** During the past month, I *have laid* down the baby regularly for a nap at this time.

majority *n.* – the greater number of, used to indicate discrete segments but never volume. Takes a singular verb.

> ➤ The majorty of shoppers waits for the big sales.

most *n.* – the greatest amount of, used to indicate both volume and number.

> ➤ Most of the water has drained out of the pool.

> ➤ Most of the shoppers wait for the big sales.

memento *n.* – souvenir, keepsake, reminder of the past.

> ➤ He gave her a seashell bracelet as a *memento* of their delightful afternoon at the shore.

momento – *there is no such word in the English language.*

quotation *n.* – the repetition or citation of someone else's exact words.

> ➤ "Friends, Romans, countrymen, lend me your ears" is a famous quotation from *The Tragedy of Julius Caesar.*

quote *v.* – to repeat or cite someone else's exact words.

➤I am tired of hearing you quote Dorothy Parker.

shrank *v.* – past tense of verb *to shrink.*

➤"Honey, I *shrank* the kids."

shrunk *v.* – past participle of verb *to shrink.*

➤"Honey, I *have shrunk* the kids."

📖 Exercise

Correct any errors in misused words. Answers on p.151.

GROUP A
1. Clara Barton was overwhelmed by the enormity of the responsibility in managing the regional office of the Red Cross.
2. Marlon Brando is liable to eat the entire box of cookies unless I hide them.
3. Was that a quote from *The Tempest?*
4. The genetic similarity of chimpanzees to humans implies that we have evolved from a common ancestor.
5. Bring the new dictionary to the library right away.
6. Everyone except Diogenes accepted the existence of UFOs.
7. The fall of the Roman Empire was a historical event that occurred in 476.
8. All the students in class corrected each other's papers.
9. Andre Agassi won less tennis tournaments than Pete Sampras had.
10. Is it likely that he is liable and will be sued?

GROUP B
1. The Queen and Margaret Thatcher complimented each other on their handbags.
2. How does the new immigration law impact our health care policy?
3. While a good fan is interested in the outcome of the game, a good referee is wholly uninterested.
4. Giorgio Armani was anxious to see the new Versace collection at the fashion show.
5. The most important thing for a healthy body is a healthy diet.
6. The imminent scientist lectured at Columbia.
7. It rained continually for two hours in San Francisco yesterday while in Edinburgh it rains continually year round.
8. The rivalry between Einstein, Oppenheimer, and Teller ended the day Einstein bowled a perfect game.
9. She aggravated her boss by refusing to work overtime on Fridays.
10. We were ready for more sightseeing after laying down for an hour's nap.

18–25 Answers to exercises

 18 Addressing the reader and choosing a voice

1. *Second person.* Change *yourself* to *oneself.* Avoid the 2nd person.
   Revision: It is essential to stretch *oneself* to the limit.
2. *Hybrid non-sexist pronoun.* Change it to the masculine, the feminine, the objective, or plural voice.
   Revision: In planning for college, *students* must give *themselves* as many academic and financial options as possible. *They* have to be aware of the competition for admissions that *they* will face and of the financial responsibility placed upon *them* by educational loans.
3. *Stilted objective voice.* Replace *one* with any standard personal pronoun (*he, she, they*).
   Revision: Einstein's theory of relativity explains what would happen to *a person* if *he* were to find *himself* hurtling through space at the speed of light.
4. *Second person.* Change *you* to the *implied you* (*consider*). Add the *we* to invite your reader to share your idea, rather than dictating to him.
   Revision: Consider the danger of judging a potential employee by appearance alone. What talents might *we* overlook that could benefit *our* company?
5. *Second person changed to impersonal voice.* Eliminate *your* and *you* in favor of the more formal impersonal voice adjusting the sentence as needed.
   Revision: Emotions affect *the* perception of situations and *encourage* unrealistic decision.

 19 Word choice

1. *Replace approximate with exact term.* The *address* is not located anywhere, but the *house* is.
   Revision: The *house* is located in a prestigious area of Southbury.
2. *Replace approximate with exact term. Objectivity* is needed for reasonable career choices. *Neutrality* is necessary for resolving conflicts between warring parties.
   Revision: An *objective* perspective on the market situation allows a reasonable rather than an emotional career choice.
3. *Replace vague with specific term. Negative* is too vague: it could mean anything. *Pejorative* is a specific type of negativity.
   Revision: He was insulted by the pejorative criticism of his play.

4. *Replace object-related word by people-related word.* Fans *decide* but support *determines*
   Revision: Fan support is one of the most important factors in *determining* whether or not a team can be called great.
5. *Replace phrasal with simple verb.* Instead of *meets together with* use *meets,* or *encounters.*
   Revision: When Don Juan *encounters* a lady, he promptly compliments her.
6. *Replace vague with specific term.* *Bad, things,* and *negative* are too vague to be meaningful.
   Revision: Her teacher's *criticism of the grammar and punctuation* in her essay *reduced* her self-confidence.
7. *Replace object-related word by people-related word.* Sentient creatures are *involved,* objects and courses are *complex.*
   Revision: Kinesiotherapy is a very *complex* area of study.
8. *Replace phrasal with simple verb.* Avoid the confusion of *get around* versus *get a round* with reference to a game of golf. Replace *get around on a golf course* with *played golf adequately.*
   Revision: Even though she did not have much experience, she knew how *to play golf adequately.*
9. *Replace vague with specific term.* Replace *thing* with *trait, being good* with *virtue,* and *more important than anything else* with *most valued.*
   Revision: Virtue was the Puritans' most valued trait.
10. *Replace approximate with exact term.* Duties are much more serious than functions. If you don't carry out a *duty,* you let people down by not living up to your responsibilities. If you don't brush and floss, you just get a cavity.
    Revision: We all lead busy lives and do not always take the time to perform essential *functions* such as flossing and brushing our teeth after every meal.

 20 Definitions and examples

1. *Using* when. Correct by using a gerund (*saying*).
   Revision: An example of Marie Antoinette's indiscretion was her *saying,* "Let them eat cake," within earshot of the peasants.
2. *Using examples accurately.* Stalin is a *dictator* not a *dictatorship.*
   Revision: Stalin is an example of *dictators who* enslave their nations.
3. *Giving definitions before examples.* Reverse the order of the 2nd and 3rd sentences.
   Revision: One of the greatest challenges of being a coach is dealing with players who do not want to work hard. These are not athletes with special needs, but rather those who are simply lazy or undisciplined. For example, they will not do the required fitness training or skills work, and yet expect to make the team.

4. *Using* where. Correct by using a gerund (*trying*).
   Revision: An experiment is actually trying out the theories in textbooks.
5. *Circular reasoning* and *using* when. *Self–esteem* is *self-respect*.
   Revision: Self-esteem means *valuing one's own abilities.*
6. *Perfect example* and *using examples accurately.* *Caesar* is a person not
   an *emotion.*
   Revision: The behavior of the mob in *Julius Caesar* exemplifies mindless emotion.
7. *Circular reasoning* and *dictionary definition.* Stilted and unhelpful.
   Define in terms specific to your approach to your topic. *Charisma* does
   not define *charismatic* but merely compounds the confusion.
   Revision: Being charismatic is using charm to attract allies and to
   disarm adversaries.
8. *Giving definitions before examples.* Reverse the order of the 2nd and
   3rd sentences.
   Revision: True love is a unique experience. True love is an overwhelming and lasting passion between two people. Examples of famous
   lovers in literature are Antony and Cleopatra, and Romeo and Juliet.
9. *Using* when. Correct by using a gerund (*feeling*).
   Revision: Sectionalism is *feeling* more loyalty to the local region than to
   the country as a whole.
10. *Using examples accurately.* The *General* is not an example of *warfare,*
    but his *march* is.
    Revision: General Sherman's march through Georgia is a typical
    example of modern warfare in which the invading army lives off the
    land.

  21 Expressing similarity and difference

1. As *starts clauses.*
   Revision: As I said, we're not growing any younger!
2. *Use* various *for more than two items.*
   Revision: I like reading about the *various* inhabitants of the future
   Earth in H. G. Wells's *The Time Machine.*
3. *No revision.* The prepositional phrase correctly begins with the
   preposition *like.*
4. *Use* different from.
   Revision: Gulliver became a very different person *from the one* he had
   been at the beginning of his travels.
5. *No revision. Like* correctly starts preposition phrase (*like his father*).
6. As *starts clauses*
   Revision: T. S. Eliot talked about literature *as if* he had a Ph.D. in
   English.

7. *Use* various *for more than two items.*
   Revision: I was fascinated by the *various* colors in an opal.
8. *Use* different from.
   Revision: In today's global village, we have to learn to be knowledge-able about customs *different from* ours.
9. *No revision.* Implied comparison between two pronunciations, the *Scottish* and the speaker's.
10. As *starts clauses.*
    Revision: The air traffic controller gave instructions *as if* she knew what she was doing.

 22 Non-standard speech

GROUP A
1. *Slang (*off of*). Cliché (*any way shape or form*).*
   Revision: The data for this project came *off* the Internet; so I refuse to be responsible for them in *any way.*
2. *Slang (*hype*).*
   Revision: People start talking and *exaggerate* rumors out of proportion.
3. *Slang (*blown...cover*).*
   Revision: Telling her the truth would have *betrayed* James Bond's *identity.*
4. *Cliché (*better safe than sorry*).*
   Revision: "Better *not take chances*," I always say.
5. *Jargon (*location-wise, lots to offer*).*
   Revision: The graphic design field offers job opportunities at many locations throughout the U.S.
6. *Slang (*feel for*).*
   Revision: After my internship, I developed a *clear understanding of* the demands of the job.
7. *Cliché (*hard and fast*).*
   Revision: A wise administrator is willing to compromise instead of relying only on *firm, unchangeable* rules.
8. *Jargon (*based on a regret minimization framework*).*
   Revision: He decided to leave Wall Street and start his own business *to reduce the possibility of future regrets.*
9. *Colloquialism (*up and leave*).*
   Revision: Free agents can *leave* their fans *abruptly* for a team that pays more.
10. *Slang (*buy into*). Colloquialism (*dead and gone*).*
    Revision: Many people *accept* the notion that seances allow them to communicate with people who are *dead.*

GROUP B
1. *Slang (*disrespected*). Colloquialism (*met up with*).*
   Revision: Ricki Lake was angry at Geraldo Rivera because he *did not treat her with respect* when she *met* him at the party.

2. *Colloquialism* (*look to be*). *Cliché* (*tender loving care*).
   Revision: Players *want* to be part of a winning team that pays high salaries and treats them *considerately.*
3. *Slang. Commit* is a transitive verb. It must take a direct object, as in "to commit a *crime.*" Note the direct object inserted into the revision.
   Revision: A no-fault divorce is intended for couples who cannot commit *themselves* to a lifetime together.
4. *Cliché* (*last but not least*). *Jargon* (*stylewise*).
   Revision: Finally, you have to improve your writing *style.*
5. *Jargon* (*psychological motivation profile, authority-averse*).
   Revision: His *psychological profile* revealed *that he tended to be hostile to people in authority.*
6. *Cliché* (*day in and day out, stuck out like a sore thumb*).
   Revision: He simply didn't fit into a prep school. He *was perpetually and painfully conspicuous.*
7. *Cliché* (*after all is said and done*). *Jargon* (*ICU, C-5, C-6*).
   Revision: Finally, the doctor puts me in the *Intensive Care Unit* and says he will have to pull back into place the *C-5 and C-6 discs in my spine.*
8. *Slang* (*suck up*).
   Revision: The noblemen in the antechamber *are obsequious* to Monseigneur in *A Tale of Two Cities.*
9. *Colloquialism* (*first off*). *Jargon* (*input, fashionwise*). *Slang* (*out of it*).
   Revision: First of all, she needs your *suggestions* because she's totally *ignorant about fashions.*
10. *Cliché* (*time and time again*). *Colloquialism* (*try and get, discuss about*).
    Revision: He *tried repeatedly* to get together *to discuss* the best way to resolve their differences

✍ 23 Ending in prepositions

1. One project is an environmental poster *for which* I won second place.
2. *No revision.* Phrasal verb (*to be involved with*).
   OR
   Qualifications depend *on the job.*
3. *No revision.* Phrasal verb (*played for*).
   OR
   In those days, people took pride *in their teams.*
4. Audie Murphy showed his courage by overcoming the enemies *by whom* his friends had been captured.
5. The airplane *onto* which the atomic bomb was loaded was called the *Enola Gay.*
6. *No revision.* Phrasal verb (*come across*).
   OR
   As you research, be sure to include any relevant statistics that you *find.*

7. The credit company *to which* I owe $5000 has cut off my membership.
8. *No revision.* Phrasal verb (*get along without*)

    OR

    My computer is *essential* to me.
9. *No revision.* Phrasal verb (*get into*).
10. *No revision.* Phrasal verb (*is about*)

    OR

    Enjoying each day should be *the essence of* life.

 24 Showing cause

1. He thinks he can give us all orders *because* he's the oldest.
2. *Because of* the storm, the shuttle blasted off later than NASA had expected.
3. I carried extra cash *because* they did not accept credit cards.
4. The gangsters tried to murder the witnesses *because* they were going to testify.
5. *Because* she loved me, she left me all her money.
6. The secret agent didn't tell the stranger his name *because* he was afraid of being betrayed.
7. A meeting at Yalta was necessary *because* Churchill, Roosevelt, and Stalin still had many problems to work out.
8. *No revision.* The *owing* is an actual debt, not a cause.
9. She might as well take the time to change her clothes *because* she's late to the party anyway.
10. They corresponded for many years *because* they had many interests in common.

 25 Frequently misused words

GROUP A

1. *Enormousness* not *enormity.* There's nothing excessively evil about the Red Cross.
   Revision: Clara Barton was overwhelmed by the *enormousness* of the responsibility in managing the regional office of the Red Cross.
2. *Likely* not *liable.* No legal responsibility is involved here.
   Revision: Marlon Brando is *likely* to eat the entire box of cookies unless I hide them.
3. *Quotation* not *quote.* You need the noun not the verb.
   Revision: Was that a *quotation* from *The Tempest*?
4. *Suggests* or *implies.* Only people *imply.*
   Revision: The genetic similarity of chimpanzees to humans *suggests* that we have evolved from a common ancestor.

    OR

    We may *infer* from the genetic similarity of chimpanzees to humans that we have evolved from a common ancestor.

5. *Take* not *bring*. *Take* away from the speaker.
   Revision: Take the new dictionary to the library right away.
6. *No revision*
7. Use either *historic* or *historical* depending on your emphasis. The 476 is *historical*, but use *historic* if your context shows that the event was influential.
   Revision: The fall of the Roman Empire was an *historic* event that occurred in 476.
8. *One another's* not *each other's*. The pairs are within the context of the entire group.
   Revision: All the students in class corrected *one another's* papers.
9. *Fewer* not *less*. Tournaments can be itemized; therefore use *fewer*.
   Revision: Andre Agassi won *fewer* tournaments than Pete Sampras had.
10 *No revision*.

GROUP B

1. *No revision*.
2. *Affect* not *impact*. Use the verb to mean *influence*.
   Revision: How does the new immigration law *affect* our health care policy?
3. *Disinterested* not *uninterested*. A fair referee does not have a stake in the outcome.
   Revision: While a good fan is interested in the outcome of the game, a good referee is wholly *disinterested*.
4. The answer depends on whether Armani is competing with Versace and is worried about his competitor's success, or is friendly and, therefore, supportive of her. If competing, no correction is needed.
   Revision: (If friendly) Giorgio Armani was *eager* to see the new Versace collection at the fashion show.
5. *Healthful* not *healthy*. People are *healthy*, diets are *healthful*.
   Revision: The most important thing for a healthy body is a *healthful* diet.
6. *Eminent* not *imminent* to mean *distinguished*.
   Revision: The *eminent* scientist lectured at Columbia.
7. *Continuously* not *continually* to mean *without a break*.
   Revision: It rained *continuously* for two hours in San Francisco yesterday while in Edinburgh it rains continually year round.
8. *Among* not *between* to list more than two.
   Revision: The rivalry *among* Einstein, Oppenheimer, and Teller ended the day Einstein bowled a perfect game.
9. *Irritated* not *aggravated* unless she made him worse.
   Revision: She *irritated* her boss by refusing to work overtime on Fridays.
10. *Lying down* not *laying down*. You *lay* down something.
    Revision: We were ready for more sightseeing after *lying* down for an hour's nap.

Structure and Sense

26 Parallel construction

What is parallel construction, and why is it important?

Parallel construction means phrasing a series of related actions or ideas in a sentence so that all have the same grammatical form. Most often, parallel construction governs lists. Its purpose is to show that all the elements of the list belong together and are of equal importance. Parallelism also helps eliminate misunderstandings.

Elements of a list can be parallel in their parts of speech, numbering, verb tense, and correlative structure.

26a Parallel parts of speech and numbering

State your lists as all *nouns*, all *adjectives*, or all *gerunds*.

NOUNS This essay discusses human development in terms of *child-*
hood, ~~growing up~~, and *adulthood*.
      adolescence

ADJECTIVES The ideal family pet is *friendly*, *loyal*, and ~~won't pee on the rug~~.
                                                          house broken

Repeat *articles, pronouns, prepositions*. Keep *numbers* in the same form.

GERUNDS *Jogging*, ~~weights~~, and *stretching* are the main components of
      weight training
a weekly physical regimen.

ARTICLES The specimens to be dissected in this experiment are *an*
earthworm, clam, and lobster.
          a   a

PRONOUNS Guidance counselors recommend colleges *that* challenge
students academically, and meet their social and emotional
needs.
                that

PREPOSITIONS The guide took us on a tour of John F. Kennedy's childhood
home and his burial place.
          of

Taking us on a tour of John F. Kennedy's childhood home *and* burial place gives the impression he had been buried *in* his childhood home.

NUMBERS   I've been to Africa three times: ~~once~~ to Kenya on safari, ~~secondly~~ *first* *second* to the Kalahari and *third* to the Sahara desert.

Alternative number forms are also acceptable: *firstly, secondly, thirdly (lastly, finally); once (the first time), the second time, the third time,* etc.

Parallel verb tenses   26b

Remain in the same verb tense when listing a variety of actions (see also §16c *Shifts in verb tense*).

➤ I *enjoy* skiing, *love* ice skating, and *am* generally active all winter.

When using tenses that take helping verbs such as *does/did, have/had,* or *will,* repeat the helping verb for added clarity.

➤ Recruits *will* undergo psychological tests, *will* learn survival techniques, and *will* be trained in first aid.

➤ I *have* traveled the world, *have* seen its wonders, and now *have* returned home.

Verbs do not have to be repeated when a single verb controls an entire list. Parallelism in such situations is obvious, and attempts to repeat the verb often result in awkward locutions.

AWKWARD   Maine had once been known as New Somerset; New Jersey had once been known as New Sweden; and Vermont had once been known as New Connecticut.

BETTER   Maine had once been known as New Somerset, New Jersey as New Sweden, and Vermont as New Connecticut.

Notice, however, that the list must still be grammatically parallel. In the above example, repeating the preposition *as* conveys the sense of parallelism.

Parallel correlative constructions   26c

Correlative constructions are phrases and clauses that work together in parallel ways within the sentence. They come in pairs and are connected by expressions such as *either...or, both...and* etc. Two rules govern their usage. First, never use one half without the other. Second, be sure that both halves of the correlation belong together idiomatically and are complete.

As...as

> Most historians believe that Tesla's inventions are ~~so~~ *as* significant as Edison's.

Both...and

> Both Amundsen ~~as well as~~ *and* Scott reached the South Pole.

As well as means *in addition to* and is redundant when used with *both*. When *and* forms half of the correlative construction *both...and,* substituting *as well as* is incorrect.

Either...or

> Either Honshu ~~but~~ *or* perhaps Hokkaido is the largest island of the Japanese archipelago.

Either...but do not belong together idiomatically.

Just as...so

> Just as Edward Lear invented words for his *Nonsense Songs,* Lewis Carroll ~~did the same~~ *so did* for *Alice in Wonderland.*

Again, *just as...the same* are a non-parallel mismatch.

Neither...nor

> "Neither Lawrence Sutterfield, ~~or~~ *nor* even the Lady March could possibly be guilty," said Miss Marple.

The word *nor* is obligatory after *neither.* But while *neither* can balance a negative proposition alone, *nor* cannot be used by itself.

> The Holy Roman Empire was not holy. ~~Nor~~ *Neither* was it Roman.

Not only...but also

> Conrad explores *not only* European exploitation of Africa, *but* *also* Kurtz's individual thirst for power.

The correlative is incomplete. *Not* matches *but,* while *only* must match *also.* The correction supplies the missing correlative *also.*

On the one hand...on the other hand

> ~~Losing~~ *On the one hand, losing* my job was a blow to my self-esteem, but *on the other hand* it provided an opportunity to change careers.

The other hand cannot be used without *on the one hand* first.

Whether...or not

> How can you tell whether ~~pasta~~ is done?
>   *or not*
>   ∧

Whether is used when the sentence presents two or more options. It must be completed by *or*. Instead of *whether* alone, use *when* or *if*.

Exercise

Correct any errors in parallel construction. Answers on p.203.

GROUP A

1. Some Americans choose their friends based on characteristics such as race, how the person dresses, and the religion of the person.
2. Physical strength is useful when trying to lift a rock, digging a ditch, or throwing a shotput.
3. The danger of tornadoes lies not only in their power but their speed.
4. The person in charge has the ability to order everyone else around as well as a lavish lifestyle.
5. Modern children acquire material possessions too easily, do not value what they have, and are needing more attention from their parents.
6. The sight of burning villages and mass gravesites in Kossovo reminds Europeans of Nazi atrocities.
7. Darth Vader is responsible for maintaining imperial control both politically and through military force throughout the galaxy.
8. Parents should provide children with what they need, not everything they want.
9. Many people object when TV presents sex as a casual experience, and that you can't get along without it.
10. Radio astronomers use massive satellites to pinpoint the nature of signals in space and what is producing them.

GROUP B

1. As long as people have egos, spread rumors, and bystanders to watch, schoolyard fights will continue to occur.
2. The aspiring driver has two options: first driver's education, secondly a responsible adult teaches him.
3. I soon discovered that the inmates were not only ignorant but also had bad manners.
4. The botanist lectured about his trip to the Congo and going to Peru.
5. As a tour guide, you must come prepared to discuss the history of the monument and with brochures to distribute.
6. Species are becoming extinct both because of natural selection and there just isn't enough room for both animals and people.
7. Two key patterns in the lives of leaders are initially how they handle rejection and secondly how they dealt with success.

8. Taxi drivers tend to drive too fast and run the car into the ground.
9. The conductor noticed improvement in our performance but that our attendance was irregular.
10. First he studies the report, then draws up the graphs, and finally gave the presentation to the board of directors.

27 Correct and complete comparisons

How can a comparison be incorrect, and how can it be corrected?

Comparisons can be drawn only between similar categories of things. Objects compare to objects, people to people, actions to actions, abstract concepts to abstract concepts, etc. In complicated comparisons, however, writers may become lost and may end up likening people to places or to objects.

The cause of an incorrect comparison is usually missing connective words. To *correct* a comparison, *complete* it by furnishing those missing words, often the helping verbs *do, have* etc., or a phrase indicating possession or location such as *that of...*, *those in....*

The most common mismatches occur after the following comparatives: *like/unlike, more than/less than, better than/worse than*. Incorrect comparisons are of four types: *person-to-object comparisons, possessive comparisons, comparisons of place and time*, and *missing* or *ambiguous comparisons*.

27a Person-to-object comparisons

People are often confused with the actions they perform or with the objects they use. Correct person-to-object mismatches by supplying the missing helping verb.

➤According to psychologists, adults need to play with toys even more
     do
than children.
       ^

In the uncorrected sentence, *toys* (object) were being equated with *children* (people). Adding *do* equates the actions of adults and children.

can
➤A trained chef can create a richer stock than Julia Child.
                                                      ^

Here, *Julia Child* is being compared to a *rich stock*. Adding *can* shifts the focus of the comparison back to the people doing the cooking.

Possessive comparisons   27b

Do not compare the effects or characteristics belonging to a person with the person himself. Correct possessive comparisons by inserting *that/those* of or by attaching the appropriate possessive suffix to the noun.

those of
➤Ernest Hemingway's mountaineering skills were better than the other journalists on Kilimanjaro.   ^

The mistake lies in comparing *skills* (abstract concept) to *journalists* (people). Inserting the phrase *those of* indicating possession completes the comparison. Alternatively, the comparison can be corrected by making *journalists* a possessive: ...*than the other journalists' on Kilimanjaro.*

's
➤Your hair looks like a sheepdog.
                              ^

Clearly the comparison is not between the person's hair and the dog itself, but between the person's hair and the dog's fur.

Comparisons with place and time   27c

People, ideas and trends should not be confused with the places and times in which they live. Correct and complete comparisons of place and time by inserting *that/those of* or *that/those in* where necessary.

those in
➤People in Rio de Janeiro are more relaxed than New York.
                                                ^

The real comparison is between the citizens of both cities, not between the person and the city. *Those in* specifies the category being compared.

those of   *of*
➤Jeans styles today are more like the 1970s than the 1980s.
                               ^   ^

27d Ambiguous or missing comparisons

Ambiguous or missing comparisons occur when a sentence implies a comparison but lacks a clear relationship between the two objects. Comparisons are often missing or ambiguous in sentences that use *like/unlike,* or *different* without *from,* or that lack a necessary verb at the end.

AMBIGUOUS   Unlike previous campaigns, the parties now are limited in the amount of money they are allowed to spend.

This sentence mistakenly compares *campaigns* to *parties.*

CLEAR   Unlike previous *campaigns,* the present *campaign* is limited by the amount of money parties are allowed to spend.

MISSING   Hubert resented being different.

Different from whom? *Different* must compare something to something else. (See §21b *Using* different from.)

PRESENT   Hubert resented being different in his attitudes *from* the other sheep in the flock.

MISSING   Salieri envied Mozart who was more talented than *him.*

The incorrect pronoun *him* is prompted by the missing verb *was.*

PRESENT   Salieri envied Mozart who was more talented than *he was.*

📖   Exercise

Correct and complete the comparisons as needed. Answers on p.205.

1. Women are more concerned about their weight than men.
2. Stronger people have the ability to overcome many more obstacles than a weak person.
3. Their technology is above other civilizations.
4. Even though these traumas occur on a smaller scale, they are just as serious as someone who was in combat.
5. Cats devour rats as successfully as coyotes.
6. The humidity in South Carolina is like Brazil.
7. In the story, Thomas did not consider his own crimes as horrible as the other people.
8. Compare this year's income with last year.
9. Being larger, dogs need more room than cats.
10. She is a better calculus student than anyone in our class.

2 8 Incomplete and self-evident thoughts

What are incomplete and self-evident thoughts?

There is always a gap between what we think and what we say. In conversation, we have the chance to ask questions, to fill in gaps and to straighten out distortions. Because readers cannot ask questions of the written word, writers must anticipate possible misunderstandings for them and leave no thought half-said.

While incomplete thoughts should not be left half-expressed, self-evident thoughts should not be expressed at all. A thought is self-evident when it is too obvious to mention. You don't write essays about the fact that the grass is green. Similar self-evident thoughts should be omitted from analytical writing.

Defend thoughts against incompletion   *28a*

In casual conversation, we can expect people to "know what we mean." In writing we must state exactly and completely what we mean. Consider the sentences below in which the writer expects the reader to intuit what she means.

➤ People tend to take the easy way out.

The easy way out of what?

➤ People can enjoy themselves more and lead happier lives.

More than what? Happier than whose? This sentence is an example of a missing comparison (see §27d *Ambiguous or missing comparisons*).

➤ People need to put aside money for the future.

For what kind of future? For whose benefit? The writer means that people need to prepare for future *hardships*.

Though incomplete and at times inaccurate, these generalizations are not inherently incorrect. The writer can still go on to expand upon the generality with specifics in a later sentence. Incomplete generalizations are a problem only when they are allowed to stand alone. To combat incomplete thoughts, ask yourself questions designed to draw out specifics such as the following:

Which one?	What kind?
So what?	How does my statement relate to this issue?
Whose?	Why is that necessarily true?
How does it work?	What does my statement mean?
Different from what?	Similar in what ways?

The result is writing that defends itself against misunderstanding.

28b   **Eliminate self-evident statements**

Expository writing seeks to persuade and explain. It can do neither with ideas that are simplistic and state the trivial or the obvious.

➤The more information we can provide to our membership, the more informed they will be.

➤Dogs bark more than cats do.

➤The Yankees have great fans who come to the ball park.

➤In the long run, prevention is the best way to stop crimes.

📖   **Exercise**

Correct any incomplete and self-evident thoughts. Answers on p.206.

1. In *Anna Karenina,* Tolstoy maintains correctly that all happy families are alike.
2. Of the 260,000 Confederate soldiers who perished, half died of disease, a disadvantage to the South.
3. I think we can win if everyone does his job, and we play the kind of basketball we're capable of playing.
4. Philosophy resolves the essential differences between the "outside" and the "inside."
5. Without love, life isn't worth living.
6. When one section of the country depends on another section for survival, it is the weaker of the two parts.
7. The more I see what's going on, the more I realize that America is going downhill. I don't even bother voting. Washington doesn't do anything for me anyway.
8. The baby toddled up with a smile on his face.
9. What other people think about us isn't important; what we think about ourselves is.
10. In the final analysis, my brother will always be my brother.

29 Fragments

What is a sentence fragment?

A sentence expresses a complete idea. By contrast, a fragment is only a part of a sentence, and it expresses only a partial idea. A group of words can be a fragment if it (1) has no subject, (2) has no verb, (3) has neither a subject nor a verb, (4) has both a subject and a verb but does not express a complete thought.

Fragments without subjects 29a

Correct these fragments by inserting a subject or by merging them with an adjacent sentence.

➤ In the dream, Sigmund was smoking a large cigar/ *and w*Was puffing happily until he was abruptly awakened.

OR

➤ In the dream, Sigmund was smoking a large cigar. *He w*Was puffing happily until he was abruptly awakened.

➤ I heard that Schubert had actually been planning to finish his

symphony/ *b*But somehow had never found the time.

Fragments without verbs 29b

Fragments that lack verbs sometimes have long descriptions with words that sound like verbs. Do not be deceived by them. Correct these by inserting a verb or by merging the group of words with an adjacent sentence.

➤ I was thoroughly frustrated that morning. The large trout *was* eluding me in the swift current, flashing silver just below the surface. ^

OR

➤ I was thoroughly frustrated that morning/ *because t*The large trout *was* eluding me in the swift current, flashing silver just below the surface. ^

➤ The atomic submarine first appeared in a story by Jules Verne. And a *another of his predictions was*

spaceship launched from Cape Canaveral a hundred years before the fact.

29c   Fragments with neither subjects nor verbs

Fragments that have neither subjects nor verbs are simply phrases masquerading as sentences. These fragments either describe or list. Correct them by merging them with an adjacent sentence, or by adding the missing subject or verb.

➤ I worried about being able to carry out my New Year's resolution/ To give up chocolate during summer vacation.

➤ If commercial breaks could be curtailed, baseball games would move much more quickly, making the game more enjoyable for many of the fans/ Especially those with short attention spans.

➤ The list of speakers featured two of the most distinguished minds of the day/ The psychiatrist, Alfred Adler, and Carl Jung, his colleague from Switzerland.

29d   Fragments with both subjects and verbs

A group of words that contains both a subject and a verb but does *not* express a complete thought is a subordinate clause. Like phrases, these fragments are corrected by being connected to an adjacent sentence, or by being turned into a new sentence.

➤ Emma played matchmaker to her friends/ While she herself was not yet married.

➤ I could always count on Norman Bates up on the hill/ Whenever I needed a friendly pat on the back or a shoulder to cry on.

➤ Mercedes never wrote to the Count of Monte Cristo, not even a simple postcard. *Her insensitivity* Which hurt his feelings and made him treat her coldly when he returned from Devil's Island.

29e   Using fragments for effect

Some expressions can lack either a subject or a verb or both, and yet, in context, express a complete thought. Such expressions are not errors. Often they appear at the beginning or end of a paragraph and are used effectively for emphasis or mood. The paragraph below contains only three complete sentences, yet is a perfectly acceptable piece of writing.

> Go, team, go! The eternal cheer! The adoring crowds! The loyalty of teammates. He treasured each memory turning it over and over in his mind. These were the timeless trophies of the college athlete. Gone now, gone forever.

Similarly, the verb or subject can be *implied* rather than stated explicitly in expressions that mimic speech: short sentences containing contrasting ideas and short responses to questions. Such sentences are not fragmentary because they express a complete thought.

➤ For better or for worse.

➤ So the State is thinking of building a new low security prison nearby? Not in my back yard!

➤ "What are diamonds?" was the first question on the geology test. Easy. A girl's best friend! Next?

Words that signal fragments   29f

Fragments often begin with words like those in the list below. When one of these words starts a sentence, check to be sure that this sentence is complete.

although	for instance	or
also	if	so that
and	in addition	such as
because	including	such that
but	in other words	that
either	instead of	that is
especially	like	which
even	mainly	who
except	namely	whose
for example	neither	when

➤ I will always love Pyramus. Even if he is late to his appointments.

➤ She managed to pass English. Although she had to attend a summer school course on grammar.

➤ We ordered many small dishes which we shared. Instead of getting individual entrees.

📖   Exercise

Correct any fragments. Answers on p.207.

1. Whenever I felt the need for a friendly pat on the back or a shoulder to cry on. I could drop by Mrs. Cleaver's house conveniently across the street.
2. When is the best time to show commercials? During the most exciting part of the match, of course!
3. At the fundraiser were many interesting people with whom I could discuss the current political situation. In particular, Shirley Temple Black and Meryl Streep with their fascinating insights into the film industry.
4. This hope is what keeps gang members loyal to their group. That the power of the gang will keep other neighborhood criminals at bay.
5. Discrimination is an action based on prejudice. Also means making fine distinctions.
6. I remember that I spent a delightful evening. With my new friends from across the lake.
7. The more technology, the higher the level of development in a civilization.
8. I look forward to trading baseball cards with people who have rare collections. Fans with a lot of baseball memorabilia.
9. I'm a Ford man because of their high quality products. If only all trucks could be as sturdy as these! Chevy? Never liked them, never will.
10. Many beginners are averse to learning how to use computers. As a result of techno-shock.

30 Transitions

What are transitions?

Transitional expressions are bridges from one idea, topic, or paragraph to another. They give polish and flow to an argument. More importantly, they signal a change of tack, telegraphing whether a following statement contradicts, agrees with, or expands upon a preceding one (see §16 *Shifts in subjects, verbs, and direction*).

Not using a transitional expression creates a gap between ideas without a bridge to unite them. Using an inappropriate transition raises questions about the logical connection between ideas (see §43c *Irrelevancy*).

Expressions that signal agreement (comparison, consequence, emphasis) *30a*

again	following the lead of	joined with
along with	for this reason	just as...so
another	furthermore	like
also	hand in hand with	likewise
and	hence	moreover
another way	in addition	of course
as a consequence	in combination with	side by side with
as a result	in common with	similarly
as well as	in concurrence with	so
at least	indeed	then
because	inevitably	therefore
besides	in fact	thus
consequently	in like manner	too
equally	in particular	undoubtedly
equally notable	in the same way that	unquestionably

Expressions that signal disagreement (contrast, conflict, contradiction) *30b*

against	in answer to	on the contrary
alternatively	in conflict with	on the other hand
although	in contrast to	opposed to
and yet	in defiance of	otherwise
as if	in disagreement with	rather
but	in opposition to	rather than
by contrast	in lieu of	still
contrary to	in place of	though
conversely	in rebuttal	unlike
counter to	in response to	while
despite	in spite of	yet
even if	instead of	versus
even though	in the face of	*vis-à-vis*
face to face with	nevertheless	
however	nonetheless	

30c   Expressions that generalize, summarize, sequence, detail

as follows	in fine	on average
bringing together	in general	on balance
eventually	initially	overarching
expanding upon	in macrocosm	specifically
finally	in microcosm	such as
first (second, third)	in retrospect	taken as a whole
for example	in sum	the following
generally	in the final analysis	to generalize
in a variety of ways	in the main	to reconsider
including	*in toto*	to review
in detail	looking ahead	variously

Exercise

Fill in the logical transitional expressions between each set of statements below. Adjust the sentences as needed. Answers on p.208.

1. On the frontier, before schools were built, settlers relied on Bible reading to educate their children.(*disagreement*) communities began to erect formal schools, usually one-room cabins that served children of all ages.
2. In the 1860s, improvements in transportation were the key to the development of American business.(*agreement*) More rapid and efficient communication facilitated the flow of information between buyers and sellers throughout the new nation. (*generalization, expansion*) the newly invented telegraph, connected the East and West Coasts through the merger of Western Union and the American Telegraph Company.
3. Grant's administration was plagued by scandal. (*detail*) Union Pacific Railroad officials created a non-existent construction company, and defrauded the public by selling shares of stock in this corporation. (*detail/agreement*) William Belknap, Grant's Secretary of War, enriched himself by conspiring with white traders on reservations to cheat Native Americans.
4. The Mugwumps were reform-minded Republicans from all walks of life(*detail*) non-professionals, (*detail*) lawyers, newspaper editors and cartoonists (*agreement*) Thomas Nast (*emphasis*). (*disagreement*) the average American voter was not greatly swayed by the Mugwumps. (*agreement*) politicians paid little attention to them.(*disagreement*) the Mugwumps were at least partially successful in reforming American politics.

31 Passive construction

What is a passive construction, and why is active better?

A passive construction pairs an inactive subject with an indirect verb. The passive subject does not act but is acted upon. The passive verb reports on an action as if it had been performed by a third party rather than acting itself. It is actually a *verb phrase* composed of a form of the verb *to be* plus a *past participle* — *have been seen, was given, is known,* etc.

Active constructions are almost always preferable to passive ones because they let the reader know who or what is performing the action. Stylistically, active subjects and verbs produce vigorous, exciting, muscular prose.

Make passive constructions active   *31a*

To activate a passive construction, first locate the person or thing that should be performing the action and make it the subject of the sentence. Then change the verb from passive to active by eliminating the form of *to be* or by using a different verb altogether.

PASSIVE   A trophy was given to Melanie by her debate coach.

   Because it is an inanimate object, *trophy* is a poor choice for an active subject. People — *Melanie* or *debate coach* — are typically active subjects.

PASSIVE   Melanie was given a trophy by her debate coach.

   Even though *Melanie* is an active subject, she is being treated as an inanimate object. The construction is still passive because it has a passive verb. If we change the verb from passive to active we must also switch subjects.

ACTIVE   The debate coach gave Melanie a trophy.

   The debate coach is now the active subject and *gave* is the active verb. Alternatively, we could activate Melanie as the subject by using a different verb from *to give.*

ACTIVE   Melanie received a trophy from her debate coach.

In place of the passive verb *was given* we now have the active verb *received*.

Some passively constructed sentences omit the active agent altogether.

➤ Last night a bomb was found in the center of Belfast.

By whom? An active subject must be supplied before the passive verb can be changed to active.

➤ Last night police found a bomb in the center of Belfast.

31b   Use passive constructions when appropriate

Passive construction is appropriate under the following circumstances:

1. When you want to give the impression of calm, or inability to resist

   ➤Ishmael *was lulled* to sleep by the gently rocking boat.

2. When you don't know who performed the action

   ➤Mr. Peacock *was murdered* in the library.

3. When you want to hide the identity of whoever performed the action

   ➤It *has been decided* to double the salaries of all elected officials.

4. When you address a topic in general and objective terms

   ➤The Puritan ethic *can be examined* from two perspectives.

📖   Exercise

Correct any passive constructions in the examples below. Construct the shortest and clearest sentences possible rewriting as needed. Answers on p.208.

1. The vehicle skidded off the road when control over it was lost.
2. The cake was ruined when the sugar was forgotten by Craig Claiborne.
3. Strategies used by Napoleon for handling flank attacks were later recommended by Clausewitz.
4. Space, as has been argued convincingly by Albert Einstein, exists as a

coefficient of time.

5. O.J.Simpson was found not guilty by a criminal court, but legally liable by a civil court.
6. The problem can be discussed in practical terms.
7. He was not recruited because he was found to be too short for the NBA.
8. Her job performance was judged to be substandard.
9. Free movie passes were given her for Thursday night.
10. Rubber was used by South American Indians long before the landing of Spanish and Portuguese explorers.

32 Sentence length, order, and type

Why vary sentences by length, and order of phrases and clauses?

Good prose has a rhythm of its own. Short, staccato sentences or phrases convey a sense of pace. Long, flowing sentences convey a sense of patient, unhurried thought. To maintain the reader's interest, these rhythms should alternate.

Vary rhythms by alternating the length of sentences, and the order of phrases and clauses.

Alternate long sentences with short ones   *32a*

Follow long compound or complex sentences by short declarative ones.

➤Little Red Riding Hood had been brought up not to fear strangers and, therefore, was not particularly alarmed when the wolf approached her from behind a nearby oak. The wolf smiled.

Alter the order of sentence elements   *32b*

The standard sentence places its subject first, then its verb, followed finally by a complement. Alternate between subject-verb-complement sentences and ones that begin with a phrase or subordinate clause.

➤The wolf was a dashing fellow. While Little Red Riding Hood had
always enjoyed her trips to Grandma's house, never before had her
little walk seemed so exciting!

(annotations over "The wolf was a dashing fellow": S. V. C.; over "had her": V.; over "little walk seemed so exciting": S. V. C.)

32c   Avoid stringy sentences

Stringy sentences are long sentences made up of a series of phrases and clauses connected by repeated conjunctions such as *and*, *but*, *or*. Repair stringy sentences (1) by combining one or more details into a single subordinate phrase or clause, and (2) by dividing an overly long sentence into two.

STRINGY   She walked on *and* looked around at the beautiful scenery *and* listened to the birds, *but* never realized that the wolf had sped ahead *or* that he had his own deadly plan in mind.

BETTER   Looking around at the beautiful scenery, she listened to the birds as she walked, never realizing that the wolf had sped ahead. He had his own deadly plan in mind.

What are sentence types?

The main idea of a sentence can appear in various places: at the beginning, divided at opposite ends, or distributed evenly throughout. These various arrangements of ideas in a sentence are called *sentence types* of which there are four: *symmetrical, loose, periodic,* and *distributive*.

32d   Vary sentences among the four types

In the examples below, the main idea of each sentence is italicized.

1. *Symmetrical sentence* – stresses similarity or contrast between main ideas that are placed at the beginning and end.

   ➤Her *habit of obedience* struggled against her *passion for adventure*.

2. *Loose sentence* – places main idea at the beginning, and then elaborates on it.

   ➤*The wolf's invitation frightened but excited her*, making her heart beat quickly and her cheeks flush.

3. *Periodic sentence* – leads up to the main idea at the end of the sentence.

> ➤ As her pulse raced and senses reeled, she took a deep breath and replied, "*No, thank you. My grandmother is expecting me.*"

4. *Distributive sentence* – distributes parts of the main idea throughout the sentence.

> ➤ Disappointed and angry, *the wolf sped* to the woodland cottage *planning to revenge himself on the grandmother* of the unsuspecting Little Red Riding Hood.

📖   Exercise

Vary the sentence length, order, and type as needed. Shorten and tighten the sentences while the retaining the essence of the story. A number of approaches can be taken in this exercise. Answers on p.209.

Once upon a time, a stray dog came upon a barn full of hay that belonged to a kindhearted old farmer who allowed the dog to live there amicably with the ox and to hunt in the nearby woods, and to drink from the fresh stream in the meadow, and to grow fat, and to forget how it felt to be hungry. The old farmer died and the dog became greedy, even though he remembered the farmer's generosity, but would not let the ox eat the hay as he guarded it day and night so that he could no longer sleep, or go out to hunt because he refused to leave the hay even for a moment until he grew too weak to hunt, and starved to death atop a mountain of hay.

33 Wordiness and word order

How are wordiness and word order problematic?

Good writing is economical. Wordy writing is indirect and inefficient; its language is an obstacle to clear expression. In revising an essay, make sure your sentences state your ideas in as few words as possible.

Another obstacle to clear expression is complex or convoluted word order (*syntax*). The strategies outlined below shorten the expression and untangle the syntax of sentences.

33a   Rewrite descriptive phrases and clauses as
                           single words

Phrases or clauses that describe or that show possession can often
be rewritten as single adjectives, adverbs or possessives (words
ending in -*'s*).

WORDY   The boy *who had a long nose* looked like Pinocchio.

REVISED   The *long-nosed* boy looked like Pinocchio.

   The adjective clause *who had a long nose* is reduced to a single
   word.

WORDY   She spent many happy hours in the attic of the house *that
   belonged to her grandparents.*

REVISED   She spent many happy hours in the attic of her *grandparents'*
   house.

   Making *grandparents* possessive eliminates a wordy adjective
   clause.

WORDY   To *show respect* for the Queen, everyone rises when she enters the
   room.

REVISED   Everyone rises *respectfully* when the Queen enters the room.

   Respectfully translates the wordy adverb clause to *show respect for.*

33b   Eliminate the indirect constructions *there are, it is,
                           one of the...* etc.

Indirect constructions, also known as *tags* or *expletives*, are phrases
that act as unnecessary prologues to an idea, although on rare occa-
sions they serve as useful transitions. *There are, it is,* and *one of the*
(*reasons, causes, effects*) *that* are the most common tags. Eliminate
them whenever possible, and state your point using an active subject. Try replacing infinitives with gerunds.

WORDY   *There is* an excellent recipe for lamb stew that calls for oranges.

REVISED   One excellent recipe for lamb stew calls for oranges.

WORDY   *There was* a clear indication that the Everglades were dying in that
   the bird population was reduced by 90%.

REVISED   A 90% reduction in the bird population clearly indicated that the
   Everglades were dying.

WORDY   *It is* an impossible task to eliminate all crime from our streets.

REVISED   Eliminating all crime from our streets is an impossible task.

Here the gerund *eliminating* replaces the infinitive *to eliminate* and shortens the sentence.

INDIRECT   *One of the most significant effects of* the OPEC oil embargo of the 1970s is that it gave a much needed boost to alternative energy research.

REVISED   The OPEC oil embargo of the 1970s gave a much needed boost to alternative energy research.

Do not separate subjects, verbs, and complements needlessly   *33c*

Beware of sentences whose flow of ideas is interrupted by phrases or clauses set off by commas. Ideally, subjects and verbs, and verbs and complements should be placed as close to each other as possible. Keep to a minimum the phrases and subordinate clauses that separate the basic parts of the sentence.

                             SUBJECT   VERB
SEPARATED   Leo Tolstoy, with *simple but powerful imagery*, reveals the hidden

COMPLEMENT
motives underlying human choices.

With simple but powerful imagery separates the subject from the verb.

                             SUBJECT   VERB
SEPARATED   Leo Tolstoy reveals, *with simple but powerful imagery*, the hidden

COMPLEMENT
motives underlying human choices.

Now, *with simple but powerful imagery* separates the verb from the complement.

                                                              SUBJECT   VERB
REVISED   *With simple but powerful imagery*, Leo Tolstoy reveals the hidden

COMPLEMENT
motives underlying human choices.

                             SUBJECT   VERB   COMPLEMENT   SUBJECT
SEPARATED   The Concorde, *in three hours*, can cross the Atlantic, a journey that,

                             VERB   COMPLEMENT
for a normal jet, would have taken seven.

	SUBJECT	VERB	COMPLEMENT		SUBJECT

REVISED   The Concorde can cross the Atlantic *in three hours*, a journey that

	VERB	COMPLEMENT

would have taken seven *for a normal jet.*

Notice that moving the intervening phrase to the beginning or end of a clause allows the subject, verb and complement to follow each other closely. Notice too that such revisions eliminate an extra comma.

📖   Exercise

Correct any errors in wordiness and word order. Answers on p.209.

GROUP A

1. The Arthur Ashe Stadium, named for the famous black tennis player who played on and captained the U.S. Davis Cup team, is the site of the U.S.T.A.'s annual U.S. Open competition.
2. A car can last a lifetime if it is pampered.
3. A good weight resistance program is, in the quest to become physically fit, the first step that should be taken.
4. Marco Polo brought back to Italy on his return from China the concept of paper money.
5. The general population considers negative treatment of people based on their race or religion to be unfair.
6. Bradbury's novel illustrates how laziness of the mind causes a person's ability to think to deteriorate.
7. Balzac portrays in *The Human Comedy*, this typical behavior of humans.
8. Civil disobedience as a moral act by people whose rights have been infringed was a lesson taught by Gandhi.
9. There are dogs, who, when they have been abused, become, in their later lives, fear-aggressive.
10. Those who figure out they want to pursue astronomy as a career must be ready for intensive academic preparation.

GROUP B

1. In many marriages, it is because people don't respect each other's needs that they reject compromise.
2. It will be shown in this study why the Marshall Plan succeeded in Europe.
3. Sexual discrimination, although efforts are made to stop it, still causes problems in the workplace.
4. There is a very pretty road from here to Boston that avoids the turnpike entirely.

5. According to the article, there are scientists who work for tobacco companies and try to cover up the truth about what they find by producing conclusions determined ahead of time.
6. Stalin explained how when a million people whom you don't know die, it is not a tragedy. A tragedy is when someone who is a friend of yours dies.
7. A person might think that he has a talent that is of no use, but suddenly it could turn out to be of great value.
8. It is a statistical fact that most women in abusive relationships continue going along with them.
9. Many pointed teeth fill Darth Maul's mouth, and there is a crown of horns that encircles his head.
10. Politicians, in responding to their voting record, tend to overlook facts that are inconvenient.

34 Rewriting heavy language

What is heavy language, and how can it be remedied?

Heavy language is the dense, overly complicated style typical of scientific articles, legal contracts, and governmental reports. Heaviness can afflict anyone writing about abstract topics that have many parts.

When writers discuss complex ideas, they often try to imitate the heavy style to lend a sense of authority to their prose. In fact, the more complex the subject the shorter and clearer should be the language.

The symptoms of heavy language are clusters of abstract terms, unnecessarily long and complicated words instead of short simple ones, and the presence of too many ideas in the same sentence. The techniques below help simplify heavy language.

Eliminate the construction *the (noun) of...*   *34a*

Whenever possible, rewrite sentences containing the construction *the (abstract noun) of...*.

HEAVY With *the break-up and reorganization of* the former Yugoslavia has come a host of problems.

LIGHTER   Yugoslavia's break-up and reorganization has caused a host of problems.

HEAVY   *The analysis* of milk has shown that the *killing of* nutrients has been caused by the *pasteurization* of the milk at unnecessarily high temperatures.

LIGHTER   Analysis has shown that pasteurizing milk at unnecessarily high temperatures kills nutrients.

HEAVY   *The buying of* large chunks of Manhattan by Japan in the 1980s was one sign of the trade imbalance.

LIGHTER   Japan's ability to buy large chunks of Manhattan in the 1980s was one sign of the trade imbalance.

34b   Change nouns to verbals

Changing nouns to verbals helps eliminate the heavy construction *the (noun) of....* Verbs are easier to understand than nouns lengthened by cumbersome suffixes. Most abstract nouns, particularly those ending in *-ing*, *-ion*, and *-ment* can be rewritten as verbals. Below are some examples.

-ING		-ION	
activating	activate	validation	validate
requiring	require	generalization	generalize
deserving	deserve	implementation	implement
solving	solve	revitalization	revitalize

-MENT	
abandonment	abandon
encouragement	encourage
accomplishment	accomplish
self-improvement	improve oneself

In the rewrites below, notice that active subjects have been substituted for passive ones when possible.

HEAVY   The *requiring* of passports from foreign visitors by governments began in the Middle Ages.

LIGHTER   Governments first *required* foreign visitors to have passports during the Middle Ages.

HEAVY   The lack of funding for the atomic supercollider in Texas led to its *abandonment*.

LIGHTER The atomic supercollider in Texas was *abandoned* for lack of funds.

HEAVY The *restoration* of the theater was the result of the *revitalization* of the local arts council.

LIGHTER The revitalized local arts council *has restored* the theater.

Avoid words ending in *-istic* and *-ness*   *34c*

Some abstract nouns began life as simpler adjectives and should be transformed back into adjectives. Some abstract adjectives began life as nouns ending in *-ism* and can be rewritten as simpler adjectives. As a general rule, convert nouns that end in *-ness* into adjectives, and simplify all adjectives ending in *-istic* by removing the suffix.

-NESS		-ISTIC	
farsightedness	farsighted	individualistic	individual
imaginativeness	imaginative	rationalistic	rational
inexpensiveness	inexpensive	naturalistic	natural
powerfulness	powerful	animalistic	animal

HEAVY The *animalistic* impulses of professional wrestlers are heightened by the cheers of the crowd.

LIGHTER The cheers of the crowd heighten the *animal* impulses of professional wrestlers.

HEAVY It was the *inexpensiveness* of the Native American burial ground that attracted real estate developers.

LIGHTER Because the Native American burial grounds were *inexpensive,* they attracted real estate developers.

HEAVY Conservatives oppose what they consider to be liberals' *radicalistic* tendencies.

LIGHTER Conservatives oppose what they consider to be liberals' *radical* tendencies.

HEAVY Few writers have had the *imaginativeness* of Jules Verne.

LIGHTER Few writers have been as *imaginative* as Jules Verne.

34d   Re-order cause and effect

Sentences that give the effect of an action before explaining its cause tend to be complicated and awkward. They often contain the heavy construction *the (noun) of.*

There are two ways to handle complicated cause-and-effect sentences: (1) place the cause *before* the effect and rewrite, or (2) leave the effect before the cause but rewrite using a causal expression — *because, because of,* or *results from.*

HEAVY
> EFFECT
> Some art historians believe that the elongation of the subjects'
> CAUSE
> limbs in Modigliani's portraits is related to his possibly having
> had an astigmatism.

CAUSE/
EFFECT
> CAUSE
> Some art historians believe that a possible astigmatism was the
> EFFECT
> reason behind the elongated limbs of Modigliani's portrait subjects.

Some sentences can be lightened either by placing cause before effect or by using a causal expression.

HEAVY
> EFFECT   CAUSE
> The moth's attraction to flame is the result of its confusion of
> artificial light with moonlight.

CAUSE/
EFFECT
> CAUSE   EFFECT
> Confusing artificial light with moonlight, the moth is mistakenly
> attracted to flame.

CAUSAL
EXPRESSION
> The moth is attracted to the flame *because* it confuses artificial
> light with moonlight.

HEAVY
> EFFECT
> Emperor Constantine's ban on the extreme violence of Roman
> CAUSE
> gladiatorial combat had its roots in his Christianity.

CAUSE/
EFFECT
> CAUSE   EFFECT
> Emperor Constantine's belief in Christianity led him to ban
> Roman gladiatorial combat on the grounds of its extreme
> violence.

CAUSAL
EXPRESSION
> The Emperor Constantine banned Roman gladiatorial combat
> *because* its gratuitous violence conflicted with his Christian
> beliefs.

Eliminate or simplify connective phrases   *34e*

Connective phrases are often helpful in making transitions. Some, however, are awkward, unnecessary, or burdened with jargon. Beware of the frequently used connective phrases below. Find simpler expressions to replace them.

as a result	⇨	because
as to	⇨	regarding
bearing on	⇨	regarding
being that	⇨	because
given the fact that	⇨	because
in conjunction with	⇨	and
in connection with	⇨	about
in the eventuality that	⇨	if, in case
in view of the fact that	⇨	because
on the part of	⇨	by, from, -'s
seeing as	⇨	because
such that	⇨	so...that
to the extent that	⇨	so...that
with regard to	⇨	regarding, concerning
with respect to	⇨	regarding, concerning

HEAVY   The filming costs of modern movies are *such that* small art films are nearly impossible to produce.

SIMPLER   Modern filmmaking is so expensive *that* small art movies are nearly impossible to produce.

HEAVY   *Seeing as* I have never performed before a large audience, dancing the Nutcracker at Lincoln Center will be frightening *to the extent that* I may forget my part.

SIMPLER   *Because* I have never performed before a large audience, dancing the Nutcracker at Lincoln Center will be so frightening that I may forget my part.

HEAVY   *In the eventuality that* my plane crashes in the ocean, I always wear my life-preserver.

SIMPLER   *In case* my plane crashes in the ocean, I always wear my life-preserver.

34f   Divide some long sentences into shorter ones

Not all long sentences should be divided. Two types of sentences, however, are good candidates for division: (1) those that discuss a single issue with many factual details or examples, (2) those with two complex ideas that are related to each other as cause and effect, problem and reason.

To divide a sentence in two, separate the fact from its reasons, the *what* from the *why*. Often these two elements are separated already by connective phrases, commas, or subordinate clauses beginning with *which* or *that*. When rewriting as separate sentences, be sure to insert a *transition* linking the *what* to the *why*.

LONG   The enmity between Carthage and Rome that had begun in the third century B.C.E. after a series of brutal wars was finally put to rest in 1985 when, 2,131 years after the destruction of Carthage, the mayors of the two cities signed a peace treaty.

The *what* or main fact of the sentence is the signing of the peace treaty between two cities. The *why* or the reasons behind the treaty involve the history of their mutual hatred.

DIVIDED   In 1985, the mayors of Rome and Carthage signed a peace treaty. In so doing, they put to an end 2,131 years of enmity begun in the third century B.C.E. after a series of brutal wars that culminated in the destruction of Carthage.

Notice the transition *in so doing* that links the two sentences.

LONG   Although a modern novel, Ernest Hemingway's *The Old Man and the Sea* is similar to the Old English epic *Beowulf* in that both can be called "songs of the last survivor": that is to say, they share the theme of an old hero's vain struggle for fame, against death and oblivion.

The *what* or main idea of this sentence is the similarity of apparently different stories. The *why* (the reason behind the similarity) is their shared themes.

DIVIDED   Although a modern novel, Ernest Hemingway's *The Old Man and the Sea* is similar in many ways to the Old English epic *Beowulf*. Both, for example, can be called "songs of the last survivor" because they share the epic theme of an old hero's vain struggle for fame, against death and oblivion.

Notice the transition *for example* that links the two sentences.

📖   Exercise

Rewrite sentences with heavy language. Suggested revisions on
p.211. Other revisions may be equally valid.

GROUP A
1. Astronomy, in terms of the scientific careers, is one of the smallest
   available fields of employment.
2. The self-promoting journalistic perspective of the American media
   has led to the marginalization of the news itself, its replacement with a
   glorification of the act of news-gathering, and, by consequence, to a
   profound cynicism on the part of modern readers and viewers toward
   the media.
3. The modernistic conception of technological preparedness in
   graphic arts is based largely on computer-oriented imaginativeness.
4. The great Confederate disadvantage was the South's lack of
   advancement in the developmental age of technology.
5. For a typical population, an unbalanced sex-ratio is optimal in that
   it does not waste resources in producing a large number of
   reproductively underutilized males.
6. The radicalistic tendencies of demonstrators in the 1960s were a
   reaction to the governmental conservativeness of the 1950s.
7. Scholastic aptitude is in direct correlation with starting income in
   initial employment.
8. Dante's vision of Hell is of a highly systematic hierarchy with a
   tyrannical ruler at the top.
9. "Authentic" is similar to yet subtly different from "genuine" in that
   something that is "genuine" refers to the realness of artifacts whereas
   something that is "authentic" refers to the truthfulness of where they
   were derived.
10. Eighteenth century French aristocrats were set in their state of mind
    that the existence of the lower classes was solely for the purpose of
    fulfilling the needs of the upper classes.

GROUP B
1. With respect to the number of five-legged frogs in the reservoir, we at
   the Dubuque Toxic Chemical Plant feel certain that the local populace
   is safe as to levels of dioxin in the drinking water.
2. Composing twelve-tone music involves choosing a row of notes that are
   ordered in accordance with a strict pattern, which, once established,
   may be played forward or backward and repeated in infinite variety.
3. Unlike insurance companies that exist as separate entities from
   doctors, HMOs utilize a cohabitation with them.
4. They do not realize that revengefulness has the possibility of killing
   themselves in addition to others.

5. The condition known as the bends is a common affliction of divers wherein the increase of internal pressure bearing on the body is disproportionate to the external pressure.

6. During the siege of Orleans in 1429, the shortage of food was to the point at which people were eating rats.

7. The character belongs to a reptilian species and holds the appearance of something that came straight out of a nightmarish experience.

8. In this famous parable is a discussion of the unmistakable behaviors of human beings with extreme complexity hidden behind what appears to be a simple children's story about a grasshopper.

9. The international implementation of UN resolutions on global warming has been slowed by institutional corruption.

10. Scientific progress has had an enormous impact upon modern society to the extent that workers today have far more leisure time due to the efficiency of computers.

35 Assertions and illustrations

What is the difference between illustrating and asserting?

"Show don't tell" is a time-honored maxim of writers. Good writing presents information that leads readers toward a conclusion but allows them to make the final judgment for themselves. When readers feel they are being dictated to instead of persuaded, they will dismiss the writer's argument out of hand.

There are several kinds of assertions that tend to alienate readers. One is to discuss an author's *intention*. Another assertion is to state your conclusions in absolute terms — such as *prove* or *show without a doubt* — that take away the reader's right to make up her own mind.

35a Illustrate characters and events

Illustrate literary or historical characters or events with specific details instead of announcing your opinions.

ASSERTION   Charles Dickens's Young Jerry Cruncher was a bully.

ILLUSTRATION Charles Dickens's Young Jerry Cruncher used to beat up children who were smaller than he was.

Reader's conclusion: he sounds like a bully.

ASSERTION   General Montgomery was a poor strategist.

ILLUSTRATION   General Montgomery's battlefield tactics frequently resulted in heavy losses that could have been avoided by a more thorough consideration of the terrain.

Reader's conclusion: poor strategist.

ASSERTION   Some administrators are totally unreasonable and narrow-minded.

ILLUSTRATION   Some administrators do not explain their decisions and are unwilling to consider objectively their workers' viewpoints.

Reader's conclusion: what unreasonable and narrow-minded people.

Avoid attributing intent   *35b*

As readers and critics, we are not mindreaders: we cannot know what writers or speakers *intend*, only what they *say*. Always discuss what people *say*, not what you think they are *thinking*. Describe *effects*, not *intentions*. Be as objective as possible in your opinions. In the examples below, the *intentional* phrases are italicized.

INTENTIONAL   Chaucer's *intent* in depicting the corruption of the Pardoner is to level criticism against the excesses of the Catholic Church and clergy.

OBJECTIVE   Chaucer's corrupt Pardoner *can be read* as a criticism of the excesses of the Catholic Church and the clergy.

INTENTIONAL   In the *Republic*, Plato recounts the myth of Gyges *in order to* frighten his readers into behaving justly rather than to persuade them.

OBJECTIVE   Plato's myth of Gyges in the *Republic seems to* frighten readers into behaving justly rather than to persuade them.

35c   Avoid overstating opinions as absolutes

Few things are more annoying to a reader than to be told that an argument has been *proven*. Avoid terms that overstate your opinion as absolutes such as *prove, show indisputably, establish beyond a doubt* etc. Instead choose words such as those listed below that guide your reader to your conclusion, but allow for differences of opinion.

argues for	connotes	is evidence of	seems to
attests to	demonstrates	is evident from	signals
bespeaks	denotes	is influential in	signifies
betokens	hints at	is symptomatic of	suggests
can be inferred from	implies	makes manifest	symbolizes
can be interpreted as	indicates	points out/to	testifies to
can be read as	is emblematic of	proposes	

➤ This essay will ~~prove that~~.... *argue for*   OR   This argument ~~is a perfect example of~~.... *attests to*

➤ That C. S. Lewis and J. R. R. Tolkien were both popular writers and medieval scholars ~~shows~~ *suggests* that modern fantasy literature is the reincarnation of medieval romance.

➤ The failure of the Weimar Republic to deliver a stable German government after W.W.I ~~establishes beyond a doubt~~ *provides strong evidence for* the ~~fact~~ *notion* that democracy cannot be imposed from without.

📖   Exercise

Correct any errors in asserting instead of illustrating. Answers on p.213.

1. Some parents think that they are infallible.
2. In "The Road not Taken," Robert Frost's purpose is to teach the reader about the human tendency toward self-deception.
3. William Faulkner's *Absalom, Absalom* proves that he is the greatest writer since William Shakespeare.
4. Southerners seceded from the Union because they feared Lincoln would end slavery.
5. In her novels, Jane Austen wants to show the injustices suffered by women who had little money or status.
6. Darwin's Theory of Evolution establishes unquestionably that human beings evolved through natural selection.

7. Thorin, the dwarf king in *The Hobbit*, is totally greedy.
8. *The Merchant of Venice* is an anti-Semitic play.
9. In the modern marketplace, people change jobs often only because they are not happy.
10. Luke Skywalker is a true hero.

36 Forms of repetition

Why should repetition be avoided?

Deliberate repetition is a useful vehicle for creating such rhetorical effects as emphasis or irony. Unintentional repetition results in awkward, cumbersome sentences clogged with too many words. Elegance in writing begins with economy of language. The goal is to be streamlined and to the point without sacrificing meaning.

What kinds of repetition are there?

There are two kinds of repetition: *redundancy* and *tautology*. A redundancy is the needless repetition of words either as the same or different parts of speech. It is also the use of synonyms that don't enhance an idea's meaning.

Repetitions of an unstated idea rather than of a word are called *tautologies*. Common *tautologies* are expressions or phrases that repeat causes (*causal overkill*), comparisons (*comparative overkill*), additional information (*additive overkill*), potentiality (*conditional overkill*).

Redundancy within a sentence   *36a*

The same word can be expressed as different parts of speech such as sad (adjective), sadness (noun), sadly (adverb) etc. Using two or more of the forms of the same word to describe the same thing is redundant.

    ADJ.   ADV.
➤ *Nervous*, Reginald gripped the armrests of the dentist's chair *nervously*.

NOUN
➤The *joy* at the birth of her first child left Samantha exhausted but *overjoyed.*

Redundancy also occurs when the writer uses multiple synonyms to describe the same thing.

➤Ernest Hemingway was a *man's man, macho* in the best sense of the word.

Saying that Ernest Hemingway is *macho* in addition to being a *man's man* does nothing to improve his reputation for masculinity.

Redundancy of synonyms in elevated speech (also called *periphrasis* and *pleonasm*) may sound elegant but should also be avoided, except for comic effect.

➤*Lovesick,* he gazed at her *intently* with all the *ardor* and *vehemence* of a man lost to *amorous desire.*

It sounds pretty, but the fact remains that *lovesick, ardor, amorous* and *desire* all relate to being in love, while *intently* and *vehemence* both describe the strength of emotion.

36b   Redundancy over consecutive sentences

Do not begin a sentence with the same word or expression with which you ended the previous one. That is to say, the same word or words should never appear on both sides of a final punctuation mark. Instead, merge the two sentences and eliminate the redundancy.

REDUNDANT	Many murders were attributed to *Lucky Luciano. Lucky Luciano* was prominent in the Mafia in the 1930s.
CONCISE	A prominent Mafioso in the 1930s, Lucky Luciano reportedly murdered many people.
REDUNDANT	Over the years, Batman *has battled many foes.* The *foes* whom he *has battled* include the Joker, the Riddler, Catwoman, and the Scarecrow.
CONCISE	Over the years, Batman has battled many foes including the Joker, the Riddler, Catwoman, and the Scarecrow.

Words with built-in limits

Some words have limits built into their meaning. Of these the most common are absolute terms. These are *natural superlatives*, that is words that express the utmost (highest or lowest) degree such as *unique, fatal, astounded, crucial* etc. Using adverbs such as *very, extremely,* or *particularly* does not intensify them but rather gives the impression that the writer does not know what the words mean.

> ➤ California is ~~one of the only~~ *one of the few* states that ~~matches~~ *match* federal welfare money to reservations dollar for dollar.

> ➤ California is ~~one of the only states~~ *the only state* OR that matches federal welfare money to reservations dollar for dollar.

The only means *one*; use either the one or the other.

> ➤ This is a beautiful and *very unique* specimen of black orchid.

Unique means *one of a kind.* The orchid cannot be more *one of a kind* than it is.

> ➤ He was a *unique* person.

Using the word *unique* to describe a person's character is redundant. As individuals, people are inherently unique.

> ➤ I was *absolutely astounded* to discover that she was a vegetarian.

Being astounded is the maximum degree of *surprise* a person can experience. So while one can be very surprised, one can never be *absolutely astounded.* The same goes for other expressions with *absolutely* such as *fabulous, delicious, wonderful.*

> ➤ The bite of the Australian blue-ringed octopus can deliver an *extremely lethal* dose of venom.

Lethal means *causing death.* A person cannot become *extremely dead.*

Another group of words with built-in limits has meanings derived from Latin or from other foreign languages. Often we use such words redundantly because we do not know their literal meanings. Common examples of this group are *alternative, et cetera (etc.),* and *déjà vu.*

> ➤ The ~~other~~ *alternative* is to get your own apartment.

Alternative means the *other option* (of two) from the Latin *alter* meaning *other.* Use *alternative* alone and then only for choices between two things. For choices of three or more, use *option.*

➤ Don't forget to buy chicken, steak, barbecue sauce ~~and~~ *etc.* for the cookout.

Etc. (et cetera) is Latin meaning *and so forth.* Using *and* before *et cetera* is redundant.

➤ This *déjà vu* made me feel as if I had already been there.

Déjà vu is French meaning already seen. To say *déjà vu* is to imply that you have already been there. The expression "it's like déjà vu all over again" makes fun of the implied repetition.

36d   Causal overkill

Causal expressions indicate the reasons or causes of things. Common causal expression include the following:

because	the effect of	the result of
consequently	the reason is	thus
so	therefore	why

Never use more than one causal expression to describe the same subject. Beware especially the common *causal overkill — the reason is because....*

➤ The reason East German athletes dominated sports in the seventies is ~~because~~ *that* they used steroids.

A reason is an explanation of why something happens. The concept of *because* is already built into the structure of *the reason is....* Instead, say *the reason is... that.... The reason why* is equally tautological but through common usage has become more accepted than the *reason is because....*

➤ Thus, when Pope Gregory XIII corrected the calendar in 1580, it was ~~consequently~~ renamed the Gregorian calendar.

➤ The ~~resulting effect~~ *result or effect* of combining potassium with water is an explosion.

36e   Comparative overkill

Comparative expressions compare or contrast people, objects, or ideas. Comparisons of two items end in *-er — stronger, higher, faster, better* etc. — or are preceded by the word *more — more intelligent, more awake* etc. Superlatives compare three or more items. They end in *-est* or are preceded by the word *most.* Do not pair *more/most* with words ending in *-er* or *-est.*

➤ Alaska is cold but Siberia is even ~~more~~ colder.

➤ Mount Everest is the ~~most~~ highest peak in the world.

➤ Do you think Bill Cosby is ~~more~~ funnier than Robin Williams?

A more sophisticated kind of comparative overkill involves the comparative expressions *rather (than), more (than), instead of, but* etc. Each of these expressions by itself signals a comparison or provides an alternative. Using more than one in a sentence is redundant. Do not combine these comparative expressions with each other or with simple comparatives ending in *-er.*

➤ It makes *more* sense to see a doctor now ~~rather~~ than to wait until the problem becomes serious.

More and *rather* should not be combined. Eliminating either one of them solves the comparative overkill.

➤ It's *cheaper* to fly to the Caribbean in the summer ~~instead of flying~~ ^{than to fly} in the peak winter months.

The comparatives *cheaper* and *instead of* are redundant alternatives.

➤ I don't think I'll have wine with dinner ~~but~~ rather a cognac afterwards.

But rather is comparative overkill. Eliminate *but* and insert a comma before *rather.*

Additive overkill   *36f*

Additive expressions introduce further information into a sentence. Below are a few common additive expressions.

also	furthermore
another	in addition
besides	moreover
further	what's more

As a general rule, avoid combining additive expressions. More than one is rarely necessary.

➤ *In addition to* sculptures by Brancusi and Rodin, the Modern Art Museum has ~~another~~ ^{one} by Moore.

➤Next Thursday is my birthday. *What's more,* I ~~also~~ have tickets to the Bulls game.

36g   Conditional overkill

Conditional expressions indicate the possibility that something will happen. The following are some of the words or phrases that signal the conditional:

as long as	may	possibly
conceivably	might	potentially
could	perchance	probably
if	perhaps	should
likely	presumably	would

Combining conditional expressions is tautological and should be avoided.

One common form of conditional overkill is using two conditionals — *would, could, should, might* — in a sentence that contains an *if* construction. Change or eliminate the first conditional after the *if*.

      had known
➤*If* I ~~would have known~~ you were rich, I would have let you pay for dinner.

➤*If* you ~~could~~ push the car, I could start it.

Like *if*, other conditional expressions from the above list are tautological when used in combination.

➤~~Perhaps~~ I'll come if ~~maybe~~ I can find a date.

Perhaps, if, and *maybe* are all conditional expressions. *Perhaps* and *maybe* are conditional overkill and can be eliminated.

       is   *will be able to*
➤There ~~might be~~ a possibility that you ~~could~~ DJ on air next week.

Might, possibility, and *could* are all conditional expressions. Change *might* and *could* from conditional to positive to eliminate the overkill.

                                   don't
➤I should be able to help you as long as you ~~wouldn't~~ embarrass me.

As long as sets up a conditional relationship between helping and embarrassment. The extra conditional *wouldn't* is unnecessary.

📖 Exercise

Correct any errors in needless repetitions and overkill. Answers on p.214.

GROUP A

1. Over and over again, the news media continue to overly glorify movie stars.
2. I could have bought Van Gogh's "Sunflowers" if I would have had an extra forty million in the bank.
3. In the long run, for most people, price is, as usual, the determining factor in any transaction.
4. For an artist, documents for job placement include a portfolio. A portfolio is a group of artworks that illustrate his skills.
5. In *The Sound and the Fury*, Dilcey's most predominant trait is endurance.
6. A large school of fish can disperse quickly to confuse and baffle a hunting shark.
7. The results of the war were beneficial in many ways, but even still resentment on both sides persisted for many years.
8. Post-traumatic stress is a very damaging and devastating disorder.
9. A job as an anthropologist and also as a businesswoman is a goal that I wish to achieve successfully.
10. In salary, sergeants average about one-third more than the average patrol officer does.

GROUP B

1. She was immovably by his side throughout their entire ordeal, passionately committed to mutually sharing life's travails together.
2. Because the Confederate forces suffered from a divided command structure, they were, therefore, unable to assemble together rapidly.
3. The room seemed gloomy because all the window glass was practically opaque.
4. The danger Mata Hari faced was far more dangerous than she could have imagined.
5. The Iraqi leader was quite adamant about refusing to negotiate and claimed that the Americans were overly obsessive about destroying his biological weapons.
6. In the Civil War, 260,000 Confederate soldiers were killed. Half the soldiers were killed as a result of disease and sickness.
7. If you would act now, you will receive a free gift in the mail, all at no cost to you.
8. ATTACK! insect spray kills bugs dead.
9. In general, after the discussion continued on for a while, the committee by and large agreed on the whole.

10. The trouble is that while taking the necessary courses, people often forget to do market research. Market research lets people know about the availability of jobs in their profession.

GROUP C

1. "As I see it," said Napoleon, "that leaves us just three alternatives: fight, surrender, or blame it all on Josephine."
2. In *A Midsummer Night's Dream*, the reason that Lysander and Hermia plan to run off and elope is because they are deeply in love and care for each other as well.
3. If you would give me just five more minutes, I could finish the exam.
4. When Toni Morrison received the Nobel Prize for literature she was totally ecstatic.
5. It is better to excel at different activities from your best friend rather than to compete constantly against each other.
6. The only reason Sir Edmund Hillary had for climbing Mount Everest was because it was there.
7. According to General MacAllister, new innovations in technology have led to the development of missiles that are more lethal than ever.
8. When he referred back to page twenty-one, he saw that he was equally as mistaken as she was.
9. When you don't word-process essays, a bad disadvantage is that it's hard to add additional information.
10. Astronauts always say that walking in space is a very unique experience unlike anything else, one which leaves a person exhilarated and feeling on top of the world.

37   Contradictions in terms

What is a contradiction in terms?

A contradiction in terms is a statement composed of two or more words or expressions that clash in meaning. Poets and essayists may use contradictions in terms called *oxymorons* intentionally for effect as in Milton's description of hell, or Shakespeare's description of love.

> ➤No light, but rather darkness visible.
> *Paradise Lost*

> ➤O heavy lightness! serious vanity!
> Mis-shapen chaos of well-seeming forms!
> *The Tragedy of Romeo and Juliet*

In expository writing, contradictions in terms generally confuse an argument and detract from its seriousness. Be aware of two kinds of contradictions: *literal contradictions* between consecutive words in a phrase, and *implied contradictions* between two statements in an argument.

Literal contradictions

37a

Self-contradictory phrases mismatch a verb or noun with a descriptive word. The description ends up contradicting the word it is meant to complement.

> ►Adolescents are harmed by ~~not enough abundance~~ *a lack* of inspiring role models.

> *Abundance* means *the state of having enough. Not enough* contradicts *abundance* and must be replaced with a more suitable expression.

> ►Psychologists were intrigued by the ~~unusual~~ *unexpected* normality of the boy who had been raised by wolves.

> *Normality* is the opposite of being *unusual. Unexpected normality* better describes the psychologists' interest.

> ► The smog ~~floated~~ *hung* heavily over greater Los Angeles.

> In order to *float* something must be *light.* The image is an unintended oxymoron. Retain the poetic imagery but correct the contradiction by choosing a verb that suggests weight such as to *hang.*

> ► Antilock brakes ~~potentially stop~~ *help prevent* an accident from happening.

> *To stop* an accident is certain prevention while *potentially* denotes uncertainty. The two words are inherently contradictory.

Implied contradictions

37b

Arguments are built out of a chain of premises or assumptions that lead logically to a conclusion. An implied contradiction is a logical conflict between the premise and the conclusion.

CONTRADICTION So much happened the night we met that I do not remember all the details. Therefore, in recounting the   _PREMISE_

CONCLUSION
events, I will not include the parts I do not recall.

The conclusion implies that the speaker *could* include the parts he did not recall which is a logical impossibility.

REVISION So much happened the night we met that I do not remember all the details and *cannot* include them in my account.

CONTRADICTION
PREMISE   CONCLUSION
History inevitably repeats itself. Hitler should have heeded this rule when he disastrously invaded Russia late in the year, just as Napoleon had over a century earlier.

If history *inevitably* repeats itself, then the *repetition* is unavoidable, and Hitler could not have helped himself. If Hitler had heeded the rule then he would not have invaded Russia disastrously. But then history would *not* have repeated itself, contradicting the premise.

REVISION History *tends* to repeat itself. Hitler should have heeded this rule when he disastrously invaded Russia late in the year, just as Napoleon had over a century earlier.

CONTRADICTION One of Malevitch's most famous paintings is *White Square on a White Background.* In it the artist is pointing
CONCLUSION   PREMISE
out the clashes in modern society by depicting the absence of contrast between the two squares.

A *clash in society* is a kind of contrast. The *absence of contrast* can never depict a contrast.

REVISION One of Malevitch's most famous paintings is *White Square on a White Background.* In it, the artist points out the *invisible* clashes in modern society by depicting the absence of contrast between the two squares.

Exercise

Correct any contradictions in terms. Answers on p.217.

GROUP A

1. The course for prospective film directors teaches students to concentrate by focusing on many different aspects of production simultaneously.

2. Anyone can potentially experience crippling arthritis.
3. In *Fahrenheit 451*, people became unable to reason because they started to stop reading.
4. Chaos formed when the Union army retreated at Centerville.
5. Greed causes legal and moral standards to become non-existent.
6. They spent the afternoon relaxing in the meadow, surrounded by the silent hum of insects.
7. *A Midsummer Night's Dream* shows some of the only times that people act irrationally when they are in love.
8. A lower set of gears was added to get the car to go faster at lower speeds.
9. The Iraqi general reported the negative advance of his troops from Kuwait as soon as they encountered American forces.
10. Whether a person is looking for a condo or a beach house, he should know what he's looking for.

GROUP B
1. The transcontinental railroad made the expanding country smaller.
2. People said he was perfect because he had so few weaknesses.
3. Many people feel depressed by the lack of the presence of God in modern consciousness.
4. Although I cannot survive without air-conditioning in my bedroom, I refuse to pay extra for it when I can just open my window.
5. As always, bonuses are usually paid for outstanding performance only.
6. The two empires shared many similarities and differences.
7. The older and cheaper a car is, the more likely teenagers are to buy it. However, teenagers want to own cars, and any car will do.
8. The main reasons for the war were many, but there were only a few really major ones.
9. It's not that he is disorganized but that he takes on more than he can handle.
10. Many businesses have collapsed during their growth while others have flourished.

38   Gilding the lily

What does gilding the lily mean?

Shakespeare gave us the ironic image of a lily painted gold to enhance its beauty. Of course, a natural lily is more beautiful than an artificially decorated one. The gilded lily stands as a metaphoric warning to writers who overdescribe their objects adding irrelevant details or inflated language in an attempt to make a passage more beautiful.

Another way to gild the lily is to overpraise contemporary, historical, or literary characters; great works of art or literature; and past or present events. The resulting exaggeration is unrealistic. It succeeds only in devaluing the virtues of the subjects. Overpraise only if you want people to mock and dismiss the merits of your subject.

38a   Eliminate irrelevant adjectives

Adjectives should be used sparingly in expository writing because it is concerned only with *relevant* details. In the examples below, compare the passage to its subject. Irrelevant details are in italics.

SUBJECT	Comparing the size and age of ancient tombs.
IRRELEVANT DESCRPTION	Built in 1648 *by Shah Jahan, the Mogul Emperor of India for his dead wife Mumtaz Mahal*, the Taj Mahal, *with its magnificent white marble façade and surrounding buildings of damask rose sandstone*, is a smaller tomb than the earlier Great Pyramid of Cheops.
	The only details relevant to the subject are size and age. The rest is ornamental.
REVISION	Built in 1648, the Taj Mahal is a smaller tomb than the earlier Great Pyramid of Cheops.
SUBJECT	Humans are not the only creatures who grow their own food.
IRRELEVANT DESCRIPTION	Those who say that humans are the only creatures to cultivate their food are mistaken. One insect that does so is the *tiny, South American* leaf-cutter ant whose enormous colonies gather leaves, *often thirty times their own weight. Back in their above-ground mounds, which can tower up to six feet high*, they use their leaves to make a *rich, fertile* compost for growing edible fungus.
	In this passage, there is no need for adjectives describing *where* and *how large* with reference to ants.
REVISION	Those who say that humans are the only creatures to cultivate their food are mistaken. One insect that does so is the leaf-cutter ant whose colonies gather leaves which they use as a compost for growing edible fungi.

Eliminate unnecessary adverbs 38b

At best, adverbs should be used frugally in expository writing. Unnecessary adverbs are another kind of irrelevant description. Essays that overuse adverbs may end up sounding like an advertisement rather than serious commentary. The adverbs in the examples below are italicized.

UNNECESSARY ADVERBS
Milton's *deeply emotionally* complex and *psychologically* conflicted Satan is *very* often considered to be a *more* attractive literary character than his *humorlessly* judgmental and *coldly* impersonal God.

Of the sentence's many adverbs, only *more* adds necessary information. Compare the following streamlined version of the sentence.

REVISION
Milton's complex and conflicted Satan is often considered to be a more attractive literary character than his judgmental and impersonal God.

Avoid overpraising 38c

Certain people and events in our lives, some famous personalities, and certain works of art or literature have earned a reputation for greatness that cannot be improved upon. Praising them excessively only annoys your reader. Worse, praise can sometimes reduce an important achievement to a cliché. Don't confuse praise with description.

PRAISE
Hamlet, the greatest play of Shakespeare, the most brilliant playwright of all time, has been called a tragedy of inaction.

We can form our own opinions about Shakespeare and *Hamlet*; we certainly don't need to be told who *Hamlet's* author is.

DESCRIPTION
Hamlet has been called a tragedy of inaction.

PRAISE
When the martyred Martin Luther King, Jr., America's greatest humanitarian, spoke the immortal words "free at last," he reminded all Americans of the broken promises of our glorious Constitution.

Focusing on Martin Luther King, Jr.'s *reputation, how great* his words were, or *how important* the Constitution is detracts from what is really important: the *meaning* and *effect* of what King said.

DESCRIPTION

When Martin Luther King, Jr. spoke the words "free at last," he reminded all Americans of the broken promises of our Constitution.

PRAISE

It is impossible to overstate the role of pets in maintaining the health and longevity of senior citizens. Caring for these warm, gentle, loving, and undemanding creatures injects a new interest into the lives of their elderly owners and reassures them about their continued usefulness and competence. Pets are the greatest possible medicine for the elderly.

Pets do help improve the health and raise the spirits of senior citizens. But, calling them *the greatest possible medicine* is an exaggeration that casts doubt on their value in general.

DESCRIPTION

Caring for a pet injects interest into the lives of senior citizens and reassures them about their continued usefulness and competence. A loving pet helps maintain the health and longevity of its elderly owner.

Exercise

Eliminate irrelevant adjectives, unnecessary adverbs, and overpraising. Answers on p.219.

1. Only a few people so intimately touch our lives as doctors do. The hundreds of different types of doctors all practice an art of great purity and share a single goal — to benefit the patient.
2. Today, you, the graduating class of 2000, are the great hope of not only our nation but of the entire world. You stand on the threshold of a new century, straining eagerly to plunge fearlessly into a universe where your limitless talents and boundless energy are sure to overcome all obstacles.
3. More than any other event, the Norman Conquest changed forever and definitively the structure and vocabulary of the English language.
4. Brilliant, brave, wily, and resourceful, Odysseus is the most famous, world-renowned hero of all time.
5. The saintly and devoted image of mother is celebrated on the glorious holiday of Mother's Day which reminds us all how these loving parents have made countless precious sacrifices for us.
6. Without the guidance of Washington, Jefferson, and Madison, the wonderful leaders whom we have the honor of calling our forefathers,

we Americans would not today be enjoying the rights and privileges unique in the modern world.

7. Being a teacher is more than just a job. It is the enactment of a daily drama of altruism and of dedication to the service of mankind.

8. A gleaming model of patriotic self-sacrifice, Nathan Hale is America's first and greatest hero who will live forever in our hearts and minds.

9. I realized that once we examine the corruption of the world in which we live, we begin to see the seraphic beauty, and the pristine purity from which it was spawned.

10. Socrates is not only the source of all Western philosophy but also its greatest practitioner. Without Socrates, there would be no Western philosophy.

39 Mixed metaphors

What are mixed metaphors?

Like other figurative expressions, metaphors enliven writing with vivid images. To be effective, however, these images must complement each other. Awkwardly matched images are called mixed metaphors. Their effect is always comic. If they are unintentional, they usually undermine the seriousness of an argument. However, mixed metaphors can be used deliberately to highlight an image.

Mixed metaphors that confuse meaning   *39a*

Often mixed metaphors are the result of combining clichés, sayings, or colloquial expressions in formal speech. To revise mixed metaphors, translate them into everyday English. Consider the combination of clichés below.

MIXED	CLICHE When the Mayor got ⌐caught with his hand in the cookie
	CLICHE jar,⌐the ⌐shoe was suddenly on the other foot.⌐
	The metaphor mixes the images of *hands* and *feet*.
TRANSLATION	When the Mayor was caught embezzling funds, he found himself suddenly on the other side of the law.

	CLICHE CLICHE
MIXED	Nobody gets a ⌐hole-in-one⌐his ⌐first time at bat.⌐

	The metaphor mixes golf with baseball.
TRANSLATION	Nobody succeeds at his first attempt.

Mixed metaphors with only one common expression, or with a common expression that has been misused are more difficult to spot and more difficult to repair.

MIXED	English is the *lingua franca* of the world.
	Lingua franca is an idiom meaning the *common language*. It comes from the Latin meaning *French language*. English cannot be the French language of the world. Retain the idiom by correcting the connotation.
REVISION	English is the *new lingua franca* of the world.
MIXED	The memory was filed away on the shelves of my brain.
	Here, the image simply doesn't work visually or idiomatically. Brains do not have shelves. The writer was looking for a half-remembered idiom and settled for this approximation.
REVISION	The memory was filed away in *the recesses of my mind.*

39b   Intentional mixed metaphors for effect

Mixed metaphors can occasionally enhance meaning. Use them to highlight only situations that are inherently contradictory or ironic.

IRONY	To get anything accomplished in Washington, you're expected to tiptoe around on your knees.
	Here the author is highlighting the fact that in Washington politics people must be careful — *tiptoe around* — as well as subservient — *on your knees*. Together, the images ironize political behavior.
IRONY	In Aesop's famous race, the Tortoise outfoxes the Hare.
	The inherent irony of a slow tortoise's victory over a quick hare is enhanced by the word *outfox*. *Outfox* means to be more clever, but also suggests that the tortoise is behaving like a fox which habitually hunts hares, an appropriately mixed metaphor.

Exercise

Translate the mixed metaphors. See answers on p.220.

1. I knew how it felt to be in her shoes, straining to win the swim meet.
2. The rabbi and his wife were as poor as church mice.
3. The mountain climbers in the competition said all they wanted was a level playing field.
4. There were so many accidents among the students, that the ambulance began doing bus runs to the school.
5. It's a dog-eat-dog rat race.
6. In a tournament, it's unfair for a disabled competitor to use a golf cart as a crutch.
7. Shakespeare stood with one foot in the Middle Ages while with the other he saluted the rising sun of the Renaissance.
8. My boss is an anatomical wonder. He manages to survive with no guts, no spine, and no heart.
9. As a great soccer player, Mia Hamm always had the upper hand in well-placed kicks.
10. When General Sherman's arm had to be amputated, Lee was very grieved. He had always thought of Sherman as his right hand.

26–39 Answers to exercises

26 Parallel construction

GROUP A

1. *Use all nouns.*
   Revision: Some students choose their friends based on characteristics such as race, *style of dress*, and religion.
2. *Use all infinitives. The* to *from* to lift *is implicit in the succeeding verbs* dig *and* throw.
   Revision: Physical strength is useful when trying to lift a rock, *dig* a ditch, or *throw* a shotput.
3. *Repeat prepositions (in) and coordinating conjunctions (not only…but also).*
   Revision: The danger of tornadoes lies not only in their power *but also in* their speed.
4. *Repeat nouns and infinitives.*
   Revision: The person in charge has the ability to order everyone else around as well as *the opportunity to enjoy* a lavish lifestyle.

5. *Parallel verb tenses.* Stay in the simple tense. Don't stray into the progressive tense (*are needing*).
   Revision: Modern children acquire material possessions too easily, do not value what they have, and *need* more attention from their parents.
6. *Parallel* the sight of *with* the discovery of. Otherwise it sounds as if the mass gravesites are burning.
   Revision: The sight of burning villages and *the discovery of* mass gravesites in Kossovo remind Europeans of Nazi atrocities.
7. *Repeat adverbs.*
   Revision: Darth Vadar is responsible for maintaining imperial control both politically and *militarily* throughout the galaxy.
8. *Repeat prepositions.*
   Revision: Parents should provide children with what they need, not *with* everything they want.
9. *Repeat adjectives.*
   Revision: Many people object when TV presents sex as a casual and *necessary* experience.
10. *Repeat nouns.*
    Revision: Radio astronomers use massive satellites to pinpoint the nature and *source* of signals in space.

GROUP B

1. *Repeat verbs.*
   Revision: As long as people have egos, spread rumors, and *perform* for bystanders, schoolyard fights will continue to occur.
2. *Non-parallel numbering (first, secondly)* and *structures (education/a responsible adult teaches him).*
   Revision: The aspiring driver has two options: first driver's education, *second lessons* by a responsible adult.
3. *Repeat adjectives* to improve style, even though the verbs are parallel.
   Revision: I soon discovered that the inmates were not only ignorant but ill- mannered.
4. *Repeat prepositions in either construction.*
   Revision: The botanist lectured about his trip to the Congo and *to* Peru.

   OR

   The botanist lectured about going to the Congo and *to* Peru.
5. *Repeat placement of infinitives.*
   Revision: As a tour guide, you must come prepared to discuss the history of the monument and *to distribute* brochure.
6. *Parallel corellative construction (both...and). Repeat nouns (natural selection* and *room).*
   Revision: Species are becoming extinct because of natural selection and *because of lack* room for both animals and people.
7. *Non-parallel numbering (initially, secondly)* and *verb tenses (handle, dealt).*

Revision: Two key patterns in the lives of leaders are initially how they handle rejection and *eventually* how they *deal* with success.

8. *Repeat infinitives* to avoid misperception.
Revision: Taxi drivers tend to drive too fast and *to run* the car into the ground.

9. *Repeat nouns* to avoid non-parallel construction (*improvement/that our attendance was irregular*).
Revision: The conductor noticed improvement in our performance but *irregularity* in our attendance.

10. *Non-parallel numbering* (*first, then, finally*) and *verb tenses* (*studies, draws up, gave*).
Revision: At first he studies the report, then draws up the graphs, and finally *gives* the presentation to the board of directors.

 ## 27 Correct and complete comparisons

1. *Person-to-object comparison — men* to *weight.*
Revision: Women are more concerned about their weight than men *are.*

OR

Women are more concerned about their weight than *they are about men.*

2. *Person-to-object comparison — person* to *obstacles —* caused by missing verb.
Revision: Stronger people have the ability to overcome many more obstacles than a weak person *has.*

3. *Missing comparative.*
Revision: Their technology is above *that of* other civilizations.

4. *Person-to-object comparison — someone* to *traumas. Missing comparative.*
Revision: Even though these traumas occur on a smaller scale, they are just as serious as *those* resulting from combat.

5. *Ambiguous comparison* incomplete because of a missing verb.
Revision: Cats devour rats as successfully as coyotes *do.*

6. *Comparison with place — humidity* is compared to *Brazil.*
Revision: The humidity in South Carolina is like *Brazil's.*

7. *Possessive comparison.*
Revision: In the story, Thomas did not consider his own crimes as horrible as the other *people's crimes.*

8. *Possessive comparison*
Revision: Compare this year's income with last *year's.*

9. *Person-to-object comparison.* Here the "person" is *cats* being compared to *room.* Complete by adding a verb.
Revision: Being larger, dogs need more room than cats *do.*

10. *Missing and ambiguous comparison.* If she is better than *anyone,* then she is better than herself. Add *else.*
    Revision: She is a better calculus student than anyone *else* in our class.

28 Incomplete and self-evident thoughts

1. *Vague.* What does Tolstoy mean by *happy?* What constitutes happiness in family life? Why are all happy families necessarily alike — is there only one generic kind of happiness?

2. *Self-evident and half-said idea.* Obviously it is a disadvantage to have your soldiers die. But why is it a larger disadvantage if they die of disease than in battle.

3. *Unexplained generalization.* What specifically is entailed in *doing his job?* What *kind* of basketball are you *capable of playing?*

4. *Vague.* "Outside" or "inside" of what/whom? What does *philosophy* have to do with location?

5. *Unexplained generalization.* Is love necessarily the primary reason for living? Without love we should kill ourselves? Without whose love? Is there no other gratification in life — intellectual, artistic, athletic?

6. *Self-evident and partially expressed idea.* Obviously dependence makes one part of the nation weaker than the other. Such a statement does not need to be said. It could, however, lead to meaningful observation if it were linked to the larger concept of *interdependence.*

7. *Vague generalization. Undeveloped idea.* What specific events are going on? Can these events be interpreted optimistically? What does *going downhill* mean? Are there objective measures for this trend, or is it merely vague intuition? Why don't you vote? Who in Washington is so unhelpful? What do you want them to do? Are there good reasons for not carrying out your wishes? Are your demands realistic in view of national or international constraints? Do your wishes conflict with those of others who are helped by the laws? Wouldn't voting help elect officials sympathetic to your opinions?

8. *Self-evident.* Where else would the baby have a smile?

9. *Unexamined and meaningless generalization.* Why isn't what other people think about us important? What does it mean to think about ourselves? Could the opinions of others be more objective than our own? List some reasons why our own assessment of ourselves is more valid or more important than that of other people?

10. *Self-evident.* Obviously, brothers are brothers. But what does *always be my brother* really mean? Is the speaker implying loyalty, affection, shared experience, heritage?

✑ 29 Fragments

1. *Lacks complete thought.* Eliminate the period, and connect the two statements with a comma between *cry on* and *I could.*
   Revision: Whenever I felt the need for a friendly pat on the back or a shoulder to cry on, I could drop by Mrs. Cleaver's house conveniently across the street.
2. *No revision. Fragment for effect* mimics speech.
3. *Lacks a verb.* Replace *with* by a verb (*had*) to create a new sentence.
   Revision: At the fund-raiser were many interesting people with whom I could discuss the current political situation. In particular, Shirley Temple Black and Meryl Streep *had* fascinating insights into the film industry.
4. *Lacks complete thought.* Connect the two statements by an em-dash instead of the period, or rewrite them as a single sentence.
   Revision: This hope is what keeps gang members loyal to their group — that the power of the gang will keep other neighborhood criminals at bay.

   OR

   What keeps gang members loyal to their group is the hope that the power of the gang will keep other neighborhood criminals at bay.
5. *Lacks a subject.* Rewrite the two statements as a single sentence. Include a *not only...but also* conjunction to emphasize the contrast between the two ideas and parallel *an action* with *a way.* Or, add a subject (*it*) and treat as two separate sentences.
   Revision: Discrimination is *not only* an action based on prejudice *but also a way* of making fine distinctions.

   OR

   Discrimination is an action based on prejudice. However, *it* also means making fine distinctions.
6. *Lacks both subject and verb.* Merge the two statements by eliminating the period between *evening* and *with.*
   Revision: I remember that I spent a delightful evening with my new friends from across the lake.
7. *No revision. Fragment for effect* creates emphasis. The verb is understood.
8. *Lacks a verb.* Add a verb and complete the sentence, or merge the two statements.
   Revision: I look forward to trading baseball cards with people who have rare collections. Fans with a lot of baseball memorabilia *are* likely to have cards that I am missing.

   OR

   I look forward to trading baseball cards with people who have rare collections, fans with a lot of baseball memorabilia.
9. *No revision. Fragment for effect.* The subject (*I*) is understood.

10. *Lacks both subject and verb.* Merge the two statements by eliminating the period between *computers* and *as.*
    Revision: Many beginners are averse to learning how to use computers as a result of techno-shock.

 30 Transitions

1. On the frontier before schools were built, settlers relied on Bible reading to educate their children. *Soon however,* communities began to erect formal schools, usually one-room cabins that served children of all ages.
2. In the 1860s, improvements in transportation were the key to the development of American business. *Equally important were innovations in communication.* More rapid and efficient communication facilitated the flow of information between buyers and sellers throughout the new nation. *In particular,* the newly invented telegraph connected the East and West Coasts through the merger of Western Union and the American Telegraph Company.
3. Grant's administration was plagued by scandal. *For example,* Union Pacific Railroad officials created a non-existent construction company, and defrauded the public by selling shares of stock in this corporation. *In addition,* William Belknap, Grant's Secretary of War, enriched himself by conspiring with white traders to cheat Native Americans on reservations.
4. The Mugwumps were reform-minded Republicans from all walks of life *including* non-professionals, *such as* lawyers, newspaper editors and cartoonists *like* Thomas Nast *in particular. Nevertheless* the average American voter was not greatly swayed by the Mugwumps. *Consequently* politicians paid little attention to them. *Still* the Mugwumps were at least partially successful in reforming American politics.

 31 Passive construction

1. *Insert the missing* driver.
   Revision: The vehicle skidded off the road when the *driver lost* control over it.
2. *Make* Craig Claiborne *the active subject.*
   Revision: Craig Claiborne ruined the cake when he forgot the sugar.
3. *Make* Napoleon *active, or make both* Napoleon *and* Clausewitz *active.*
   Revision: The strategies *Napoleon used* for flank attacks were later recommended by Clausewitz.

OR

Clausewitz recommended flank attack strategies that *Napoleon had used* earlier.

4. *Make* Einstein *active.*
   Revision: Space, as *Albert Einstein has argued* convincingly, exists as a coefficient of time.

5. *Make the* courts *active.*
   Revision: A *criminal court found* O. J. Simpson not guilty, but a *civil court found* him legally liable.

6. *No revision for general, objective statement.*

7. *Insert some* recruiters.
   Revision: The *NBA recruiters* considered him too short.

8. *Insert the missing evaluators.*
   Revision: They judged her job performance to be substandard.

9. *Make the recipient active,* although we still don't know from whom she received those passes.
   Revision: She received free movie passes for Thursday night.

10. *Make both the* Indians *and the* explorers *active.*
    Revision: South American Indians had used rubber long before *Spanish and Portuguese explorers landed.*

 ## 32 Sentence length, order and type

The revision below is one of a number of possibilities.
Once upon a time, a stray dog came upon a barn full of hay. Its owner, a kindhearted old farmer, allowed the dog to live there amicably with the ox. Hunting in the woods and drinking from the fresh stream in the meadow, the dog grew fat. He forgot hunger.

After the farmer died, the dog's greed struggled against his recollection of the farmer's generosity. Greed won. He denied the ox the hay. Guarding the hay day and night, the dog neither slept nor fed until he became too weak to hunt. He starved to death atop a mountain of hay.

 ## 33 Wordiness and word order

GROUP A

1. *Place subject and verb next to each other.* Move the clause *named for the famous, black tennis player who played on and captained the U.S. Davis Cup team. Shorten clause.* Replace *who played on and captained.*
   Revision: Named for the famous, black tennis player and captain of the U.S. Davis Cup team, the Arthur Ashe Stadium is the site of the U.S.T.A.'s annual U.S. Open competition.

2. *Shorten clause to single adjective.* Change *if it is pampered* to *pampered.*
   Revision: A *pampered* car can last a lifetime.

3. *Place verb and complement close to each other.* Eliminate *in the quest.* *Convert infinitive* to become *to the gerund* in becoming. *Delete excess words.*
   Revision: *In becoming physically fit,* the first step is a good weight resistance program.

4. *Place verb and complement close to each other.* Move *on his return from China.*
   Revision: *On his return from China,* Marco Polo brought back to Italy the concept of paper money.

5. *Shorten clauses and phrases.* Replace *negative treatment of people based on their race or religion,* and *the general population.*
   Revision: The public considers *racial or religious discrimination* to be unfair.

6. *Shorten clauses and phrases.* Replace *laziness of the mind,* and *ability to think.*
   Revision: Bradbury's novel illustrates how *intellectual laziness* causes one's *reasoning ability* to deteriorate.

7. *Place verb and complement close to each other.* Move the title. *Shorten phrase.* Replace *of humans.*
   Revision: In *The Human Comedy,* Balzac portrays this typical *human* behavior.

8. *Eliminate excess words. Place subject and verb close to each other* by removing the intervening clause. Make Gandhi active.
   Revision: *Gandhi taught that civil disobedience was a moral act* by people whose rights have been infringed.

9. *Eliminate indirect construction* there are. *Shorten clauses and phrases.* Replace *who when they have been abused. Place verb and complement close to each other.* Move *in their later lives.*
   Revision: In *their later lives, abused* dogs become, fear-aggressive.

10. *Reduce wordiness.* Convert *figure out they want to pursue* to *choose.*
    Revision: Those who *choose* astronomy as a career must be ready for intensive academic preparation.

GROUP B

1. *Eliminate indirect construction* it is.
   Revision: In many marriages, *people reject compromise* because they don't respect each other's needs.

2. *Eliminate indirect construction* it will be. This also eliminates the passive construction.
   Revision: *This study will show* why the Marshall Plan succeeded in Europe.

3. *Place subject and verb next to each other.* Move the clause *although efforts are made to stop it.*
   Revision: *Although efforts are made to stop it,* sexual discrimination, still causes problems in the workplace.

4. *Eliminate indirect construction* there is.
   Revision: A very pretty *road* from here to Boston *avoids* the turnpike entirely.
5. *Eliminate indirect construction* there are. *Shorten clauses and phrases.* Replace *who work for tobacco companies, to cover up the truth, about what they find, determined ahead of time.* Use a gerund (*findings*).
   Revision: According to the article, *tobacco company* scientists try to *hide their findings* by producing *predetermined* conclusions.
6. *Shorten clauses and phrases.* Replace *how when a million people whom you don't know,* and *who is a friend of yours. Eliminate indirect construction* it is.
   Revision: Stalin explained that a *tragedy is the death of a single friend, not of a million strangers.*
7. *Shorten clauses and phrases.* Replace *that is of no use, could turn out to be,* and *of great value.*
   Revision: A person might *consider* his talent *useless,* until *suddenly* it *proves very valuable.*
8. *Eliminate indirect construction* it is. *Shorten phrases.* Replace *in abusive relationships,* and *going along with them.*
   Revision: Statistically, most *abused* women continue these relationships.
9. *Eliminate indirect construction* there is.
   Revision: Many pointed teeth fill Darth Maul's mouth, and a *crown of horns encircles* his head.
10. *Place subject and verb next to each other.* Move the phrase *in responding to their voting record.*
    Revision: In responding to their voting record, politicians tend to overlook inconvenient facts.

34 Rewriting heavy language

GROUP A

1. *Eliminate connective phrase* in terms of. *Eliminate* one of the. *Reduce* scientific.
   Revision: Astronomy offers the fewest career opportunities among the sciences.
2. *Divide into shorter sentences. Change nouns to verbals. Eliminate* -istic. *Reduce the number of* the noun of *constructions. Place cause before result.*
   Revision: Journalists in the American media tend to promote themselves. They reduce the importance of the news while glorifying news-gathering. As a result, modern readers and viewers have become profoundly cynical about the media.
3. *Eliminate* -istic, -ness. *Eliminate abstract cluster* (*computer-oriented*). *Change nouns to verbals.*

Revision: Modern graphic arts courses prepare students to use computer technology imaginatively.

4. *Re-order cause-and-effect using* because. *Eliminate the lack of construction. Eliminate unnecessary and heavy adjectives and word clusters (developmental age of technology).*
   Revision: Because it lagged in technology, the South suffered a great disadvantage.

5. *Divide into shorter sentences. Eliminate heavy word clusters and expressions (unbalanced sex-ratio, reproductively underutilized). Note cause-effect sequence in the second sentence of the revision.*
   Revision: Ideally, a typical population should have fewer men than women. Such a ratio maintains the society's capacity to reproduce but does not waste its resources.

6. *Eliminate the tendencies of. Eliminate* -istic, -ness.
   Revision: Radical demonstrators in the 1960s were reacting to the conservative government of the 1950s.

7. *Eliminate heavy word clusters (in direct correlation with, initial employment).*
   Revision: Achievement in school directly affects one's first salary.

8. *Eliminate heavy word clusters (systematic hierarchy, tyrannical ruler). Eliminate* vision of. Replace it by a verb *(views)*
   Revision: Dante views Hell as a hierarchy ruled by a tyrant.

9. *Divide into shorter sentences. Eliminate connective phrases (in that). Eliminate -ness (realness, truthfulness). Simplify word clusters (truthfulness of, where they were derived).*
   Revision: "Authentic" is similar to yet subtly different from "genuine." While "genuine" refers to the existence of artifacts, "authentic" refers to their origins.

10. *Eliminate* their state of, the existence of, the purpose of, the needs of. *Convert noun to verb. Replace* state of mind *with* believed.
    Revision: Eighteenth century French aristocrats firmly believed that the lower classes existed solely to serve them.

GROUP B

1. *Eliminate connective phrases (with respect to, as to). Replace the* number of *with* many. *Replace word cluster the* local populace *with* our.
   Revision: We at the Dubuque Toxic Chemical Plant feel certain that the levels of dioxin in our drinking water are safe despite the many five-legged frogs in our reservoir.

2. *Divide into shorter sentences. Eliminate connective phrases (in accordance with). Replace heavy cluster (involves choosing).*
   Revision: A twelve-tone composition uses a row of notes ordered in a strict pattern. Once established, this pattern may be played forward or backward and repeated in infinite variety.

3. *Replace heavy cluster (utilize a cohabitation with, exist as separate entities).*
Revision: Insurance companies are wholly separate from doctors, while HMOs incorporate them into their organizations.

4. *Eliminate -ness (revengefulness). Eliminate the possibility of. Notice the cause/effect sequence.*
Revision: They do not realize that revenge may kill both themselves and others.

5. *Place cause (pressure) before effect (bends). Eliminate connective phrase (known as).*
Revision: When the pressure inside a diver is greater than the pressure outside, it causes the bends.

6. *Eliminate connective phrase (to the point at which). Replace with so severe.*
Revision: During the siege of Orleans in 1429, the shortage of food was so severe that people ate rats.

7. *Eliminate heavy word cluster (belongs to a reptilian species, holds the appearance of, nightmarish experience). Eliminate the appearance of.*
Revision: The character is a type of reptile and looks like something out of a nightmare.

8. *Eliminate a discussion of, the behaviors of. Eliminate heavy word clusters (unmistakable behaviors, extreme complexity).*
Revision: This simple children's story of a grasshopper is a parable about complex human behavior.

9. *Change nouns to verbals. Implementation becomes to implement/implementing; corruption becomes to corrupt/corrupting. Convert adjectives ending with, or containing -tion, -istic, or -ic International becomes worldwide). Re-order cause (corrupt companies) and effect (implementing the resolution).*
Revision: Corrupt companies have slowed the effort to implement worldwide the UN's resolutions on global warming.

10. *Divide into shorter sentences. Re-order cause (computers) and effect (more leisure). Eliminate the efficiency of. Eliminate connective (to the extent that).*
Revision: Scientific progress has had an enormous impact upon modern society. Efficient computers, for example, provide added leisure time for today's workers.

 35 Assertions and illustrations

1. *Illustrate instead of judging.* What makes us believe that this is what they think?
Revision: Some parents *do not examine their decisions* and *are unwilling to admit that they are mistaken.*

2. *Don't attribute intent.* We don't know the poet's purpose. We do know what the poem does.
   Revision: In "The Road not Taken," Robert Frost *comments on* the human tendency toward self-deception.
3. *Don't overstate.* Sure, he's great writer. Anything else is opinion, not fact.
   Revision: Absalom, Absalom places William Faulkner firmly *in the ranks of major writers* in the English language.
4. *Don't overstate.* That's only one of many reasons.
   Revision: The South's fear that Lincoln would end slavery was *one of the reasons* for secession.
5. *Don't attribute intent and don't overstate.*
   Revision: Jane Austen's novels indicate a concern about injustices suffered by women who had little money or status.
6. *Don't overstate.* Theories *propose* – they do not *establish unquestionably.*
   Revision: Darwin's Theory of Evolution *proposes* that human beings evolved through natural selection.
7. *Illustrate characters.* Show don't tell.
   Revision: Thorin, the dwarf king in *The Hobbit,* is willing to sacrifice the lives of his people to avoid sharing his treasure with his neighbors.
8. *Illustrate characters and don't overstate.*
   Revision: The Merchant of Venice treats Shylock, the Jew, more generously than other contemporary plays do; nonetheless, it presents him as greedy, vengeful, and ungenerous by nature.
9. *Don't overstate. Happiness* is too broad a term for a meaningful judgment. Does it mean that they don't like their boss or their co-workers? Do they want to earn more money? Are they looking for prestige? Are they bored? Do they feel unappreciated? And why *only*?
   Revision: In the modern marketplace, people change jobs to achieve greater satisfaction in one way or another.
10. *Illustrate characters.* Show don't tell. Define heroism.
    Revision: A gifted and charismatic figure, Luke Skywalker is willing to face unimaginable horror and to sacrifice himself in order to restore freedom to his world.

 36 Forms of repetition

GROUP A

1. *Redundancy.* Multiple synonyms describe the same thing (*over and over again = continue*). Eliminate one of them. *Words with built-in limits (glorify).*
   Revision: Over and over again, the news media glorify movie stars.
2. *Conditional overkill.* Eliminate *would have* from *if clause.*
   Revision: I could have bought Van Gogh's "Sunflowers" if I had had an extra forty million in the bank.

3. *Redundancy.* Multiple synonyms describe the same thing. *In the long run = for most people = as usual = any.* Eliminate all but one.
Revision: For most people, price is the determining factor in a transaction.

4. *Redundancy over consecutive sentences.* Eliminate one *portfolio.*
Revision: For an artist, documents for job placement include a portfolio *which* is a group of artworks that illustrate his skills.

5. *Words with built-in limits (predominant).* Eliminate *most.*
Revision: In *The Sound and the Fury,* Dilcey's predominant trait is endurance.

6. *Redundancy.* Multiple synonyms describe the same thing. *Confuse = baffle.* Eliminate one of them.
Revision: A large school of fish can disperse quickly to baffle a hunting shark.

7. *Additive overkill (even/still). Persisted* and *for many years* seem redundant but are not.
Revision: The results of the war were beneficial in many ways: still resentment on both sides persisted for many years.

8. *Comparative overkill (most/worst). Redundancy.* Multiple synonyms describe the same thing. *Very damaging = devastating.* Eliminate one of them.
Revision: The worst of all types of stress, post-traumatic stress is a devastating disorder.

9. *Additive overkill (and/also).* Eliminate *also. Redundancy.* Multiple synonyms describe the same thing. *Achieve = successfully.* Eliminate *successfully.*
Revision: My goal is a job as both an anthropologist and a business-woman.

10. *Redundancy using the same word as different parts of speech. Average* is used as a verb and as an adjective. Replace *average* with *typical.*
Revision: In salary, sergeants average about one-third more than the *typical* patrol officer does.

GROUP B

1. *Redundancy of synonyms in elevated speech. Loyally = passionately committed, ordeal = travails, by his side = mutually = sharing = together.* Eliminate most of them. *Redundancy using multiple synonyms. Throughout = entire.* Pick one. *Words with built-in limits. Committed* includes the notion of *passionately.*
Revision: Loyally by his side throughout their ordeal, she was committed to sharing his hardships.

2. *Causal overkill (because/therefore). Redundancy of synonyms (assemble = together).*
Revision: Because the Confederate forces suffered from a divided command structure, they were unable to assemble rapidly.

3. *Words with built-in limits. Opaque* means no light can get through; there's no *practically* about it. Try *darkly tinted.*
   Revision: The room seemed gloomy because all the windowglass was *darkly tinted.*
4. *Redundancy using the same word as different parts of speech (danger* and *dangerous).* Replace with *serious.*
   Revision: The danger Mata Hari faced was far more *serious* than she could have imagined.
5. *Words with built-in limits. Adamant, obsessive.* Neither can be modified.
   Revision: The Iraqi leader was adamant about refusing to negotiate and claimed that the Americans were obsessive about destroying his biological weapons.
6. *Redundancy over consecutive sentences (soldiers were killed).*
   Redundancy of synonyms. Disease = sickness.
   Revision: Of the 260,000 Confederate soldiers who perished in the war, half died of disease.
7. *Conditional overkill.* Eliminate *would* from *if clause. Redundancy of synonyms Free = gift = at no cost.* Choose one.
   Revision: Act now, and you will receive a gift in the mail.
8. *Words with built-in limits and multiple synonyms. Kills* is absolute and means *dead.*
   Revision: ATTACK! insect spray kills bugs.
9. *Redundancy.* Multiple synonyms describe the same thing. *In general = by and large = on the whole. Continued on = for a while.* Reduce each equation.
   Revision: After *extended* discussion, the committee *generally* agreed.
10. *Redundancy over consecutive sentences.* Eliminate one *market research.*
    Revision: The trouble is that while taking the necessary courses, people often forget to do market research in order to learn about the availability of jobs in their profession.

GROUP C

1. *Words with built-in limits. Alternative* means two choices only.
   Revision: "As I see it," said Napoleon, "that leaves us just three *options*: fight, surrender, or blame it all on Josephine."
2. *Redundancy of synonyms. Run off = elope, in love = care for. Causal overkill (reason is...because). Additive overkill (and/as well).*
   Revision: In *A Midsummer Night's Dream*, Lysander and Hermia plan to elope because they are deeply in love.
3. *Conditional overkill.* Eliminate *would* from *if clause.*
   Revision: If you give me just five more minutes, I could finish the exam.
4. *Words with built-in limits. Ecstatic* is already superlative. Don't modify it. Remove *totally.*
   Revision: When Toni Morrison received the Nobel Prize for literature, she was ecstatic.

5. *Comparative overkill (better/rather)*. Eliminate *rather. Redundancy with multiple synonyms. Compete* means *against*.
   Revision: It is better to excel at different activities from your best friend's than to compete constantly.
6. *Causal overkill (reason is...because)*. Replace *because* with *that*.
   Revision: The only reason Sir Edmund Hillary had for climbing Mount Everest was *that* it was there.
7. *Words with built-in limits (innovations* and *lethal)*. Eliminate *new* and change *lethal* to *powerful*.
   Revision: According to General MacAllister, innovations in technology have led to the development of missiles that are more *powerful* than ever.
8. *Words with built-in limits. Refer* means *back.* Eliminate *back.*
   Redundancy. Equally = *as.* Eliminate *as.*
   Revision: When he referred to page twenty-one, he saw that he was as mistaken as she was.
9. *Conditional overkill*. Remove *would* from *if clause. Redundancy (advantage* = *good)*.
   Revision: If you word-process instead of writing long hand, you have an advantage when you revise your work.
10. *Redundancy using multiple synonyms. Unique* = *unlike anything else, exhilarated* = *feeling on top of the world. Words with built-in limits. Unique* is an absolute degree. Eliminate *very.*
    Revision: Astronauts always say that walking in space is a unique and exhilarating experience.

 37 Contradictions in terms

GROUP A

1. *Implied contradiction. To focus* and to *concentrate* mean to converge on one thing not on *many* things, and certainly not *simultaneously.* The implication is that the course teaches students to do the impossible.
   Revision: The course for prospective film directors teaches students to concentrate on *each of* the many different aspects of production.
2. *Literal contradiction. Experience* is actual, and it contradicts *potentially.* Replace *potentially* with *practically.*
   Revision: Practically anyone can experience crippling arthritis.
3. *Literal contradiction. Started to stop* is an oxymoron. Replace it with *gradually stopped.*
   Revision: In *Fahrenheit 451,* people became unable to reason because they *gradually stopped* reading.
4. *Literal contradiction. Chaos* means dissolution *not* formation. Replace *formed* with *erupted.*
   Revision: Chaos erupted when the Union army retreated at Centerville.

5. *Literal contradiction. Become* means *exist.* Replace *become non-existent* with *eliminates* or *undermines.*
   Revision: Greed *undermines* legal and moral standards.
6. *Literal contradiction.* A *hum* can't be *silent.* Eliminate *silent.*
   Revision: They spent the afternoon relaxing in the meadow, surrounded by the hum of insects.
7. *Literal contradiction. Some* and *only* are opposites. Eliminate both and replace with *can.*
   Revision: A Midsummer Night's Dream shows that people *can* act irrationally when they are in love.
8. *Literal contradiction.* Cars go more slowly at lower speeds, not more quickly. *Implied contradiction.* A lower gear is for slower speeds. This construction implies that it is for more speed.
   Revision: A lower set of gears was added *to provide a wider range of speed.*
9. *Literal contradiction.* A *negative advance* is an oxymoron.
   Revision: The Iraqi general reported *the retreat* of his troops from Kuwait as soon as they encountered American forces.
10. *Implied contradiction.* The statement suggests that in one case, a person knows *what he's looking for,* but in the other case he does not, and *should know.* Alternatively, the statement suggests he does not know if he wants a condo or a beach house.
    Revision: Regardless of what type of property a person is looking for, he should know ahead of time what he wants.

GROUP B

1. *Literal and implied contradiction. Expanding* is the opposite of *smaller.* The implication is that countries *expand* by shrinking.
   Revision: The transcontinental railroad *maintained contacts within* the expanding country.
2. *Literal contradiction. Perfect* means having no weaknesses at all.
   Revision: Because he had *no* weaknesses, people said he was perfect.
3. *Literal contradiction. Lack of the presence* is oxymoronic and simply means *absence.*
   Revision: Many people feel depressed by the absence of God in modern consciousness.
4. *Implied contradiction.* The implication is that she would rather open her bedroom window and die than pay for air-conditioning.
   Revision: Although I *suffer* without air-conditioning in my bedroom, I refuse to pay extra for it when I can just open my window.
5. *Literal contradiction. Always* is absolute. There is no *usually* about *always.* Choose one.
   Revision: As always, bonuses are paid for outstanding performance only.
6. *Literal contradiction.* You can share *similarities* but not *differences.*
   Revision: The two empires shared many similarities despite their differences.

7. *Implied contradiction.* The illogical implication is that teenagers prefer older and cheaper cars but out of desperation would settle for a shiny new expensive car which would have to do.
   Revision: The older and cheaper a car is, the more likely teenagers are to buy it. However, teenagers want to own cars, *and are willing to spend more than they planned.*

8. *Literal contradiction. Main* means *major.* Substitute *important* and *key.*
   Revision: There were many *important* reasons for the war; but of these only a few were *key.*

9. *Implied contradiction.* The implication is that disorganization depends on the number of jobs rather than on a way of structuring those jobs.
   Revision: Not only is he disorganized, but *he also* takes on more than he can handle.

10. *Literal contradiction. Collapsed* contradicts growth. Replace *during their growth* with *new.*
    Revision: Many *new* businesses have collapsed while others have flourished.

38 Gilding the lily

1. *Inflated language (art of great purity). Unrealistic exaggeration.* Statement gives the impression that doctors are interested exclusively in serving humanity, not, for example, in making money, and that they all excel at their profession.
   Revision: Only a few people so intimately touch our lives as doctors do. Doctors are committed to healing humanity, and many of them are skilled and caring professionals.

2. *Unrealistic exaggeration.* It is highly unlikely that the world or even the nation relies on a single graduating class from one institution. Overcoming *all obstacles* is equally unlikely. *Too many adverbs and adjectives (eagerly, fearlessly, limitless, all).*
   Revision: Today, you, the graduating class of 2000, stand on the threshold of a new century, eager to overcome all obstacles. We believe in your large talents and youthful energy; and we are optimistic about your success.

3. *Unrealistic exaggeration.* Yes, the Norman Conquest did change the English language. But did it do so more than the Roman, Saxon, or Danish conquests have done? More than the 20th century migrations have done? This is an exaggerated and unreliable claim. *Too many adverbs. Forever* is not necessary.
   Revision: The Norman Conquest changed definitively the structure and vocabulary of the English language.

4. *Unrealistic exaggeration.* Unquestionably, Odysseus is a great hero — but *the most famous*? A good argument can be made for classic contenders such as Theseus, Hercules, Aeneas, not to mention more con-

temporary characters. *Too many adjectives (brilliant, brave, wily, resourceful, famous, world-renowned).*
Revision: Brave and resourceful, Odysseus is a world-renowned hero whose feats have been admired for millennia.

5. *Unrealistic exaggeration.* It's hard to exaggerate the virtues of a mother, but this statement manages to do so. The surfeit of praise and description reduces motherhood to greeting card sentimentality. *Too many adjectives (saintly, devoted, glorious, loving, countless, precious).*
Revision: Mother's Day celebrates the love and devotion of mothers and reminds us of their countless sacrifices.

6. *Unrealistic exaggeration.* The undeniable merit of the Founding Fathers is undermined by exaggeration. Also, American rights and privileges are precious and rare, but not unique. *Inflated language (have the honor of calling).*
Revision: Without the guidance of Washington, Jefferson, and Madison, we Americans might not today be enjoying rights and privileges rare in the modern world.

7. *Unrealistic exaggeration.* Certainly teaching is a job that demands both emotional and intellectual commitment. Saying more than that risks mockery. *Inflated language (enactment of a daily drama, altruism, service of mankind).*
Revision: Being a teacher is more than just a job. It demands both intellectual commitment to one's subject and emotional commitment to one's students.

8. *Unrealistic exaggeration.* While Nathan Hale is a model hero, it is hard to say that he is the *first and greatest. Live forever in our hearts and minds?* Well, maybe. *Too many adjectives (gleaming, patriotic, first, greatest). Clichés don't help (in our hearts and minds).*
Revision: A model of patriotic self-sacrifice, Nathan Hale is perhaps America's first hero immortalized by history.

9. *Inflated language (seraphic beauty, pristine purity, was spawned).*
Revision: I realized that when we examine the corruption of the world we begin to see the beauty and purity from which it sprang.

10. *Unrealistic exaggeration.* While the teachings of Socrates are an important source of Western culture, they are not its *only* source. And, it is absurd to claim that without Socrates Western philosophy would not exist. *Greatest?* Hard to say.
Revision: The philosophy of Socrates is crucial to Western thought.

 ## 39 Mixed metaphors

1. *Explanation:* It sounds as if the speaker makes a habit of swimming with her shoes on. In fact, she's empathizing with the competitor in the meet.
Translation: I know how she felt, straining to win the meet.

2. *Explanation:* The mixed metaphor places a Jewish clergyman (*rabbi*) into a Christian house of worship (*church*)
   Translation: The rabbi and his wife were *very* poor.
3. *Explanation:* The metaphor mixes mountains with flat terrain (*level playing field*).
   Translation: The mountain climbers in the competition said all they wanted was a *fair chance.*
4. *Intentional mixed metaphor.* Equating an ambulance with regularly scheduled school buses emphasizes the frequency of the accidents.
5. *Explanation:* In this mixed metaphor, dogs and rats are mixed pell mell in a cannibalistic competition.
   Translation: The competition is *merciless and unrelenting.*
6. *Explanation:* It's not only unfair *to use a golf cart as a crutch,* but very hard to do.
   Translation: In a tournament, using a golf cart *gives competitors an unfair advantage, even if they are disabled.*
7. *Explanation:* A classic mixed metaphor, it balances Shakespeare precariously on one foot while the other foot waves a salute.
   Translation: Shakespeare's *writing provides a literary transition* from the Middle Ages to the Renaissance.
8. *Intentional mixed metaphor.* The metaphor is so apt that it is barely a mixed one. It points out that the man is cowardly (*no guts*), indecisive (*no spine*), and unkind (*no heart*).
9. *Explanation:* This mixed metaphor has Mia kicking with an *upper hand.*
   Translation: As a great soccer player, Mia Hamm always had *an advantage* in placing kicks accurately.
10. *Explanation:* This sounds as if there had been only one right hand between the two generals. This metaphor mixes the amputation with the figurative meaning of *right-hand* as most important assistant.
    Translation: When General Sherman's arm had to be amputated, Lee was very grieved. He had always thought of Sherman as his most important officer.

A *rhetorical fallacy* is a misleading argument. Often an inadvertent error in reasoning, it can also be a deliberate tactic calculated to make a weak argument appear stronger. Fallacies rely on strategies other than logic to persuade. They thrive in the language of politics, propaganda, advertising, and business, not to mention in daily conversation. Gradually they find their way into history, science, the humanities, and popular beliefs. An important first step toward making valid judgments is to be able to recognize fallacies and arguments and to learn how they mislead us. Learning their basic patterns and most common types is essential to becoming a good writer and a clear thinker.

This section will discuss the most common arguments and fallacies grouped by type: *emotional fallacies, invalid standards of proof, sequence and consequence, diversionary tactics, semantic slithers,* and *misconstruing the argument.*

40 Emotional fallacies

What are emotional fallacies?

Emotion is the enemy of objectivity. Good writing strives at all times to keep emotions in check, to maintain an objective view on its subject, and to encourage the same clear thinking in its audience. Emotional fallacies accomplish precisely the opposite: they appeal to the audience's passions — anger, greed, fear — rather than to rational judgment. They signal the writer's willingness to prejudice his argument and mislead his audience.

40a   Argument against the person (*ad hominem*)

The *ad hominem* argument moves from a condemnation of a person's opinions to a condemnation of her character.

➤ The angry, antisocial behavior Salinger ascribes to Holden Caulfield in *Catcher in the Rye* reflects the author's own twisted values, not those of a generation of American youth.

The attack on the author Salinger begins as a criticism of his novel but loses objectivity immediately when it becomes personal.

➤ The review of my restaurant was limited and skewed because the reviewer is a snobbish, small-minded, self-important little man with no knowledge of ethnic food.

➤ The chief prosecutor who accused my client of corruption is motivated not by a search for justice but by his selfish desire to promote himself politically.

Argument by force (*ad baculum*)   *40b*

The argument *ad baculum* makes an explicit or implicit threat of violence. Its purpose is to persuade not by reasoning but by fear.

➤ If protesters do not give up their plans to march, we, the police, will be forced to jail them for incitement to riot. We cannot be held responsible for the safety of demonstrators who disobey the law.

In this example, the police have delivered a veiled threat, implying that harm will come to protesters. Consider the other implied threats in the following examples.

➤ I have tried reasoning politely with you about your loud parties. Next time, I will not be so reasonable or polite.

➤ Resist by any means necessary.

Argument to shame (*ad verecundiam*)   *40c*

In the argument *ad verecundiam*, the writer appeals to the reader's sense of personal modesty or collective shame, often in contrast to some moral ideal.

> The Good Lord raised this mighty Republican Republic to be a home for the brave and to flourish as the land of the free — not to stagnate in the swampland of collectivism, not to cringe before the bully of Communism.   — Barry Goldwater, Presidential candidate 1964

Goldwater shames any American who tolerates communism or "collectivism" as a coward and an opponent of freedom.

Responding to arguments *ad verecundiam* requires caution. One is tempted to agree in order to avoid embarrassment. Consider these examples that invite an embarrassing response:

➤When you say that you are correct, you are, therefore, suggesting that everyone else is wrong, among them people who are older and more experienced than you.

➤What do you mean you disagree with my account of the accident? I saw it for myself. Are you calling me a liar?

40d   Argument to the wallet (*ad crumenam*)

The argument *ad crumenam* seeks to persuade its audience to act or to dissuade them from acting based upon the amount of money that action would cost. It establishes money as the most important basis for judgments.

> Why should the U.S. spend a huge portion of its 1999 budget surplus on intervention in Kossovo? The alleged atrocities by the Serbs against the ethnic Albanians are the result of centuries of grudges and injuries by both groups against each other. We should not be taking sides and wasting precious national resources that we ourselves need, on a conflict which is not our business and where we do not know all the facts.

The speaker here manages to alarm his audience with the prospect of spending *a huge portion* of the annual budget surplus without accounting for specific costs. He also does not consider the ethical problem of ignoring genocide. The argument is equally financial and emotional.

Not all arguments *ad crumenam* are fallacies. Topics such as canceling Third World debt or dealing with welfare and workfare are legitimately economic and must take into account financial consequences. Fallacies occur when the speaker exaggerates and emotionalizes the effect money has on a problem.

➤For just fifty cents a day, your contribution to *Feed the Hungry* can help stop famine in Africa.

African famines are complex political and environmental problems. Money may help feed individuals, but it does not solve the long-term problems.

➤Global warming may be a reality, but the American people cannot afford to give up their cars. That would destroy the economy.

It is equally true that Americans cannot afford the consequences of global warming. Nor is giving up the car an inevitable consequence of solving environmental problems (see §42a *If...then*).

📖　Exercise

Identify and explain each of the following fallacies. Answers on p.248.

1. The Vietnam vet claims that the Veterans' Administration has withheld his benefits for over a year. The Veterans' Administration denies the claim and points out that this man also maintains a Web page that discusses UFOs.
2. Put your statue on the front lawn? We can't. What would the neighbors say?
3. Unless you honor the warranty on this defective car, you'll hear from my attorney.
4. The only way to save the Everglades from dying is to dismantle the system of dams that has been diverting fresh water from the wetlands. But such a project is impossible to carry out because it would cost billions of dollars.
5. Regardless of what you think is fair to the other students, if you do not allow my child to retake her English exam, I will speak to the School Superintendent about your attitude.
6. You think that the state's new workfare program increases the self-esteem of the participants? What do you know about any of these issues? What knowledgeable people do you talk to all day? All you do is keep house and take care of our children.
7. I don't care if you like this outfit. Nice girls do not wear such short tight skirts.
8. We need to invest in a national drug rehabilitation program because it costs less to rehabilitate an addict than to imprison her.
9. How can you consider his opinions on prison reform when he's probably a criminal himself?
10. So you think that the word "potato" does not have an -e at the end? Well let's just step outside and settle this once and for all.

41 Invalid standards of proof

What are invalid standards of proof?

Examples, facts, and expert opinions are the evidence upon which an argument is built. However, not all examples are relevant, not all facts are true, and not all expert opinions are correct. Arguments that use false or misleading evidence employ *invalid standards of proof*.

41a   Argument by authority

The *argument by authority* is a dressed up version of the classic response "because I said so." Instead of exploring the merits of an issue, the speaker glorifies the non-specific reputation of an authority.

Sometimes the authority is the speaker himself.

➤You can't win because I'm the world champion.

More often the authority is a famous third person or well-reputed institution. These arguments by authority could be legitimate if they explained the reason behind the authoritative opinion.

➤Democracy is an inferior form of government. Aristotle makes this argument in his famous *Politics*.

What else did Aristotle say about democracy? Why did he think it was inferior?

➤The play is a masterpiece. It got top reviews in the *New York Times*.

Have you seen the play? Is the *New York Times* infallible?

➤Don't argue with Sarah about politics; she studied at Stanford.

Did Sarah study politics at Stanford? Does she have a background in this subject?

41b   Argument by definition

Defining one's terms is a key part of making an argument. In a valid argument, however, every definition must be explained and supported with examples. *Arguments by definition* use as proof unexplained, unsupported definitions which are a type of generalization (see §45e *Generalization*).

DEFINITION
➤Right and wrong is a matter of opinion. A person who believes he is doing the right thing can never be guilty of a crime.

DEFINITION
➤There's no reason to disagree because deep down we all have the same hopes and desires.

DEFINITION
➤I've decided to bleach my hair. After all, blondes have more fun.

The definitions in these examples are arbitrary and unexamined. The arguments they support are true only if one accepts the definition.

Argument by popularity   *41c*

Fashions and trends make an opinion popular; research and careful thought make an opinion valid. The *argument by popularity* mistakes majority opinion for informed opinion.

➤ Most people who hear Schönberg's twelve-tone composition *Altered Night* think it sounds terrible. It cannot, therefore, be good music.

➤ Why shouldn't I smoke cigarettes? Everybody else does.

In both cases the speaker asks us to accept two misleading assumptions: (1) that there is indeed a majority consensus, and (2) that right and wrong, good and bad, should be decided by majority opinion not objective evidence.

Hypothetical argument   *41d*

The *hypothetical argument* likens the situation under discussion to an imagined scenario in which the details are similar, but the outcome is different. Truth, however, is often in the details; rarely is one situation exactly like another. The hypothetical argument uses imagined evidence to prove an actual case.

Let's say two people are stranded on a desert island with only enough water for three days for both of them. A rescue boat will be sent in one week. One of them could survive if the other gave up her share. A good friend would be willing to sacrifice herself to save her friend. I would be willing to do that for you. So why can't you sacrifice a little and lend me a hundred dollars?

Hypothetical arguments are valid only when the imagined scenario is realistic and comparable. The desert island scenario is neither.

Some hypothetical arguments seem reasonable but in fact presume the unpredictable.

➤ If I were you, I'd skip college to become a professional basketball player.

➤ You wouldn't speak to me that way if I were a complete stranger.

Each of the examples above makes assumptions that can be neither predicted nor verified.

41e   Implied argument

The *implied argument* is a fallacy that rests on principles that are never explicitly stated, and whose validity thus cannot be examined. Often the implied argument has its origin in sayings, commonly held beliefs, or prejudices repeated without scrutiny from one generation to the next.

> ➤ I can't make an exception for you because I'd have to do the same for everyone else.

The example above seems to be about making an exception for someone. In fact, it assumes principles of fairness that remain unexamined. The implied argument here — that justice requires the same treatment for everyone regardless of individual circumstances — is patently false. Killing someone, for example, may be an act of self-defense or an act of murder.

Implied arguments can be particularly damaging when they conceal prejudice. The following extract is from a speech given by a white Prime Minister of South Africa in the days of apartheid.

> What would [a multiracial state] involve? A South African Army and a South African police force under black generals; an air force under a black air marshal; a government with black Cabinet Ministers; a Parliament with black Members of Parliament; administrators and mayors, all black! Now I ask the Honorable Leader of the Opposition: with such an end in view, what hope would there be for the white man? [...] if there is an emergency, [...] he would be under the domination and under the superior power of the army, navy, air force, police service, government — nation-wide — of the black man.
>
> — Hendrik Verwoerd, South African Prime Minister 1958-66

The argument implies that the races are naturally prejudiced against one another and naturally treat each other vindictively. Verwoerd assumes that if blacks were in control of government, they would behave as prejudicially as the whites did. History has proven this implied argument wrong.

41f   Proof by absence

The *proof by absence* fallacy assumes that the lack of evidence is itself a kind of proof.

> ➤ The safe is empty. Therefore, its contents must have been stolen.

Did the safe ever have anything in it? Did the owner remove its contents? While the absence of facts may be the sign of a problem, we cannot know what that problem is and, therefore, cannot make assumptions about cause or motive.

The proof by absence fallacy is also a frequent cause of misunderstanding between the sexes.

➤I know he hated my dinner because he didn't say how much he enjoyed it.

📖　Exercise

Identify and explain each of the following fallacies. Answers on p.249.

1. Real men don't eat quiche. Look at him — he's eating quiche.
2. QUESTION: "How do you know that she's not a good friend for me?" ANSWER: "Because I'm older than you."
3. The SONY Playstation will be around for a long time because it is the turn of the millennium and people are looking for new experiences.
4. How can you say that I am selfish? If I were to win this week's $5 million dollar jackpot, I would contribute half of it to charity. That's how generous I am!
5. More people buy Nikes than any other athletic shoes. Nikes are the best athletic shoes in America.
6. He doesn't care about our home because he didn't even take out the garbage while I was at work.
7. Nikes are the best basketball shoes of all because Michael Jordan wears them, and he's the greatest basketball player of all time.
8. If a dog protects the home, then he's worth spending money on. What good is Old Spot? All he does is love you and give companionship.
9. You say you love me. But would you say that if I gained 20 pounds and lost my job?
10. Of course he has bad, teeth. He's English, isn't he!

42 Sequence and consequence

What are fallacies of sequence and consequence?

In an essay, thinking is much like being a detective. The writer comes to a conclusion by building a chain of logically connected ideas called premises that advance the argument bit by bit. Each premise must follow logically from the last. If the chain of reasoning misses a link or presents the premises in the wrong order, the whole argument collapses. *Fallacies of sequence and consequence* are errors in logical order and missing links in the chain of reasoning.

42a   *If...then*

The *if...then* fallacy artificially limits the possible consequences of an action to one result: *if* a given event occurs, *then* a particular consequence is inevitable. Life tends to be more complicated; actions often have many consequences not all of which are inevitable. In the following examples compare consequences that really are inevitable to *if...then* fallacies.

FALLACIOUS   If we hadn't dropped the bomb on Hiroshima, we would never have won the war in the Pacific.

The fact is that we would probably have won the war by other, albeit lengthier, methods.

LOGICAL   If you hadn't hit the brakes, we would have run down that pedestrian.

FALLACIOUS   If you go out in the rain without a raincoat, you will catch a cold.

Many people go out in the rain without a raincoat and never catch a cold. What if one went out with an umbrella instead?

LOGICAL   If the polio vaccine hadn't been invented, many people would have been crippled by the disease.

Non sequitur   **42b**

Non sequitur means "it does not follow" in Latin. It refers to a missing link in the chain of reasoning. A non sequitur surprises the reader with a conclusion that doesn't follow from its premise.

➤I know that he is an honest man because he is a socialist.
                 CONCLUSION   PREMISE

➤Iraq won't invade Syria because it didn't invade Saudi Arabia.
   CONCLUSION   PREMISE

➤The car won't start. We must be out of gas.
     CONCLUSION   PREMISE

In each case, the speaker is missing logical steps on the way to his conclusion. For the first statement to be valid, the speaker must explain that all socialists in his experience are honest. In the second statement, he would have to explain why Iraq's relationship to Syria is similar to its relationship to Saudi Arabia. In the final example, he must assure the reader that he has ruled out all other possible reasons the car won't start. Without these intervening premises, the conclusions are arbitrary.

Post hoc fallacy   **42c**

The Latin phrase *post hoc ergo propter hoc* means "after this therefore because of this." A *post hoc fallacy* is an error in consequence. It assumes that events happening *after* a fact necessarily occur *because* of it. *Post hoc* is the logic of superstition applied to simple coincidence.

➤As soon as they hired that new guy in the office, things started to disappear from my desk. He must be responsible.

➤Fire broke out in the building after children were seen playing basketball in the back lot.

➤Statistics show an increase of UFO sightings around the time of earthquakes.

In each case, a coincidence is treated as a cause-and-effect relationship. Although it is possible that one incident is the direct result of another, it is by no means certain. The conclusion does not necessarily follow from the premise. A cause-and-effect connection should be neither suggested nor deduced based on the sequence of events alone.

42d   Slippery slope

The *slippery slope* is a longer version of the *if...then* fallacy. It assumes that a given act or decision will trigger a series of inevitable and progressively more serious consequences. Actions, according to the slippery slope, are connected like dominoes in a line. The argument fails, however, to examine the cause-and-effect of each connection. Consider Shakespeare's famous speech about the importance of hierarchy or degree:

> Take but degree away, untune that string,
> And hark what discord follows! Each thing melts
> In mere oppugnancy: the bounded waters
> Should lift their bosoms higher than the shores,
> And make a sop of all this solid globe;
> Strength should be lord of imbecility,
> And the rude son should strike his father dead;
> Force should be right; or, rather, right and wrong —
> Between whose endless jar justice resides—
> Should lose their names, and so should justice too.
> Then everything includes itself in power,
> Power into will, will into appetite[...].

Troilus and Cressida (1.3.109–120)

Here Ulysses is arguing that universal chaos will result from the most minor infraction of social order. Poetic but illogical.

The same *slippery slope* reasoning was behind American involvement in the Vietnam War. According to the "domino theory" if one Southeast Asian country were taken over by communists, the other countries in the region would fall too like a row of dominoes. Vietnam did, eventually, fall under communist control, but other Southeast Asian countries did not follow suit, disproving the domino theory's slippery slope.

The most common example of slippery slope, however, is to be found in daily conversation.

➤If I let her pierce her ears, soon she'll be wearing nose rings and tattoos, and staying out all night.

📖 Exercise

Identify and explain each of the following fallacies. Answers on p.250.

1. She was very beautiful because he couldn't stop looking at her.
2. I'd better not allow you to take tomorrow off to lecture at another school. I'm concerned that you might become very well known, and many other schools might invite you, so that you'll be absent from our classroom all the time..
3. She began to win the chess game after she had put on her lucky bracelet.
4. How could he have given me a D when I studied so hard?
5. QUESTION: "Why can he ride his bike to the playground, but I can't?" ANSWER: "Because he's a boy."
6. If there's smoke, there's fire.
7. As soon as he got his driver's license, the accident rate in town went up.
8. This book was extremely exciting because I couldn't put it down.
9. Medical evidence shows a glass of red wine with your dinner several times a week reduces the risk of heart attack. But, if you begin to drink this wine you will get to like it and will go on to whisky and brandy, so that eventually you will become an alcoholic.
10. That old lady is a jinx. The moment she came to visit, four of my electrical appliances stopped working.

43 Diversionary tactics

What are diversionary tactics?

If you can't win an argument with reasoning and proof, you can divert attention from its weaknesses. *Diversionary tactics* are designed to confuse the audience and prevent careful analysis of an argument's flaws.

Begging the question   43a

Begging the question means asserting in advance what has yet to be proven.

➤My talented daughter deserves an art scholarship.

The speaker prejudices the case by calling the daughter *talented*. Talent must be established before its merit can be rewarded.

The most famous example of begging the question is René Déscartes' famous proof of his own existence.

➤ I think, therefore I am.

If the philosopher wants to prove he exists, he cannot begin with the word *I* which assumes in advance that he exists.

43b   Circular reasoning

Circular reasoning is a cause-and-effect error. Instead of showing how a cause leads to an effect, circular reasoning repeats the effect in different words and passes it off as the cause; it rephrases a premise as a conclusion without adding any further information.

                EFFECT   CAUSE
➤ He was reluctant to try out for the team because he didn't want to.

Reluctant means *he didn't want to.* The cause merely restates the effect.

                                                    EFFECT
➤ The reason Julius and Ethel Rosenberg were executed for treason

                CAUSE
was that they had betrayed their country.

Treason means *to betray one's country.* Again the cause restates the effect.

            EFFECT   CAUSE
➤ The President made the decision because he realized it had to be done.

Here the cause — *it had to be done* — is implied in the effect — *made a decision.*

43c   Irrelevancy

Irrelevancies are often true statements that happen to have nothing to do with the issue at hand. They distract, confuse, and often attempt to mislead.

➤ Senator Andersen is an ideal person to head the foreign trade committee. She is an intelligent, well-traveled, experienced business-woman and a loving mother.

Motherhood is not a relevant qualification for foreign trade.

➤Mata Hari, who was executed for spying for Germany against the French in World War I, is among the world's most famous spies, even though she was a woman.

Her gender is irrelevant to her fame as a spy.

➤The space shuttle will make history today when it completes its longest mission ever in space. This long mission is especially historic because only one of the crew has been in space previously.

Whether the crew has been in space before or not is irrelevant to the historic length of the mission.

Red herring   43d

The expression "red herring" comes from foxhunting in which a smelly fish was sometimes dragged across the scent trail to confuse the hounds. In rhetoric, a *red herring* is an exercise in misdirection and an effective way of ignoring the real question. It diverts attention from a weak argument by sidetracking it into a tangential issue. Often this new issue is emotionally charged.

➤An American tourist visiting Moscow during the cold war years comments to his Soviet guide that the subway runs very seldom. Indignant, the guide retorts, "And what about your lynchings in Mississippi?"

Obviously the problems of the Moscow subway have nothing to do with lynchings in Mississippi. The guide is just diverting the criticism.

➤How can this Olympic committee form a policy on doping in light of the recent bribery scandal involving members of the past Olympic committee?

The actions of the previous Olympic committee have no bearing on those of the current one. Bribery is no excuse for permitting doping.

📖   Exercise

Identify and explain each of the following fallacies. Answers on p.251.

1. Because he had a low I. Q., he was not very intelligent.
2. SPEAKER A We know that George Gershwin is a great composer because all the best critics say so.
   SPEAKER B How do you know they're the best critics?
   SPEAKER A Because they appreciate great music like Gershwin's.

3. OK, so I spent too much on long-distance calls this month. But how about the way you just ran the red light? If you'd been caught by a cop, the ticket would have cost us a lot more than my phone calls did.
4. If Lincoln believed that slavery was wrong, why did he allow the use of black soldiers in the Civil War?
5. Being unchangeable makes love real because if love keeps changing and doesn't stay constant then it is not genuine.
6. Why didn't they publish such a brilliant novel? It was written just like Ernest Hemingway's *The Sun also Rises*, and he won the Nobel Prize.
7. Joe taught you how to save the tree from the ant infestation? Why did you seek information from a man who didn't even go to college?
8. The South outclassed the North in cavalry because they had better horsemen.
9. My dogs kept you up all night? What about your baby whose crying bothers me all the time?
10. She was a wealthy woman because she had large financial assets.

44 Semantic slithers

What are semantic slithers?

Semantics is the study of word meanings. *Semantic slithers* are clever and misleading shifts in the meaning of words designed to confuse the audience and prejudice the argument.

44a   Equivocation

Equivocation means repeating the same word or phrase using different meanings. By giving the repeated expression a different and *usually disparaging* connotation, the writer can shift the direction or emphasis of the argument without seeming to do so. Such a shift may sound clever, but it is a dishonest and often slanderous tactic.

> ►Both my opponent and I wish to represent you at our party's convention. However, while we may both be members of the same *party*, my chief business is not to *party*.

> By changing *party* from a *political group* to a verb meaning *to drink and have a good time*, the speaker implies that his opponent is irresponsible and not hardworking.

➤What my opponent calls common *sense* I take to be *common* sense indeed. His proposals are ordinary and stale. There is nothing innovative about his ideas.

By changing emphasis in the expression *common sense*, the speaker changes its connotation from praise to criticism. "Common *sense*" means *clear thinking*; "*common* sense" means *run-of-the-mill* or *unoriginal* thinking.

➤I am not saying that homeless people should be *put out* on the street, but neither should the average taxpayer on the street be *put out* by the homeless.

In the first instance *put out* means *expelled, left outside*; in the second instance *put out* means *disturbed* or *inconvenienced*. The speaker shifts the emphasis from the problems homeless suffer, to the problems they cause to taxpayers.

However, if the same word is used a second time with a different meaning that is *not* intentionally disparaging, it is not equivocation.

➤During the Crusades, *different* countries put aside their *differences* to promote Christianity.

Here, *different* simply means *various*, and *differences* means *disagreements*. These are statements of fact without unpleasant implications.

Loaded terminology   *44b*

Loaded terminology prejudges issues, events, or individuals by tagging them with an adjective that arouses strong emotions. Rather than describe the subject in objective terms, these tags describe the speaker's feelings about the subject. Loaded terminology is used purely for effect, not to analyze a topic reasonably. There are two kinds of loaded terminology: *name calling* and *glittering generalizations*.

In *name calling*, the tags have unpleasant social or political connotations intended to anger the audience. Common examples of name calling include *fascist argument, racist attitude, capitalist exploitation, liberal guilt* etc.

➤I resent the *fascist attitudes* of the police who force you to submit to a breath test even when you haven't committed any offense.

➤Our town is controlled by the *garbage Nazis*. Ever since the Green Party won seats on the council, recycling has become mandatory.

In *glittering generalizations*, the tags are so-called virtue words designed to trigger reflexive approval rather than thoughtful reflection. Common glittering generalizations include *social justice, equal opportunity, fair employment, right to work, the moral majority, the American way* etc. While these phrases may appeal vaguely to our sense of fairness or national pride, they are non-specific slogans hiding complex political motives. What does "the American way" mean? Is there only one "American way" as the slogan suggests? Consider the glittering generalizations in the following excerpt.

> Duty — Honor — Country. Those hallowed words reverently dictate what you ought to be, what you can be, what you will be. They are your rallying points; to build courage when courage seems to fail; to regain faith when there seems to be little cause for faith; to create hope when hope becomes forlorn.
>
> — General Douglas MacArthur, 1962

What makes *duty, honor, country* glittering generalizations is that MacArthur neither explains nor justifies them. They are presented as slogans or "rallying points" instead of thought-provoking ideals.

Exercise

Identify and explain each of the following fallacies. Answers on p.252.

1. We deserve to have an advantage because last time they took advantage of us.
2. SPEAKER A You've let your emotions affect your judgment.
   SPEAKER B I'm not the one making judgments, you are.
3. I stand for healthy children, education, and the environment.
4. He says that he believes in God, but God knows what he really has in mind!
5. "That is a typical, American, imperialist attitude," said Fidel Castro scornfully.
6. How sound is a poem if it's only a sound?
7. Is it better to be pro-choice or pro-life?
8. According to President Bush, Iran is part of the Axis of Evil.
9. He has a kind heart — the question is what kind.
10. Energy suppression groups are standing in the way of oil drilling in Alaska.

45 Misconstruing the argument

What does it mean to misconstrue an argument?

To misconstrue an argument is to interpret its meaning incorrectly, often intentionally. An argument can be misconstrued by limiting the ways it can be interpreted, by rephrasing the argument in different and misleading terms, by oversimplifying the argument's ideas, or by exaggerating its claims.

Attributing intent

45a

There is a subtle but important distinction between statements and the intentions behind them. We know what people say, but can only guess or infer what they intend. To *attribute intent* is to rephrase a statement in terms of what you think the writer or speaker means to say rather than what she says.

BOSS Productivity has been slipping in your sector.

EMPLOYEE I have always worked very hard and resent your criticism.

The employee has assumed that his boss intended to criticize him, and has responded to the assumed intention rather than to the actual statement. The statement was merely factual. Any hint of criticism would depend on a much broader context. For example, is this boss in the habit of criticizing the employee?

Often, critics attribute intent to authors or artists rather than analyze their work (see §35b *Avoid attributing intent to authors*).

INTENTIONAL In *Catch-22*, Joseph Heller *meant to* criticize all bureaucracies, not just the air force.

REVISED *Catch-22* criticizes all bureaucracies through the example of the air force.

INTENTIONAL Steven Spielberg's *intent* in *Schindler's List* was to celebrate humanity in the face of barbarism.

REVISED Steven Spielberg's *Schindler's List* celebrates humanity in the face of barbarism.

45b   Decontextualizing

The meaning of an idea always depends upon what is said before or after. Taken out of context, an expression may be incomplete. We cannot know the speaker's full or true intent from a fragment. A favorite tactic of tabloid journalists, decontextualizing commonly occurs when a writer quotes parts of a sentence.

> GENERAL   I have heard those who claim that gays are unfit to serve in the army, and I have always maintained that such statements are pure bigotry.

> JOURNALIST In speaking of bigotry, the General stated that "gays are unfit to serve in the army."

Although the words the journalist cites were indeed spoken by the General, he goes on to deny that gays are unfit to serve in the military.

At the height of the cold war, the Soviet premier Nikita Khruschev said regarding America, "We will bury you." It was clear from the context that he meant communism would outlast capitalism, but taken out of context, it could have meant that the Soviet Union was planning to destroy America militarily. Similar decontextualizing occurs in quotations from literature and history.

> ➤ In his famous soliloquy, Hamlet considers suicide as something to be wished for, "Tis a consummation/ Devoutly to be wished — to die[...]."

The writer decontextualizes the quotation making it appear as though Hamlet is resolved to die. In fact, the Prince later makes known his irresolution to die, "Thus conscience does make cowards of us all."

When quoting from a source, discuss the context beforehand. Then quote a representative portion of the text, even if it limits the argument you hope to make.

45c   *Either...or*

The *either...or fallacy* artificially limits one's choices to two; it traps one into binary thinking. It bullies the reader into accepting opposite alternatives while ignoring other viable possibilities.

> ➤ In war, one either fights or surrenders.

> What about negotiation?

> ➤ America — love it or leave it.

How about improving it with constructive criticism or community involvement?

➤Evolution is a controversial theory. Either you accept Darwin or you believe in God.

It is entirely possible to believe in God *and* to subscribe to the theory of evolution.

False analogy 45d

A false analogy assumes wrongly that because two people, things, or events are alike in some ways, they must be alike in every way.

➤People are like fine wines. They improve with age. There is no reason, therefore, to force older drivers to retake their driving tests.

Like fine wines, people improve with age insofar as their life experience is concerned. However, fast reflexes, which are essential to safe driving, deteriorate with age.

Often false analogies result from comparisons between things that have similar qualities but in different degrees. A firecracker is similar to an atomic bomb: both explode, but the explosions are unlike in degree.

➤Saddam Hussein is the Hitler of the late twentieth century.

Saddam Hussein and Hitler are both dangerous megalomaniacs, but Saddam operates on a much smaller scale.

➤There's no difference between smoking a cigarette and taking drugs. Both are addictive.

It is true that both cigarettes and drugs are addictive. Drugs, however, are much more powerful and dangerous than cigarettes, and foster a criminal subculture.

When drawing an analogy, limit the terms of comparison to the aspects that are indeed alike. Make analogies specific, not general.

Generalization 45e

The *generalization* is a kind of *overstatement*. It assumes that a few examples or even a clear trend proves a universal truth. The speaker arrives at a conclusion based on incomplete evidence. When applied to people, generalizations deny differences among individuals, and treat them instead as groups that behave alike in predictable ways. As with overstatements, generalizations often employ the absolute words *all, always, every, never, none* etc.

➤Generalizations are always wrong.

Some generalizations are accurate as long as they bear out the evidence. How about this generalization?

➤That Greek housepainter did a terrible job on my kitchen. I'll never hire a Greek housepainter again.

The speaker falsely assumes that the housepainter acted not as an individual but as a member of a large group all of whom behave identically.

➤I've been cheated on by two boyfriends. Men are incapable of being faithful.

Two examples do not prove a universal rule.

Use generalizations for a broad perspective, but avoid applying them to individual people or cases.

45f   Oversimplification

Oversimplification reinterprets an idea in a simplified form, losing some of the necessary subtleties and details. This fallacy reaches a conclusion based on superficial and distorted analysis.

➤He was lucky to win that Olympic medal.

While luck may be a factor in any victory, the speaker's conclusion disregards the athlete's training and intrinsic ability.

➤The reason I drink too much is stress.

Many people experience stress; few become alcoholics. The cause of her alcoholism clearly is more complicated than the speaker implies.

➤The American Civil War was about right and wrong: the South was fighting for slavery and the North against it.

The Civil War was waged for many reasons, the most important of which was states' rights over the authority of the federal government. It is an oversimplification to say that the war was fought over slavery, although slavery was one of the issues in dispute. It is even more of an oversimplification to say it was about right and wrong.

Overstatement 45g

Overstatement exaggerates the claims of an argument; it goes beyond its evidence. Often overstatements are designed to add a sense of moment, grandeur, or importance.

➤You, the graduating class of 2000, are the future of America. The whole country depends on your accomplishments.

Realistically, the speaker's claims are untrue, as they are in the following example.

➤Tonight's party is for Washington insiders. Everybody with any influence will be there.

Overstatements can cause crucial misunderstanding in serious writing. Beware of such absolute words as *all, always, every, never, none* etc. as possible overstatements.

➤History always repeats itself. No matter how much we study the past, we will never be able to apply its lessons to the future.

The threadbare wisdom that *history always repeats itself* is exaggerated. World leaders have often learned from the mistakes of the past.

➤After the stock market crash of 1986, new measures have been taken to prevent another crash from happening ever again.

The speaker's assurance that another stock market crash will *never* happen is overstated.

Statistics 45h

There is some truth to the saying, "There are three types of lies: lies, white lies, and statistics." Statistics are not facts; they are interpretations of facts that describe one part of a larger, more complex problem. To be valid and useful, statistics must be explained in context. Often, they give only partial truths that can be as misleading as lies.

➤Scientists have finally proven that vegetarianism is more healthful than meat-eating. Studies reported by the Vegetarian Society suggest that lifelong vegetarians go to the hospital 22% less than meat-eaters do.

Is the frequency of visiting hospitals a valid test of health? Could the statistic be explained by other factors such as the tendency of vegetarians to take more vitamin supplements? Could it be that vegetarians tend to be younger than meat-eaters? Statistics comparing the incidence of various common diseases among vegetarians and meat-eaters would be more valid and easier to interpret.

Consider the various alternative interpretations of the following statistics.

➤City dwellers are five percent heavier than people who live in the country. Clearly, the availability of fast food is to blame.

What about the possibility that country dwellers lead more active lives?

➤The temperature of the environment has been shown to be a key factor in green turtle survival. A much higher percentage of green turtles survives to the next breeding season in cold waters than in warm waters.

Is it possible that warm waters attract more tourists to the beaches, disturbing the turtles' breeding grounds?

45i   Straw man

The *straw man* fallacy restates an opposing argument as a weak proposition, as shaky and helpless as a "straw man." The restatement is a distortion of the original.

STATEMENT   A divorced man should not be forced to pay alimony to his able-bodied ex-wife.

STRAW MAN   In other words, men should be allowed to renege on their legal responsibilities.

STATEMENT   There are more people listed as needing organ transplants than there are available organs. The Health Commission has decided to give preference to younger patients over older ones.

STRAW MAN   The Health Commission actively discriminates against older people on the organ transplant list.

A more sophisticated use of a straw man is to propose a weak argument that you then knock down, making it seem as though you have considered all the angles. The arguments below seem comprehensive, but they present only a straw man alternative instead of all the reasonable considerations.

➤Some say that to argue against the divorced man's obligation to pay alimony to his able-bodied ex-wife is to encourage men to renege on their legal responsibilities. Quite the contrary, arguing for the rights of divorced men ensures equal protection under the law for both women and men.

➤The problem of long waiting lists for organ transplant has no easy solution. Those who argue against giving preference to younger transplant patients over older ones maintain that it constitutes unfair discrimination. Others recognize the reality: younger patients have a better chance of surviving the operation.

📖 Exercise

Identify and explain each of the following fallacies. Answers on p.253.

GROUP A

1. STATEMENT I don't want you to take this job.
   REPLY You're telling me that you want me to be dependent on you all my life.
2. QUESTION "Why can't we go to Australia? You promised we could go in January."
   ANSWER "I said we could go if we had enough money."
3. HUSBAND You look amazingly beautiful today
   WIFE Thanks for telling me that I usually look ugly!
4. Their success means that either they know the right people, or they're very lucky.
5. All city officials are corrupt, which is why Mayor Martin is probably no different from the rest of them.
6. Only 15% of the population suffers from hemorrhoids which means it is not a serious problem.
7. Because euthanasia is legal to use on animals, it should also be legal to use on people.
8. Cleanliness is next to godliness.
9. He got 1600 on his SATs? What a good guesser!
10. By not giving money to that homeless person, you have shown me that you care nothing for the plight of the homeless.

GROUP B

1. You must be as rich as Bill Gates. He, too, drives a Mercedes.
2. Congress is again debating whether or not to make flag burning a criminal act. To set this issue into rational historical perspective, we need only remember the infamous Nuremberg laws passed by the Nazis when they first came to power. One of the key Nuremberg laws was that treating the Nazi flag with disrespect was a criminal act. Need more be said?
3. This serial killer is a victim of social injustice. Society should be on trial here instead of him.
4. Women comprise nearly 60% of the American population, but less than 10% of the US Senate. Either women are not good at public speaking or they simply do not understand political issues.

5. Why should I have to call a plumber when there's a man in the house?
6. FIRST SPEAKER I think this advertising campaign has potential. But I think you should hold off proposing it to the Board until you have more market research to support it.
   SECOND SPEAKER I will absolutely make my proposal today. And, I advise you to try not to feel threatened by my initiative and creativity.
7. There are more suicides per capita in Sweden than in any other European country. Sweden must have the worst living conditions in Europe.
8. My mother-in-law was the kindest, most generous person in the world. She was a living saint.
9. Events are never black and white. There is always right and wrong on both sides.
10. FIRST STUDENT That was a brilliant answer. How did you come up with it?
    SECOND STUDENT I'm not as stupid as you think.

40–45 Answers to exercises

Many statements may contain more than one fallacy. The answers below list the most obvious.

40 Emotional fallacies

1. *Ad hominem* (and *Irrelevancy*).
   Explanation: Instead of dealing with the *problem*, the Veterans' Administration tries to cast doubt on the *man's credibility* and even his sanity by suggesting that he believes in UFO's. In addition, the subject of his Web page is irrelevant to the subject of his claim.
2. *Argument to shame/Ad verecundiam.*
   Explanation: The decision not to place the statue on the front lawn is based not the *merit* of the statue, but on the *embarrassment* in case the neighbors disapprove.
3. *Argument by force/Ad baculum.*
   Explanation: The *force* in this case is the threat of *legal action* by the dissatisfied customer against the reluctant car dealer.
4. *Argument to the wallet/Ad crumenam.*
   Explanation: The speaker is arguing that the *value of money* is greater than the *value of the natural wonder.*
5. *Argument by force/Ad baculum.*
   Explanation: The irate parent is not interested in discussing the situation, but is seeking to persuade by force in threatening to complain to the teacher's boss.
6. *Ad hominem.*

Explanation: The speaker attacks the *person* instead of the *idea.* The subject should be the effects of workfare, not the intellectual life of the person.

7. *Argument to shame/Ad verecundiam.*
   Explanation: The speaker is attempting to persuade the girl into not wearing the skirt by shaming her.

8. *Argument to the wallet/Ad crumenam.*
   Explanation: The speaker seeks to persuade not in terms of *moral validity* but in terms of *financial good sense.* The fallacy lies in the inappropriate mode of appeal. Both morality and finances must be considered.

9. *Ad hominem.*
   Explanation: Instead of dealing with the merits of the *opinion* on prison reform, the speaker launches an attack on the *person's honesty.*

10. *Argument by force/Ad baculum.*
    Explanation: The threat of force here is the challenge to fight in order to determine the correct spelling of a word.

 41 Invalid standards of proof

1. *Argument by definition.*
   Explanation: If you accept the definition that a *real man* is identified by his eating habits, then the conclusion follows logically that this person is *not a real man,* regardless of the physical reality.

2. *Argument by authority.*
   Explanation: The answer makes the assumption that age automatically confers greater knowledge. This argument must be examined before it is accepted.

3. *Implied argument.*
   Explanation: The implication is that the SONY Playstation will always be innovative.

4. *Hypothetical argument.*
   Explanation: This hypothetical argument proves nothing at all. He will show his generosity only if *after actually winning* the jackpot, he makes the contribution.

5. *Argument by popularity.*
   Explanation: The fact that most people buy Nikes proves their popularity not their quality. The argument assumes that popularity determines quality. It is fallacious because it does not consider other contributing factors, e.g., advertising strategy.

6. *Proof by absence.*
   Explanation: He could have been busy building bookshelves for your home proving that he does care about your home.

7. *Argument by authority.*
   Explanation: Michael Jordan is the authority whom the speaker wants us to trust mindlessly.

8. *Argument by definition.*
   Explanation: A pet's love and companionship help people live longer and happier lives. However, these virtues are irrelevant if you accept the definition that the only worthwhile dog is a watchdog.
9. *Hypothetical argument.*
   Explanation: The question is impossible to answer definitively. The speaker creates a hypothetical situation. Any response will be necessarily meaningless.
10. *Implied argument* (and *Irrelevancy*, and *Hasty generalization*).
    Explanation: His nationality is irrelevant to his teeth. Just because some English have bad teeth doesn't mean that all do. The *implied argument*, which is never explicitly stated, attacks English dental practices.

 ## 42 Sequence and consequence

1. *Non sequitur.*
   Explanation: She was beautiful because she was born that way. His looking at her was the *result* of her beauty, not its *cause*.
2. *Slippery slope.*
   Explanation: This argument is built on the assumption that an action has hypothetical results that somehow, inevitably, lead from one consequence to the next.
3. *Post hoc.*
   Explanation: There is no logical connection between putting on a bracelet and winning at chess.
4. *If...then.*
   Explanation: Studying hard does not automatically lead to success.
5. *Non sequitur,* (and *Irrelevancy*).
   Explanation: So what if he's a boy? Where's the causal connection? Gender seems irrelevant to bike riding.
6. *If...then.*
   Explanation: In a literal sense, the appearance of smoke can be created by other processes such as dry ice. In a figurative sense, just because there are rumors, for example, doesn't mean that there's any truth to them.
7. *Post hoc.*
   Explanation: There is no logical connection between his receiving his license and the increase in the accident rate.
8. *Non sequitur.*
   Explanation: The book was exciting because of the way the author wrote it, *not* because you couldn't put it down.
9. *Slippery slope.*
   Explanation: This argument *assumes the inevitability of disaster* from a series of *hypothetical consequences*.

10. *Post hoc.*
    Explanation: There is no logical connection between the visit and the breakdown of the appliances. One event simply *precedes* the others: that does not mean that it *causes* them.

 43 Diversionary tactics

1. *Circular reasoning.*
   Explanation: I.Q. *is* a measure of intelligence, not a reason for it. Low I.Q. *means* not very intelligent.
2. *Begging the question* (and *Circular reasoning*).
   Explanation: Calling the critics *best* without any proof *begs the question.* This statement is also clearly circular when it maintains that Gershwin is great because the critics say so, and the critics are best because they think that Gershwin is great.
3. *Red herring* (and *If...then*).
   Explanation: Changing the subject to running the red light is a red herring. The subject was *talking* not *driving.* The if...then fallacy is — if a policeman had caught them then he would not necessarily have given them a ticket as costly as the phone calls.
4. *Irrelevancy* (and *Non sequitur*).
   Explanation: Recruiting black soldiers is *not relevant* to the question of slavery. Soldiers are volunteers. Even draftees are not slaves. The statement is also a *non sequitur*, because the one idea does not follow from the other.
5. *Circular reasoning.*
   Explanation: This statement does not explain its meaning. It simply replaces the original words with synonyms (*unchangeable=constant, real=genuine*). All it says is that "real love is unchangeable because it's real and unchangeable.
6. *Begging the question* (and *Argument by authority*).
   Explanation: The speaker *presupposes* that her novel is brilliant. That assessment is yet to be proven. To write in the style of Ernest Hemingway is not the same as having his talent. The reference to *Hemingway* is also a nod in the direction of an *argument by authority.*
7. *Irrelevancy* (and *Implied argument*).
   Explanation: The argument is *irrelevant* because Joe's academic credentials have nothing to do with how much he knows about trees. It is an *implied argument* in that it assumes that only people who go to college know anything.
8. *Circular reasoning.*
   Explanation: Instead of proving with facts, the statement repeats the same idea in different words. The only way to *outclass* someone *in cavalry* is by having *better horsemen.*

9. *Red herring.*
   Explanation: The *crying baby* changes the subject from the *barking dogs.* In any event, the situations seem parallel but are not. Dogs can be restrained whereas a baby cannot.

10. *Circular reasoning.*
    Explanation: Wealthy *means* having large financial assets. The statement does not prove anything. It merely repeats the idea.

   ## 44 Semantic slithers

1. *Equivocation.*
   Explanation: The word *advantage* is repeated with two different meanings. The first use means "favor, benefit," while the second is disparaging and means "exploitation."

2. *Equivocation.*
   Explanation: The first speaker uses the word *judgment* to mean reasoning or sense. The second speaker uses *judgments* to mean unpleasant evaluations.

3. *Loaded terminology/glittering generalization.*
   Explanation: Who doesn't support healthy children etc.? But what exactly do these glittering generalizations mean in terms of legislative action? They are merely an emotional appeal.

4. *Equivocation.*
   Explanation: God only knows means *who knows?* and has a derogatory implication, quite different in meaning from *God,* the deity.

5. *Loaded terminology/name calling.*
   Explanation: The expression *American imperialists* speaks for itself.

6. *Equivocation.*
   Explanation: The first *sound* means *free from defect.* The second *sound* means *an aural vibration.*

7. *Loaded terminology/glittering generalization.*
   Explanation: Both political euphemisms evoke desirable reactions in listeners.

8. *Loaded terminology/name calling.*
   Explanation: Calling enemies *evil* automatically establishes one's own virtue.

9. *Equivocation.*
   Explanation: The first *kind* means *benevolent.* The second *kind* casts doubt on that benevolence.

10. *Loaded terminology/name calling.*
    Explanation: Energy suppression groups suggests that conservationists want to sabotage America's energy supplies.

45 Misconstruing the argument

GROUP A

1. *Straw man argument.*
   Explanation: False restatement of the speaker's argument. The speaker said nothing about dependency. If there is such an implication, it must be analyzed not simply asserted.

2. *Decontextualizing.*
   Explanation: Context includes an *if* clause (*if we had enough money*) which the speaker ignores. He takes the promise out of its context.

3. *Attributing intent.*
   Explanation: The wife attributes to the husband an intention that the statement, taken by itself, does not justify.

4. *Either...or* (and *Oversimplification*).
   Explanation: There are more than those two options. They could have been clever, talented, knowledgeable, hardworking.

5. *Generalization.*
   Explanation: How many people constitute *all city officials*? Are there no exceptions? Just because corruption is widespread doesn't mean that Mayor Martin is corrupt.

6. *Statistics.*
   Explanation: It is a serious problem for those people who suffer from hemorrhoids. The statistics minimize the severity of the problem.

7. *False analogy.*
   Explanation: While people and animals are alike in certain basic physiological ways, they are different from one another in various complex ways: intellectually, legally, etc.

8. *Overstatement.*
   Explanation: No it's not! Wit, truth, steadfastness, beauty, courage, and integrity all precede cleanliness among human virtues. Notice that no one has ever written a play, or poem, or novel celebrating cleanliness.

9. *Oversimplification.*
   Explanation: Guessing is a simplistic explanation for a perfect SAT score. Other, more likely possibilities are intelligence, years of extensive reading and study etc.

10. *Straw man* (and *Implied Argument*).
    Explanation: The speaker's specific action is generalized and distorted. He is put into a weak position just like a straw man. Other reasonable explanations are possible. He may indeed be insensitive to the plight of the homeless, or he may make donations to established charities instead. Perhaps he was short of money. Or, perhaps he knows something specific about the person that the speaker does not know. The *implied argument* is that one shows one's concern only by giving to individual homeless people.

GROUP B

1. *False analogy.*
   Explanation: Just because people are alike in their taste in cars doesn't mean they are equally wealthy.
2. *Straw man* (and *Loaded terminology*).
   Explanation: Instead of directly attacking the Congressional proposal, this argument equates the American proposal with a Nazi law and then attacks the Nazis. The loaded teminology is in the words *rational historical perspective.* Totalitarianism and democracy are not analogous. Judge the proposal on its own merits, in its own time and culture.
3. *Overstatement.*
   Explanation: Social injustice is one contributing factor. Indeed, it may be a mitigating factor in the sentencing. But the one who committed the crimes should be the one who stands trial and pays the legal penalty.
4. *Either...or.*
   Explanation: Those are two possibilities. Other possibilities are lack of public acceptance of women in leadership positions, greater difficulty in raising funds, traditional attitudes that want to keep women in the home etc. All need to be examined. Binary thinking is limited thinking.
5. *Generalization.*
   Explanation: The generalization here is implied: that all men know how to fix the plumbing.
6. *Attributing intent.*
   Explanation: The first speaker may have a hidden motive for his comment; but, any such motive can be evaluated only in the context of the entire relationship. On its face, this statement does *not* indicate the unpleasant intention attributed by the second speaker.
7. *Statistics.*
   Explanation: The statistics may be accurate but their interpretation is not because it fails to take into consideration a host of factors other than *living conditions.* In fact, Sweden has some of the best *living conditions in the world* in terms of vacation time, health care, housing, food, social institutions etc. The answer is clearly not in the statistics.
8. *Overstatement.*
   Explanation: The lady in question may have been kind and generous, but no doubt there existed in her lifetime other equally kind and generous people. Certainly this is an overstatement born of enthusiasm. Sainthood is even more unlikely, especially as it is never conferred on the living.
9. *Generalization.*
   Explanation: Not so. The Nazis were totally in the wrong in trying to place all Europe under their tyranny and in pursuing genocide. They have *no* justification whatsoever as the Nuremberg court first ruled.
10. *Attributing intent.*
    Explanation: In fact, the first student's remark does not indicate that he thinks his colleague is stupid. Rather, *in itself* it indicates admiration.

Rhetorical Figures

Rhetoric is the art of persuading an audience through speech and writing. The previous chapter on rhetorical fallacies was about arguments that persuade by misleading. This chapter on *rhetorical figures* is about persuading with stylish and vivid language. *Rhetorical figures of speech* are arrangements of words around an image or verbal pattern designed to heighten the effect of an argument. They emphasize meaningful connections, contrasts, and repetitions. The rhetorical figures selected below are particularly applicable to expository writing.

46 Analogies

What is an analogy?

An *analogy* is a comparison between things that are not obviously similar. Its purpose is to reveal an unexpected quality in the subjects being compared. Analogies can be parallel on several levels: the most superficial level is *figurative speech*; the second level is the so-called *analogy by translation*; the deepest level includes the *extended simile and metaphor*.

46a   Figurative speech

Figurative speech injects into a phrase a quick, suggestive image that adds a new dimension of meaning. Its visual relevance is implied but not explained.

> ➤The vicar was a *giant* of a man. He *towered* over his congregation.
>
> Both *giant* and *towered* are images that suggest size in a more vivid and compelling way than *big* or *tall*.

> ➤Starting up our new website was a *tiger's leap* into the future for our company.
>
> A *tiger's leap* means an *important movement forward*. The imagery of a tiger leaping, however, suggests a dimension of danger and boldness.

Analogy by translation   *46b*

An effective way to convey an idea is to translate an abstraction into concrete terms. This is what an *analogy by translation* does. It makes numerical facts easier to grasp by transferring them into common experience. The numbers become more meaningful when they are compared to familiar images or to situations with which readers can identify. *Analogies by translation* are useful in conveying notions of size, age, value, time, and cost. Compare the facts below with the analogies that explain them.

FACT   Before the 1967 war, Israel's land area measured approximately 8000 square miles.

TRANSLATION   Before the 1967 war, Israel was smaller in area than Massachusetts.

FACT   Her Mercedes-Benz cost $80,000.

TRANSLATION   To her, $80,000 meant one vehicle to take her shopping. To me, it meant my entire college education.

FACT   Noah's ark was 450 feet long.

TRANSLATION   Noah's ark was the length of one-and-a-half football fields.

Extended simile   *46c*

Extended similes show not one but several points of likeness between images. They make their comparisons explicit by using the words *like, as, similar to* etc.

➤The human body is like a house. Its skeleton is like the structural framework; its circulatory system like the plumbing; its digestive and excretory systems like the sewers. Its nervous system is similar to electrical circuitry. Its eyes are comparable to windows.

➤Modern authors depend on the great authors of the classical past. We are like pygmies standing on the backs of giants. Although smaller in stature, we manage, with their support, to take the art of literature higher.

Extended similes can show not only a series of one-to-one comparisons, but also compound comparisons. The extended simile below compares pairs of qualities.

➤He is a man of splendid abilities, but utterly corrupt. He shines and stinks like rotten mackerel by moonlight.

— Congressman John Randolph, about New York mayor Edward Livingston

46d   Extended metaphor

Like an *extended simile*, an *extended metaphor* follows a comparison through many parallel points. The extended metaphor, however,
makes its comparison by having the subject *become* the image or
experience to which it is compared.

➤Hope is a thing with feathers that perches on the soul.

— Emily Dickinson

➤Life is a box of chocolates. After a while, when you have tried them all,
the sweetness and variety wear off and you begin to feel sick. But then
again, it's such a nice present you really can't refuse, and despite the
nausea of the last box, you begin to wish you could have another.

📖   Exercise

Identify and explain each analogy. Answers on p.264.

1. There is a 5-hour difference between New York and London. In other
   words, when I am first waking up at 6 a.m., you are getting ready to go
   to lunch.
2. The dining area is L-shaped.
3. My grandfather was the oak tree whose shade protected me from the
   heat of life's cruelties, but never limited the light of outside influences.
   So I, the little acorn, grew tall and strong spreading the branches of my
   talents and hopes in my own configuration.
4. "My heart is like a singing bird/Whose nest is in a watered shoot;/
   My heart is like an apple tree/Whose boughs are bent with thickest
   fruit [...]" (Rossetti, "A Birthday").
5. In response, she smiled a *Mona Lisa* smile that left me still wondering
   what the truth could be.

47 Irony

What is irony, and when should it be used?

Irony is a figure of speech in which the writer says something different from what he means. He signals the reader to read *counter* the literal meaning by giving *ironic cues* — words that exaggerate the situation.

In expository writing, irony is particularly useful for criticizing the behavior of people or institutions with humor and thus without obvious offense. Although humorous, irony belongs to the kind of comedy that is in the service of truth.

The most common types of irony are *hyperbole, understatement,* and *situational irony.*

Hyperbole   47a

Hyperbole is an exaggeration that overplays the image. It is different from an overstatement which is a fallacy (see §45g *Overstatement*) because it is ironic. In some hyperboles the irony is more obvious than in others.

➤ Before taking off to play golf, my boss left me *a mountain* of letters to type.

➤ I told you *five million times* to pick up your socks!

In writing, hyperbole's ironic cues tend to be subtle, noticeable mainly from context.

➤ I adore my mother-in-law and am impatient to hear once again her long and helpful lectures about my more obvious inadequacies.

The writer underscores his irony with such exaggerations as *adore* and *impatient, long, helpful, more obvious.* The subject itself indicates irony because no one likes to be criticized.

➤ Spending lottery money on building a sumptuous new city hall was a wise decision motivated by a profound appreciation of the educational needs of our city. Now at last, students can take class trips which show them that not all buildings have to be as dilapidated as their schools are.

The exaggerations *wise, profound appreciation, at last, not all buildings have to be* are clues to the writer's true feelings that the lottery money should have been spent on improving schools.

47b   Situational irony

Irony of situation depends less upon what people *say* than on what they *do*. In situational irony, fate appears to punish people for their misdeeds or to thwart their hopes.

➤Returning from the historic peace accords, the President tripped over his fighting toy poodles, hitting his head on the gangplank to Air Force One.

Readers will appreciate the ironic contrast of *peace accords* with the trivial violence of *fighting toy poodles*. The irony suggests that despite resolving one war, there is always another waiting. Equally ironic is the contrast between the indignity of the scene and the importance of the President.

➤Tweety bird squeezed through the white, pointed bars and sat down on the moist, red rug. At last he felt safe.

The alert reader will notice that the details resemble a cat's teeth and tongue.

➤Robert Oppenheimer returned home late from the laboratory once again. He opened the door to the bedroom silently, knowing that the slightest sound might set off his wife.

Oppenheimer developed the atomic bomb, and yet he is afraid of his wife's exploding in anger. The irony may be asking us to consider the more serious consequences of the bomb's explosion.

47c   Understatement

Understatement is a reverse exaggeration that underplays an image or quality. Clues to the irony lie in the ordinary descriptions of extreme qualities.

➤It is safe to say that Einstein was a *reasonably proficient* mathematician.

➤The riots in Los Angeles were *a tap on the shoulder*, reminding us of the racial tensions that still exist in America.

Another type of understatement is the *litotes*, created by combining *not* with a disparaging term. The two negatives produce a positive effect.

➤It is only right that Bill Gates donate something to charity. After all, he is *not* a *poor* man.

➤1492 is a date that has *not* gone *unremarked* by historians.

📖 **Exercise**

Identify and explain each instance of irony. Answers on p.265

1. While there were various causes of the Civil War, slavery did have something to do with it.
2. FIRST STUDENT Dissecting lab rats drives me insane. I'd rather commit suicide than do another dissection.
   SECOND STUDENT I think that dissecting rats is a beautiful and spiritual experience. Ah, the aroma of formaldehyde that clears your passages better than Channel No. 5 even if it does cause some of us to vomit on the carcass.
3. As James Bond walked in, instead of his beautiful date he saw Goldfinger flanked by thugs armed with Uzis.
4. To show his interest in education, Mr. Rockefeller endowed our university with $50 million. We can certainly consider this a step in the right direction.
5. Come in, gentlemen. Marcia, John's blind date, has also just arrived. I know they'll really like each other. She too is recovering from a recent messy divorce.... What do you mean you've met her before, John?... Marcia is your ex-wife?

48 Figures of contradiction

How can contradictory figures clarify an idea?

Considering one idea against its opposite, called *dialectical thinking*, helps us define what something *is* by contrast with what it *is not*. Irony, as above, is an implied contradiction. Other contradictory figures such the oxymoron and the paradox are more obvious. They have an explicit contrast at their core. At first glance, oxymorons and paradoxes appear absurd. Upon closer examination, the contradiction is resolved, revealing an unexpected truth.

48a

Oxymoron

An *oxymoron* is an expression that employs contradictory terms to construct seemingly contradictory images.

➤A sophomore, meaning *wise fool*, describes perfectly the student in the second year of study.

The word sophomore is an oxymoron. Its contradiction is intended to point out that second year students think they are wise before they have enough experience to be truly wise.

➤"Feather of lead, bright smoke, cold fire, sick health!" (*Romeo and Juliet*).

Romeo describes the experience of love as a series of contradictions.

➤There is nothing more relaxing than the *sound* of *silence*.

Silence means *without sound*. The *sound of silence* however, suggests that the absence of sound is as perceptible as sound.

48b

Paradox

A *paradox* is a seemingly illogical statement made up of contradictory propositions both of which are valid and point out a truth. Paradoxes are usually ironic.

➤Liars understand the truth better than honest people do. To lie is to be aware of the limits of the truth; to be honest is to be merely factual.

➤Love and hate are opposite sides of the same emotion. Both are kinds of passion.

➤In *Catch-22*, wartime pilots can apply for a discharge from the Air Force if they are insane; but by applying for the discharge, the pilots prove that they are sane and, therefore, ineligible.

Exercise

Identify and explain each figure of contradiction. Answers on p.265.

1. He had lost so much money in Las Vegas that he had to laugh.
2. Misery is the measure of contentment.
3. At the end of July, she took a two-week working vacation.
4. It is in a crowd that we can feel most alone.
5. During the 1960s, the Cold War dominated our foreign affairs while passive resistance in the civil rights movement made news on the domestic scene.

49 Figures of attention

What are figures of attention?

Writers may draw attention to an idea in a variety of ways. *figures of attention* such as *anaphora* and *rhetorical question* point out repetition or propose overarching themes.

Anaphora   **49a**

Anaphora is the repetition of a key word or phrase throughout a passage. A favorite of public speakers, anaphora emphasizes a phrase like a song's refrain.

> All over the world, particularly in the newer nations, *young men* are coming to power — *men who are not bound* by the traditions of the past — *men who are not blinded* by the old fears and hates and rivalries — *young men who* can cast off the old slogans and delusions and suspicions.
>
> — John F. Kennedy, "A New Frontier," July 15, 1960

Anaphora in the essay need not repeat exactly the same words or phrase. In the example below, the repeated structure is the negative *do not, cannot, will not.*

> The mysteries of the mind *do not* lie under the lens of a microscope, they *cannot* be found neat and whole in a Freudian volume, they *do not* reveal themselves clearly in the world of dream, they *will not* yield to the surgeon's knife.

Rhetorical question   **49b**

Writers ask a *rhetorical question* to phrase a problem clearly and succinctly in the mind of the reader. While it may not have a definitive answer, the rhetorical question invites the reader into discourse with the writer.

> What is a single life worth? Despair whispers in my ear: "Not a lot." But I refuse to give in to despair[…]. Or again: What minority is smaller and weaker than a minority of one?
>
> — Salman Rushdie, 1991

It can be answered immediately in the text, or can hang over the passage as a reminder of the theme, often recurring in the conclusion.

> ➤Mark Twain's *Huckleberry Finn* asks us to consider the questions: Where do I come from? Where am I going?

> ➤Who knows what shadows lurk in the minds of men?

📖   **Exercise**

Identify and explain each figure of attention. Answers on p.266.

1. Do not weep when I am gone. Do not feel remorse for your indifference. Do not seek to expunge your casual, small cruelties. Regret belated is regret in vain.
2. At some point in his life every man asks himself, "What is love?"
3. A penny saved is a penny earned.
4. Through a fog of pain and anesthesia I heard the nurse say, "Unless there is a miracle, she won't make it." And I thought, "So this was life? That's all there is? What did it all mean?"
5. This bill on patients' rights is the way that this Congress can protect these working poor. This bill is the fulfillment of our sacred trust to this nation.

46–49 Answers to exercises

✎   **46 Analogies**

1. *Analogy by translation.*
   Explanation: The numerical difference is translated into meaningful life activities.
2. *Figurative language.*
   Explanation: L-shaped provides a quick and clear image.
3. *Extended metaphor.*
   Explanation: The grandfather = the oak, the child = the acorn, shade = protection, sun's heat = cruelty, sun's light = influence of others, branches = talents and hopes, configuration = individuality.
4. *Extended simile.*

Explanation: Each comparison is made at more than one point: *heart* is like *singing bird,* and the bird's *nest* is in a *watered shoot* (a swift, turbulent part of a stream). In other words, the poet's heart is in a state of excitement. In the second simile, *heart* is compared to *an apple tree* with *boughs* rich with fruit. That is her heart is full of the love that grows there.

5. *Figurative language.*
   Explanation: Leonardo da Vinci's painting, the *Mona Lisa* is famous for the mysterious smile of its subject.

 47 Irony

1. *Understatement.*
   Explanation: Slavery was one of the major causes of the Civil War. The words *did have something to do with it* are an ironic understatement.
2. *Hyperbole.*
   Explanation: Both statements are hyperbolic. Obviously, the first student is exaggerating wildly in preferring *suicide* to *another dissection.* The ironic elements are much more obvious in the second student's exaggerated expressions such as *beautiful* and *spiritual* and in the comparison of *formaldehyde* to *Channel No.5.*
3. *Situational irony.*
   Explanation: The irony in the situation is clear. Bond was sure of a romantic evening. Instead he had walked into a life-threatening trap.
4. *Understatement.*
   Explanation: Clearly an understatement! Fifty million dollars is a lot more that *a step* in any circumstances.
5. *Situational irony.*
   Explanation: The irony is, of course, that the expectation of a pleasant evening with a compatible stranger turns out to be its opposite in every respect.

 48 Figures of contradiction

1. *Paradox.*
   Explanation: The response is a contradictory reaction to a loss. Yet it conveys the absurdity and helplessness that the person feels.
2. *Paradox.*
   Explanation: The paradox lies in the truth that contentment is comparative. An occasional shot of misery reminds us of how content we were. For example, it is only when we suddenly develop backpain that we realize what a pleasure it has been to be painfree.
3. *Oxymoron.*
   Explanation: The oxymoron is *working vacation.*
4. *Paradox.*

Explanation: Sometimes when we are surrounded by people, we suddenly realize that we have nothing in common with them, that they neither understand nor want to understand what we need or think or feel. The sense of aloneness is sharpest in a crowd because it is unexpected.

5. *Oxymoron.*
   Explanation: The two oxymorons are *Cold War* and *passive resistance.*

49 Figures of attention

1. *Anaphora.*
   Explanation: Repetition of *do not* and of *regret that is* is anaphoristic.
2. *Rhetorical question.*
   Explanation: It is an impossible question to answer perhaps because it has too many answers.
3. *Anaphora.*
   Explanation: Poor Richard's Almanack provided this anaphoristic saying 250 years ago. The anaphora is in the repetition of *a penny* followed by the verb in the past tense.
4. *Rhetorical question.*
   Explanation: An impossible question to answer perhaps because it has no answer at all.
5. *Anaphora.*
   Explanation: The anaphora is in the repetition for rhetorical effect of *this*: *this bill, this Congress, these working poor, this bill, this nation.*

50   Spelling rules and homophones

50a   Choosing *ie* or *ei*

Choose *ie* if the sound is a long *-e*.

➤achieve   brief   fiend   lien   piece   pier   yield

EXCEPTIONS   After *-c*; either, neither, seize, weird

➤deceive   receive

Otherwise, choose *ei*.

➤weight   height   foreign   heirloom

50b   Words ending in *-cede*

The standard way to spell this word ending is *-cede*.

➤accede   concede   intercede   secede

EXCEPTIONS supersede   exceed   proceed   succeed

50c   Prefixes

Prefixes are added to the beginning of the basic word. Add the prefix to the basic word without changing its spelling and without any hyphens. Common prefixes: *il-, in-, im-, un-, dis-, mis-, re-, over-, pre-, some-, inter-, intra-*.

➤enter ⇨ reenter   do ⇨ undo   allow ⇨ disallow

EXCEPTION Italicize and hyphenate a prefix that stands alone and modifies a word that already contains a prefix (whether hyphenated or not).

We collected all the *six-* and eight-legged creatures we could find.

50d   Suffix that never changes the spelling of the basic word

Suffixes are added at the end of the basic word. Only one suffix does not change the spelling of the basic word: *-ful*. Notice that *-ful* at the end of a word has only one *-l*.

➤wonderful   fearful   beautiful

Suffixes that change the spelling of the basic word   **50e**

With the exception of *-ful*, suffixes affect the spelling of a word in various ways. Some common suffixes are *-able, -al, -ed, -er, -est, -eth, -hood, -ing, -less, -ly, -ment, -ness, -ous.* The ending of a word determines how its spelling changes when you add a suffix.

WORDS ENDING IN *-E*

Keep the *-e* if the suffix starts with a consonant

➤ tire ⇨ tireless   love ⇨ lovely

Drop the *-e* if the suffix starts with a vowel

➤ move ⇨ movable   hope ⇨ hoping

EXCEPTION Keep the *-e* to preserve the soft sound of *-c* or *-g*

➤ peace ⇨ peaceable   courage ⇨ courageous

WORDS ENDING IN *-Y*

Keep the *-y* if the word is a one-syllable adjective

➤ shy ⇨ shyness   dry ⇨ dryly or drily

Keep the *-y* if the suffix is *-ing*

➤ try ⇨ trying   apply ⇨ applying

Keep the *-y* if a vowel precedes the *-y*

➤ obey ⇨ obeying   delay ⇨ delayed   employ ⇨ employable

Change *-y* to *-i* and add the suffix if the word ends in *-ast.*

➤ hasty ⇨ hastily   nasty ⇨ nastily

Change *-y* to *-i* to add a suffix that begins with *-e: -er, -est, -eth.*

➤ heavy ⇨ heavier   pretty ⇨ prettiest   thirty ⇨ thirtieth

Usually change *-y* to *-i* to add *-ness.*

➤ happy ⇨ happiness   lovely ⇨ loveliness

Double the final consonant when *all* of the following conditions exist:

◆ suffix begins with a vowel (*-eth, -ing, -ed, -er, -able, -ous, -al*)
◆ the basic word has only one syllable, *or* the accent is on the final syllable
◆ a single vowel precedes the final consonant

➤ begin ⇨ beginning   red ⇨ redder   compel ⇨ compellable
   drag ⇨ dragged

50f Plurals

Common and proper nouns are pluralized in the same ways usually by simply adding -*s* to the singular word.

➤brother ➪ brothers   William ➪ Williams

Otherwise, the plurals are determined by the ending of the word.

WORDS ENDING IN: -*S*, -*X*, -*Z*, -*CH*, -*SH* Add -*es*

➤bushes   fezzes   roaches   boxes   losses

EXCEPTION ox ➪ oxen

WORDS ENDING IN CONSONANT + -*Y* Change -*y* to -*i* and add -*es*

➤party ➪ parties   dummy ➪ dummies

WORDS ENDING IN -*O*

Consonant + -*o*: Add -*es*

➤potato ➪ potatoes   hero ➪ heroes

EXCEPTION hello ➪ hellos

Vowel + -*o*: Add -*s*

➤radio ➪ radios

WORDS ENDING IN -*F* /-*FE* Usually change to -*ves*

➤leaf ➪ leaves   wife ➪ wives   half ➪ halves

Often just add -*s*

➤handkerchiefs   tariffs   roofs

Sometimes both -*ves* and -*s* are correct

➤dwarfs   dwarves   hoofs   hooves

WORDS ENDING IN -*IS* Change to -*es*

➤analysis ➪ analyses   crisis ➪ crises   stasis ➪ stases   thesis ➪ theses

WORDS ENDING IN -*US* /-*USS* Usually add -*es*

➤bus ➪ buses   fuss ➪ fusses

Sometimes change -*us* to -*i*

➤syllabus ➪ syllabi   alumnus ➪ alumni   radius ➪ radii
amicus ➪ amici

Sometimes both of the above are acceptable

➤thesaurus ⇨ thesauri   thesauruses

WORDS ENDING IN *-UM* Grammatical: change *-um* to *-a*

➤agendum ⇨ agenda   datum ⇨ data   gymnasium ⇨ gymnasia,
curriculum ⇨ curricula   auditorium ⇨ auditoria   bacterium ⇨
bacteria

Acceptable:

➤Plurals — gymnasiums   auditoriums   condominiums   sanctums
forums

➤Singular — agenda

WORDS ENDING IN *-EX* Grammatical: change *-ex* to *-ices*

➤index ⇨ indices   appendix ⇨ appendices

Acceptable: add an *-es*

➤indexes   appendixes

WORDS ENDING IN *-A* Grammatical: Change *-a* to *-ae*

➤alumna ⇨ alumnae   antenna ⇨ antennae (meaning an insect's
appendages)   persona ⇨ personae   curia ⇨ curiae

Equally correct: add an *-s*

➤drama ⇨ dramas   vista ⇨ vistas   miasma ⇨ miasmas
mimosa ⇨ mimosas   antenna ⇨ antennas (referring to receptors
for television sets)

WORDS CONNECTED BY HYPHENS Add *-s* to the main part of the expression

➤editors-in-chief   brothers-in-law

(See also §56f *Pluralizing words as words,* 56g *Pluralizing abbreviations,* §56h *Pluralizing letters,* §56i *Pluralizing numbers,* §56j
Pluralizing signs.)

50g List of commonly misspelled words

A
a lot
absence
acceptance
accessible
accidentally
accommodate
acknowledge
acquainted
across
addresses
affectionate
agreeable
all right
among
analysis
anticipate
apology
appearance
approach
arrangement
assurance
attendance
authority

B
beginning
believe
benefited
boundary
Britain
business

C
calendar
campaign
categories
characteristic
chief
choice
circuit
colleagues
column
commissioner
committee
competition
completely
conceivable

conscience
conscious
consistency
continuous
cooperate
correspondence
criticize
cylinder

D
debtor
decision
definite
description
disappearance
disappointed
discipline
disgusted
doesn't
duplicate

E
each other
eighth
eligible
embarrassment
employee
environment
equipped
especially
essentially
evidence
exaggerated
excellent
excessive
excite
extension
extraordinary

F
fascinating
financial
foreign
fourth

G
government
gracious
graduation

grammar
gymnasium

H
hasten
heavily
height
hypocrite

I
icy
immediately
incidentally
inconvenience
indispensable
inevitably
innocence
inquire
insurance
intelligence
interfere
Israel

J
jealous
judgment

K
knowledgeable

L
leisure
lieutenant
loneliness

M
maintenance
malicious
maneuver
marriage
mechanic
medieval
mortgage
muscle
mutual

N
narrate
necessary
neurotic

niece
noticeable

O
obstacle
occasionally
occurrence
official
opportunity
optimistic
optimum
orchestra
originate
outwardly

P
paid
pamphlet
percentage
perspiration
persuade
pleasant
possession
possibility
practical
precision
preferred
prejudiced
preparation
primitive
privilege
probably
procedure
proceed

professional
professor
psychological
pursuit

Q
questionnaire
quiescent

R
realistic
really
reasonable
receipt
receive
recognize
recommend
reference
refrigerator
remembrance
renown
requirement
resistance
responsibility
rhythm

S
sacrifice
sacrilege
scarcely
scheme
scholarship
scissors
secretaries

sensibility
separate
shepherd
sheriff
similar
sincerely
skiing
solemn
source
sponsor
straighten
subtle
success
sufficient
surprise

T
thorough
thoughtful
transferring
truly
trying

U
unconscious
undoubtedly
unnecessary
using

V
vacuum
valuable
various

Homophones   **50h**

Homophones are words that sound exactly like other words but are spelled differently and have different meanings. Electronic spellchecks will not highlight homophone errors because the mistake is in the meaning, not in the spelling. Below is a list of commonly confused homophones. (See also §25 *Frequently misused words.*)

adapt – *v.* to adjust or fit to a specific situation or purpose.

➤Let's *adapt* the clamp to make it fit the hose.

adopt – *v.* make a member of one's family, take up and apply to one's needs.

➤ Let's *adopt* this adorable child.

➤ Let's *adopt* this excellent plan.

advice – *n.* opinion or suggestion.

➤ My *advice* is to invest in blue chip stocks only.

advise – *v.* to inform, to suggest.

➤ I *advise* you to invest in blue chip stocks only.

affect – *v.* to influence, move (*most frequent usage*).

➤ My words do not *affect* his behavior.

effect – *n.* result, consequence (*most frequent usage.*)

➤ The *effect* of my speech was to make him do the opposite of what I said.

allusion – *n.* indirect reference.

➤ The professor made an *allusion* to Thomas Hardy.

illusion – *n.* mistaken perception.

➤ That vision is not real; it's just an *illusion.*

already – *adv.* by a given time.

➤ It is *already* too late to repair the damage.

all ready – *adj.* prepared.

➤ Are we *all ready* to hear the news?

altar – *n.* raised area for religious ceremonies.

➤ They were married at the *altar* in a traditional religious ceremony.

alter – *v.* to change.

➤ The seamstress *altered* the dress to make it fit me better.

altogether – *adv.* entirely, on the whole.

➤ It was *altogether* appropriate to serve the salad before the main course.

➤ *Altogether,* it was a very pleasant evening.

all together – *adj.* everyone gathered as a group.

➤ We were gathered *all together* at the railroad station to give the orchestra a proper farewell.

a while – *n.* An undetermined amount of time; can be the object of a prepositional phrase.

➤The customer waited *for a while* and then left the store abruptly.

awhile – *adv.* An undetermined amount of time; never the object of a preposition.

➤The customer waited *awhile* and then left the store abruptly.

bare – *adj.* naked, without decoration, undisguised.

➤He walks in the snow in his *bare* feet.

bear – *v.* to tolerate, to give birth to.

➤I can't *bear* to think how cold his bare feet are.

breaks – *v.* smashes.

➤That's a valuable vase. Make sure that no one *breaks* it.

brakes – *n.* device for stopping vehicles.

➤I need to get the *brakes* repaired on my car.

business – *n.* place of work or commerce, affair.

➤Her new *business* is an elegant pastry shop.

busyness – *n.* condition of being occupied.

➤My *busyness* keeps me from visiting anyone.

by – *prep.* via, near.

➤I walked *by* the antique shop several times.

buy – *v.* purchase.

➤Finally I went in to *buy* that pitcher I liked.

capital – *n.* city which is the seat of the government, money.

➤The *capital* of Connecticut is Hartford.

➤I invested my *capital* in Internet stocks.

capitol – *n.* building in the capital where the government transacts its business.

➤It's easy to recognize the *capitol* because it has a gold dome.

cite – *v.* to quote, to mention, to commend.

➤You forgot to *cite* the title of the text.

sight – *n.* view, vision.

➤The Washington Monument was a breathtaking *sight*.

site – *n.* location, place.

➤Which state is the *site* of the Battle of Gettysburg?

choose – *v.* select.

➤I *choose* my friends carefully.

chews – *v.* masticates.

➤He *chews* thoroughly before swallowing.

coarse – *adj.* not refined.

➤That is a *coarse* expression. Polite people do not use such language.

course – *n.* track, way.

➤The *course* they followed was difficult but satisfying.

compliment – *n., v.* praise, to express admiration.

➤He *complimented* me gallantly, and I enjoyed this *compliment*.

complement – *n., v.* that which completes, to complete or to fulfill.

➤My father is great at planning, while my mother actually does the work. They *complement* each other.

counsel – *n.* advice, discussion, guidance; *v.* to advise.

➤He *counseled* the graduates to remember their ideals, and I took his *counsel* to heart.

council – *n.* a government body or assembly.

➤The governing *council* of the organization included representatives from each state.

dessert – *n.* after-dinner sweet.

➤We'll have apple pie for *dessert*.

desert – *n.* arid and barren terrain.

➤The *desert* is cold at night.

devise – *v.* invent, contrive.

➤He *devised* a clever escape plan.

device – *n.* an object such as a machine, a contrivance; an emblem.

> ➤The *device* was a primitive flying machine.

> ➤The stranger had a strange *device* embroidered on her dress.

die – *v.* perish, stop living.

> ➤Mortals all eventually *die*.

dye – *v.* change the color of; *n.* chemical used to change a color.

> ➤She *dyed* the dress royal purple using a mulberry *dye*.

discreet – *adj.* judicious, prudent.

> ➤He was *discreet* and never revealed my secret.

discrete – *adj.* consisting of unconnected parts.

> ➤We put together the *discrete* pieces of the puzzle to form a single picture.

eminent – *adj.* outstanding, notable.

> ➤The *eminent* composer received another award.

imminent – *adj.* about to occur.

> ➤We'd better hurry because the awards ceremony is *imminent*.

hanger – *n.* an object used to hang items such as clothes.

> ➤Hang your coat on this *hanger*.

hangar – *n.* a garage for airplanes.

> ➤The airplane is in the *hangar*.

illicit – *adj.* illegal.

> ➤You can be arrested for *illicit* activities.

elicit – *v.* draw out from.

> ➤I tried to *elicit* an emotional response from my audience.

insure – *v.* guarantee a person payment for loss.

> ➤Did you *insure* the car against collision?

ensure – *v.* make certain.

> ➤Check the numbers to *ensure* their correctness.

its – *possessive pronoun.*

> ➤*Its* name is Lassie.

it's – *contraction* for "it is."

> ➤*It's* getting late.

led – *v.* guided.

> ➤The Sherpa guide *led* us up Mount Everest.

lead – *n.* a metal.

> ➤*Lead* is poisonous and can cause brain damage.

lessen – *v.* to reduce.

> ➤Let's *lessen* the load on the donkey by removing some of the baggage.

lesson – *n.* that which is learned.

> ➤This was a good *lesson*. I learned a lot.

libel – *n.* written defamation of a person's character.

> ➤What he wrote about me was pure *libel*. It was untrue and meant to damage me.

liable – *adj.* legally responsible.

> ➤Each person is *liable* for her own actions.

lightning – *n.* bolt of light in the sky.

> ➤The *lightning* lit up the night sky for a moment. We knew the storm was near.

lightening – *adj.* becoming less dark.

> ➤The sky is *lightening* in the East. Morning is near.

loose – *adj.* not tight.

> ➤This fitting is *loose*. No wonder the lamp doesn't work.

lose – *v.* misplace.

> ➤Do not *lose* this key. It's my only one.

minor – *n.* one who is not legally an adult.

> ➤*Minors* cannot vote.

miner – *n.* one who digs for minerals underground.

> ➤Coal miners often get black lung disease.

naval – *adj.* of the sea.

> ➤The *naval* base stored some old ships as well as new submarines.

navel – *n.* belly button.

> ➤Be sure to wash your *navel* when you shower.

one – *adj.* single unit; *pron.* someone.

> ➤*One* can always trust *one's* common sense.

> ➤There was only *one* tomato left.

won – *v.* triumphed, was victorious.

> ➤We *won* the competition.

passed – *v.* moved ahead.

> ➤They *passed* us on the road.

past – *n.* time gone by.

> ➤For the *past* five years we have lived in La Jolla.

piece – *n.* a portion of.

> ➤Give me a *piece* of bread.

peace – *n.* opposite of war.

> ➤Stop arguing. Let's make *peace*.

plain – *n.* large flat land region; *adj.* simple, unadorned, obvious.

> ➤The arctic *plain* seemed to stretch forever.

> ➤The outfit was very *plain* with no decoration.

plane – *n.* geometric surface, carpenter's tool, short for airplane.

> ➤The carpenter smoothed the surface of the door with his *plane*.

pray – *v.* to talk to a deity, to beg.

> ➤He *prayed* for good fortune.

prey – *v.* to hunt; *n.* a quarry.

> ➤He *preyed* on those weaker than he was.

> ➤The *prey* lay still hoping the predator will not notice it.

principle – *n.* basic law, belief, code.

> ➤It's not the money but the *principle* that counts.

principal – *n.* highest in rank, administrator of a school, money that is the main part of an estate.

➤The *principal* let school out early today.

➤The bank paid me $200 interest on the *principal* in my account.

shown – *v.* indicated.

➤Your statistics have been *shown* to be wrong.

shone – *v.* glowed.

➤The fire *shone* brightly.

stationary – *adj.* standing still.

➤The sailboat was *stationary* because there was no wind.

stationery – *n.* writing paper.

➤This is elegant engraved *stationery*!

then – *adv.* after a time.

➤First we ate, *then* we brushed our teeth.

than – *conj. indicating a comparison.*

➤Her teeth are whiter *than* mine.

they're – *contraction for* they are.

➤*They're* very happy together.

their – *pron.*

➤*Their* baby is called Nicholas.

there – *adv.* at that place, not here.

➤He is not *there* yet.

threw – *v.* past tense of *to throw.*

➤He *threw* the ball.

through – *prep.*

➤The ball went *through* the window.

throne – *n.* royal seat.

➤The princess sat on a golden *throne*.

thrown – *v.* flung.

➤The baseball was *thrown* into the stands.

to – *prep.*

> ➤We went *to* the movie which was *too* scary for my taste.

too – *adv.* very, extremely, also.

> ➤Did you go *too*?

two – *adj.* one plus one.

> ➤The *two* of us went to the movies.

vary – *v.* change, differ.

> ➤Temperatures *vary* greatly in New England, as much as ten degrees in a single day.

very – *adv.* to a great degree, extremely.

> ➤Today is a *very* hot day.

waive – *v.* give up.

> ➤I *waived* my right to an attorney.

wave – *v.* flutter or flap; *n.* undulation, curve, swell of water.

> ➤The towel *waved* in the wind.

> ➤The *wave* of salt water hit me unexpectedly.

waiver – *n.* deliberate giving up of a claim or right.

> ➤He signed a *waiver* to the property, so that it became entirely mine.

waver – *v.* to be indecisive.

> ➤He *wavered* unsure of which way to turn.

waste – *v.* to use recklessly and unnecessarily; *n.* trash, a barren place or ruin.

> ➤Don't *waste* water.

> ➤The place was a *wasteland* where nothing grew, and which people had littered with *waste*.

waist – *n.* place on the body where a belt is worn.

> ➤She had a tiny *waist*.

weather – *n.* atmosphere on a given day; *v.* to resist or withstand, to become discolored.

> ➤The *weather* was sunny.

> ➤We *weathered* the storm by taking shelter in the *weathered* barn.

whether – *conj.* in the case that, if.

➤Time passes *whether* or not we want it to.

week – *n.* a period of seven days.

➤Last *week* I worked only three days.

weak – *adj.* lacking strength.

➤They felt *weak* after their illness.

who's – *contraction* for "who is."

➤*Who's* coming to dinner?

whose – *pron.*

➤*Whose* friend is coming to dinner?

yoke – *n.* burden; *v.* to join or harness together.

➤This *yoke* is too heavy for me.

➤The peasant *yoked* the oxen and began to plow.

yolk – *n.* yellow center of an egg.

➤This egg has a double *yolk*.

your – *pron.*

➤*Your* sister looks just like you.

you're – *contraction* for "you are"

➤*You're* the winner of this contest.

yore – *n.* former times, long ago

➤In days of *yore*, the knights were all bold and the ladies all virtuous.

📖 Exercise

Select the correct homophones. Answers on p.293.

GROUP A

1. Let's (adapt, adopt) Robert's Rules of Order for our meetings, just as they are without (adapting, adopting) them.
2. I (advice, advise) you to keep quiet and let your lawyer do the talking. After all, you're paying her for her (advice, advise).
3. The Mayor's policy (affected, effected) us in a very helpful way. Its (affect, effect) was to increase job openings in our town.
4. My wife is under the (allusion, illusion) that everyone is waiting for her instructions.
5. It is (already, all ready) past six, and the rest of us have been (already, all ready) for half an hour.
6. Let's walk down the aisle to the (altar, alter) before you (altar, alter) your decision.
7. The family was gathered (all together, altogether), and there were (all together, altogether) too many of us to fit comfortably at the table.
8. (Baring, bearing) children is a painful process, and that's the simple, (bare, bear) truth.
9. He doesn't step on the (brakes, breaks) and consequently (brakes, breaks) down the garage wall.
10. I may be occupied all the time, but my (business, busyness) is none of his (business, busyness).

GROUP B

1. Did you (by, buy) that car at the dealership (by, buy) the theater?
2. The (capital, capitol) of our state has a beautiful (capital, capitol) building.
3. I recognized the Lincoln Memorial on (cite, sight, site) and was inspired to (cite , sight, site) all the architects who have praised it. The monument has been standing on this (cite , sight, site) for many years.
4. My mother and I (choose, chews) to spend a lot of time at the dinner table because, like me, she (choose, chews) her food slowly and thoroughly.
5. Of (coarse, course) I use (coarse, course) salt in my marinades!
6. They (compliment, complement) each other perfectly. She pays him (compliments, complements), and he accepts them.
7. The city (counsel, council) met and listened to the (counsel's, council's) suggestions.
8. (Dessert, desert) tribesmen like to eat figs for (dessert, desert).
9. We will have to (devise, device) an original (devise, device) for our new firm's logo.
10. I will (die, dye) of embarrassment if you (die, dye) your hair purple.

GROUP C

1. She was too (discrete, discreet) to tell anyone how I made a fool of myself.
2. The (eminent, imminent) professor was going to lecture on the (eminent, imminent) political crisis.
3. He tried to (illicit, elicit) information from the prisoner about the (illicit, elicit) activities of the gang.
4. Can you (ensure, insure) that the company will (ensure, insure) this painting?
5. (It's, its) time for the cat to get (it's, its) rabies shot.
6. She (lead, led) us to the buried treasure. But it proved to be not silver but (lead, led).
7. The (lessen, lesson) is to lose weight and (lessen, lesson) the strain on your heart. That means fatty egg (yokes, yolks) should no longer be on your menu.
8. People should not be able to (libel, liable) others. They should be (libel, liable) for what they write.
9. The (lightening, lightning) in the East is not the dawn; it is a (lightening, lightning) and thunder storm.
10. I told you several times that the catch on your bracelet is (loose, lose) and that you will (loose, lose) the bracelet.

GROUP D

1. (Miners, minors) are too young to vote.
2. She has a boyfriend at the U.S. (Naval, Navel) Academy.
3. The (one, won) who (one, won) the trophy was a (one-, won-) time Olympic champion.
4. The truck that (past, passed) us was a classic vehicle out of the (past, passed).
5. They signed a (piece, peace) treaty on a (piece, peace) of parchment.
6. The (plain, plane) truth was that he didn't know that this flat piece of land was a (plain, plane).
7. She (preyed, prayed) to the God of her ancestors in (Whose, Who's) power she had great faith.
8. The basic (principal, principle) of investment is to protect your (principal, principle).
9. The signal they had (shone, shown) me (shone, shown) in the tower of the Old North Church.
10. Then (yore, your, you're) train stopped moving. It was (stationery, stationary).

GROUP E

1. (Then, than) we turned right, rather (then, than) left because we trusted our own judgment more (then, than) the old map.
2. (They're, their, there) are not many people who know (they're, their, there) way around the back roads of (they're, their, there) own county.

3. When you (through, threw) up on the carpet, I thought the lady would go (through, threw) the roof.
4. He gave up the (thrown, throne) when he was (thrown, throne) out of the royal family for marrying a commoner.
5. We were (very, vary) happy to (very, vary) our diet by adding fresh vegetables.
6. The flag (waived, waved) in the wind above the (waives, waves).
7. He (waivered, wavered) about signing the (waiver, waver).
8. Having a small (waist, waste) is a (waist, waste) if there's no one around to admire it.
9. (Whether, weather) or not you like the (whether, weather) makes no difference. We have to stay because the rental fee is non-refundable.
10. I felt very (weak, week) all last (weak, week).

51 Capitalization

Always capitalize   *51a*

1. First letter of a sentence, of a sentence within another sentence, and of a fragment intended to convey a complete thought.

   ➤Zelda said to herself, "No, Gatsby wasn't all that great!"

   ➤Does Bill Clinton really expect me to lie? And if so, to the grand jury?

2. First letter of a word in quotation marks if

   ♦ the quotation starts a quoted writer's sentence
   ♦ the quotation starts your own sentence
   ♦ the original is capitalized

   ➤Bill Gates e-mailed his broker, "Let's buy a million shares of Netscape."

   ➤"To be or not to be" is an existential question.

   ➤Robert Frost may have been referring to his own complex choices when he noted the two roads that "diverged in a yellow wood."

3. In titles of works or their subtitles, all important words especially the first and the final words both parts of hyphenated words

   ➤"The Management of Post-Secondary Institutions: Section 504 and the Disabled Student"

4. All proper nouns including:

♦   Courses of study

➤Introduction to Drawing, Music 101

♦   Groups of people

➤Greenpeace, Daughters of the Revolution, Act Up

♦   Nationalities

➤Turkish, Malaysian, Chilean

♦   Organizations and their departments

➤United Nations, Joe's Diner, Metropolitan Opera, Tulane University, Physics Department

♦   People

➤Dr. Watson

♦   Places

➤Paris, France

♦   Sacred books, deities, pronouns referring to deities

➤the Bible, God ("He" when referring to the biblical God)

5. Names of family members when a proper noun can be substituted for them

➤Did you see Mother at the party?

Mother is capitalized because it stands for her name which can be replaced by a proper noun.

6. Adjectival forms of names when they refer specifically to the noun from which they are derived

➤Elizabethan era

➤Translation from the Aramaic manuscript

➤Rabelaisian humor

➤European fashions

7. Titles of people when they precede the name or when they stand for a particular person

➤Queen Beatrix of the Netherlands

➤The Queen entered first.

8. Titles of high positions

➤The President of the United States

➤The Pope

➤The Chief Justice

9. Historical or literary events, movements, or periods

➤The Impressionists

➤The Roaring Twenties

➤The Antebellum South

➤The Lake Poets

10. Dates

◆ Days and months

➤on Saturday, next June

◆ Holidays

➤Fourth of July, Labor Day

11. Geographic direction if it indicates a specific area, not a general course or bearing

➤South of France

➤Midwest

➤Northwest Territory

Do *not* capitalize unless the terms meet the above requirements   **51b**

1. The first letter that follows a colon, unless it signals a proper noun.

➤Edgar Allan Poe: the Ushers Revisited

2. The first letter of a quotation if its meaning is *not* set apart from your sentence but flows into it

➤He was forced to believe her words, that she loved him only "as a friend."

3. In titles of works: articles, prepositions, and conjunctions unless they are the initial words

➤"The Fall of the House of Usher"

4. Names of family relationships that cannot be replaced by a proper noun

   ➤Did you see my mother at the party?

5. Titles or ranks that do *not* refer to specific people or to the names of high offices

   ➤the general

   BUT
   ➤General Patton

6. Organizations or institutions used as common nouns

   ➤He was a student at a local art school.

   ➤She ran a steel mill before her children were born.

   ➤The staff of the institute went on strike.

   (Institute can be capitalized if it is used as a proper noun.)

7. Seasons

8. Numerical parts of dates written in words

9. Words for general disciplines as opposed to specific courses. Languages, however, are always capitalized.

   ➤He enjoyed computer science.

   ➤She had a particular aptitude for mathematics.

   ➤We were always good in French.

10. Adjectival forms of sacred names unless they refer to a specific location or to an individual

    ➤godlike attributes

    ➤biblical analysis

    BUT
    ➤Christlike patience

    ➤Olympian indifference

11. References in the text to the divisions of a book, play, or poem

    ➤appendix, bibliography, chapter, glossary, index, introduction, preface

    ➤prologue, act, scene

    ➤verse, stanza, canto

12. References to general groups of people as opposed to specific clubs

➤ societies

➤ reformers

➤ conservationists

➤ homeless

➤ middle class

➤ senior citizens

➤ college freshmen

13. General geographic directions

➤ She lives east of here.

➤ Saratoga lies to the north of Albany.

52 Abbreviations

Standard abbreviations are commonly used in citing and documenting sources of information. In the main text, however, abbreviations should be used sparingly and in carefully controlled ways.

Words that may be abbreviated in the main text   *52a*

COMMON TITLES THAT PRECEDE NAMES may be abbreviated as below, and must have a space between the title and the name.

Mr.	Messrs.
Ms.	Dr.
Mrs.	St.

➤ Mr. John Wilkins

➤ Dr. Angela Wood

➤ St. Theresa

PERSONAL AND ACADEMIC TITLES THAT FOLLOW NAMES may be abbreviated. Separate the initials of the titles by periods but not spaces. A comma and space must separate the name from the title. Below are some common examples.

D.D.S.	M.A.
Esq.	M.D.
J.D.	Ph.D.
Jr.	Sr.

➤Charles Addams, Jr.

➤Naomi Rosen, J.D.

➤Robert Hertz, Esq.

INITIALS BEFORE LAST NAMES are separated by periods and spaces.

➤e. e. cummings

➤T. S. Eliot

➤J. R. R. Tolkien

PLACE NAMES may be abbreviated with or without periods depending on how commonly they are referred to by initials. In either case, do *not* separate the initials by spaces.

➤USA OR U.S.A.

➤LA OR L.A.

➤DC OR D.C.

➤UK OR U.K.

ORGANIZATIONS COMMONLY KNOWN BY THEIR INITIALS do not require either spaces or periods, and each initial must be capitalized.

➤PTA, CBS, NATO, NAACP, FBI, UNICEF

TIME ABBREVIATIONS ASSOCIATED WITH NUMBERS are always written together with the numbers. The initials are separated by periods but not by spaces. They are separated from the number by a period and a space.

◆ Always capitalized

➤600 B.C.

➤30 B.C.E.

➤A.D. 450

(A.D. precedes the date.)

◆ Capitalization that depends on the writer's preference, but which must be consistent throughout the text.

➤a.m. OR A.M.

➤P.M. OR p.m.

SPEED ABBREVIATIONS are always used with a number, but may be written without periods or intervening spaces.

➤80 mph OR 80 m.p.h.

➤80 rpm OR 80 r.p.m.

MISCELLANEOUS TERMS

➤etc. – May be italicized if the writer considers it a foreign expression.

➤IOU — Always capitalized, no periods, no spaces.

➤viz or viz. – May be italicized or not and may be written with or without a period.

Words that may *not* be abbreviated in the main text   *52b*

NAMES

➤Charles (*not* Chas.), Robert (*not* Robt.), Irving (*not* Irv.)

POLITICAL AND MILITARY TITLES

➤President (*not* Pres.), Senator (*not* Sen.), Admiral (*not* Adm.)

TITLES PRECEDED BY *THE*

➤the Reverend Dr. King (*not* Rev.), the Honorable Margaret Smith (*not* Hon.), the Archbishop of Canterbury (*not* Arch.)

PLACE NAMES (except as noted above)

➤Philadelphia (*not* Phila.), Michigan (*not* Mich.)

STREET NAMES

➤Avenue (*not* Ave.), Street (*not* St.), Boulevard (*not* Blvd.), Turnpike (*not* Tpke.)

ACADEMIC COURSES

➤Geography (*not* Geog.), Sociology (*not* Soc.), Psychology (*not* Psych.)

HOLIDAYS

➤Christmas (*not* Xmas), Memorial (*not* Mem.) Day

DAYS AND MONTHS

➤Tuesday (*not* Tues.), February (*not* Feb.)

MEASUREMENTS

➤inches (*not* in.), feet (*not* ft.), pounds (*not* lbs.), minutes (*not* mins.), months (*not* mos.)

MISCELLANEOUS WORDS

➤versus (*not* vs., v.)

52c Abbreviations in citation and documentation

ABBREVIATION	IN FULL	MEANING
anon.		anonymous
bibliog.		bibliography
c., ca.	*circa*	about, around (used with dates)
can.		canto
cf.	*confer*	compare
ch., chs.		chapter(s)
comp.		compiled, compiler
diss.		dissertation
ed., eds.		edited by, edition(s), editor(s)
e.g.	*exempli gratia*	for example
esp.		especially
et al.	*et alibi*	and elsewhere
	et alii	and others
etc.	*et cetera*	and so forth
et seq.	*et sequens*	and the following
f., ff.		and the following page(s)
fac.		facsimile
fn.		footnote
front.		frontispiece
gloss.		glossary
ib., ibid.	*ibidem*	in the same place
i.e.	*id est*	that is
ill.		illustrated, illustration
include.		including, inclusive
ind.		index
inf.	*infra*	below
introd.		introduction

jour.		journal
l., ll.		line(s)
loc. cit.	*loco citato*	in the place cited
ms., mss., MS, MSS		manuscript(s)
n., nn.		note(s)
N.B.,	*nota bene*	note well, take notice
n.d.		no date (in an imprint)
No., no., nos.	*numero*	number (s)
op.	*opus*	work
op. cit.	*opere citato*	in the work cited
p., pp.		page(s)
pl., pls.		plate(s)
pref.		preface
pt., pts.		part(s)
pub.		published, publisher
q.v.	*quod vide*	see elsewhere in this text
Q.E.D.	*quod erat demonstrandum*	which was to be demonstrated
Sic, sin		so
R.I.P.	*requiescat in pace*	may he/she rest in peace
viz, viz.	*videlicet (videre licet)*	namely

50 Answers to exercises

 ## 50h Homophones

GROUP A

1. Let's *adopt* Robert's Rules of Order for our meetings, just as they are without *adapting*, them.
2. I *advise* you to keep quiet and let your lawyer do the talking. After all, you're paying her for her *advice*.
3. The Mayor's policy *affected* us in a very helpful way. Its *effect* was to increase job openings in our town.
4. My wife is under the *illusion* that everyone in town is waiting for her instructions.
5. It is *already* past six, and the rest of us have been *all ready* for half an hour.
6. Let's walk down the aisle to the *altar* before you *alter* your decision.
7. The family was gathered *all together*, and there were *altogether* too many of us to fit comfortably at the table.
8. *Bearing* children is a painful process, and that's the simple, *bare* truth.

9. He doesn't step on the *brakes*, and consequently *breaks* down the garage wall.
10. I may be occupied all the time, but my *busyness* is none of his *business*.

GROUP B

1. Did you *buy* that car at the dealership *by* the theater?
2. The *capital* of our state has a beautiful *capitol* building.
3. I recognized the Lincoln Memorial on *sight*, and was inspired to *cite* all the architects who have praised it. The monument has been standing on this *site* for many years.
4. My mother and I *choose*, to spend a lot of time at the dinner table because, like me, she *chews* her food slowly and thoroughly.
5. Of *course* I use *coarse* salt in my marinades!
6. They *complement* each other perfectly. She pays him *compliments* and he accepts them.
7. The city *council* met and listened to the *counsel's* suggestions.
8. *Desert* tribesmen like to eat figs for *dessert*.
9. We will have to *devise* an original *device* for our new firm's logo.
10. I will *die* of embarrassment if you *dye* your hair purple.

GROUP C

1. She was too *discreet* to tell anyone how I made a fool of myself.
2. The *eminent* professor was going to lecture on the *imminent* political crisis.
3. He tried to *elicit* information from the prisoner about the *illicit* activities of the gang.
4. Can you *ensure* that the company will *insure* this painting?
5. *It's* time for the cat to get *its* rabies shot.
6. She *led* us to the buried treasure. But it proved to be not silver but *lead*.
7. The *lesson* is to lose weight and *lessen* the strain on your heart. That means fatty egg *yolks* should no longer be on your menu.
8. People should not be able to *libel* others. They should be *liable* for what they write.
9. The *lightening* in the East is not the dawn; it is a *lightning* and thunder storm.
10. I told you several times that the catch on your bracelet is *loose* and that you will *lose* the bracelet.

GROUP D

1. *Minors* are too young to vote.
2. She has a boyfriend at the U.S. *Naval* Academy.
3. The *one*, who *won* the trophy was a *one*-time Olympic champion.
4. The truck that *passed* us was a classic vehicle out of the *past*.
5. They signed a *peace* treaty on a *piece* of parchment.

6. The *plain* truth was that he didn't know that this flat piece of land was a *plain*.
7. She *prayed* to the God of her ancestors in *Whose* power she had great faith.
8. The basic *principle* of investment is to protect your *principal*.
9. The signal they had *shown* me *shone* in the tower of the Old North Church.
10. Then *your* train stopped moving. It was *stationary*.

GROUP E

1. *Then* we turned right, rather *than* left because we trusted our own judgment more *than* the old map.
2. *There* are not many people who know *their* way around the back roads of *their* own county.
3. When you *threw* up on the carpet, I thought the lady would go *through* the roof.
4. He gave up the *throne* when he was *thrown* out of the royal family for marrying a commoner.
5. We were *very* happy to *vary* our diet by adding fresh vegetables.
6. The flag *waved* in the wind above the *waves*.
7. He *wavered* about signing the *waiver*.
8. Having a small *waist* is a *waste* if there's no one around to admire it.
9. *Whether* or not you like the *weather* makes no difference. We have to stay because the rental fee is non-refundable.
10. I felt very *weak* all last *week*.

Punctuation

Writing with incorrect punctuation is like driving without road signs or traffic lights, or, worse still, with the wrong signs and lights. Mispunctuated writing is disorienting and misleading. Correct punctuation divides a sentence into groups of words that fit together logically. It signals when a person is speaking and for how long, when a sentence begins and ends, whether the sentence is a question or a statement.

53 Commas

What do commas do?

Commas perform the following functions:

- ◆ Separate complete thoughts (independent clauses) in a sentence to prevent a run-on sentence
- ◆ Set apart introductory material
- ◆ Set apart incidental information
- ◆ Indicate the person being addressed
- ◆ Introduce dialogue informally
- ◆ Separate items in a list
- ◆ Separate repeated or similar words that may create confusion

53a Avoid run-on sentences and comma splices

A *run-on* sentence occurs when two or more sentences are punctuated as if they were a single sentence. If two or more complete ideas (independent clauses) are closely related to each other in meaning, the author may keep them in the same sentence. However, she must separate them by a *comma* and a *conjunction* such as *and, but, or, nor, yet, so.*

➤Robert may have been tardy today *but* he is usually punctual.

Using a comma without the conjunction is called a *comma splice,* and also results in a run-on sentence.

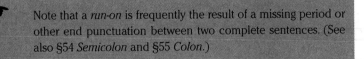

Note that a *run-on* is frequently the result of a missing period or other end punctuation between two complete sentences. (See also §54 *Semicolon* and §55 *Colon.*)

EXCEPTIONS No conjunction is needed if the two complete ideas are close in meaning and also seem to contradict each other.

➤The more she thought about it, the angrier she became.

➤Macbeth's courage is impressive, however repellent his crimes.

The word *however* in this example is not a conjunction meaning *but*, but an adverb meaning *regardless* or *in spite of.*

No comma is needed between short ideas that state or suggest a contrast. The first two examples below are complete sentences, not fragments, because their verbs are implied.

➤The later the better.

➤The more the merrier.

Set apart introductory material 53b

Introductory material takes a comma if it is an interjection, a lengthy phrase, a subordinate clause, or a standard transitional expression: *namely, e.g., i.e., in other words, that is, specifically, otherwise, consequently, accordingly, especially, in particular* etc.

INTERJECTION	*Ugh,* I hate worms!
PHRASE	*Having eaten only an hour before,* I simply was not hungry enough for a large meal.
SUBORDINATE CLAUSE	*While the teacher was lecturing,* John took a nap.
TRANSITIONAL EXPRESSION	*Specifically,* your color, technique, and balance need work. *Otherwise,* you have a beautiful painting.
	In other words, you're saying that you hate my painting.

Do *not* use a comma after short introductory expressions.

➤*On Mondays* he never went to the office.

Set apart incidental material 53c

Incidental information is not vital to the meaning of the sentence. Unlike essential information in *restrictive* phrases and clauses, incidental information can be removed from a sentence without changing its basic meaning. Clauses and phrases containing incidental information are sometimes called *non-restrictive*. Enclose incidental clauses and phrases in commas.

INCIDENTAL CLAUSE	The ballet, *which had a beautiful prima ballerina*, made a lasting impression on him.

BUT

ESSENTIAL CLAUSE	Jerry *who never obeys traffic signs* was hit by a car.
INCIDENTAL PHRASE	I want to hear every word he said, *regardless of its importance*.

➤Discussing problems protects, *rather than endangers*, children.

➤Our neighbor, *the gardener*, weeds early each morning.

53d   Identify a speaker by commas

Place a comma either before or after the name of the person being addressed. If the name is in the middle of the sentence, place commas both before and after it.

➤*Miles*, you're being obnoxious!

➤Let's go to a movie, *Adele*.

➤I think, *my dear,* that you are mistaken.

53e   Commas in dialogue and with quotations inside quoted speech

Short or informal dialogue like a short quotation or a casual conversation is set off by a comma. (See also §63 *Punctuating and capitalizing with quotations.*)

➤Ellen ran into the room and called out, "We have a guest!"

If the end of the dialogue coincides with the end of the sentence, place an appropriate end punctuation mark — a period, an exclamation point, or a question mark — inside the quotation marks, as in the example above. Otherwise, place a comma before the close-quotation marks.

➤"Mother's upstairs," said Anthony Perkins.

If a quotation inside quoted speech is a complete sentence, it is preceded by either a comma or a colon. (See also §64 *Punctuating a quotation-within-a-quotation.*)

➤Looking at the overgrown flower garden, Mother said sadly, "I know, 'Tis an unweeded garden grown to seed.'"

> *Before* a quotation, the comma precedes the open-quotation mark. *After* a quotation, the comma precedes the close-quotation mark.

Using commas in a list 53f

Use commas when a list or series contains *three or more items.* Place a comma before the conjunction connecting the last two items in the list. Do not use a comma in a list that has only two items.

➤Mary, Ellen, and Marcia spent the day at the carnival.

➤I recall returning the book to Bob, John, or Bill.

(For punctuating lists that contain both semicolons and commas, see §54a.)

Use commas to avoid confusion with repeated or ambiguous words 53g

Separate with a comma two identical words when they appear next to each other in a sentence. Also use a comma to avoid ambiguity.

➤The new resident didn't like the way he was stared *at, at* the town meeting.

➤In tests the Mustang's rear suspension dominated in *turning, over* the Camaro's.

Notice how the comma between *turning* and *over* corrects the misperception that the Mustang's rear suspension turned over the Camaro's rear suspension.

EXCEPTION Do *not* place commas inside a verb phrase even when the conjugated verb is repeated.

➤I remembered that just the month before we had (*no comma*) had wonderful rapport.

53h   When commas are not used

Commas should not come between the following parts of the sentence:

SUBJECT AND A VERB unless the commas enclose an incidental clause or phrase.

➤Many of my friends who like jazz (*no comma*) also enjoy opera.

                                        BUT

➤Many of my friends who like jazz, *like Martin, Ralph, and Eleanor,* also enjoy opera.

VERB AND A COMPLEMENT unless the commas enclose an incidental clause or phrase.

➤The unpleasant rumor about Shoeless Joe Jackson was (*no comma*) that he shaved runs off his performance in the World Series to pay off gambling debts.

                                        BUT

➤The unpleasant rumor about Shoeless Joe Jackson was, *according to one gossip columnist,* that he shaved runs off his performance in the World Series to pay off gambling debts.

PARTS OF A TWO-PART COMPOUND SUBJECT, VERB, COMPLEMENT

➤Joseph (*no comma*) and several of his brothers fished in the Nile.

➤Joseph camped in the desert (*no comma*) and fished in the Nile.

➤Joseph caught not only fish (*no comma*) but even a crocodile.

MONTH AND A YEAR, OR A SEASON AND A YEAR

➤We saw the Statue of Liberty for the first time in *April 1947.*

➤Five years later we became citizens in *summer 1952.*

WORD AND THE PHRASE OR CLAUSE THAT DESCRIBES IT and is *essential* to its meaning

➤The recollection (*no comma*) of his triumph (*no comma*) made him flush with pleasure.

➤The gramophone was one of the inventions (*no comma*) that made Thomas Edison famous.

PARTS OF A TWO-PART LIST

➤ That year Serena Williams took first place both at Wimbledon (*no comma*) and at the U.S. Open.

(See also §63d *No punctuation before quotation marks.*)

📖 Exercise

Correct any errors in commas. Answers on p.339.

GROUP A

1. Space travel opens limitless vistas for exploration. The moon today, the cosmos tomorrow.
2. Whenever Arnold and I lifted weights he removed his shirt revealing his biceps usually the most impressive in the gym.
3. "Wow Dad this tropical fruit drink is unusually sweet yet it is refreshing" I said.
4. Billiards or pool a game I could never master requires a strong sense of spatial relations much as geometry does.
5. That young woman in the gold evening gown, is the guest of honor at this reception.
6. "Batman" said Robin "it might be a good idea to take off your utility belt the next time you shower."
7. The desserts at Thanksgiving included peach pie vanilla ice cream and brownies.
8. He ignored the older members of the family i.e. those over thirty.
9. His aunt was the person he ran to to say that he was hurt.
10. I first met the man who became my husband at the Harvest Festival in spring, 1998.

GROUP B

1. The hotel register showed that the tour group members had signed in in pairs.
2. Her eyes shining with pride Nadia wearing her medal posed with her coach for the photograph.
3. At first, I was angry, and hurt at not having been chosen for a speaking part in the play.
4. He used his charm to win over enemies.
5. Whoever he may be he looks like someone accustomed to giving orders.
6. In June, 1995, he graduated from high school, and went to work.
7. Attila the Hun of course never called back after our first date so I didn't get the chance to tell him what I thought of his behavior.
8. In August Mother, Tom, and David vacationed on Cape Cod.
9. There were many causes for the Civil War from the South's insistence on states' rights to slavery.
10. After a long and pleasant reunion, my former college roommates, and I promised to e-mail, and phone one another at least once a month.

54 Semicolon

When do you use a semicolon?

Semicolons separate *complete thoughts* that are too dependent upon each other for a period, but whose meaning is not related closely enough for a comma. Semicolons can also separate items in lists. Semicolons may be — but do not need to be — accompanied by conjunctions.

54a   Semicolons between complete thoughts and in lists

Use semicolons between *complete thoughts* of *equal importance*. Sometimes these independent clauses are joined by such adverbial conjunctions as *indeed, therefore, however, consequently, but, thus, then, hence.*

➤I never phoned the train station; consequently, I missed the train.

➤Freedom enhances the imagination; structure disciplines it.

Also, use semicolons in a list to separate information that contains commas.

➤Leading the protest were Donna Presnell, founder of the League for Stray Animals; Tom Snyder, the antiquarian; and Caroline Evanson, author of *The Computer Expert.*

📖   Exercise

Correct any errors in semicolons. Answers on p.341.

1. Her appearance proclaimed her self-confidence her resolve was weakened by secret misgivings.
2. Reportedly Marilyn Monroe always felt insecure, despite the fact; that she was renowned for her beauty.
3. Her guest list included Christian Barnard, a young surgeon, William Rehnquist, who had just passed his bar exam, and Ella Fitzgerald, an aspiring singer.
4. The trip was a depressing trek over miles of run-down motels and greasy fast food joints the return home a re-entry into sanity.
5. He decided that the three films he had enjoyed the most were *Casablanca, Sex, Lies, and Videotape,* and *Unforgiven.*

6. At Gettysburg the Confederates attacked the Union forces on Cemetery Ridge; which is adjacent to Cemetery Hill, a strategically important site.

7. The course was advertised as an introduction for beginners, it proved to be an exercise in graduate education.

8. For many tourists, the most important items to pack are their camera; their dictionary; and their favorite shampoo, which may be hard to find in out-of-the-way locations.

9. His smile was like a ray of sunlight, his frown like the dark of the moon.

10. Just as Coleridge was writing down the poem that had come to him in his dream; the knock at the door interrupted him; consequently, the poem was never completed.

55 Colon

How is the colon different from the semicolon?

Both the semicolon and the colon must be preceded by an independent clause. However, the colon does *not* have to be followed by a complete thought. Another difference between them is that the thought which follows the colon *is less important* than the thought in the first clause. The second clause merely elaborates on or explains the meaning of first clause. In addition, while a semicolon separates groups of items *within* a list, a colon *precedes* a list. The colon also precedes certain quoted remarks.

Colons preceding supplementary information   *55a*

Use a colon after an independent clause when the secondary clause merely explains or provides more information about the primary clause.

➤ As late as the 1950s, individuals in the Soviet Union seldom had personal privacy: entire families lived in a single room in communal apartments.

➤ Peggy was tormented by a serious ethical consideration: whether or not to reveal her friend's misbehavior.

55b ## Colons preceding lists

Use colons in front of lists, especially after such expressions as *follows, following, including, to wit.*

➤ The chef checked off the ingredients needed for the sponge cake: flour, sugar, eggs, vanilla, and orange juice.

➤ In choosing our apartment, we must consider the following: cost, neighborhood, proximity to our jobs, availability of parking.

55c ## Introducing quotations and salutations formally

Use a colon before a quotation of *three lines or longer* that is set apart from the rest of the text. Such a quotation does not require quotation marks.

Use a colon instead of a comma before a short quotation or before formal dialogue that is part of your sentence *but whose grammar or sentence structure is different from yours.* In the example below, the text is in the past tense, while the quoted material is in the future tense.

➤ The news reports of that day recorded General MacArthur's promise: "I shall return."

Use a colon after a formal salutation in a business letter.

➤ Dear Mr. Birnbaum:

➤ Dear Sir or Madam:

55d ## Referring to time and citing texts

Use a colon between

HOUR AND MINUTE

➤ 10:15 a.m.

VOLUME AND NUMBER (OR PAGE NUMBERS)

➤ *Newsweek* 12:3

BIBLICAL CHAPTER AND VERSE

➤ Exodus 1:5

TITLE AND SUBTITLE

➤ *Recollection: Memory in the Work of William Faulkner*

Using colons incorrectly 55e

Never use more than one colon per sentence.

➤To equip my home office, I purchased the following electronic equipment:
a computer, a laser printer, a scanner, and a voice mail ~~system: it~~ *system. It* was a
large investment.

Never use a colon after a preposition.

➤My students rejected the notion of homework ~~on: weekends~~ *on weekends*, holidays,
and before school dances.

Never use a colon after the relative pronoun *that.*

➤The note announced ~~that: he~~ *that he* refused to work overtime, wanted a raise,
and was going fishing on Monday.

Never use a colon after a verb, unless that verb precedes
dialogue in quotation marks.

➤For my birthday I ~~received: rollerblades~~ *received rollerblades*, a book on origami, and tickets
to a Broadway show.

BUT

➤The President's birthday greeting was as pleasant as it was unexpected.
He wrote: "Happy birthday, and thank you for helping me with my
proposal on education."

Exercise

Correct any errors in colons. Answers on p.342.

1. For their camping trip Lewis and Clark bought: cooking gear,
   dehydrated food, two sleeping bags, and hiking boots.
2. Homer describes Telemachus's journey to Sparta saying "They came
   into the plain full of wheat [...]."
3. The weather discouraged travel the skies grew ever darker and
   lightning illuminated the empty road.
4. He improved his nutrition with: whole grain rice, fresh vegetables, and
   fish in his diet.
5. Horace Greeley's command proved distinctly prophetic, "Go West,
   young man!"
6. Three main ways to judge the all-time greatest baseball team are: fan
   support, individual player success, and overall team success.
7. The reason Jesse James turned to robbing trains is easy to explain; as a
   child, he didn't have a train set of his own.

8. Safety features are important in that: they help both to prevent accidents and to reduce their seriousness.
9. She was already late for class accordingly, she skipped breakfast.
10. Dear Dr. Maxwell: In response to your query, my seminar addresses three topics: first, the danger of global warming, second, deforestation, and third the need for alternative energy sources: all issues that correspond to your research.

56 Apostrophe

What do apostrophes do?

Apostrophes perform three functions. They show possession; indicate contractions; and pluralize abbreviations, letters, numbers, and signs.

56a   Possessives of common nouns

To show possession in nouns, add an -'s to singular nouns, and an apostrophe alone to plural nouns.

SINGULAR NOUNS	PLURAL NOUNS
this girl's chess club	all the girls' clubs
the fox's den	the robbers' hideout
this tourist's guide book	all the tourists' bags

EXCEPTIONS Possessives of irregular plurals may end in -'s.

➤ women's clubs

➤ honoraria's provisions

If a noun ending in -s sounds too sibilant when you add -'s, keep the apostrophe and drop the final -s.

➤ for goodness' sake

Possessives of proper nouns 56b

Possessives of singular *proper* nouns end in -'s even if the noun itself ends in an -s or in an -x.

➤ Tsarina Catherine's ukases

➤ Christopher Columbus's voyages

➤ Groucho Marx's humor

EXCEPTION As above, if the addition of -'s makes the proper noun too sibilant, add only an apostrophe and drop the -s.

➤ Ulysses' voyage

➤ Demosthenes' speeches

Possessives of plural proper nouns end in an apostrophe only.

➤ The *Joneses'* house was the only residence on the block.

Never use an apostrophe to pluralize a personal name. Use -s or -es as needed.

➤ The *Joneses* had no one to keep up with.

Possessives of compound nouns 56c

To show possession in a compound noun, add an apostrophe at the *end* of the compound noun regardless of whether or not it is hyphenated.

➤ Son-in-law's new job

➤ Dean of Graduate Studies' signature

Do not mistake possessives for plurals. To *pluralize* a compound noun, add the -s to the root word — three *sons*-in-law, several *deans*-of-graduate studies.

Possessives of jointly owned property 56d

When two people own the *same* property and both owners' names are used, add -'s to the final name only.

➤ Grosset and Dunlap's texts

➤ Sam and Tom's restaurant

When one of the owners is represented by a name and the other by a pronoun, add the *-'s* only to the name.

➤Sarah's and his business

➤His and Sarah's business

➤Joe's and her marriage

➤Her and Joe's marriage

56e   Indicating contractions

The apostrophe indicates that two words have been merged and a letter or letters have been left out. Place the apostrophe at the spot where the letters are omitted.

➤does not ⇨ doesn't

➤who is ⇨ who's

➤he will ⇨ he'll

Treat omitted numbers in the same way as omitted letters by replacing them with an apostrophe. Apostrophes showing contraction always curl clockwise.

➤1975 ⇨ '75

➤1776 ⇨ '76

Avoid contractions in formal writing. Commonly found in informal speech and writing, contractions are inappropriate in a formal essay. Use *is not, do not, have not, cannot, I will, she will,* and so forth instead of *isn't, don't, haven't, can't, I'll, she'll.*

56f   Pluralizing words used as words

There are three ways to pluralize words used as words. Whether or not you use an apostrophe, *do not italicize* the -s.

1. If you have *italicized* the word, simply add the *-s* or *-es* in a non-italicized font.

➤There are too many *and*s in this sentence.

➤Foreigners often use *the*s incorrectly.

2. If you have placed the word inside quotation marks, do *not* italicize it, but add an apostrophe and -*s*.

➤There are too many "and's" in this sentence.

➤Foreigners often use "the's" incorrectly.

3. For standard, commonly used expressions just add -'*s*.

➤Don't give me any and's, if's, or but's!

Pluralizing abbreviations   *56g*

Pluralize the abbreviation of a single word, by simply adding an -*s*.

➤vol. ⇨ vols.

➤no. ⇨ nos.

➤ed. ⇨ eds.

Pluralize an abbreviated expression consisting of several words in two ways.

Eliminate the periods, and add an -*s*.

➤M.A. ⇨ MAs

➤Ph.D. ⇨ PhDs

➤M.D. ⇨ MDs

➤I.R.A. ⇨ IRAs

Retain the periods, and add an -'*s*.

➤M.A. ⇨ M.A.'s

➤Ph.D ⇨ Ph.D.'s

➤M.D ⇨ M.D.'s

➤I.R.A. ⇨ I.R.A.'s

Certain irregular pluralizations double the *only* or the *final* letter.

➤p. for page — becomes pp. for pages

➤ms. for manuscript — becomes mss. for manuscripts

56h   Pluralizing letters

To pluralize letters, you may choose to use an apostrophe or not, but be consistent in style throughout your text. In general, italicize the letter or letters, then use a non-italicized font for the *-s*, regardless of whether or not you include an apostrophe.

➤I'd like the initial *t*'s in larger point type.

➤You have reversed the *b*'s and the *d*'s.

OR

➤I'd like the initial *t*s in larger point type.

➤You have reversed the *b*s and the *d*s.

For standard, common expressions, *italicize the letters or not* as you wish, *but always use an apostrophe.*

➤Mind your *p*'s and *q*'s.

➤You need to learn the *abc*'s of this business.

OR

➤Mind your p's and q's.

➤You need to learn the abc's of this business.

56i   Pluralizing numbers

Do not use an apostrophe to pluralize numbers. Just add an *-s*.

➤How many 2s are there in 18?

➤It happened in the early 1990s.

➤It happened in the early '90s.

56j   Pluralizing signs

Always italicize the sign when you pluralize it. However, using an apostrophe to pluralize signs is optional. Select whichever method is least confusing, and be consistent once you have made your choice.

➤The *#*'s line is to record your account number.

➤Place the *%* 's after the numbers.

OR

➤The *#*s line is to record your account number.

➤Place the *%*s after the numbers.

📖 **Exercise**

Correct any errors in apostrophes. Answers on p.343.

Answers on p.343.

GROUP A
1. There are too many "perhapses" in this paragraph.
2. The childrens playground was nearly empty.
3. She hadnt read all of Henry James novels, but shed planned to do so that summer.
4. Only a superstitious person would suffer any of the hexs harmful effects.
5. The secretaries convention is in Hawaii this year.
6. What did you do with Jess hat?
7. I was bitten by the Robinsons cat.
8. She bragged about her daughter-in-laws talents.
9. Is this Jane Samuels umbrella?
10. No, this umbrella is Becky Rabinowitzs.

GROUP B
1. This is Bobbys and Sams bedroom.
2. Friedrich Engels writings are nearly as well-known as Karl Marxs.
3. I was impressed by all the PhDs and M.D.'s at the conference.
4. In general the winters in the 1990's have been fairly severe, although'96 was unusually mild.
5. Dot your i's and cross your t's.
6. Write out your ands instead of using &s.
7. The number line is a sequence of 2's and 3's, and their multiples'.
8. Arent you related to the MacIntosh's from Culver City?
9. Your *v*'s and *u*'s are practically interchangeable.
10. Domenicos Theotocopoulos's nickname was El Greco.

57 Parentheses

What is the purpose of parentheses?

Parentheses are used for incidental but illuminating information, citations of source materials, numbering, foreign words or phrases and their English definitions.

57a Parentheses for marginal or lengthy incidental information

Like commas, parentheses set apart incidental information that adds to the sentence but is not vital to its meaning — examples, definitions, explanations.

Choose *commas* for information that is more closely connected to the meaning of the sentence and which is not too long to make the sentence confusing.

Choose *parentheses* for information that is more distant from the content of the sentence or which is so lengthy as to muddle the sense of the sentence. Comments that begin with such terms as *i.e., e.g., namely, to wit, in other words, that is* may be placed inside parentheses.

➤Margarita, originally a Russian immigrant, still speaks English with a foreign accent.

➤Margarita (whose poetry was published by Columbia University Press) still speaks English with a foreign accent.

In these examples, Margarita's being an immigrant is closely related to her foreign accent; therefore it is set apart by commas. However, the publication of her poetry is only distantly connected to her foreign accent; it is marginal information and is, therefore, in parentheses.

➤Margarita (originally a Russian immigrant who came to the U.S. as a child) still speaks English with a foreign accent.

Here the parenthetical material is still closely related to Margarita's accent, but is too long to be separated from the rest of the sentence by commas. For purposes of clarity, the material is enclosed in parentheses.

Parentheses for citing source materials   **57b**

Parenthetical information identifies where ideas, facts, or quotations come from. It can be inserted into the middle of the sentence, or it can appear at the end of a sentence or quotation. It is usually punctuated as part of the sentence (see §72 *Models of parenthetical references*).

➤The rise in unemployment (see chart p. 32) coincides with the sharp increase in stocks traded on Wall Street.

➤In his autobiography, the Senator admits that "mistakes were made" (Randall 37).

Parentheses for numbering   **57c**

Use double parentheses around numbers and letters when they are in a numbered list like those in the example below. Letters in a list are italicized (*a*). The example below uses semicolons instead of commas because each numbered item is an independent clause in the list.

➤He disliked air travel because (1) it was too expensive; (2) it placed him at the mercy of airline and travel agents; and (3) it usually required a lot of walking.

Parentheses for foreign words or phrases, and their   **57d**
English definitions

All foreign words do not need to be defined. Define them or list them only when they are important in context. In the examples below, they are "significant."

➤Significantly, the protagonist is named El Brujo (*Magician*).

➤Significantly, the protagonist is the magician (*El Brujo*).

Punctuating sentences that contain parentheses   **57e**

Punctuate the rest of the sentence exactly as you would if it had not contained parentheses. Do *not* place any punctuation before an open-parenthesis mark inside a sentence unless the parentheses are around numbers or letters in a list (see example above under §57c *Parentheses for numbering*).

➤Beverly Sills/ (once nicknamed Bubbles) is recognized as one of opera's greatest sopranos.

Also, never use parentheses inside other parentheses (see below §58 *Brackets*).

57f　　　　Punctuating material inside parentheses

The punctuation of parenthetical material depends on whether it is inserted into a sentence, or is a complete sentence between two other sentences.

When a parenthetical remark is inserted into a sentence *do* use *commas, question marks, exclamation points* as needed inside the parentheses.

➤Charles (who later became a serial killer!) was a model student in high school.

➤Although Charles was a model student in high school, he later became a serial killer (who could have foreseen it?).

Do *not* use a *period* inside such parentheses even if the remark is a complete sentence, unless it shows an abbreviation.

➤Charles's psychotherapist took a legal stance (she testified that his psychological condition excused his crimes) that the judge rejected.

When the parenthetical remark is a complete sentence between two other sentences, use *any* ending punctuation applicable to a standard sentence, including a period, and place this punctuation *inside* the parentheses.

➤Charles, the model student in high school, grew up to be a serial killer. (According to his guidance counselors, psychological testing could have predicted it.) After his conviction, he again became a model of good behavior (this time in a psychiatric institution!).

📖　　Exercise

Correct any errors in parentheses. Answers on p.344.

1. I met some abused youths under the auspices of the state's Child and Family Services who had suffered severe emotional trauma as small children.

2. A successful parent's three key principles are 1) not to relinquish his authority, 2) not to evade his responsibility, and 3) not to forget how it felt to be the child.

3. The children were taught formal ballroom dancing that they interspersed with less gracious activities namely, name calling making faces, and pinching.

4. Despite the fact that the North finally won the Civil War, the years 1861 to 1865 were filled with hardship for Lincoln as commander-in-chief. In 1861, South Carolina spurned Lincoln's overtures, and its militia fired on Fort Sumter starting the Civil War. (in addition, Lincoln suffered a personal tragedy during the war when he lost his eleven-year old son to disease). Reacting to Confederate victories in the early years of the war, the press reviled and ridiculed Lincoln's leadership daily.

5. The D on the sociology test, which tested us on material never covered in class, seriously affected my grade average.

6. Announcing "L'état c'est moi" (I am the state), France's Louis XIV summarized his absolutist views.

7. There was great merriment in Tehran despite the wartime conditions, the year was 1942, and much partying.

8. The more information we can provide to our members, who have written and e-mailed in large numbers wanting to know the facts, the more likely they will be to support our proposal.

9. Eighteenth and nineteenth century South Carolina planters justified slavery as an economic necessity. Even planters opposed to slavery in principle record in their diaries that it was impossible to find free workers to perform the hard labor on rice, cotton, and tobacco plantations. (See Appendix D.)

10. General Winfield Hancock born in 1824 was a Union commander; who fought at Gettysburg.

58 Brackets

What are brackets used for, and how do they differ from parentheses?

Brackets are square parentheses used for information that is *within parentheses or quotation marks*. Do *not* use brackets outside of parentheses or quotation marks. Do *not* use parentheses inside other parentheses — use brackets [ ]. If quoted or parenthetical material (such as documentation) contains parentheses, change these to brackets.

58a ### Pointing out errors in quoted text

Bracketed information points out a mistake in a quoted text by the insertion of [sic] after the error.

➤According to the article:"History will recognize Harry Turman [sic] as one of America's greatest presidents."

58b ### Referring readers to parenthetical source materials

Bracketed information refers the reader to source materials, appendices, charts, and other addenda listed in parentheses.

➤The plan for the Allied invasion of Europe (at Normandy, June 6, 1944 [see Appendix A]) was named Operation Overlord.

58c ### Providing additional information

Within parentheses or quotation marks, bracketed information provides explanations, examples, dates, translations of foreign expressions, and other data.

➤The mayor admitted that "it [the charter school plan] still has not overcome the reservations of certain city councilmen."

➤The judge ruled the confession of the drunkard admissible saying "*in vino veritas* [in wine is truth]."

Indicating changes in quotations **58d**

Indicate syntactical changes to a quotation by bracketing them. Initial letters may be changed from upper to lower case and vice versa. Connectives such as *and, but, or* may be inserted as long as they are bracketed. Deleted material is indicated by a bracketed ellipsis (see §68d *Indicating deletions in fragmentary quotations,* §68e *Indicating deletions at the end of a quotation,* and §68f *Indicating deletion of a sentence or more*).

ORIGINAL   After discussing the contract, the board chairman noted that the cost of living index warrants increased health benefits for employees. He also recommended an increase in the starting salary of employees.

QUOTATION   "[T]he cost of living index," according to the board chairman, "warrants increased health benefits for employees [...] [and] an increase in the starting salary [...]."

📖   Exercise

Correct any errors in brackets. Answers on p.345.

1. The coach said, "If a player can handle the pressure from the fans, he is on his way to becoming an intregal part of the team."
   (Obviously the word "intregal" should be "integral." Indicate in your revision that you know this is a mistake.)
2. There was great merriment in Tehran (the wartime conditions 1942–1944 notwithstanding) and much partying.
3. In his lecture, the noted archeologist expressed the opinion that "Along with the Theory of Evolution we need to consider the principles of Catastrophism."
   (Change the *-a* in *along* to lower case to make it fit into the flow of the sentence. Indicate that you have made the change.)
4. The letter to our first president referred to him as "President Washineton"; it sold for $200,000 at auction.
5. The original text discovered in 1860 see Appendix B indicates that Richard III probably had not murdered his nephews.

59 Dashes

Aren't all dashes alike?

There are two kinds of dashes: the shorter *en dash* and the longer *em dash*. The length of a dash determines its function.

59a The en dash

The en dash has two functions. It links the names of people, nations, events, and places.

➤ The Mason–Dixon Line

➤ The Washington–Boston express

➤ The Anglo–Japanese alliance

It also shows distance or span from one point to another.

➤ The 1929–1939 economic depression

➤ Volumes *A–F* of the encyclopedia

➤ Pages 36–72

59b The em dash

The em dash inserts incidental commentary into a sentence. It can set off a *word*, a *phrase*, or a *clause*. Comments set off by an em dash are more emphatic and more conversational than those set off by parentheses.

EMPHATIC OR SUDDEN BREAK IN THOUGHT SUCH AS AN ASIDE

➤ Her best friend — if indeed she is her friend — will certainly rise to her defense.

ELABORATION OF A PRECEDING IDEA IN THE SENTENCE by an explanation, a definition, or an example (in place of parentheses)

➤ Her best friend will certainly rise to her defense — she will testify on her behalf at the hearing.

➤Her best friend — they had sworn eternal friendship in kindergarten — will certainly rise to her defense by testifying on her behalf at the hearing.

INTERRUPTION IN DIALOGUE

➤"I'm in danger! They're coming! They're — " she shouted into the receiver. The connection was severed abruptly.

INSERTION OF A SURPRISING LIST

➤Again he itemized his equipment — a garrote, a Browning automatic, and several live grenades.

➤A garrote, a Browning automatic, and several live grenades — never leave home without them, recommends *Survivalist Magazine.*

Using other punctuation with a dash   **59c**

Punctuate and phrase sentences in a way that makes sense without the material set off by dashes.

In the *middle of a sentence,* material set off by dashes can end in a question mark or an exclamation point but never in a comma or in a period (unless it marks an abbreviation).

➤The speaker's contention — extraordinary as it seemed to the audience! — was that children are merely short adults.

➤The speaker's contention — however did he reach that conclusion? — was that children are merely short adults.

At the *end of a sentence,* eliminate the final dash and use a period, question mark, or exclamation point as is appropriate to the meaning of the sentence.

➤The Republican Party did finally agree on one winning campaign strategy — no new taxes!

☞   *Never* use a dash next to a period, a comma, a semicolon, or a colon. *Never* use more than one remark set off by dashes in a sentence.

📖   **Exercise**

Correct any errors in using dashes. Answers on p.346.

1. My father — whom I adored when I was small, sang Italian love songs as my mother accompanied him at the piano.
2. I recall vividly who could forget the enthusiastic applause of the guests.
3. In August 1939 the Stalin/Hitler pact stunned Europe.
4. I started to say, "Your behavior last night," but never finished because she walked away even as I was speaking.
5. I could not understand exercises 7/14 in the calculus assignment.
6. The guest speaker who towered over the students was seven feet tall.
7. The children were taught formal ballroom dancing that they interspersed with less gracious activities name calling, making faces, pinching.
8. Privately Nixon's aides maintained that Nixon resigned the presidency because he had been certain Jerry Ford would pardon him — they had little doubt about it — !
9. Our conversation, such as it was — was punctuated by the exploding fireworks — a drawback of the Fourth of July extravaganza.
10. Was this set such a good buy when it is missing series *K-P*?

60 Hyphens

Can hyphens be used interchangeably with dashes?

Hyphens are not interchangeable with dashes. Use hyphens to divide a word at the end of a line, to alter the meaning of a root word, to avoid confusion, to merge existing words into new words, and to write out numbers.

60a   Dividing a word at the end of a line

Sometimes it is necessary to divide a word at the end of a line, even when word-processing. To divide words, use the following rules:

DO NOT DIVIDE ONE-SYLLABLE WORDS

➤NOT dra-pe BUT drape

DO NOT HAVE A SINGLE LETTER REMAIN ALONE

➤NOT e-normity BUT enor-mity

DO NOT CREATE SEPARATIONS WITHIN NAMES, BETWEEN FIRST AND LAST NAMES, OR BETWEEN TITLES AND NAMES

➤NOT Ambassador Al-bright BUT Ambassador Albright

➤NOT Made-leine Albright BUT Madeleine Albright

➤NOT Mr. (line break) Albright BUT Mr. Albright

DO DIVIDE BETWEEN DOUBLE CONSONANTS

➤NOT rapp-ort BUT rap-port

DO DIVIDE BETWEEN SYLLABLES

➤NOT und-ertake BUT under-take

DO DIVIDE ROOT WORDS FROM THEIR PREFIXES OR SUFFIXES

➤NOT elo-pement BUT elope-ment

Altering the meaning of a root word **60b**

To *define*, *expand*, or *contradict* the meaning of root words, place a hyphen between the root word and the prefix, or between the root word and the suffix *-elect*.

all-knowing	far-sighted
anti-American	president-elect
counter-intelligence	pseudo-intellectual
ex-wife	self-critical

 Self- is always hyphenated if it is not part of root word like *selfish*.

Italicize any hyphenated prefix that stands alone and modifies a word that already contains a prefix (hyphenated or not).

➤*Anti-* and pro-war protesters picketed the senator's office.

➤The researchers compared the *over-* and underdeveloped musculature of the laboratory mice.

60c Use a hyphen with most prefixes ending in vowels

Prefixes that end in vowels (such as *anti-, co-, de-, pre-* etc.) are sometimes attached to words beginning with a vowel, often the same one. This combination may confuse pronunciation. To avoid confusion, place a hyphen between prefixes ending in vowels and root words beginning in vowels.

Separate a prefix *ending* in the same vowel that *begins* the root word.

co-opt	pre-empt
de-emphasize	re-elect
multi-intentioned	semi-invalid

However, through common usage some words have dropped their hyphens. Here are a few examples.

biennial	extraordinary
cooperative	proactive
coordinate	reenter

60d Using a hyphen with the prefix *re-*

The prefix *re-* can be attached to almost any verb to show an action that occurs again. Sometimes, however, the new compound can become confused with unhyphenated words spelled the same way. Insert a hyphen after the prefix *re-* to distinguish between words that share the same spelling but have different meanings (*homonyms*). Below are a few examples.

re-collect OR recollect	re-form OR reform
re-cover OR recover	re-lay OR relay
re-dress OR redress	re-mark OR remark
re-fine OR refine	re-pay OR repay

60e Use hyphens with prefixes to capitalized words

Prefixes added to capitalized words must have a hyphen.

pre-Raphaelite	post-Renaissance
neo-Tudor	pro-Islam
all-American	pan-African

Merging existing words into new words   **60f**

To merge existing words into new words, hyphenate many compound nouns, verbs, adverbs, and adjectives. However, remember these are words in transition that eventually may drop their hyphens. Below are a few examples.

NOUNS THAT RETAIN HYPHENS	NOUNS THAT HAVE DROPPED HYPHENS
extra-terrestrial	textbook
know-it-all	snowboard
tête-à-tête	grandmother
word-processing	blueberry

VERBS THAT RETAIN HYPHENS	VERBS THAT HAVE DROPPED HYPHENS
bad-mouth	shoplift
claim-jump	skydive
water-ski	footnote
jump-start	override

Hyphenate compound adverbs that do *not* end in *-ly*, and/or that *precede* the word they describe.

➤ five-foot long

➤ sat vis-à-vis

➤ walked arm-in-arm

➤ learned step-by-step

Hyphenate compound adjectives that *precede* the word they describe.

➤ *out-of-date* dictionary

➤ *hoof-and-mouth* disease

➤ *picture-perfect* scene

➤ *time-honored* custom

➤ *state-of-the-art* computer

➤ *rapid-fire* speech

➤ *one-syllable* words

➤ five *inch-high* beetles OR *five-inch-high* beetles

EXCEPTION Current usage favors dropping the hyphen when the compound adverb or adjective *follows* the described word.

➤The dictionary was *out of date*.

➤The child was *well behaved*.

BUT

➤The old lady was *even-tempered*.

➤The computer was *state-of-the-art*.

60g   Writing out numbers

Numbers *twenty-one* to *ninety-nine* are always hyphenated whether they stand alone or are part of a larger number.

➤I voted for the first time on my *twenty-first* birthday.

➤The designer shoes cost *one hundred and seventy-five* dollars.

Hyphenate the number and the word it modifies when both describe yet another word.

➤It was a *twenty-mile* hike to town.

➤The *six-year* old entered first grade.

Hyphenate a number that is merged with a noun to form a new noun.

➤The nursery school admits *three-and-a-half-year* olds only into the *half-day* program.

➤The Lamaze class was full of *thirty-somethings*.

Hyphenate fractions only when they are modifiers.

➤The *four and three-fifths* foot bookshelf was *one-half* inch too long.

BUT

➤The answer to the problem was *three fifths*.

📖   Exercise

Correct any errors in using hyphens. Answers on p.347.

1. The students formed groups to discuss the pro and anti tax resolutions.
2. During the investigation, the exwife deemphasized her drinking problem and accused her exhusband of neverending criticism.

3. Robin Hood's step by step mastery of archery amazed me.
4. Even after repaying me the two hundred dollars, he still owed me fifty seven more.
5. The seven foot tall basketball player towered over the seventh graders.
6. How much is three fifths of twelve?
7. Some politicians are hand in glove with big companies who contribute to their campaigns.
8. They walked down the street hand-in-hand.
9. They acted without considering both the short and long term consequences of damaging Mrs.Robinson's fence.
10. At twenty one, I felt totally in control of my own destiny, ready to plunge into the rough and tumble world of Wall Street wheeling and dealing.

61 Italics

What are italics used for?

Before word-processing became common, writers underlined rather than italicized. Underlining is still acceptable, but italicizing is more current. Use italics to emphasize key terms and prefixes; to refer to numbers as numbers, letters as letters, and words as words; for foreign words; for certain names; for some literary titles.

Italics for emphasis   *61a*

Italicize to draw attention to key words or expressions either in your own text or in a quotation. However, when you add italics to a quotation, inform the reader with the words: "italics mine," or "italics added," or "emphasis added," or "my emphasis."

➤Homer's opening verse establishes Odysseus as "the man of *twists and turns*"(emphasis added).

Italics also emphasize any prefix that stands alone and describes a word which already contains a prefix.

➤On the eve of Revolution, heated *pro-* and anti-monarchist debates raged in the American colonies.

61b   Italics for numbers as numbers, letters as letters, and words as words

At times we refer to numbers, letters, or words not as concepts, but as items or signs. To indicate our intention, we italicize them.

➤The teacher mistook my *1* for a *7*, and my *a* for a *d*.

➤*Here* and *there* are never subjects except in a sentence like this one.

61c   Italics for foreign words

Italicize foreign words that are scholarly or technical. Do not italicize words of foreign origin that have become part of standard English and which may be readily understood in casual conversation. (Authorities may differ on which foreign words are part of standard English. For example, some italicize *etc.*, others do not.)

➤Thrasymachus's argument in Plato depends on whether the Greek term *kreitonos* means "stronger" or "better."

➤The young lawyer's first *voir dire* was a stressful experience.

BUT

➤We met at the restaurant for a tête-à-tête.

➤President Thomas Jefferson had a laissez-faire attitude toward the Executive Branch's influence on legislation.

Do not italicize quotations in foreign languages, or names and titles in foreign languages.

➤The Marquis de Lafayette was a hero of the American Revolution.

61d   Italics for literary titles

Italicize or underline any of the following that are *published as complete in themselves:* titles of books, magazines, plays, films, radio or television presentations, newspapers, long poems.

➤Thomas Mann's *Buddenbrooks* is famous for its irony.

In the above example, the title of a book published by itself is italicized.

➤I have a beautifully illustrated edition of the *Rubáyat of Omar Khayyám*.

The title of a long poem published by itself is italicized in the example above.

Book titles referred to as *part of a collection*, or book titles that appear *in the titles of other books* are neither italicized nor underlined.

➤A Tale of Two Cities, which appears in the third volume of *The Collected Works of Charles Dickens*, is reviewed in *The Boston Globe*.

The example above illustrates the title of a book that appears as part of a collection.

➤*Perspectives on Irony in Dickens's* A Tale of Two Cities

In the title of a book about a novel, above, the name of the novel is *not* italicized.

Book titles included *in the titles of articles* are italicized.

➤ "Perspectives on Irony in Dickens's *A Tale of Two Cities*"

Titles of films, plays, and radio and television programs are italicized.

➤I have been watching re-runs of *Star Trek*.

Italics for names   61e

Italicize the names of art exhibits and art works.

➤Did you know that madmen periodically attack the *Mona Lisa*?

➤Have you seen the *Gauguin in the South Seas* exhibit?

Italicize the names of musical compositions *not* listed by form, number, and key.

➤Beethoven's *Moonlight Sonata* is our favorite piece of music.

Italicize the names of airplanes, ships, trains, spacecraft

➤*The New York Times'* theater critic gave glowing reviews to Robert Brownell's new play, *In Ariadne's Footsteps*, which premiered on the cruise ship *Titanic II*.

EXCEPTIONS Use standard print, *not* italics or quotation marks, for buildings and monuments; conferences; courses; documents; instrumental music listed by form, number, and key; literary series; sacred texts; societies.

➤He discovered one of the earliest copies of the Declaration of Independence in his grandparents' attic.

➤The pianist played Beethoven's Serenade in D Opus 41.

➤They studied the Bible paying particular attention to Exodus.

📖   Exercise

Correct any errors in using italics. Answers on p.348.

1. On the program at *Lincoln Center* was Dvořák's New World Symphony.
2. Like Sherlock Holmes, we are fascinated by why the dog didn't bark.
3. In Meyer's play Art Comes Alive, the pièce de resistance was the dance of the Mona Lisa.
4. The hors d'oeuvres consisted of Italian and Hungarian specialities.
5. Let's listen to Richter's recording of Mozart's *Piano Concerto No. 20 in D Minor*.
6. My article is entitled, "The Perception of Duality in Conrad's The Secret Sharer."
7. While we waited to *rendezvous* with the others at the *Lincoln Memorial*, he edited my speech removing some of the ands.
8. The Washington Post is running a series of articles on the *Koran*.
9. According to one German critic, Weltschmerz is sadness experienced by people who have nothing better to do.
10. Shakespeare in Love has received more Oscars than any other film in recent years.

62 Quotations marks

62a   Uses of quotation marks

Quotation marks are used in the following situations:

DIALOGUE WITHIN A TEXT indent for each new speaker.

➤ "I love you madly!" John exclaimed.

➤ "You love everyone madly," Marcia responded. "That's why I won't marry you."

(See below §70 *Quoting drama* for punctuating dialogue quoted from a play.)

AROUND QUOTATIONS of fewer than five lines of text that are *not* set off in a separate paragraph.

➤ Successful dieters have learned to "just say no."

➤ "Two B or not two B," mused Watson, looking for the address.

UNPLEASANT, OUTMODED, OR IRONIC EXPRESSIONS

➤They called their mass murder "ethnic cleansing."

➤Slavery was referred to as the South's "peculiar institution."

➤Is breaking up with me part of "reorganizing" your life?

NICKNAMES AND DESCRIPTIVE ASSOCIATIONS uniquely associated with a person, place, time, or product.

➤Mae West is often referred to as "the last of the Red Hot Mamas."

➤I may not be a saint, but like Ivory Soap, I am "ninety-nine and forty-four one-hundredths per cent pure."

WORDS USED AS WORDS

➤Are "here" or "there" ever the subjects of a sentence?

Alternatively, words used as words may be italicized.

TITLES OF PUBLICATIONS that form part of a larger work: chapter titles; episodes in radio or television series; unpublished work; short pieces such as articles, short stories, essays, lectures, short poems, songs.

➤"Re-evaluating the Dolphin," in this month's *National Geographic* changed my image of dolphins as benevolent, non-violent creatures.

➤Simon and Garfunkel's "Mrs. Robinson" in *The Graduate* became an anthem for the disaffected youth of the 1960s.

Exercise

Correct any errors in using quotation marks. Answers on p.349.

1. The expression gosh was coined to avoid taking the Lord's name in vain.
2. Norman Mailer thought Jack London's hero in To Build a Fire behaved like a sissy.
3. I hear them coming, I said. I have to hang up now.
4. I think that I was the bastard he was ranting about.
5. Quoting, If at first you don't succeed try, try again, my brother encouraged me to fly off the roof of the garage once more.
6. She spent her vacation in Alaska, The Land of the Midnight Sun.
7. My favorite tale in The Arabian Nights is The Story of the Magic Horse.
8. Mirror, mirror on the wall, she kept asking who's the fairest of them all?
9. My great-grandmother used to tell me about her girlhood in the Gay Nineties, and about Clara Bow, the silent film star, who was said to have It.
10. Many people confuse the words discrete and discreet.

63 Punctuating and capitalizing with quotations

Do capitalization and punctuation change when they are inside quotation marks?

Changes in punctuation depend on whether the punctuation belongs to the quotation itself, to a quotation-within-the-quotation, or to your own sentence. Avoid changing the case of the initial letter of a quotation. If a quotation is integrated into your sentence, some authorities permit changing the upper case to lower, and enclosing the change in brackets. Altering your own language to avoid such a change, however, is clearer and more graceful. When quoting poetry, always retain the original capitalization.

63a   Capitalizing quotations

The first letter of the first word of any sentence is always capitalized. This rule may become confused when you quote capitalized or uncapitalized statements *in the middle* of your own sentence.

QUOTING A COMPLETE SENTENCE

> ACCEPTABLE We wrote that "[w]e all miss being home."

> PREFERABLE We wrote: "We all miss being home."

QUOTING A FRAGMENT INTEGRATED INTO YOUR OWN SENTENCE

> ➤ In his postcard, he pretended to "miss being home."

63b   Punctuation placed inside quotation marks

Punctuation that shows the meaning or tone of the quoted text is placed inside quotation marks. That is, if the quoted text is a question, the question mark goes inside the quotation marks etc. The examples below indicate the placement of punctuation marks when the quotation comes at various locations in your own sentence.

QUESTION MARK WHEN THE QUOTED TEXT IS A QUESTION

> ➤ "Did something happen, Willy?" asks Linda (*Death of a Salesman* 1).

➤Linda asks:"Did something happen,Willy?" when her husband returns home discouraged.

➤In *Death of a Salesman,* Linda asks her husband: "Did something happen,Willy?"

OR

➤Linda Loman asks her husband:"Did something happen,Willy?" (*Death of a Salesman* 1).

EXCLAMATION POINT WHEN THE QUOTED TEXT IS AN EXCLAMATION Exclamation points follow the same rules as question marks do. In the example below, the quoted speech comes at the beginning of the sentence. See the examples above for punctuating quoted exclamations that come in the middle of your sentence, and that coincide with the end of your sentence.

➤ "Bad dog!" our neighbor shouted at Fidel who was digging up the tulips.

COMMA THAT FOLLOWS IMMEDIATELY A QUOTED STATEMENT

➤ "I love you, and I will never forget you," he said.

PERIODS always go inside quotation marks, even when the end of the quotation coincides with the end of your own sentence.

➤She laughed when she heard Pavarotti sing,"On top of Old Smoky."

BUT

➤Lord Acton warned that "absolute power corrupts absolutely" (*Life and Letters of Mandell Creighton* 1.372).

Here, the end of the sentence seems to be after the word "absolutely." In fact, the parenthetical citation is part of the sentence, so that the end of the quotation and the end of the sentence do *not* coincide.

SEMICOLONS AND COLONS THAT ARE PART OF A QUOTATION

➤The former hostage said,"At first I was afraid of being alone; later I was afraid of not being alone."

➤ "Belgium," he smiled,"is known for three things: beer, waffles, and Jean-Claude Van Damme."

Punctuation placed outside quotation marks   **63c**

Use common sense in punctuating. If punctuation expresses the tone and sense of the quotation, it goes *inside* the quotation marks (see above). But, if the punctuation belongs to your own sentence, and *not to the quotation*, it goes outside the quotation marks.

There is no problem in punctuating quotations that come at the beginning or in the middle of your own sentence. However, when the *end of the quotation* and the *end of your own sentence* coincide follow the general rules below. Specific examples follow.

◆ If the quotation is a *statement* inside your own sentence which is a *question*, put the question mark after the close-quotation mark. Treat exclamation points in the same way.

➤Did you hear him say, "I enjoy hurricanes"?

➤I was astounded to hear him say, "I enjoy hurricanes"!

◆ If the quotation is a question or an exclamation inside your own sentence which is a statement, drop your own final period. Let the sentence end with either the question mark or the exclamation point inside the quotation marks.

➤One of the questions on the survey asked: "Do you enjoy hurricanes?"

➤She was amused when he exclaimed: "I enjoy hurricanes!"

Never double-up final punctuation — question marks, exclamation points, semicolons, commas, periods — at the end of a sentence as occurs in the following: *The survey asked, "Do you enjoy hurricanes?"*.

EXCEPTION Periods always go *inside* the quotation marks when a quoted *statement* (not exclamation or question) coincides with the end of your own sentence.

➤Napoleon referred to the English as "a nation of shopkeepers."

SEMICOLONS AND COLONS NOT PART OF A QUOTATION

➤My advisor said, "You have not handed in the last six assignments"; then she told me I was failing out of college.

➤The experienced cook includes in her "arsenal": sharp knives, fresh spices, and copper-bottom pots.

QUESTION MARKS AND EXCLAMATION POINTS NOT PART OF A QUOTATION

➤Did you hear Melvin say, "The postman rang twice"?

➤How presumptuous of our neighbor to refer to Fidel as "a bad dog"!

COMMANS AND COLONS THAT PRECEDE QUOTED SPEECH

➤Mother looked sadly at Fidel and said,"That dog needs to be trained."

➤Crusoe's telegram read:"Please send a man immediately STOP Friday if possible STOP."

PERIODS (See exception above.)

➤Mr. Duchamp was thrilled the first time little Marcel said,"Da-da."

No punctuation before quotation marks   **63d**

Quotations that simply complete the thought of the sentence, without any introduction, do not require punctuation marks in front of them. The quotation is followed by an end punctuation mark if it coincides with the close of the sentence.

➤Our little boat drifted"as silent as a painted ship upon a painted ocean" on that hot afternoon in San Diego Bay.

➤Our little boat in San Diego Bay was"as silent as a painted ship upon a painted ocean."

➤Was your little boat really "as silent as a painted ship upon a painted ocean"?

➤It is astounding how closely our little boat resembled Coleridge's "painted ship upon a painted ocean"!

Do *not* use punctuation in front of quotations preceded by a relative pronoun: *who, whom, whose, which, that, whoever, whomever, whichever.*

➤People often disagree with Shakespeare's quixotic sentiment *that* "love is not love which alters when it alteration finds."

➤Macbeth is killed by Macduff *who* "was from his mother's womb untimely ripp'd."

Eliminate adjacent quotation marks   **63e**

Never have two adjacent sets of quotation marks. Use your own text to separate two quotations that are distant from each other in the source. Or, if the two quotations are in close proximity to each other, as within the same paragraph, include both inside the same set of quotation marks, and use an ellipsis between them. (See §67

Guidelines for changes in quoted material, §68 *Quoting prose,* §69
Quoting poetry and song lyrics, §70 *Quoting drama.*)

➤Edward Lear's Jumblies "went to sea in a ~~sieve," /~~ *sieve [...] on* a stormy day."

See below for Exercises §63 and §64.

---

64   Punctuating a quotation-within-a-quotation

How do you punctuate quotations-within-quotations?

When you place a quotation inside another quotation, turn the original double quotation marks into single ones. Be sure to *place a space between single and double quotation marks.* The examples below show the appropriate punctuation when a quotation appears at the beginning and in the middle of another quotation, and when it coincides with the end of the host quotation.

64a   Punctuation of quotation-within-the-quotation

All punctuation that belongs to the quotation-within-the-quotation goes inside the single quotation marks.

COMMAS

➤"Today I re-read 'Hills Like White Elephants,' " Mariel noted in her diary.

EXCLAMATION POINTS AND QUESTION MARKS The same rules apply to both.

➤" ' Quick, phone the police!' was what I heard them yell, and I dialed 911," she explained to the detective.

➤"I heard them yell, 'Quick, phone the police!' and I dialed 911," she explained to the detective.

Notice that the first example above has a comma after yell, to prevent a run-on. However, the second example drops this comma to avoid double punctuation (police!',).

➤She said to the detective, "I dialed 911 as soon as I heard them yell, 'Quick, phone the police!' "

PERIODS always belong inside the single quotation marks when the ends of the two quotations coincide.

> ➤I enjoyed reading Igor Ivanov's "Reflections on Gogol's 'The Overcoat.'"

Punctuation of main quotation   *64b*

Punctuation that belongs to the main quotation, *not* to the quotation-within-the-quotation, obeys the following rules.

COMMAS THAT IMMEDIATELY FOLLOW A QUOTATION-WITHIN-A-QUOTATION are always placed inside the single close-quotation mark.

> ➤"Today I read 'Hills Like White Elephants' and 'The Bear,'" wrote Mariel in her diary.

COLONS, SEMICOLONS, DASHES

> ➤"Today I read 'Hills Like White Elephants' — which, in fact, is not about elephants at all," wrote Mariel.

> ➤"Today I read 'Hills Like White Elephants': a story which is not about elephants at all," wrote Mariel.

> ➤"Today I read 'Hills Like White Elephants'; it is not about elephants at all," wrote Mariel.

QUESTION MARKS AND EXCLAMATION POINTS go *between* the final single and double quotation marks.

> ➤Warren Buffet asked, "Did that salesman say, 'No exchanges on purchases made with gift certificates'?"

> ➤Marlon Brando bragged, "I improvised Antony's soliloquy, 'Friends, Romans, Countrymen'!"

PERIODS always belong inside the single quotation marks when the ends of the two quotations coincide.

> ➤I enjoyed reading Igor Ivanov's "Reflections on Gogol's 'The Overcoat.'"

Final punctuation when the ends of quotations coincide   *64c*

Never use two consecutive end punctuation marks (for example, a period and an exclamation point) when a quotation and a quotation-within-a-quotation coincide at the end of a sentence.

WHEN QUOTATION-WITHIN-THE-QUOTATION IS A QUESTION OR AN EXCLAMATION drop your own final period.

> ➤Ishmael said, "I heard Captain Ahab ask, 'Does everyone know how to swim?' "

Drop the less important single-quotation punctuation to avoid double end punctuation. In this case, eliminate the original exclamation point inside the single quotation marks, and keep the question mark inside the double quotation marks.

> ➤I asked my grandfather, "Did you actually hear President Roosevelt exclaim that 'the only thing we have to fear is fear itself'?"

WHEN QUOTATION-WITHIN-THE-QUOTATION IS A STATEMENT place your period inside the single close-quotation mark.

> ➤"Remember," he said, "that Hamlet refers to 'the undiscover'd country' in 'To Be or Not To Be.' "

📖 Exercise

Correct any errors in punctuating and capitalizing with quotations, and errors in quotations-within-quotations. Answers on p.349.

1. Plato's *Protagoras* identifies the saying Know thyself as belonging to the Delphic Oracle.
2. Sancho said Don Quixote didn't you hear that windmill go Squeak!?
3. A penny saved is a penny earned quoted my father.
4. I rose early in order to see Fort McHenry by the dawn's early light as the poet had seen it when he wrote The Star-Spangled Banner.
5. The Vietnam veteran told us that war is hell.
6. Scholars ask themselves does Hitler's *Mein Kampf* give clear evidence of his intended solution to the Jewish Question?
7. The Duchess of Malfi announced I love all fruit then she admitted that apricots were her favorite.
8. But the room was locked *from the inside.* Said Monsieur Poirot emphatically!
9. As you can imagine said the folklorist the proverb a stitch in time saves nine was popular with quilters.
10. Can you remember the end of Emily Dickinson's poem I heard a fly buzz when I died?

53–64 Answers to exercises

 ## 53 Commas

GROUP A

1. *Eliminate comma between short, contrasting ideas.*
   Revision: Space travel opens limitless vistas for exploration. The moon today the cosmos tomorrow.

2. *Introductory clause* and *non-restrictive phrase.* Place comma after introductory clause, (*whenever Arnold and I lifted weights*) and around incidental information (*usually the most impressive in the gym.*)
   Revision: Whenever Arnold and I lifted weights, he removed his shirt revealing his biceps, usually the most impressive in the gym.

3. *Run-on caused by a missing comma independent clauses separated by the conjunction (yet). Missing comma after interjection(wow). Missing commas around person being addressed (Dad). Missing commas before close-quotation mark.*
   Revision: "Wow, Dad, this tropical fruit drink is unusually sweet, yet it is refreshing," I said.

4. *Non-restrictive clause.* Enclose in commas incidental information (*a game I could never master*).
   Revision: Billiards or pool, a game I could never master, requires a strong sense of spatial relations, much as geometry does.

5. *Eliminate comma between subject and verb.*
   Revision: That young woman in the gold evening gown is the guest of honor at this reception.

6. *Missing comma after name of person being addressed, and before quoted speech.*
   Revision: "Batman," said Robin, "it might be a good idea to take off your utility belt the next time you shower."

7. *Missing commas in a list.*
   Revision: The desserts at Thanksgiving included peach pie, vanilla ice cream, and brownies.

8. *Missing commas before explanatory information and after i.e.*
   Revision: He ignored the older members of the family, i.e., those over thirty.

9. *Identical words (to) next to each other create confusion and require a comma.*
   Revision: His aunt was the person he ran to, to say that he was hurt.

10. *Eliminate comma between a season and a year.*
    Revision: I first met the man who became my husband at the Harvest Festival in spring 1998.

GROUP B

1. *Missing comma between identical words creates confusion.*
   Revision: The hotel register showed that the tour group members had signed in, in pairs.

2. *Missing commas after introductory phrase and around incidental information.*
   Revision: Her eyes shining with pride, Nadia, wearing her medal, posed with her coach for the photograph.

3. *Eliminate comma between parts of a two-part compound verb (angry/hurt). There is no comma after the short introductory expression at first.*
   Revision: At first I was angry and hurt at not being chosen for a speaking part in the play.

4. *A comma determines the meaning of the sentence.* Does *win over enemies* mean draws them over to his side? Or, does it mean he conquers them with his charm? It could mean either. Without a comma, it means draws them over to his side. Insert a comma between *win* and *over*, and it means he conquers them.

5. *Missing comma after introductory clause (whoever he may be).*
   Revision: Whoever he may be, he looks like someone accustomed to giving orders.

6. *Eliminate comma between month and year, and between parts of a two-part compound verb (graduated/went).*
   Revision: In June 1995, he graduated from high school and went to work.

7. *Missing comma between independent clauses causes run-on. Missing commas around incidental material (of course).*
   Revision: Attila the Hun, of course, never called back after our first date, so I didn't get the chance to tell him what I thought of his behavior.

8. *No revision.* The three-part compound subject needs commas to avoid confusion. The introductory phrase *in August* is too short for a comma.

9. *Missing comma in a list creates confusion.* Place a comma between *rights* and *to.*
   Revision: There were many causes for the Civil War from the South's insistence on states' rights, to slavery.

10. *Eliminate comma between parts of a two-part subject (roommates/I), and between parts of a two-part complement(e-mail/phone).* Comma after the long introductory phrase is correct.
    Revision: After a long and pleasant reunion, my former college roommates and I promised to e-mail and phone one another at least once a month.

54 Semicolon

1. *Two independent clauses of equal importance require a semicolon.*
   Revision: Her appearance proclaimed her self-confidence; her resolve was weakened by secret misgivings.

2. *No semicolon needed.* There is only one main clause in this sentence. Also eliminate the comma, because her being *renowned for her beauty* is essential information.
   Revision: Reportedly Marilyn Monroe always felt insecure despite the fact that she was renowned for her beauty.

3. *Semicolons must separate a list of items containing commas.*
   Revision: Her guest list included Christian Barnard, a young surgeon; William Rehnquist, who had just passed his bar exam; and Ella Fitzgerald, an aspiring singer.

4. *Use a semicolon between two equally important independent clauses.* Place semicolon between *joints* and *the.* Note that in the second clause the verb is implicit.
   Revision: The trip was a depressing trek over miles of run-down motels and greasy fast food joints; the return home a re-entry into sanity.

5. *Separate with semicolons items that contain commas.*
   Revision: He decided that the three films he had enjoyed the most were *Casablanca; Sex, Lies, and Videotape*; and *Unforgiven.*

6. *Eliminate semicolon.* Semicolons separate main clauses. The second clause here (beginning with *which*) is a subordinate clause and is preceded by a comma.
   Revision: At Gettysburg the Confederates attacked the Union forces on Cemetery Ridge, which is adjacent to Cemetery Hill, a strategically important site.

7. *Use a semicolon between two equally important independent clauses.*
   Revision: The course was advertised as an introduction for beginners; it proved to be an exercise in graduate education.

8. *No revision.* This list includes commas *within* the items. It needs the semicolons to separate the items from one another.

9. *Use a semicolon between two equally important independent clauses.* Note that in the second clause the verb is implicit.
   Revision: His smile was like a ray of sunlight; his frown like the dark of the moon.

10. *Eliminate the first semicolon.* The first clause (*just as Coleridge was writing down the poem that had come to him in his dream*) is subordinate — it is not a complete thought. Place a comma after it. Retain the second semicolon at the start of the final main clause.
    Revision: Just as Coleridge was writing down the poem that had come to him in his dream, the knock at the door interrupted him; consequently, the poem was never completed.

55 Colon

1. *Eliminate colon after a verb (bought).*
   Revision: For their camping trip Lewis and Clark bought cooking gear, dehydrated food, two sleeping bags, and hiking boots.
2. *Use a colon before a quotation that differs grammatically from the rest of the sentence and whose introduction sounds formal.* Here the sentence is in the present tense while the quotation is the past tense.
   Revision: Homer describes Telemachus's journey to Sparta saying: "They came into the plain full of wheat [...]."
3. *Use a colon between two independent clauses, the second of which explains or enlarges on the meaning of the first.* Use a comma before the conjunction *and* to avoid a run-on.
   Revision: The weather discouraged travel: the skies grew ever darker, and lightning illuminated the empty road.
4. *Do not use a colon after a preposition (with).*
   Revision: He improved his nutrition with whole grain rice, fresh vegetables, and fish in his diet.
5. *Use a colon to introduce formal dialogue, especially when it changes the tense of the sentence.*
   Revision: Horace Greeley's command was distinctly prophetic: "Go West, young man!"
6. *Eliminate colon after a verb (are).*
   Revision: Three main ways to judge the all-time greatest baseball team are fan support, individual player success, and overall team success.
7. *Replace the semicolon with a colon.* The second clause beginning with *as a child* is less important that the first: it merely explains the first clause.
   Revision: The reason Jesse James turned to robbing trains is easy to explain: as a child, he didn't have a train set of his own.
8. *Eliminate colon* The word *that* may *not* be followed by a colon.
   Revision: Safety features are important in that they help both to prevent accidents and to reduce their seriousness.
9. *Use a colon to separate a more important clause from a less important clause.* Here, the second clause (*accordingly, she skipped breakfast*) merely refers to and explains the first clause.
   Revision: She was already late for class: accordingly, she skipped breakfast.
10. *Eliminate the second colon in the sentence.* A sentence may not have more than one colon. Replace the colon between *sources* and *all* with an em dash instead of a comma to avoid confusion. The colon after the formal salutation (*Dear Dr. Maxwell*) is correct, as is the one preceding the list.
    Revision: Dear Dr. Maxwell: In response to your query, my seminar addresses three topics: first, the danger of global warming, second, deforestation, and third the need for alternative energy sources — all issues that correspond to your research.

56 Apostrophe

GROUP A

1. *A pluralized word, used as a word in quotation marks, needs an -'s.*
   Revision: There are too many "perhaps's" in this paragraph.
2. *Possessive of an irregular plural noun (children) takes an -'s.*
   Revision: The children's playground was nearly empty.
3. *In contractions an apostrophe marks the omission (hadn't, she'd).*
   Add -'s to a singular proper noun ending in -s (James) unless the
   addition sounds too sibilant.
   Revision: She hadn't read all of Henry James's novels, but she'd
   planned to do so that summer.
4. *Singular possessives (hex) take an -'s.*
   Revision: Only a superstitious person would suffer any of the hex's
   harmful effects.
5. *Show possession in plural nouns by adding an apostrophe alone.*
   Revision: The secretaries' convention is in Hawaii this year.
6. *Add -'s to a singular proper noun ending in -s (Jess) unless the*
   addition sounds too sibilant.
   Revision: What did you do with Jess's hat?
7. *Possessive plural proper nouns (Robinsons) end in an apostrophe only,*
   without an additional -s.
   Revision: I was bitten by the Robinsons' cat.
8. *For possession in singular compound nouns (daughter-in-law's) add -'s*
   at the end.
   Revision: She bragged about her daughter-in-law's talents.
9. *Leave off the final -s to avoid undue sibilance.*
   Revision: Is this Jane Samuels' umbrella?
10. *Adds -'s to show possession in a singular proper noun (Rabinowitz)*
    unless the addition sounds too sibilant.
    Revision: No, this umbrella is Becky Rabinowitz's.

GROUP B

1. *For jointly owned property, add -'s to final name only.*
   Revision: This is Bobby and Sam's bedroom.
2. *Apostrophize in accordance with pronunciation.*
   Revision: Friedrich Engels' writings are nearly as well-known as
   Karl Marx's.
3. *Be consistent.* Use either the one style or the other.
   Revision: I was impressed by all the PhDs and MDs at the conference.
   OR
   I was impressed by all the Ph.D.'s and M.D.'s at the conference.
4. *Pluralize numbers by adding an -s.* Eliminate the apostrophe from
   1990.
   Revision: In general the winters in the 1990s have been fairly severe,
   although '96 was unusually mild.

5. *In one style, no correction is needed for commonly used proverbial expressions. For the other style, correct as follows:*
   Revision: Dot your *i*'s and cross your *t*'s.
6. *Be consistent in whichever of the two styles you choose.*
   Revision: Write out your *and*s instead of using *&*s.

   OR

   Write out your *and*'s instead of using *&*'s.
7. *Just add -s without an apostrophe for pluralizing numbers.* No apostrophe on *multiples.*
   Revision: The number line is a sequence of 2s and 3s, and their multiples.
8. *Apostrophe replaces deleted letters in a contraction (aren't). Do not use apostrophe to pluralize a proper noun.*
   Revision: Aren't you related to the MacIntoshes from Culver City?
9. *In both styles, the -s is not italicized.* In this situation, the -'s is preferable because without it the letters could look confusing.
   Revision: Your *v*'s and *u*'s are practically interchangeable.
10. *Use only an apostrophe.* An extra -s would make the name too sibilant.
    Revision: Domenicos Theotocopoulos' nickname was El Greco.

57 Parentheses

1. *Place parentheses around marginal incidental information.*
   Revision: I met some abused youths (under the auspices of the state's Child and Family Services) who had suffered severe emotional trauma as small children.
2. *Use double parentheses for numbering.*
   Revision: A successful parent's three key principles are (1) not to relinquish his authority, (2) not to evade his responsibility, and (3) not to forget how it felt to be the child.
3. *Enclose incidental examples in parentheses.* The examples may also be set aside with an em dash.
   Revision: The children were taught formal ballroom dancing that they interspersed with less gracious activities (namely, name calling, making faces, and pinching).
4. *A parenthetical remark that is a complete sentence between other sentences must be punctuated and capitalized like any normal sentence.* Inside the parentheses, capitalize *in* and place a period after *disease*, inside, *not* outside, the parentheses.
   Revision: Despite the fact that the North finally won the Civil War, the years 1861 to 1865 were filled with hardship for Lincoln as commander-in-chief. In 1861, South Carolina spurned Lincoln's overtures, and its militia fired on Fort Sumter starting the Civil War. (In addition, Lincoln suffered a personal tragedy during the war when he lost his eleven-year-old son to disease.) Reacting to Confederate victories in the early years of the war, the press reviled and ridiculed Lincoln's leadership daily.

5. *The incidental remark is so distant from the content of the sentence that it requires parentheses, not commas.* Place parentheses around *which tested us on material never covered in class,* and add an appropriate exclamation point of surprise, inside the parentheses. The word *which* is not capitalized because the parenthetical remark is not a complete sentence but a fragment.
   Revision: The D on the sociology test (which tested us on material never covered in class!) seriously affected my grade average.

6. *No revision.* The translation is correctly enclosed in parentheses. The comma that follows the translation is correctly placed *outside* the parentheses.

7. *Enclose marginal incidental commentary in parentheses.* The remark *the year was 1942* is too distant from the sense of the sentence for commas. Place it in parentheses. The parenthetical remark is *not* capitalized and does *not* end in a period because it is inserted inside a sentence.
   Revision: There was great merriment in Tehran despite the wartime conditions (the year was 1942) and much partying.

8. *Use parentheses, not commas, for lengthy remarks inside sentences.* The clause *who have written and e-mailed in large numbers wanting to know the facts* is too long to be set aside meaningfully in commas. Enclose it in parentheses.
   Revision: The more information we can provide to our members (who have written and e-mailed in large numbers wanting to know the facts), the more likely they will be to support our proposal.

9. *Punctuate the parenthetical citation as part of the sentence.* Use a lower case -s on *see,* and place the final period outside the parentheses.
   Revision: Eighteenth and nineteenth century South Carolina planters justified slavery as an economic necessity. Even planters opposed to slavery in principle record in their diaries that it was impossible to find free workers to perform the hard labor on rice, cotton, and tobacco plantations (see Appendix D).

10. *Enclose in parentheses relatively distant incidental information. Eliminate semicolon.*
    Revision: General Winfield Hancock (born in 1824) was a Union commander who fought at Gettysburg.

✍ 58 Brackets

1. *Point out error in text by inserting a bracketed* sic *immediately after the mistake.*
   Revision: The coach said, "If a player can handle the pressure from the fans, he is on his way to becoming an intregal [sic] part of the team."

2. *The years 1942–1944 provide additional information that interferes with the flow of the parenthetical remark and should be bracketed.*
   Revision: There was great merriment in Tehran (the wartime conditions [1942–1944] notwithstanding) and much partying.

3. *Bracket changes in quotations.*
   Revision: In his lecture, the noted archeologist expressed the opinion that "[a]long with the Theory of Evolution we need to consider the principles of Catastrophism."
4. *Bracket correction (sic) in quotation.*
   Revision: The letter to our first president referred to him as "President Washineton [sic]"; it sold for $200,000 at auction.
5. *Bracket additional information inside parentheses.*
   Revision: The original text (discovered in 1860 see [Appendix B]) indicates that Richard III probably had not murdered his nephews.

59 Dashes

1. *Set aside in em dashes the incidental and conversational commentary and include appropriate punctuation.*
   Revision: My father — whom I adored when I was small! — sang Italian love songs as my mother accompanied him at the piano.
2. *Set aside in em dashes the incidental and conversational commentary and include appropriate punctuation.*
   Revision: I recall vividly — who could forget? — the enthusiastic applause of the guests.
3. *Use en dash.*
   Revision: In August 1939 the Stalin–Hitler pact stunned Europe.
4. *Insert an em dash to show an interruption in dialogue.* Also eliminate the comma. Do not use a dash next to a comma.
   Revision: I started to say, "Your behavior last night — " but never finished because she walked away even as I was speaking.
5. *Use en dash to indicate span from one point to another.* I could not understand exercises 7–14 in the calculus assignment.
6. *No revision.*

   OR

   Revision: The guest speaker — who towered over the students — was seven feet tall.
7. *Set aside with an em dash a surprising list.* Alternatively, the list may be enclosed in parentheses.
   Revision: The children were taught formal ballroom dancing that they interspersed with less gracious activities — name calling, making faces, pinching.
8. *Eliminate final dash when incidental remark coincides with the end of the sentence.* Conclude this sentence with an exclamation point or with a period.
   Revision: Privately Nixon's aides maintained that Nixon resigned the presidency because he had been certain Jerry Ford would pardon him — they had little doubt about it!

9. *The aside should be enclosed in em dashes on both sides. Use only one remark set off by dashes per sentence.* Replace the comma with an *em* dash. Replace the dash after *fireworks* with a comma or with parentheses.
 Revision: Our conversation — such as it was — was punctuated by the exploding fireworks, a drawback of the Fourth of July extravaganza.
10. *Show span from one point to another by using an en dash.* Replace hyphen with *en* dash.
 Revision: Was this set such a good buy when it is missing series *K–P*?

✍ 60 Hyphens

1. *Hyphenate prefixes that stand alone and describe a word that also contains a prefix (whether or not it be hyphenated).* Also italicize such a prefix. (See §61 *Italics*.)
 Revision: The students formed groups to discuss the *pro-* and anti-tax resolutions.
2. *Divide a word at the end of a line by hyphenating between the prefix and root word (de-emphasize). Hyphenate to contradict the meaning of a root word (ex-wife, ex-husband). Hyphenate to avoid confusing spellings (de-emphasized, never-ending).*
 Revision: During the investigation, the *ex-wife de-emphasized* her drinking problem and accused her *ex-husband* of *never-ending* criticism.
3. *Hyphenate compound adjectives that precede the words they describe (step-by-step mastery).*
 Revision: Robin Hood's *step-by-step* mastery of archery amazed me.
4. *Hyphenate numbers twenty-one to ninety-nine.*
 Revision: Even after repaying me the two hundred dollars, he owed me *fifty-seven* more.
5. *Hyphenate the number and the word it describes when both describe yet another word (seven-foot).*
 Revision: The *seven-foot* tall basketball player towered over the seventh graders.
6. *No revision.* In this sentence, *three fifths* does not describe any other word and, therefore, should not be hyphenated.
7. *No revision.* Do not hyphenate compound adjectives that *follow* the word they describe.
8. *Do not hyphenate compound adverbs that follow the words they describe.*
 Revision: They walked down the street hand in hand.
9. *Hyphenate and italicize a prefix that stands alone (short-). Place a hyphen between a prefix and the root word whose meaning it changes (long-term).*
 Revision: They acted without considering both the *short-* and long-term consequences of damaging Mrs. Robinson's fence.

10. *Hyphenate numbers from twenty-one to ninety-nine. Hyphenate compound adjectives that precede the words they describe (rough-and-tumble).*
Revision: At *twenty-one,* I felt totally in control of my own destiny, ready to plunge into the *rough-and-tumble* world of Wall Street wheeling and dealing.

 61 Italics

1. *Do not italicize names of buildings* (Lincoln Center). *Do italicize the name of a composition not listed by form, number, and key.*
Revision: On the program at Lincoln Center was Dvořák's *New World Symphony.*
2. *Italicize for emphasis.*
Revision: Like Sherlock Holmes, we are fascinated by why the dog *didn't* bark.
3. *Italicize foreign words which are not yet standard English expressions. Italicize titles of plays.*
Revision: In Meyer's play, *Art Comes Alive,* the *pièce de resistance* was the dance of the Mona Lisa.
4. *No revision. Hors d'oeuvres* has become a standard English expression.
5. *Do not italicize compositions listed by form, number, and key.*
Revision: Let's listen to Richter's recording of Mozart's Piano Concerto No. 20 in D Minor.
6. *Italicize the title of a book that is part of the title of an article.*
Revision: My article is entitled "The Perception of Duality in Conrad's *The Secret Sharer."*
7. *Do not italicize foreign words that are standard English expressions* (rendezvous). *Do not italicize the names of buildings and monuments. Do italicize words used as words* (ands).
Revision: While we waited to rendezvous with the others at the Lincoln Memorial, he edited my speech removing some of the *and*s.
8. *The names of sacred books are not italicized* (Koran). *Do italicize the name of a newspaper.*
Revision: The Washington Post *is running a series of articles on the Koran.*
9. *Italicize foreign words that are not standard English expressions.*
Revision: According to one German critic, *Weltschmerz* is sadness experienced by people who have nothing better to do.
10. *Italicize the names of films.*
Revision: Shakespeare in Love *has received more Oscars than any other film in recent years.*

62 Quotation marks

1. *Words used as words are enclosed in quotation marks.*
   Revision: The expression "gosh" was coined to avoid taking the Lord's name in vain.
2. *Titles of short stories are enclosed in quotation marks.*
   Revision: Norman Mailer thought Jack London's hero in "To Build a Fire" behaved like a sissy.
3. *Dialogue is in quotation marks.*
   Revision: "I hear him coming," I said. "I have to hang up now."
4. *Unpleasant, tasteless, or ironic expressions are in quotation marks.*
   Revision: I think that I was "the bastard" he was ranting about.
5. *Quotations are in quotation marks.*
   Revision: Quoting, "If at first you don't succeed try, try again," my brother encouraged me to fly off the roof of the garage once more.
6. *Nicknames or descriptive associations are in quotation marks.*
   Revision: She spent her vacation in Alaska, "The Land of the Midnight Sun."
7. *Titles of short stories published as part of a collection are in quotation marks.*
   Revision: My favorite tale in *The Arabian Nights* is "The Story of the Magic Horse."
8. *Dialogue is in quotation marks.*
   Revision: "Mirror mirror on the wall," she kept asking, "who's the fairest of them all?"
9. *Nicknames or descriptive associations are in quotation marks.*
   Revision: My great-grandmother used to tell me about her girlhood in the "Gay Nineties," and about Clara Bow, the silent film star, who was said to have "It."
10. *Words used as words are enclosed in quotation marks.*
    Revision: Many people confuse the words "discrete" and "discreet."

 63, 64 Punctuating and capitalizing with quotations, and punctuating a quotation-within-a-quotation

1. *Capitalize quotations in the middle of a sentence if they are complete sentences in themselves.*
   Revision: Plato's *Protagoras* attributes the saying, "Know thyself " to the Delphic Oracle.
2. *Commas that precede quoted speech are placed before the open-quotation mark (Quixote, "didn't). Commas that follow quoted speech are always inside quotation marks (Sancho," said). Eliminate the less important (!) end punctuation to avoid doubly punctuating the sentence. Place the quotation within the dialogue in single quotation*

marks ('Squeak'). Place the question mark outside the single quotation marks because the entire sentence is the question.
Revision: "Sancho," said Don Quixote, "didn't you hear that windmill go 'Squeak'?"

OR

Sancho said, "Don Quixote, didn't you hear that windmill go 'Squeak'?"

3. *Enclose in single quotation marks a quotation within quoted speech. Separate the two sets of quotation marks with a space. Place the comma inside the single quotation marks.*
Revision: " 'A penny saved is a penny earned,' " quoted my father.

4. *There is no comma in front of the quotation because you do not place punctuation before a quotation that simply flows into your own sentence. Enclose the quotation (by the dawn's early light) in quotation marks, but do not capitalize it because it is a fragment. Enclose the anthem title in quotation marks.*
Revision: I rose early in order to see Fort McHenry "by the dawn's early light" as the poet had seen it when he wrote "The Star-Spangled Banner."

5. *Enclose the veteran's statement in quotation marks, but do not place a comma after the relative pronoun (that).*
Revision: The Vietnam veteran told us that "war is hell."

6. *Enclose the entire question (does...question) in double quotation marks. Enclose the unpleasant expression (the Jewish Question) in single quotation marks. The question mark goes between the single and double end quotation marks to indicate that the scholars are asking a question. A colon instead of a comma precedes this formal quoted speech.*
Revision: Scholars ask themselves: "Does Hitler's *Mein Kampf* give clear evidence of his intended solution to 'the Jewish Question'?"

7. *Enclose the quoted speech in quotation marks preceded by a comma. After the close-quotation mark, place a semicolon for the second and closely related part of the statement. Semicolons are placed outside of quotation marks unless they are part of the quotation.*
Revision: The Duchess of Malfi announced, "I love all fruit"; then she admitted that apricots were her favorite.

8. *Enclose the quoted speech in quotation marks. Because it is an exclamation, place the exclamation point inside the quotation marks. Said is not capitalized because the entire statement is a single sentence regardless of the exclamation point. End with an appropriate period.*
Revision: "But the room was locked *from the inside!*" said Monsieur Poirot emphatically.

9. *Enclose the quoted speech in quotation marks with commas after the word* imagine, *and* folklorist. *The proverb is capitalized because it is a complete sentence, and is enclosed in single quotation marks. It is preceded and followed by a comma. Note the space between the single and double close-quotation marks.*

Revision: "As you can imagine," said the folklorist, "the proverb, 'A stitch in time saves nine,' was popular with quilters.

10. *Enclose the entire sentence in double quotation marks and the poem's title in single quotation marks. A comma precedes the title of the poem. The question mark is placed after the single close-quotation mark to indicate that the entire statement is a question.*

Revision: "Can you remember the end of Emily Dickinson's poem, 'I heard a fly buzz when I died'?"

65   Plagiarizing and documenting

What is the purpose of quoting and documenting?

Quoting authorities illustrates and strengthens our arguments and allows us to examine critically the opinions of others. Instead of just making assertions, serious writers support their ideas by quoting or otherwise referring to the work of knowledgeable people respected in the field.

Documentation should be honest and informative. It gives credit where due and directs interested readers to related sources of information for further study. Footnotes or endnotes provide readers with extra information that cannot be inserted into the text without digressing.

What exactly is plagiarism, and how can you avoid it?

Plagiarism is using other people's words or ideas without giving them credit. It is intellectual robbery, and it is illegal. The sources of ideas must be documented even when these sources are not quoted directly but provide merely background information.

Ideas may be paraphrased without using quotation marks, but the paraphrase cannot just juggle pre-existing words or replace certain words with synonyms. You must capture the idea entirely in your words and in an original sentence construction, and then document it. Other people's language (groups of words) must be enclosed in quotation marks and documented.

Can you plagiarize your own work?

Yes! Strange as it may seem, once you have put your ideas down on paper, they become an authority. When you return to quote them in a later paper, you must acknowledge their source in a citation. The most common kind of self-plagiarism is *double submission* in which the student submits the same paper in more than one course without the permission of the instructor.

How much documentation is necessary? Is more better?

All quotations, paraphrases, and insights that are not your own must be attributed, or you will be guilty of plagiarism. However, quote only what is absolutely necessary to support your ideas, and limit informative notes to strictly essential material. Don't ramble merely to prove your erudition.

Some students "pad" their notes and bibliographies with books and articles cited by other authors. Note and bibliography padding is dangerous and dishonest when you have not actually read the sources yourself. Padded documentation is obvious to the instructor and often clearly uninformed or irrelevant.

What is the "right" way to document material?

There are various accepted styles of documentation: *MLA*, *APA*, *Chicago*, *Turabian*. Your instructor will tell you which style she prefers.

This text describes and illustrates the *MLA* style. There are a few issues of documentation, however, on which the *MLA* differs from the common practice adopted by scholarly journals. In such cases, this text presents the common practice as a possible alternative to the *MLA* protocol.

Why do people sometimes use footnotes/endnotes and sometimes parenthetical citations in the text?

In citing sources, writers use one of two equally valid techniques:

◆ Endnotes and footnotes (referred to below as *notes*)
◆ Parenthetical citations in the text (sometimes called *running text*)

Which form you use depends on your instructor's and your own preference, and especially on your material. People choose the form that seems to create the least interruption in the flow of their language and ideas. Often the decision is dictated by whether or not you plan to use content notes — additional information that supplements the text (see §73 *Models of footnotes and endnotes*). Content notes require footnoting, and thus the use of the footnote/endnote style of citation. Once you have chosen a form, be consistent in using it.

66   Using quotations effectively

How do you know when and what to quote?

Quote material to show that your assertions are based on authoritative sources. However, examine these authorities critically. Do not simply repeat their opinions. Just because someone is an authority does not mean that you cannot question his opinion. In fact, you will usually find authorities who contradict one another on every subject.

Quote language that is particularly vivid, that uses words in unusual ways, that illustrates your point precisely, that is directly relevant to your argument. Trim the quotation of irrelevancies by using *ellipses* [...] judiciously.

66a   Introduce and explain longer quotations

Quotations illustrate and support your discussion; *they do not replace it.* A quotation of two or three words may be simply inserted into your text as part of the sentence. For longer quotations, two rules apply: (1) prepare the reader for longer quotations with a short introduction that sets the scene identifying the speakers and the occasion; (2) explain the quotation immediately afterward. Remember that a meaningful explanation draws out the implications of the words and reaches reasonable conclusions based on them.

In the example below, the introduction is inadequate — it fails to set the scene — and the explanation is missing.

UNCLEAR   Macbeth shows that he is worried by saying, "Listening to their fear, I could not say 'Amen,' / When they did say, 'God bless us' " (2.2.39-40).

REVISED   To his dismay, Macbeth discovers that after killing Duncan, he is suddenly unable to pray, "Listening to their fear, I could not say 'Amen,' / When they did say, 'God bless us' " (2.2.39-40). His inability to pray is a portent of his damnation.

Make quotations relevant **66b**

Make sure that the details of your quotation are relevant to your argument. In the example below, the argument concerns Macbeth's insomnia, but the quotation deals with nightmares. Because nightmares occur only during sleep, the quotation effectively contradicts the argument.

```
Contributing to Macbeth's self-destruction is
                        peacefully
his inability to sleep as he comments to his
                       ^
wife about "these terrible dreams / That

shake us nightly [...]" (3.2.20-21).
```

Adding the word *peacefully* changes the subject from *inability to sleep* to the *quality* of Macbeth's sleep — a subject borne out by the quotation.

 When quoting fewer than three lines of verse, indicate the line breaks with a slash (/) and retain the capital letter of the new line's first word as above.

Integrate quotations into text **66c**

Quotations should flow as naturally as possible from your words into those of the authority. To the reader, the quotation should seem to be completing your own idea. Avoid isolating short quotations in separate sentences without a few words of your own.

ISOLATED
```
According to scientists in Edinburgh,
genetic flaws in the cloned sheep Dolly
have revealed problems with the viability
of current cloning methods. "We haven't yet
entered the age of foolproof cloning."²
```

INTEGRATED
```
Genetic flaws in the cloned sheep Dolly
have revealed problems with the viability
of current cloning methods. Scientists in
Edinburgh admitted that they "haven't yet
entered the age of foolproof cloning."²
```

The subject and verb tense of your own text must fit with those of your quotation. If necessary, alter your own text to make it grammatically compatible with the quotation.

SHIFT IN SUBJECT	`Hamlet tells Polonius to use people "after your own honour and dignity: the less they deserve, the more merit is in your bounty" (2.2.484-86).`
REVISED	`Hamlet instructs Polonius to treat people better than they deserve: "Use them after your own honour and dignity: the less they deserve, the more merit is in your bounty" (2.2.484-86).`
SHIFT IN SUBJET AND VERB	`Cleopatra decided to kill herself explaining that "I have / Immortal longings in me […]."`[1]
REVISED	`When Cleopatra decides to kill herself, she explains: "I have / Immortal longings in me […]."`[1]

66d   Quote to add factual details

Sometimes, a statement seems wholly unreasonable unless clarified by a quotation. In the example below, the writer cannot simply state that Macduff was not born of a woman. What could that mean? Human experience demands an explanation from the text.

```
Macbeth battles Macduff confidently because
the apparition predicted that "none of woman
born / Shall harm Macbeth" (4.1.86-87).
However, his confidence fails him when he
learns that Macduff was not born of a woman
but "was from his mother's womb / Untimely
ripp'd" (5.8.19-20).
```

66e   Quotations as completed ideas

Whether your quotation flows into your own sentence or stands apart from your text, make sure that it is not merely a fragment of an idea. Even when quotations are broken up by ellipses or otherwise foreshortened, they must always present completed ideas. The model below has a non-specific introduction and no explanation. The substance of the quotation is incomplete — a fragment of an idea.

INCOMPLETE   After Macbeth murders Duncan, events take a turn for the worse. According to Ross, "And Duncan's horses […] beauteous and swift, the minions of their race […] contending 'gainst obedience, as they would make / War with mankind" (2.4.16-21).

REVISED   After Macbeth murders Duncan, unnatural events pervade Scotland. Daylight seems to vanish entirely, so "That darkness does the face of earth entomb […]" (2.4.10). And animals behave out of character like Duncan's horses that "Turn'd wild in nature […] / Contending 'gainst obedience, as they would make / War with mankind" (2.4.19-21). The kingdom reflects the unnatural behavior and psychological disturbance of its king.

67 Guidelines for changes in quoted material

What specific kinds of changes may be made in quotations?

In using quotations, writers sometimes find that they need to make certain adjustments to the quoted text. Very few adjustments are permitted in quotations. Alter quotations only as follows:

- ◆ Font or size
- ◆ Punctuation
- ◆ Spacing or placement on a page
- ◆ Change of initial letters of the first word from lower to upper case or vice versa
- ◆ Indication of typographical errors
- ◆ Insertion or deletion of certain information (see below)

Why are changes in quotations made, and how are these changes signaled?

Changes in quotations are made to clarify meaning by adding language, to add emphasis, to eliminate irrelevant information, to make

the text and the quotation compatible grammatically and typo-
graphically (see §66c *Integrate quotations into text*). All documentation styles require that changes in quotations be bracketed, except
for changes in punctuation other than ellipses. In making changes
in quotations:

◆ Preserve the meaning of the quotation
◆ Change its typographical form but not its language
◆ Preserve the grammatical integrity of the quoted text

*Why do you leave out parts of quotations, and how do you
show these deletions?*

Sometimes parts of quotations must be deleted for the sake of
elegance, relevance, economy. Use deletions to eliminate extraneous
or adjacent quotation marks (see §63e *Eliminating adjacent quotation marks*). As always, the deletions must preserve the meaning and
grammar of the quotation and must be indicated by appropriate
punctuation. Use the ellipsis mark inside square brackets [...] to
show that you have deleted (elided) material from a quotation.

68 Quoting prose: citations, placement, deletions, insertions

What is prose, and how is it different from poetry?

Prose is any writing — literature, criticism, history, news etc.— that is
not poetry. Unlike poetry, prose does not have meter — a rhythmical
pattern of stresses — or rhyme.

Drama, particularly Renaissance drama such as Shakespeare's,
is often written both in prose and in verse (poetry). Each must be
quoted using a different format. You will recognize prose in drama
by the fact that it is punctuated as a normal sentence, unlike verse
which begins each new line with a capital letter regardless of
preceding punctuation.

Citing and placing prose quotations of four lines or fewer 68a

Prose quotations of four lines or fewer may be incorporated into your paragraph without being set off from your text. They may be complete sentences or just key words or phrases. They may be inserted as an entire uninterrupted quotation, or the quoted words may be separated by your own text.

USING PARENTHETICAL REFERENCES If the quotation ends in a period, place that period *after* the close-parenthesis mark, *not* inside the quotation marks.

➤Martha wrote, "Today I met the perfect English gentleman" (*Young Americans Abroad* 27).

➤Roberta Thompson reminds us that Odysseus was named "by his maternal grandfather, Autolychus, who was known to be the greatest liar and perjurer of ancient Greece" (37).

➤Significantly, Odysseus became a "liar and perjurer" just like "his maternal grandfather, Autolychus" who had given him both a name and an identity (Thompson 37).

If the quotation is a question or exclamation, place the appropriate mark inside the quotation marks, and place your own period after the close-parenthesis mark.

➤Martha wrote, "Will I ever meet the perfect English gentleman?" (*Young Americans Abroad* 27).

USING NOTES Superscript the note number immediately after the reference. All final punctuation, including quotation marks, *precedes* the note. There is no punctuation after the note.

➤Autolychus, "the greatest liar and perjurer of ancient Greece,"[5] named his grandson Odysseus.

Citing and placing prose quotations longer than four lines 68b

Prose quotations longer than four lines are always set off from your own text.

◆ Long quotations are usually — but not always — preceded by a colon or a period.

◆ Indent the quotation one inch (10 spaces) from the left margin of your text. Optionally, you may also choose to indent the right margin of your quotation by an inch.
◆ Do *not* enclose the quotation in quotation marks.
◆ Use end punctuation as needed throughout the quotation.
◆ At the conclusion of the quotation, place the end punctuation mark *before* the parenthetical reference or note.
◆ The parenthetical reference is separated by a space from the end of the quotation.
◆ There is no additional space before the note.

The *MLA* recommends that quotations be double-spaced. Many stylists, however, strongly favor single-spacing long quotations. Check with your instructor concerning her preference. If you single-space, skip an additional line between your text and the set-off quotation.

```
Another way to facilitate disabled students'

access to coursework is with assistive devices

as mandated by Section 504:

     A recipient [...] may not impose upon
     handicapped students other rules, such
     as the prohibition of tape recorders in
     classrooms or of dog guides in campus
     buildings, that have the effect of limiting
     the participation of handicapped students
     in the recipient's education program or
     activity. (HEW Agency Regulations,
     subpart E, section 84.44 [b] 22684)
```

68c   Prose quotations longer than one paragraph

◆ Indent by a quarter inch (3 spaces) the first line of the first paragraph if it is the start of a new sentence, but not if it merely continues the sentence in your text.
◆ Indent (3 spaces) the first line of each of the following paragraphs.
◆ In quoting *dialogue* longer than one paragraph, use open-quotation marks at the start of each paragraph, but use close-quotation marks *only* at the end of the final paragraph.

Indicating deletions in fragmentary quotations 68d

A fragmentary quotation is a bit of cited text whose beginning — and sometimes end — the writer leaves out in order to integrate it into his sentence. Deletions in short unindented quotations are formatted differently from those in long indented quotations.

No ellipses are needed for short, unindented, quoted fragments or phrases that flow into your sentence without a perceptible break.

➤ Faulkner believes that the duty of the writer is to celebrate humanity's "compassion and sacrifice and endurance." [4]

➤ Americans look back cynically on Nixon's promise that he was "not a crook."

However, quoted fragments that are formally introduced should be preceded by an ellipsis and followed by one as needed.

➤ Juliet warns Romeo to leave the orchard: "[…] the place is death, considering who thou art […]." [3]

For longer, indented fragments, place the ellipsis at the beginning of the quotation to show deletion.

In "Lecture 14" on English prose style, Coleridge insists that

> […] the primary role and condition is not to attempt to express ourselves in language before we thoroughly know our own meaning; — when a man perfectly understands himself, appropriate diction will generally be at his command. (237)

Indicating deletions at the end of a quotation 68e

Use an ellipsis mark at the end of a longer quotation either (1) when you omit the end of the quoted sentence or (2) for a long quoted fragment, if the material coincides with the end of your own sentence.

ORIGINAL

> Section 504 does not require the finest accommodations possible for disabled students. However, it does require access to all educational facilities including dormitories, dining halls, theaters.

ELIDED AND FOOTNOTED TEXT

> According to the article, the law "does not
> require the finest accommodations possible
> for disabled students. However, it does
> require access to all educational facilities
> [...]."[9]

ELIDED TEXT WITH PARENTHETICAL REFERENCE

> According to the article, the law "does not
> require the finest accommodations possible
> for disabled students. However, it does
> require access to all educational facilities
> [...]" (35).

68f   Indicating deletion of a sentence or more

To show a deletion of a sentence, or a paragraph or more of prose
use a bracketed ellipsis [...]. Be aware, however, that pasting parts of
quotations together from distant parts of a book is misleading. Do
not delete sentences or paragraphs from a quoted source in an
attempt to conceal contradictions.

68g   Punctuating an elided quotation

Keep the original punctuation of an elided quotation. Insert the
ellipsis [...] where appropriate. Thus all of the following variants are
possible: . [...] or , [...] or [...]? or [...]: etc.

68h   Indicating insertions in quotations

Information may be inserted into a quotation when necessary in
order to clarify or correct it. Information inserted into either prose or
verse must be placed in brackets. For comments outside quotation
marks use parentheses.

TO ADD CLARIFICATION

➤ "It was a judicial decision [Roe v. Wade] that
  altered forever the lives of American women."

➤ "Eventually Carl Jung's relationship with him
  [Freud] deteriorated to the point of enmity."

TO POINT OUT TYPOGRAPHICAL ERRORS IN THE ORIGINAL TEXT Insert *sic* immediately after the mistake.

➤The antiques catalogue listed the rocking chair as "President Jeferson's [sic] favorite piece of furniture."

TO ADD EMPHASIS TO IMPORTANT WORDS When making a close reading of the text, writers may choose to italicize important words in a quotation to make them stand out. To indicate this formatting change in the original quotation, place the words *emphasis added* or *italics mine* in parentheses directly after the quotation marks, but before the final punctuation.

Vonnegut's *Cat's Cradle* begins with a series of echoes that translate old literary traditions into a new idiom, biblical and Melvillean heroes into modern characters: "Call me *Jonah*. My parents did. Or nearly did. They called me *John*"[10] (emphasis added).

69 Quoting poetry and song lyrics: citations, placement, deletions, insertions

How are poetry and song lyrics different from prose?

Both poetry and song lyrics are kinds of verse. In other words, their language has a rhythmic pattern (called *meter*) or rhyme or both.

Unlike quoting prose, quoting verse requires that you indicate the beginning of each new line with a slash (/) even when the sentence has not ended. In order to appreciate the quotation fully, the reader needs to know not merely what the poem says but what the pattern of accents or meter is — a pattern which is measured from the beginning of the line.

Quoting three lines of verse or fewer   **69a**

◆ Do *not* set off the quotation from your text.
◆ Enclose it in quotation marks.

♦ Separate the lines with a slash (/) leaving a single space on either side.

♦ Do not change capitalized letters in verse into lower case, namely, the capitals following a slash.

♦ In parenthetical references, cite either the author and collection, or the author and the poem.

♦ In parenthetical references, place the final period outside the quotation marks and after the close-parenthesis mark.

♦ For poetry fragments, cite the author's name and the poem title, and list the line numbers.

```
The poet expresses succinctly the paradox
of divine passion and individual freedom
when he tells his God: "for I/ Except you
enthrall me, never shall be free" (John
Donne, "Batter my Heart" 12-13).
```

♦ If the author is cited in the preceding text, do not cite him again in the parenthetical reference.

```
Politicians would do well to heed Frost's
ironic observation that he never "dared to
be a radical when young / For fear it
would make me a conservative when old"
("Precaution" 1-2).
```

♦ Using notes, place the final period inside the quotation marks.

```
Politicians would do well to heed Frost's
ironic observation that he never "dared to
be a radical when young / For fear it
would make me conservative when old."6
```

69b   Quoting more than three lines of verse

♦ The last sentence before the quotation should end either with a colon or a period. If the quotation is a continuation of the sentence, a comma will do.

♦ Set the quoted verse off on the line following your text.

♦ Indent quotation so that it is centered on the page insofar as possible. But retain an even left margin for all capitalized lines.

♦ Do *not* enclose the set-off verse in quotation marks.

♦ Using parenthetical reference, cite either the author and collection, or the author and the poem.

- If the author is cited in the preceding text, do not cite her again in the parenthetical reference.
- Lines that are too long to fit before the right margin are carried over to the next line and indented three spaces.
- Reproduce as far as possible the original set up of the poem on the page. Shaped poems, for example, should retain their original shape in quotation.
- For poetry fragments, cite poem title and list the line numbers.
- Place the final punctuation mark (usually a period) immediately after the last word of the quotation.
- Leave one space between the final punctuation mark and the parenthetical reference.
- When the parenthetical reference is too long to fit on the same line as the end of the quotation, place it on a new line at the left margin of the poem.
- There is *no punctuation* after the parenthetical reference.
- For a note reference, place end punctuation at the end of the poem. Place the note directly after the end punctuation, without any intervening space.
- The quotation may be double-spaced to conform to *MLA* protocol, or single-spaced to follow common practice.

```
Here,  the  poet's  mesmeric  litany  of  senses  and

images  experienced  in  an  archetypal  childhood

gropes  after  the  prophetic  sublime.

     Out  of  the  cradle  endlessly  rocking,

     Out  of  the  mocking-bird's  throat,  the  musical

          shuttle,

     Out  of  the  Ninth-month  midnight,

     Over  the  sterile  sands  and  the  fields  beyond,

          where  the  child  leaving  his  bed  wander'd

          alone,  bareheaded,  barefoot,

     Down  from  the  shower'd  halo,

     Up  from  the  mystic  play  of  shadows  twining

          and  twisting  as  if  they  were  alive,
```

```
Out of the patches of briers and blackberries,

From the memories of the bird that chanted

    to me[...].

(Walt Whitman, "Out of the Cradle
Endlessly Rocking," 1-8)
```

As with prose quotations, many stylists favor single-spacing. If you choose to single-space, skip a line between your text and the quotation.

```
Here, the poet's mesmeric litany of senses and

images experienced in an archetypal childhood

gropes after the prophetic sublime.

    Out of the cradle endlessly rocking,
    Out of the mocking-bird's throat, the musical
        shuttle,
    Out of the Ninth-month midnight,
    Over the sterile sands and the fields beyond,
        where the child leaving his bed wander'd
        alone, bareheaded, barefoot
    Down from the shower'd halo,
    Up from the mystic play of shadows twining
        and twisting as if they were alive,
    Out of the patches of briers and black-
        berries,

    From the memories of the bird that chanted
        to me[...].³
```

69c   Indicating deletions and insertions in quoted verse

FOR DELETIONS IN QUOTATIONS OF POETRY INTEGRATED INTO THE TEXT (3 LINES OR FEWER)
Show a deletion from either the middle or end of the quotation by placing an ellipsis in brackets, following the same rules as for prose (see §68d *Indicating deletions in fragmentary quotations*, and §68e *Indicating deletions at the end of a quotation*).

FOR DELETIONS IN QUOTATIONS OF POETRY SET ASIDE FROM THE TEXT (4 LINES OR MORE)
All ellipses must be enclosed in brackets. Show the omission of a line or more in the middle of the poem by inserting a full line of bracketed double-spaced points the length of the poetic line.

Remember to indicate separately the line numbers of *each part* of the elided quotation in the parentheses that follow.

```
Chaucer begins his poem with an open question

concerning the truth of dreams:

    God turne us every drem to goode!
    For hyt is wonder, be the roode,
    To my wyt, what causeth swevenes
    [.   .   .   .   .   .   .   .   .]
    And why th'effect folweth of somme,
    And of somme hit shal never come [...].
    ("House of Fame" 1-3, 5-6)
```

FOR INSERTIONS IN VERSE QUOTATIONS Treat insertions in verse in the same way as insertions in prose (see above §68h *Indicating insertions in quotations*).

70 Quoting drama: citations, placement, deletions, insertions

Do the rules for quoting prose and poetry apply to drama as well?

The same rules apply except in quoting dialogue of two or more characters. Some drama may contain both prose *and* verse. (You will recognize verse by the capital letter at the beginning of each line.) Dramatic verse should be quoted as poetry, and dramatic prose as prose.

Parenthetical citations of passages in drama use Arabic numerals only and list *act, scene,* and *lines* as follows: (3.5.37-42).

Quoting an excerpt from one character's speech   *70a*

In quoting a single character, the same rules apply in drama as in poetry and prose.

DRAMATIC PROSE Unlike Olivia, Malvolio is attuned to the presence of anagrams as names.

```
          M.O.A.I. This simulation is not as
          the former. And yet, to crush this a
          little, it would bow to me, for
          every one of these letters are in my
          name. Soft! Here follows prose.
          (Twelfth Night 3.1.136-39)
```

Notice that the quotation does not capitalize the first word of each line as it would for poetry.

DRAMATIC
VERSE
```
          Twelfth Night opens with Orsino's conceit of
          music as an anaphrodisiac: "If music be the
          food of love, play on / Give me an excess of
          it that, surfeiting, / The appetite may
          sicken and so die" (1.1.1-3).
```

70b   Quoting two or more characters

◆ Dialogue is set off from the text and is usually preceded by a colon.
◆ Characters' names:
   — are indented one inch (10 spaces) from left text margin
   — are entirely capitalized (in small caps)
   — are followed by a period and two spaces
◆ The first line of each character's dialogue starts on the same line as the character's name.
◆ Subsequent lines are indented an additional three spaces, to a total of 13 spaces from the left text margin.
◆ Do *not* enclose dialogue in quotation marks.
◆ Format verse dialogue as in the original.
◆ Parenthetical reference comes after the final punctuation which is followed by two spaces. There is no punctuation after the parenthetical reference.
◆ Note is superscripted after the final punctuation.
◆ Double-space dialogue to conform to *MLA* protocol, but as with prose and poetry, some stylists prefer single spacing. If you choose to single-space, precede and follow your quotation with a skipped line.

```
Jacobs' characters parody the frothy dialogue

of Noel Coward society:

   JOHN. I love you madly.
```

MARCIA. You love everyone madly. That's why

I can't marry you. (1.3.22-25)

Indicating deletions and insertions in quoted drama   *70c*

To show deletions or insertions in quoted drama, use the same technique as in treating prose or verse quotations. (See above §68d – 68h, see also §69c *Indicating deletions and insertions in quoted verse.*)

71   Citing titles in text

When referring to a title, how do you know whether it should be underlined, italicized, or placed in quotation marks?

When you cite titles in your essay, a general rule is to italicize titles of "long" works, and to place quotation marks around titles of "short" works. Underlining is no longer necessary with computer formatting. Within that general rule are variations that require careful scrutiny. Specific rules also apply to capitalizing words in titles.

The *MLA* recommends underlining as equivalent to italicizing. Underlining, however, is left over from the days of typewriters and should no longer be considered an alternative to italics.

Capitalizing words in titles   *71a*

Always capitalize the first and last words and main words of all titles and subtitles. Also capitalize in accordance with parts of speech.

CAPITALIZED PARTS OF SPEECH	NOT CAPITALIZED PARTS OF SPEECH
nouns	articles
pronouns	prepositions
verbs	coordinating conjunctions
adjectives	*to* in infinitives
adverbs	subordinating conjunctions

➤"To Be or Not to Be"

➤*In Search of an Mrs.: College Girls from 1900-1960*

➤*Folk-Lore in the Old Testament*

➤"The Land between the Oceans"

➤"With Hatred in Between"

➤"Batter My Heart"

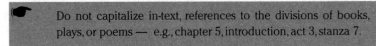

Do not capitalize in-text, references to the divisions of books, plays, or poems — e.g., chapter 5, introduction, act 3, stanza 7.

71b   Titles that are italicized

Italicize the types of titles listed below:

◆ Works published as complete in themselves (as opposed to those that are part of a collection): books, long poems, plays
◆ Magazines, newspapers, pamphlets
◆ Musicals, opera, ballets, films, radio and television programs
◆ Art exhibits, names of paintings and sculptures
◆ Airplanes, ships, trains, spacecraft

➤*The New York Times'* theater critic gave glowing reviews to Robert Brownell's new play, *In Ariadne's Footsteps* which premiered on the cruise ship *Titanic II*.

71c   Titles enclosed in quotation marks

Enclose in quotation marks titles of texts published not separately but as part of a collection. Usually these are short texts such as chapters, articles, short stories, essays, lectures, songs, short poems. The example below illustrates the reference to chapters in a novel.

➤Dickens juxtaposes "A Fellow of Delicacy" and "A Fellow of No Delicacy" to emphasize the irony in the social circumstances and characters of Carton and Stryver.

Titles in standard print   **71d**

Use standard print — *not* italics or quotation marks — for buildings and monuments; conferences; courses; instrumental music listed by form, number, and key; literary series; political documents; sacred texts; seminars; societies; workshops.

➤He discovered one of the earliest copies of the Declaration of Independence in his grandparents' attic.

➤The pianist played Brahms' Klavierstücke, Opus 119 in B minor.

➤The Sacred Writings Seminar on the Bible paid particular attention to Exodus.

Citing titles within titles   **71e**

FOR A SHORT STORY TITLE WITHIN THE TITLE OF AN ARTICLE Use single quotation marks around the title of the short story. Always separate the two sets of quotation marks by a space.

➤"Social Implications of Shirley Jackson's 'The Lottery' "

FOR A BOOK TITLE INCLUDED IN THE TITLE OF AN ARTICLE Italicize.

➤"Perspectives on Irony in Dickens' *A Tale of Two Cities*"

(an article about a novel)

FOR A BOOK TITLE INCLUDED IN ANOTHER BOOK TITLE De-italicize (use standard print).

➤*Perspectives on Irony in Dickens'* A Tale of Two Cities

(a book about a novel)

72 Models of parenthetical references

What is a parenthetical reference, and where do you place it?

A parenthetical reference is an alternative to a footnote or endnote. It gives the source of a quotation or idea directly after the citation. Place it in parentheses, and punctuate it *as part of the preceding sentence.* Make parenthetical citations as brief as possible. List only the author's name or first word of the title, depending on the way the source appears in the *Works Cited,* but include the page number(s) if available. The *complete* reference, with all the necessary information appears in the *Works Cited,* which is the final section of your work. If the *Works Cited* lists a magazine article by its title, "The Dilemma of Assisted Suicide," and the quotation is on page 29, the parenthetical reference is ("Dilemma" 29). (See also in poetry §69a and §69b, and in drama §70 *faq.*)

INTERNET WEB SITE ARTICLE Name the author or first word of the title of the article and, in angle brackets, <the electronic address>.

> ➤The review describes *The Passion of the Christ*, as "an orgy of violence" (Kramer <www.filmclips.org>).

IF THE AUTHOR'S NAME IS STATED IN YOUR TEXT Do *not* repeat it in the parenthetical reference, but use page numbers only.

> ➤Bonessi supports this argument (125-26).

IF THE AUTHORS' NAMES ARE NOT IN YOUR TEXT Include their names.

> ➤Some scientists contend that three-year olds can learn to decode words(e.g., Bonessi and Rodican 125-26).

IF TWO CITED AUTHORS HAVE THE SAME LAST NAME Add the first initial.

> ➤One researcher disagrees with the analysis (J. Rodican 267-8).

IN CITING TWO WORKS BY A SINGLE AUTHOR Include enough of the title to indicate which work you mean.

> ➤Clemens' work on adolescent psychology maintains that teenagers are less tolerant than adults in judging deviant behavior (*Absurdity* 77-93).

IN CITING A CORPORATE AUTHOR List as you would a single author.

➤The governor expressed concern with the decline of the population in the state (U.S. Census Bureau 196).

IF NO AUTHOR IS NAMED AND THE WORK IS ALPHABETIZED BY TITLE IN YOUR WORKS CITED List it by the complete title if it is short, or by the first word of a long title.

➤*The Hartford Courant* hailed the production as "ingenious and innovative, confirming the theater's reputation as a leader of experimental drama among regional companies" ("Rapunzel" B3).

IN CITING A MULTIVOLUME WORK Cite both *volume* and *page* number, separating them by a *colon* and a *space*.

➤(Toynbee 2: 13-60).

IN CITING AN ENTIRE VOLUME Include a *comma* and the abbreviation "vol." as follows:

➤(Toynbee, vol. 2).

TO REFER TO AN INDIRECT SOURCE (AN AUTHOR CITING SOMEONE ELSE'S WORDS OR IDEAS) Insert the abbreviation "qtd. in" in front of the secondary source.

➤(qtd. in Chang 2: 127, 212-213).

IN CITING CLASSIC PROSE LITERATURE, HISTORY, OR PHILOSOPHY Cite *parts and chapters* because they are more useful to readers than a page number alone. These works are widely available in many editions with various paginations. Therefore, list the *page number* followed by a *semicolon* and *additional information*.

➤(Tolkien 822; bk.5, ch.3).

➤(Kant 162; bk.2, pt.1, sec.43).

IN CITING GREEK AND LATIN CLASSICS OF LITERATURE, HISTORY, OR PHILOSOPHY Cite the book title in italics omitting the page number. Then cite the divisions of the book from largest to smallest — line numbers, if given — with numbers separated by periods. If the divisions are given in Roman numerals, translate them into standard Arabic numerals.

➤*(Aeneid* 4.6-30).

➤*(The Peloponnesian War* 2.50).

IN CITING SACRED TEXTS LIKE THE BIBLE List chapter and verse. *Never* abbreviate the name of a sacred work in your own writing, but *do* abbreviate it in the parenthetical reference.

> Marriage, according to St. Paul, is only slightly more pleasant than a poke in the eye with a sharp stick. When possible, men should have nothing to do with women (1 Cor.7.1-3).

TO CITE MORE THAN ONE WORK IN A SINGLE PARENTHETICAL REFERENCE Use one of the forms above, and separate your citations with a *semicolon* and a *space.*

> While some traditional scholars maintain the biblical supremacy of the male over the female because "woman was taken out of man," many feminists point out that neither is superior to the other as God is both male and female simultaneously. "So God created man in His own image [...] male and female created He them" (Gen.2.23; Gen.1.27).

CITE INTERVIEWS BY THE NAME OF THE PERSON INTERVIEWED For clarity, include the word "Interview."

> ➤(Nielson, Interview).

TO INDICATE NON-PRINT CITATIONS (E.G., BROADCAST, FILM, ELECTRONIC SOURCES) Use the same form as for print citations. However, for purposes of clarity, identify the *non-print* nature of the source in your own text.

> The swiftly moving collage of violent images in Serengeti's first film juxtaposes the escalating fear and the dwindling self-esteem of people in a totalitarian state (*Total Terror*).

73 Models of footnotes and endnotes

How are footnotes and endnotes different from one another?

Footnotes and endnotes differ only in their location. Footnotes are placed at the bottom of each page. Endnotes appear at the end of an essay, a chapter, or a book. Often both footnotes and endnotes are referred to simply as "notes."

Do I need to format my own footnotes and endnotes if my computer does it automatically?

Most high school students and all university students today use computers for their written assignments. All modern word-processing applications format footnotes and endnotes automatically. This text presents both computer formatting options, and traditional manual formatting instructions.

Placing and formatting footnotes using the computer   *73a*

Signal footnotes in the text with superscript numbers (raised above the line). They correspond to numbered notes just below the text set off with a line running one third of the way across the page.

When formatting your footnotes on the computer, choose the following options:

◆ Autonumbering: numbers footnotes consecutively throughout the text, not by page.
◆ Arabic numerals: standard numbers (1, 2, 3 etc.) should be used in preference to Roman numerals or special symbols.
◆ Start at 1.
◆ If your word processing application does not number automatically starting at one, select *continuous numbering*.

Place the footnote mark at the end of the phrase, clause, or sentence that contains the cited material. All punctuation marks, *except dashes*, precede the note numbers. Do *not* place any punctuation mark immediately after the note number or around it.

Placing and formatting endnotes using the computer   *73b*

Endnotes are signaled in the text exactly like footnotes (see above). When formatting endnotes on the computer, choose the same format options as for footnotes.

While word processing applications place endnotes at the end of the text, they will not begin on a separate page. To conform to *MLA* protocol, adjust the placement of computer endnotes manually as follows:

◆ The endnote references are placed on a page entitled *Notes* which comes directly after the end of an essay, chapter, or book. The title, *Notes*, should be centered on the page.

◆ . The *Notes* page *precedes* the *Works Cited* page.

73c   Formatting footnotes and endnotes manually

If you choose not to use the automatic computer options, format your notes as follows:

◆ Indent the first line one-half inch (5 spaces). Note that this text uses computer formatting in its examples

◆ Single-space after the superscripted number

◆ Single-space between the lines within each footnote

◆ Double-space between footnotes

◆ To continue a footnote onto the following page: (1) double-space after the text and type a solid line across the page, (2) double-space again and continue the footnote from the preceding page without indenting.

◆ Place footnotes from the new page after this continuation with the usual double-space between them

◆ Number footnotes/notes consecutively throughout the essay

73d   Location and format of the *Notes* page

The Notes page comes after the text but before the Works Cited. The page is numbered consecutively with the text. The title is centered and placed one inch from the top of the page. The first endnote is double-spaced down from the title of the page. Number all pages and all notes in sequence.

73e   Two types of footnotes or endnotes

There are two kinds of notes, *content* notes and *bibliographic* notes.

CONTENT NOTES Provide additional information without interrupting the flow of the text. They are superscripted and numbered just as bibliographic notes are.

[1] The term "wasteland" in medieval literature is potentially misleading. The land is "waste" not because it is inherently infertile, but

```
because, as forest, it is not arable.
"Wasteland" most closely translates the
medieval Latin brolium.
```

BIBLIOGRAPHIC NOTES (DESCRIBED IN FULL BELOW) Contain author, title, and other publication data, but may also contain other information pertinent to the subject of the essay.

```
2 For an authoritative discussion of theories
of price, see John Baldwin, "Medieval Theories
of Just Price" in Transactions of the American
Philological Society, vol. 49 (1959).
```

Information in a first bibliographic footnote or endnote   *73f*

The first reference to a text consists of five parts:

◆ Note number followed by a space
◆ Author's first and last name, followed by a comma and a space
◆ Title of the work italicized, or in quotation marks as needed, space.
◆ Open-parenthesis, location of the publisher, colon, name of publisher, comma, date of publication, close-parenthesis, space
◆ Page number(s) followed by a period
◆ Footnotes should be single-spaced, while endnotes may be *single-* or double-spaced.

```
➤1 Barbara Clemens, Absurdity and Other Adolescent
Afflictions (Buffalo: Malcolm Press, 1997) 37.
```

 There is no page number if you are citing the text as a whole.

Indicating missing information   *73g*

Sometimes information such as the publisher, or publication date is not available. Sometimes too, a source many be unpaginated. If so, in the place where you would normally list this material, indicate that the information is missing. Use the abbreviations below as needed.

ABBREVIATION	MEANING	CITATION FORM
n.p.	No place of publication	N.p.: Yale UP, 1999
n.p.	No publisher	New Haven: n.p., 1999

```
n.d.          No date of publication New Haven: Yale UP, n.d.

n.pag.        No pagination          New Haven: Yale UP, 1999.
                                     N.pag.
```

73h   Information listed in subsequent bibliographic footnotes or endnotes

All subsequent references are also indented and double-spaced down from the preceding note. The references are abbreviated to provide just enough information to identify the text and the page number.

TO CITE ONLY ONE TEXT BY A GIVEN AUTHOR Last name and the page number followed by a period are sufficient.

➤¹ Clemens 43-44.

TO CITE TWO OR MORE TEXTS BY THE SAME AUTHOR Identify the title *in abbreviated form*. The citation lists the following in order: superscripted note number, space, author's last name, comma, space, abbreviated title, space, page number, period.

➤¹ Clemens, *Absurdity* 43-44.

TO CITE AN ANONYMOUS LISTED BY TITLE Use the first word of the title and the page number.

➤¹ *Absurdity* 43-44.

73i   Books and pamphlets: model footnote or endnote

Book and pamphlet titles are treated identically. Below is the model of a footnote or endnote for a book or pamphlet which is cited for the first time. Notice that it includes the five parts listed above.

Following this model are examples that show you how to adapt each part of this basic model to indicate other types of references. This model footnote is for a single-author book.

➤¹ Barbara Clemens, *Absurdity and Other Adolescent Afflictions* (Buffalo: Malcolm Press, 1997) 37.

BOOK BY TWO OR MORE AUTHORS   Simply add the names of the other authors, and continue the model.

➤¹ Barbara Clemens, Robert Sato, and Aaron Swift,

BOOK BY AN ORGANIZATION (INCLUDING THE GOVERNMENT) Replace the author's name (Clemens) by the name of the organization, and retain the rest of the model.

➤¹ Ford Foundation,

ANONYMOUS BOOK If you have no listed author, start with the title. Otherwise, the model is unchanged.

➤¹ *Absurdity and Other Adolescent Afflictions*

EDITED ANTHOLOGY OF WORKS BY VARIOUS AUTHORS Start with the name of the editor followed by the abbreviation "ed." and a comma. If there are more than two editors, name one and add "et al." Pluralize "ed." to "eds." Then continue with the original model.

➤¹ Barbara Clemens, ed., *Absurdity and Other Adolescent Afflictions*

➤¹ Barbara Clemens et al, eds., *Absurdity and Other Adolescent Afflictions*

WORKS OF A SINGLE AUTHOR THAT HAVE BEEN EDITED BY ANOTHER WRITER Start with either the name of the original author, or the name of the editor, but be sure to include both names. Add a comma after the title. Otherwise keep to the model.

➤¹ Barbara Clemens, *Absurdity and Other Adolescent Afflictions*, ed. Carl Loving

➤¹ Carl Loving, ed., *Absurdity and Other Adolescent Afflictions*, by Barbara Clemens

TRANSLATION In the model, after the title, simply add a comma and the word "trans." Then add the name of the translator(s).

➤¹ Barbara Clemens, *Absurdity and Other Adolescent Afflictions*, trans. Carl Loving and Sandra Knispel

MULTIVOLUME WORK Add the volume number (vol. 7) after the title. If the editor's or translator's name comes after the title, place a comma, then add the word "vol." and the number of the volume after the comma. Add a space, and continue with the model.

➤¹ Barbara Clemens, *Absurdity and Other Adolescent Afflictions*, trans. Carl Loving and Sandra Knispel, vol. 7

73j   Portions of books: model first footnote or endnote

Portions of books can include a short story, an essay, or a play in an anthology; an encyclopedia article; a preface; a foreword; an afterword etc. Treat chapters similarly. (See also §71c.)

WORK IN AN ANTHOLOGY   If the entire anthology is by a single author, simply place the name of the short story, essay, play etc. after the author's name in the model.

> ➤¹ Barbara Clemens, "First Love," *Absurdity and Other Adolescent Afflictions*

If the anthology is an edited collection of the work of various authors, list the following:

- ◆ The author of the quoted piece
- ◆ The title of the quoted piece in quotation marks (followed by a comma)
- ◆ The editor (followed by a comma)
- ◆ The title of the anthology

Then continue with the model.

> ➤¹ Barbara Clemens, "First Love," ed. Jack Rodican, *Absurdity and Other Adolescent Afflictions*

INTRODUCTION, PREFACE, FOREWORD, AFTERWORD   If the same author has written the entire work, you can either replace the page number with the words "introduction, preface, foreword, afterword," or insert one of these words before the page number.

> ➤¹ Barbara Clemens, *Absurdity and Other Adolescent Afflictions* (Buffalo: Malcolm Press, 1997) afterword.

If someone other than the author of the text has written the cited section, begin with that person's name, followed by the section of the book, then the title of the book, and author. Separate the entries with commas. The remainder of the note follows the model.

> ➤¹ Sandra Knispel, Introduction, *Absurdity and Other Adolescent Afflictions*, by Barbara Clemens

ARTICLE IN A REFERENCE BOOK Begin with the author if one is listed; otherwise, strip the model down to the 3 parts below. Include only the following information:

- Article title and comma in quotation marks
- Italicized title of the reference work (followed by a comma)
- Year of the edition

> ➤¹ Barbara Clemens, "Adolescent Afflictions,"
> *Parents' Encyclopedia*, 1993 ed.

> ➤¹ "Adolescent Afflictions," *Parents' Encyclopedia*,
> 1993 ed.

Articles in periodicals: general notation guidelines   *73k*

Note references to articles in periodicals have 6 parts:

- Indented and superscripted note number followed by a space
- Author's first and last name, comma, space
- Title of the article and comma in quotation marks, space
- Italicized name of the periodical, space
- Volume /series / issue (if any), date, colon, space
- Page number(s), period
- For articles on discontinuous pages — list the first page number of the article followed immediately by a plus sign (12+)
- For short, unpaginated texts, cite by paragraph numbers preceded by the abbreviation *par(s)* — e.g., par.18.

For newspapers only: if the name of the newspaper does *not* include its city, insert that name in brackets after the name of the newspaper.

Magazine articles: model first footnote or endnote   *73l*

Below is a standard *MLA*-style note for a magazine article. Adaptations of this note follow this model.

> ➤¹ Bianca Bonessi, "Teaching Reading to First
> Graders," *Journal of Early Learning* Jan.-Feb.
> 1998: 66.

ANONYMOUS MAGAZINE ARTICLE If no author is listed, start with the title, then continue the model.

> ➤¹ "Teaching Reading to First Graders," *Journal of
> Early Learning* Jan.-Feb. 1998: 66.

JOURNAL ARTICLE IN A PERIODICAL WITH SERIES / ISSUE / VOLUME NUMBERS Insert these numbers into the model after the name of the periodical and before the date. When these journals do *not* list months, place the year in parentheses.

> ➤¹ Bianca Bonessi, "Teaching Reading to First Graders," *Journal of Early Learning* 3rd ser. 49 (1998): 66.

EDITORIAL IN A MAGAZINE Start with the title, as in an anonymous article, then insert the word "editorial" followed by a comma. Then complete the model.

> ➤¹ "Teaching Reading to First Graders," editorial, *Journal of Early Learning* Jan.-Feb. 1998: 66.

LETTER TO THE EDITOR IN A MAGAZINE Use the model, but replace the article title with the word "letter."

> ➤¹ Bianca Bonessi, letter, *Journal of Early Learning* Jan.-Feb. (1998): 66.

SERIALIZED ARTICLE IN A MAGAZINE Stay with the model as usual, but list chronologically each of the issues where the series of articles appears. If the magazine is issued by volumes, use those numbers (as below), if by months list the specific months. Separate the listings by semicolons. Add authors as needed.

> ➤¹ Bianca Bonessi and Jack Rodican, "Teaching Reading to First Graders," *Journal of Early Learning* 54 (1997): 25-33; 59 (1998): 66-70.

REVIEW IN A MAGAZINE After the title of the article, insert the words "rev. of" and the title of the work being reviewed in italics, comma, the author's name, comma. Then complete the model.

> ➤¹ Bianca Bonessi, "Teaching Reading to First Graders," rev. of *Adventures in Elementary Education*, by Larisa Polonskaya, *Journal of Early Learning* Jan.-Feb. 1998: 66.

ANONYMOUS REVIEW Begin with the title of the article, and proceed with the model as usual.

> ➤¹ "Teaching Reading to First Graders," rev. of *Adventures in Elementary Education*, by Larisa Polonskaya, *Journal of Early Learning* Jan.-Feb. 1998: 66.

Newspaper article: model first footnote or endnote *73m*

Stay with the magazine model up to and including the name of the newspaper, then list as follows:

◆ City in brackets if it is not part of the newspaper's name — insert immediately after the name of the newspaper and follow with a space
◆ Date by day, month (abbr.), year, comma, space
◆ Type of edition (if any), colon, space
◆ Section and page number, period

> ➤[1] Bianca Bonessi, "Teaching Reading to First Graders," *The Herald* [Buffalo] 22 Ap. 1997, late ed.: B6.

ANONYMOUS ARTICLE IN A NEWSPAPER Drop the author, but otherwise copy the model. In the example below, the newspaper's name includes its home city and, therefore, does *not* require the city's name in brackets as in the model above.

> ➤[1] "Teaching Reading to First Graders," *The Buffalo Herald* 22 Ap. 1997, late ed.: B6.

EDITORIAL IN A NEWSPAPER List in the same way as an anonymous article, but add "editorial" and a comma, and then continue with the model.

> ➤[1] "Teaching Reading to First Graders," editorial,

LETTER TO THE EDITOR IN A NEWSPAPER Start with author, comma, and the word "letter" and comma. Drop the title. Otherwise the model is unchanged.

> ➤[1] Bianca Bonessi, letter,

SERIALIZED ARTICLE IN A NEWSPAPER Keep the entire model, but add to it. Change the final period to a semicolon and add the following information:

◆ Part in the series, comma
◆ Title of the series, comma
◆ Date when the series began, period

> ➤[1] Bianca Bonessi, "Teaching Reading to First Graders," *The Buffalo Herald* 22 Ap. 1997, late ed.: B6; pt. 3 of a series, Innovations in Buffalo Schools, begun 5 Ap. 1997.

REVIEW IN A NEWSPAPER IF THE AUTHOR OF THE REVIEW IS KNOWN:

◆ Begin with his name and the title of the article, as usual
◆ Insert italicized title of the work being reviewed, comma
◆ Add the author or editor of the reviewed work, comma

If the review is in a supplement, include the name of this supplement in place of the usual edition and section.

> ➤¹ Bianca Bonessi, "Teaching Reading to First Graders," rev. of *Adventures in Elementary Education*, ed. Jack Rodican, *The Buffalo Herald Education Supplement* 22 Ap. 1997: 28.

REVIEW IN A NEWSPAPER IF THE AUTHOR OF THE REVIEW IS NOT LISTED:

Begin either with the title of the article and the words "rev. of," or begin with the words "Rev. of" and leave out the article title. Otherwise follow the listing immediately above.

> ➤¹ "Teaching Reading to First Graders," rev. of *Adventures in Elementary Education*, ed. Jack Rodican, *The Buffalo Herald Education Supplement* 22 Ap. 1997: 28.

> ➤¹ Rev. of *Adventures in Elementary Education*, ed. Jack Rodican, *The Buffalo Herald Education Supplement* 22 Ap. 1997: 28.

73n　　Letters in collections and to the author: model first footnote or endnote

> ➤¹ V. I. Lenin, "To Krupskaya," 14 June 1919, letter 379 of *The Collected Letters of V. I. Lenin*, ed. Gary Light, vol. 1 (Moscow: Novoe Izdatelstvo, 1996) 260-62.

> ➤⁹ William Faulkner, letter to the author, 25 October 1928.

73o　　Interviews: model first footnote or endnote

FORMAL, PUBLIC INTERVIEWS Citations consist of 4 parts:

◆ Name of the person interviewed, comma
◆ The words "interview with" and the interviewer's name, comma

- ◆ Site where interview material was obtained — broadcast, magazine with commas. (For personal interviews see below.)
- ◆ Date the interview took place

Follow the spacing, capitalization, and punctuation of the models below.

> ➤¹ Bianca Bonessi, interview with Jack Rodican, *60 Seconds*, ABC, New York, 23 Dec. 1998.

PERSONAL INTERVIEWS CONDUCTED BY THE AUTHOR Use citations that consist of 3 parts:

- ◆ Name of the person interviewed, comma
- ◆ Personal interview, comma
- ◆ Date the interview took place

> ➤¹ Bianca Bonessi, Personal interview, 23 Dec. 1998.

> ➤¹ Bianca Bonessi, Telephone interview, 23 Dec. 1998.

Lectures, speeches / addresses: model footnote or endnote   *73p*

These citations consist of 6 parts:

- ◆ Name of the speaker, comma
- ◆ Title of the lecture, or the word "address", comma
- ◆ Name of the forum (if any), and name of the convention, comma
- ◆ Location, comma
- ◆ Date of the speech, comma

Follow the spacing, capitalization, and punctuation of the models below.

> ➤¹ Bianca Bonessi, "Teaching Reading to First Graders," Elementary Education Forum, National PTA Convention, De Soto Convention Center, Miami, 16 Oct. 1998.

> ➤¹ Bianca Bonessi, address, Elementary Education Forum, National PTA Convention, De Soto Convention Center, Miami, 16 Oct. 1998.

73q

Electronic references

Before using electronic references for support, evaluate their credibility even more thoroughly than you do the credibility of print references. As a rule, information in print tends to be more trustworthy than electronic information. A more permanent and therefore more responsible medium, a print source is more readily verified, and most printed material benefits from editorial review before publication. Unedited electronic publications are readily accessible to anyone with a link to the Internet. Consider the following questions about the author, the treatment of the subject, and the publication:

- What are the author's qualifications, and can they be verified?
- Is the author an expert in this subject?
- Is the information accurate and up-to-date?
- Is the topic treated fairly, objectively, and broadly?
- Who are the publishers?
- What is the purpose of the publishers? Do they have personal agenda they wish to promote?

If you decide to cite an electronic publication, download or print out a hard copy for future reference and record the date of this search.

73r

Electronic references: model footnote or endnote

INTERNET REFERENCE WITHOUT PRINT SOURCE

> ➤³ Grove, Josephine, "Reading Readiness in
> Kindergarten," n. pag., pars. 25. 28 Jan. 2000
> <http://www.cea.org>.

For electronic references with print sources, use one of two techniques:

1. Retain the print model, but convert final period to a comma and add electronic reference.

2. Keep the author and title section of the model, but replace the print publisher, location, and date with the same information about the electronic company.

 Electronic texts are often unpaginated. When no pagination is available, cite by paragraph numbers preceded by the abbreviation *par(s)* — e.g., *par. 18*.

Follow the punctuation, capitalization, and spacing in the models below.

BOOK ON DISKETTE OR ON MAGNETIC TAPE

Print model

➤¹ Barbara Clemens, *Absurdity and Other Adolescent Afflictions* (Buffalo: Malcolm Press, 1997) 37.

Electronic model

➤¹ Barbara Clemens, *Absurdity and Other Adolescent Afflictions*, diskette, (Chicago: New Media, 1997) 37.

What has changed?

After the title, the rest of the model has been replaced by the electronic information.

 If the book is on magnetic tape, replace the word *diskette* with the words *magnetic tape*.

WORK IN AN ANTHOLOGY ON CD-ROM

Print model

➤¹ Barbara Clemens, "First Love," *Absurdity and Other Adolescent Afflictions* (Buffalo: Malcolm Press, 1997) 37.

Electronic model

➤¹ Barbara Clemens, "First Love," *Absurdity and Other Adolescent Afflictions* Buffalo: Malcolm Press, 1997) 37, *Adolescent Psychology Full-Text Database*, rel. 3, CD-ROM (Burbank: Metro, 1997).

What has changed?

The entire model is retained, and the electronic reference is inserted at the end.

MAGAZINE ARTICLE ACCESSED THROUGH A COMPUTER NETWORK

Print model

> ➤[1] Bianca Bonessi, "Teaching Reading to First Graders," *Journal of Early Learning* Jan.-Feb. 1998: 66.

Electronic model

> ➤[1] Bianca Bonessi, "Teaching Reading to First Graders," *Journal of Early Learning* Jan.-Feb. 1998: 66, online, GALENET, 20 Ap. 1998.

What has changed?

The entire model is retained, and the electronic data are inserted at the end.

Replace the name of the computer network as needed, e.g., Internet, Bitnet, SIRS etc.

NEWSPAPER ARTICLE FROM A DATABASE ON CD-ROM

Print model

> ➤[1] Bianca Bonessi, "Teaching Reading to First Graders," *The Buffalo Herald* 22 Ap. 1997, late ed.: B6.

Electronic model

> ➤[1] Bianca Bonessi, "Teaching Reading to First Graders," *The Buffalo Herald* 22 Ap. 1997, late ed.: B6, *The Buffalo Herald Ondisc*, CD-ROM, UMI-ProQuest, Jl. 1997.

What has changed?

The electronic information is simply added at the end.

E-MAIL

Print model of letter

> ➤[9] Carlton Smith, letter to the author, 25 October 1928.

Electronic mail

➤⁹ Carlton Smith, e-mail to the author, 25 October 1928.

Broadcasts and live performances: model footnote or endnote   *73s*

TELEVISION OR RADIO PROGRAM

➤⁵ "American Klezmer," *Jewish Culture in America*, writ. and narr. Naomi Bloom, perf. Klezmer 2000, Learning Channel, 18 Sept. 1999.

FILM OR VIDEO RECORDING

➤⁶ Kolja Muller, dir., *Pythons*, Jennifer Voskov and Rolfe Chaplin, 1977, videodisc, RKO, 2000.

LIVE PERFORMANCE

➤² Gordon Martino, perf., *Uncle Vanya*, by Anton Chekhov, trans. Gary Light, dir. Matthew Parkhill, Sharon Playhouse, Sharon, CT 4 July 1998.

74 Works Cited / bibliography

What is Works Cited, and where is it located?

Works Cited, sometimes called *bibliography*, lists in full all the source references in your text. It is the final section of your essay, placed after the appendices and after the *Notes* page. Some instructors believe that the footnote or endnote form precludes the need for *Works Cited* because the first citations already include complete references to each source. Check your instructor's preference. The parenthetical reference form, however, always requires a *Works Cited* section to which all the in-text citations are keyed.

Formatting the Works Cited section   *74a*

◆ Leave a one-inch margin all around the page.
◆ Center the title: Works Cited.

- Start your first entry two lines below the title.
- Double-space throughout — both within and between entries.
- In each entry, start the first line at the margin, then indent by one-half inch (5 spaces) all the lines after the first line.
- For multiple entries by the same author or editor, use 3 en dashes followed by a period, instead of repeating the first and last names. Or, use a one-half inch (5 spaces) underline followed by a period.

74b   Listing the entries

The entries are all bibliographic notes. However, their formatting differs from that of footnotes and endnotes.

- Alphabetize by the author's (or editor's) last name, or anonymous work by title.
- In citing more than one work by an author, arrange them alphabetically by title (ignore *A*'s and *The*'s), and replace the author's name by 3 en dashes and a period, or by a one-half inch (5 spaces) underline followed by a period.
- In case an author is also the co-author of another cited work, list the single-author book first.
- When an author has co-authored two books each with a different co-author, list them alphabetically by the co-author's last name.
- When there is no author or editor listed, alphabetize by the title of the book, the article, or the work in an anthology.

74c   Indicating missing information

As we said earlier with reference to footnoting, sometimes information such as the publisher, or publication date is not available. Sometimes too, a source may be unpaginated. If so, in the place where you would normally list this material, indicate that the information is missing. Use the abbreviations below as needed.

ABBREVIATION	MEANING	CITATION FORM
n.p.	No place of publication	N.p.: Yale UP, 1999
n.p.	No publisher	New Haven: n.p., 1999
n.d.	No date of publication	New Haven: Yale UP, n.d.
n.pag.	No pagination	New Haven: Yale UP, 1999.

Supplying missing information from an alternate source 74d

If you can make an educated guess about missing bibliographic information, or if you find this missing information in a different source, by all means use it in your reference. However, indicate this different source by bracketing it.

➤New Haven: Yale UP, [1999].

Any uncertain information should be signaled by a question mark, and, as usual, bracketed. Estimated dates are preceded by the abbreviation *c.* for *circa*.

➤New Haven: [Yale UP?], 1999.

➤New Haven: Yale UP, [c.1999].

Differences between *Works Cited* notes and 74e footnotes/endnotes

They are nearly identical in terms of information. The changes are in punctuation, in spacing, and in listing authors by last names first. Below are two model citations for the same book by a single author:

FIRST FOOTNOTE REFERENCE FOR A BOOK WITH A SINGLE AUTHOR

➤[1] Barbara Clemens, *Absurdity and Other Adolescent Afflictions*, vol. 7 (Buffalo: Malcolm Press, 1997) 37.

WORKS CITED REFERENCE FOR THE SAME BOOK

➤Clemens, Barbara. *Absurdity and Other Adolescent Afflictions*. Vol. 7. Buffalo: Malcolm Press, 1997.

What has changed?

- ◆ The note number is no longer needed.
- ◆ The author is listed last name first (to help with alphabetizing).
- ◆ The indentation is reversed (to call attention to the alphabetical order).
- ◆ The commas have become periods (except between last and first names, and between publisher and date).
- ◆ The parentheses are gone.
- ◆ The page number is gone (except for a work in an anthology).

- Periods are followed by two spaces instead of one space.
- If a period is followed by a word, that word is always capitalized.
- The entries are double-spaced.
- The second and subsequent lines of the entry are indented one-half inch.

Using the list of changes above, you can easily adapt any footnote or endnote to a *Works Cited* entry. However, if you prefer, you may consult the models below.

74f   Books and pamphlets: models of *Works Cited* references

TWO OR MORE BOOKS OR PAMPHLETS BY THE SAME AUTHOR

➤Clemens, Barbara. *Absurdity and Other Adolescent Afflictions*. Buffalo: Malcolm Press, 1997.

➤- - - . *Surviving Adolescence*. Buffalo: Malcolm Press, 1997.

OR

➤_____. *Surviving Adolescence*. Buffalo: Malcolm Press, 1997.

BOOK BY TWO OR MORE AUTHORS If the book has *more than 3 authors*, name the first one only and add the words *et al* followed by a period.

➤Clemens, Barbara, Robert Sato, and Aaron Swift. *Absurdity and Other Adolescent Afflictions*. 2nd edition. Buffalo: Malcolm Press, 1997.

➤Clemens, Barbara, et al. *Absurdity and Other Adolescent Afflictions*. 2nd edition. Buffalo: Malcolm Press, 1997.

BOOK BY AN ORGANIZATION (INCLUDING THE GOVERNMENT)

➤Ford Foundation. *Absurdity and Other Adolescent Afflictions*. 2nd edition. Buffalo: Malcolm Press, 1997.

ANONYMOUS BOOK

➤*Absurdity and Other Adolescent Afflictions*.

    2nd edition. Buffalo: Malcolm Press, 1997.

TITLE WITHIN A TITLE Do *not* italicize the title of a book which is contained within the larger title.

➤Baker, Emily. *The Black and White Family*

    Structure in William Faulkner's Absalom,

    Absalom! Buffalo: Malcolm Press, 1999.

EDITED ANTHOLOGY OF WORKS BY VARIOUS AUTHORS

➤Clemens, Barbara, ed. *Absurdity and Other*

    Adolescent Afflictions.2nd edition. Buffalo:

    Malcolm Press, 1997.

WORKS OF A SINGLE AUTHOR WHICH HAVE BEEN EDITED BY ANOTHER WRITER

➤Clemens, Barbara. *Absurdity and Other Adolescent*

    Afflictions. Ed. Carl Loving. 2nd edition.

    Buffalo: Malcolm Press, 1997.

➤Loving, Carl, ed. *Absurdity and Other Adolescent*

    Afflictions. By Barbara Clemens. 2nd edition.

    Buffalo: Malcolm Press, 1997.

TRANSLATION

➤Clemens, Barbara. *Absurdity and Other Adolescent*

    Afflictions. Trans. Carl Loving and Sandra

    Knispel. 2nd edition. Buffalo: Malcolm

    Press, 1997.

MULTIVOLUME WORK

➤Clemens, Barbara. *Absurdity and Other Adolescent*

    Afflictions. Trans. Carl Loving and Sandra

    Knispel. Vol. 7. Buffalo: Malcolm Press, 1997.

WORK IN AN ANTHOLOGY BY A SINGLE AUTHOR Notice the need for page numbers.

➤Clemens, Barbara. "First Love." *Absurdity and*
    Other Adolescent Afflictions. Buffalo:
    Malcolm Press, 1997. 204-27.

WORK IN AN EDITED ANTHOLOGY OF THE WORK OF VARIOUS AUTHORS

➤Rodican, Jack. "First Love." Ed. Barbara
    Clemens. *Absurdity and Other Adolescent*
    Afflictions. Buffalo: Malcolm Press, 1997.
    204-27.

INTRODUCTION, PREFACE, FOREWORD, AFTERWORD ETC.

➤Clemens, Barbara. *Absurdity and Other Adolescent*
    Afflictions. Buffalo: Malcolm Press, 1997.
    Afterword.

➤Knispel, Sandra. Introduction. *Absurdity and*
    Other Adolescent Afflictions. By Barbara
    Clemens. Buffalo: Malcolm Press, 1997.

ARTICLE IN A REFERENCE BOOK

➤"Adolescent Afflictions." *Parents' Encyclopedia*.
    1993.

➤Clemens, Barbara. "Adolescent Afflictions."
    Parents' Encyclopedia. 1999.

74g   Magazine references: *Works Cited* models

MAGAZINE ARTICLE Notice that there are parentheses around dates which
are identified by year only. Note the colon before page numbers.

➤Bonessi, Bianca. "Teaching Reading to First
    Graders." *Journal of Early Learning*
    Jan.-Feb. 1998: 66-68.

ANONYMOUS MAGAZINE ARTICLE

➤"Teaching Reading to First Graders." *Journal of
    Early Learning* (1999): 66-69.

JOURNAL ARTICLE IN A PERIODICAL WITH SERIES/ISSUE/VOLUME NUMBERS

➤Bonessi, Bianca. "Teaching Reading to First
    Graders." *Journal of Early Learning* 3rd ser.
    49 (1998): 66.

EDITORIAL IN A MAGAZINE

➤"Teaching Reading to First Graders." Editorial.
    Journal of Early Learning Jan.-Feb. 1998:
    66-68.

LETTER TO THE EDITOR IN A MAGAZINE

➤Bonessi, Bianca. Letter. *Journal of Early
    Learning* Jan.-Feb. 1998: 66-69.

SERIALIZED ARTICLE IN A MAGAZINE

➤Bonessi, Bianca, and Jack Rodican. "Teaching
    Reading to First Graders." *Journal of Early
    Learning* 54 (1997): 25-33; 59 (1998): 66-70.

REVIEW IN A MAGAZINE

➤Bonessi, Bianca. "Teaching Reading to First
    Graders." Rev. of *Adventures in Elementary
    Education* By Larisa Polonskaya. *Journal of
    Early Learning* Jan.-Feb. 1998: 66-68.

74h   Newspaper references: *Works Cited* models

Adapt the magazine models to newspaper references using the sample below as a standard.

NEWSPAPER ARTICLE

➤Bonessi, Bianca. "Teaching Reading to First

    Graders." *The Buffalo Herald* 22 Ap. 1997,

    late ed.: B6.

74i   Interviews, lectures, speeches / addresses: *Works Cited* models

Adapt the footnote form in the same way as above by changing the indents, starting with the last name, converting commas to periods followed by 2 spaces and capital letters, double-spacing between lines. List by the *last name of the person being interviewed*.

➤Bonessi, Bianca. Interview with Jack Rodican.

    60 Seconds. ABC. New York. 23 Dec. 1998.

➤Bonessi, Bianca. Personal interview. 23 Dec.

    1998.

➤Bonessi, Bianca. Internet interview. 23 Dec.

    1998.

➤Bonessi, Bianca. Telephone interview. 23 Dec.

    1998.

➤Bonessi, Bianca. "Teaching Reading to First

    Graders." Elementary Education Forum.

    National PTA Convention. De Soto Convention

    Center. Miami. 16 Oct. 1998.

➤Bonessi, Bianca. Address. Elementary Education

    Forum. National PTA Convention. De Soto

    Convention Center. Miami. 16 Oct. 1998.

Electronic *Works Cited* references   *74j*

In general, adapt the standard *Works Cited* reference sometimes by replacing the publication information with the electronic information, and sometimes by simply adding the electronic information to the existing print model. Cite whatever information is available. To indicate the information that is not available use the abbreviations (see §74c *Indicating missing information*). Use paragraph numbers (*par.*) if pagination is missing.

    For online publications, list the uniform resource locator (URL). This is the network address where the reader can access the cited electronic source. The URL is enclosed in angle brackets and begins with the access-mode identifier (*http, ftp, telnet, gopher, bitnet news*). If the address is longer than the line of print in your text, divide it *only after* a slash.

    Always cite the date on which you download the electronic source. This date precedes the angle-bracketed URL address without any intervening punctuation mark.

    Below are specific electronic models and guidelines for citing information from CD-ROM, diskette, magnetic tape, commercial online databases, and Internet sources.

CD-ROM, diskette, magnetic tape — non–periodical   *74k*
publication / single issue

Include as much of the following information as is available. Remember, that you may choose to include or omit the print information. Punctuate as in the examples below.

- ◆ Author
- ◆ Title, italicized or in quotation marks
- ◆ Title of product italicized (e.g., *Davka Classic Author Series*)
- ◆ Edition, release, version, publication medium (CD-ROM or diskette)

- City of publication
- Name of publisher
- Year of publication

BOOK, PAMPHLET

Print model

➤Clemens, Barbara. *Absurdity and Other Adolescent*

    Afflictions. Vol.7. Buffalo: Malcolm Press,

    1997.

Electronic models

➤Clemens, Barbara. *Absurdity and Other Adolescent*

    Afflictions. Magnetic tape. Chicago: New

    Media, 1997.

➤Jones, Franklin. "Adventures of Paul Bunyan."

    Microsoft Legendary Americans. 1998 ed.

    CD-ROM. Ashland: Microsoft, 1998.

➤Jones, Franklin. "Adventures of Paul Bunyan."

    Microsoft Legendary Americans. 1998 ed.

    Diskette. Ashland: Microsoft, 1998.

74l CD-ROM, diskette, magnetic tape — periodically updated

For periodicals originally from a printed source, list the following if available, and punctuate as in the examples below.

- Author
- Print publication information
- Database title or Computer service name italicized
- CD-ROM, diskette, or magnetic tape
- Vendor name
- Electronic publication date

WORK IN AN ANTHOLOGY

Print model

➤Clemens, Barbara. "First Love." *Absurdity and Other Adolescent Afflictions*. Buffalo: Malcolm Press, 1997. 204-27.

Electronic model

➤Clemens, Barbara. "First Love." *Absurdity and Other Adolescent Afflictions*. Buffalo: Malcolm Press, 1997: 204-207. *Adolescent Psychology Full-Text*, rel. 3, Diskette. Burbank: Metro, 1997.

NEWSPAPER ARTICLE

Print model

➤Benet, Carl. "Vitamin E and the Youth Culture." *Plainville Daily News* 27 Feb. 1997: A 5+.

Electronic model

➤Benet, Carl. "Vitamin E and the Youth Culture." *Plainville Daily News* 27 Feb. 1997: A 5+. *Plainville Daily News Ondisc*. CD-ROM. UMI-ProQuest. May 1997.

Online databases

74m

For periodicals originally from a printed source, list the following if available, and punctuate as in the examples below.

◆ Author
◆ Print publication information
◆ Database title or computer service name italicized

- Online
- Vendor name
- Electronic publication date

NEWSPAPER ARTICLE ACCESSED THROUGH AN ONLINE DATABASE

Print model

➤Benet, Carl. "Vitamin E and the Youth Culture."

  Plainville Daily News 27 Feb. 1997: A 5+.

Electronic model

➤Benet, Carl. "Vitamin E and the Youth Culture."

  Plainville Daily News 27 Feb. 1997: A 5.

  Plainville Daily News Online. Online.

  Nexis. May 1997.

MAGAZINE ARTICLE ACCESSED THROUGH AN ONLINE DATABASE

Print model

➤Bonessi, Bianca. "Teaching Reading to First

  Graders." *Journal of Early Learning* Jan.-Feb.

  1998: 66-68.

Electronic model

➤Bonessi, Bianca. "Teaching Reading to First

  Graders." *Journal of Early Learning* Jan.-Feb.

  1998: 66. Online. GALENET. 20 Ap. 1998.

FOR PERIODICAL MATERIALS WITH NO SPECIFIED PRINTED SOURCE OR ANALOG List the
following if available and relevant:

- Author
- Title of material accessed, in quotation marks
- Date of the material
- Title of database italicized
- Publication medium (e.g., *Prodigy*)

◆ Name of vendor
◆ Electronic publication date

➤Jones, Franklin. "Stocks in Flux." Dec. 1997.

  J.V. Market Reviews Online. Prodigy.

  Dawson, Inc. Dec. 1997.

Sources accessed through Internet — world wide web (www), file transfer protocol (ftp), gopher, telnet, e-mail and other messages   **74n**

Include the following standard electronic information if it is available:

◆ Author, with e-mail address in angle brackets
◆ Title of document or message, period, enclosed in quotation marks
◆ Publication date
◆ Date of access — double-spaced after the publication date
◆ Address — URL in angle brackets, or other electronic path *not* bracketed. In formatting, divide URL *only after a slash*.

ELECTRONIC JOURNALS, NEWLETTERS, CONFERENCES WITH PRINT INFORMATION ON THE WORLD WIDE WEB Cite these as you do similar print references, but *add the electronic information above.*

◆ Author
◆ Title of article or document in quotation marks
◆ Title of journal, newsletter, conference — italicized
◆ Volume number, issue number, etc.
◆ Year or date of publication in parentheses
◆ Number of pages or paragraphs (if available). Add *n. pag.* if material is not paginated
◆ Electronic data (see above)

➤Grove, Josephine. "Reading Readiness in

  Kindergarten." *The Educator's Newsletter* 3.

  47 (15 Jan. 1998): n. pag., pars. 25.

  28 Jan. 2000 <http://www.cea.org>

ELECTRONIC TEXTS WITHOUT PRINT SOURCE INFORMATION

◆ Author
◆ Title in quotation marks
◆ Publication date if available
◆ Pagination if available
◆ Date of access
◆ Electronic address in angle brackets

> ➤Underwood, Anne. "Fabric of Freedom." n.d.: 2.
>
>   13 April 1999 〈http://newsweek.washington-
>
>   post.com...e/05_99a/tnwtoday/ex/ex)1sa_1.htm〉

ELECTRONIC TEXTS ON A FILE TRANSFER PROTOCOL SITE

◆ Author
◆ Title and period in quotation marks followed by the letters *ftp* and a space
◆ Date of access
◆ Complete electronic path (not bracketed)

> ➤James, Robert. "In Search of Daisy Mae."
>
>   12 Oct. 1999 ftp/ unh.newhaven.eduusers/lib

GOPHER OR TELNET SITE REFERENCE WITH PRINT PUBLICATION DATA

◆ Author
◆ Title and period in quotation marks
◆ Standard print publication information
◆ Date of access
◆ URL address in angle brackets, or the word *gopher* and the site and access path
◆ For a telnet site substitute *telnet* for *gopher*, then the path with the usual slashes

> ➤Atkins, Arnold "Freedom's Way." Published in
>
>   *Anthropos* 14 June 2000. 28 June 2000
>
>   gopher/Evanston University/InreKALASinBondage/
>
>   Projects/anthropos

ELECTRONIC MESSAGE SUCH AS AN E-MAIL, NEWSGROUP, LISTSERV

- ◆ Writer's name
- ◆ Date of access
- ◆ E-mail address in angle brackets (not required by *MLA*)
- ◆ Subject in quotation marks
- ◆ Publication date
- ◆ For an e-mail message, write the word *e-mail* or *personal e-mail*, or the name of the recipient
- ◆ For a newsgroup message, list the newsgroup address in angle brackets
- ◆ For a listserv message, include listserv address in angle brackets

➤Wales, Sandler. 23 Dec. 1999 <sandler@att.net>

"Final draft." Personal e-mail.

Electronic interviews   *74o*

List by the last name of the person being interviewed. Name the interviewer. Include the title, if any, and date of the interview. Indicate the medium of the interview. For Internet interviews provide either URL or e-mail address.

➤Bonessi, Bianca. Internet interview with the

author. 23 Dec. 1998.

➤Bonessi, Bianca. Telephone interview with the

author. 23 Dec. 1998.

➤Bonessi, Bianca. Interview with Leslie Steel.

"Teaching Reading." *60 Seconds*. ABC. New

York. 23 Dec. 1998.

Film and videotape   *74p*

- ◆ Title italicized, period
- ◆ Director, period
- ◆ Lead actors, period, and writer, period
- ◆ Company distributing the work, comma
- ◆ Date, period

➤*Hamlet*. Dir. Charles Gould. Perf. Carl Evans,

 Madeleine Horne. TriStar, 1994.

74q   Television and radio programs

- ◆ Name of specific episode, period, enclosed in quotation marks
- ◆ Title of program italicized, period.
- ◆ Writer, narrator, actors, etc.
- ◆ Network, period
- ◆ Local station, comma
- ◆ City, period
- ◆ Date of broadcast, period

➤"American Klezmer." *Jewish Culture in America*.

 Writ. and Narr. Naomi Bloom. Perf. Klezmer

 2000. CBS. Learning Channel, New York.

 18 Sept. 1999.

Glossary

ad baculum (*§40b*) an argument that seeks to persuade by threatening violence.

ad crumenam (*§40d*) an argument that bases action on financial cost.

additive overkill (*§36f*) repetitive, tautological expressions used to introduce further information about a single idea.

ad hominem (*§40a*) an attack against the person instead of against the ideas.

ad verecundiam (*§40c*) argument that seeks to shame people into agreement.

agreement (*§1,§2*)subject and verb, or a pronoun and its antecedent are in the same person and number.

adjective describes nouns and pronouns

analogy (*§46*) a comparison between things that are not obviously similar, in order to reveal unexpected qualities in the subjects.

analogy by translation (*§46b*) converts numbers into common experiential images.

anaphora (*§49b*) repetition of a key word or phrase for rhetorical effect.

antecedent (*§2, §6, §7*) noun or pronoun to which another noun or pronoun refers.

apodosis (*§12f*) the logical effect of a possible action in a sentence.

appositive (*§4h*) noun or pronoun (or phrase) that describes another noun or pronoun that immediately precedes or follows it.

adverb describes verbs, adjectives, and other adverbs.

anon. (*§52c*) anonymous.

anthology (*§73, §74*) a collection of writings — essays, letters, plays, poems, short stories — by one author or by a number of authors.

argument by authority (*§41a*) an argument that assumes that people in authoritative positions are right by virtue of their position.

argument by definition (*§41b*) an argument that uses unsupported definitions as proof.

argument by popularity (*§41c*) an argument that assumes that majority opinions must be correct.

attributing intent (*§45a*) a fallacious restatement of an opinion based not on what the speaker said but on one's assumptions about what he meant.

begging the question (*§43a*) asserting in advance something that is not yet proven.

bibliographic note (*§73e*) footnote or endnote that specifically identifies source texts.

binary thinking (*§45c*) thinking artificially limited to two options as in *either...or* situations.

causal overkill (*§36d*) repetitive, tautological expressions used to show cause.

circa (*§52c*) about, around (used with dates).

circular reasoning (*§20b, §43b*) illogical reasoning that simply rephrases the effect of an action instead of showing its cause; explanations that use in their definitions the very words they are trying to define.

citation (*§68–§74*) a quotation itself, as well as a specific reference to the source of a quotation.

clichés (*§22b*) expressions worn-out and stale from overuse.

collective nouns (*§1b*) group nouns.

colloquialisms (*§22a*) non-standard, informal, imprecise speech specific to particular groups of people or to particular regions of a country.

comma splice (*§53a*) a run-on that results from separating two main clauses by a comma alone and without a conjunction.

comparative overkill (*§36e*) repetitive, tautological expressions used to show comparison.

complement (*§4*) completes the meaning of the subject or verb, e.g., direct object, predicate nominative etc.

concessive subjunctive (*§15f*) a verbal mood used to show yielding of opinion or concession of fact.

conditional overkill (*§36g*) repetitive, tautological expressions used to show the possibility that something will happen.

conditional tense (*§11*) indicates events or conditions that do not exist at the time of the statement but might exist under certain circumstances.

confer (*§52c*) compare.

content note (*§73e*) footnote or endnote that provides additional information about the topic and may or may not include the source reference.

correlative constructions (*§26c*) phrases and clauses that work together in parallel ways within a sentence. They come in pairs and are connected by expressions such as *either...or, both...and* etc.

dangling modifier (*§9c, §9d*) a modifier that describes a word that does not exist in the sentence.

decontextualizing (*§45b*) a false restatement of an idea taken out of context.

dialectical thinking (*§48 faq*) thinking that balances an idea against its opposite and helps define what *is* by contrasting it with what *is not*.

distributive sentence (*§32d*) sentence in which parts of the main idea are distributed throughout.

documentation (*§68–§74*) identification of source materials in research.

e.g. (*§52c*) for example.

either...or (*§45c*) a logical fallacy that artificially limits one's options to one of two possibilities.

emotional fallacies (*§40a–d*) arguments that appeal to the emotions instead of to rational judgment.

endnote (*§65, §73*) superscripted note in the text and the citation to which it refers at the end of the essay, chapter, or book; can be a content note or a bibliographic note.

equivocation (*§44a*) a way of giving a false impression by repeating an expression and using it with a different and disparaging definition.

essential clause (*§7a, §53c*) also called *restrictive*. A subordinate clause important to the meaning of the sentence. Not set aside in commas.

expletive (*§1, §33b*) sometimes called *tag*. A word or phrase empty of grammatical function in a sentence, other than to mark a beginning or an end.

extended metaphor (*§46d*) a comparison made at two or more levels between two essentially unlike phenomena. Here, the object or person actually *becomes* that to which it is compared.

extended simile (*§46c*) a comparison made at two or more levels between two essentially unlike phenomena using such comparative terms as *like, similar to, as* etc.

fallacy (*preface to Rhetorical fallacies*) a deliberately misleading argument, or inadvertent error in reasoning.

false analogy (*§45d*) a false assumption that because two people or events are alike in some ways, they must be alike in all ways.

faq (*Index*) a frequently asked question, signals an explanatory passage at the beginning of many sections of this text.

figurative speech (*§46a*) enriches meaning by providing a verbal image.

footnote (*§65, §73*) superscripted note in the text and the citation to which it refers at the foot of the page; can be a content note or a bibliographic note.

fragment (*§29*) an incomplete sentence.

ftp (*§74j*) file transfer protocol. A standard way to send and receive files on the Internet. An "ftp client program" is needed to transfer files via ftp.

generalization (*§45e*) an overstatement that does not allow for individual exceptions to apparently universal patterns.

gopher (*§74j*) similar to the world wide web, gopher is a hierarchical addressing scheme for resources on the Internet. However, unlike the web, gopher is rooted at the University of Minnesota where it was invented. Although still in use, it has been largely supplanted by the web.

gerund (*§8a*) a verbal that ends in *-ing* and acts like a noun.

grammar (*§1–§18*) the rules that describe and govern language.

heavy language (*§34*) dense, overly complicated style.

homonym a word that has the same sound and usually the same spelling as another word but a different meaning.

homophone (*§50h*) a word that has the same sound as another word but a different meaning.

hyperbole (*§47a*) an ironic exaggeration.

hypothetical argument (*§41d*) uses imagined evidence as proof for actual cases.

ibid. (*§52c*) in the same place.

i.e. (*§52c*) that is.

if...then fallacy (*§42a*) a sometimes fallacious and sometimes valid form of reasoning that limits possible consequences to a single outcome.

imperative mood (*§15*) verb form used for commands and instructions.

implied argument (*§41e*) a fallacious argument that rests on an unexamined foundation.

incidental clause (*§7a, §53c*) also called *non-restrictive*. Subordinate clause not vital to the meaning of the sentence. Set aside in commas.

indicative mood (*§15*) verb form used for objective and factual discourse, is used most frequently in communication.

infinitive (*§10a*) the "to" form of a verb e.g., *to do, to be* etc.

irony (*§47*) a figure of speech in which what is said is different from what is meant. In poetic irony, a harmful or mischievous intent or expectation redounds on the perpetrator.

irrelevancies (*§43c*) true statements that have nothing to do with the question under discussion.

jargon (*§22c*) technical terms specific to each profession and often incomprehensible to outsiders.

jussive subjunctive (*§15b*) expresses wishes and strong suggestions.

litotes (*§47c*) an ironic understatement that combines *not* with a disparaging term to create a positive effect.

linking verb (*§4c*) verb that shows a condition instead of an action, usually a *to be* verb or one that can be replaced by a *to be* verb while retaining the essential meaning of the sentence.

loaded terminology (*§44b*) an emotional fallacy that seeks to persuade listeners by using either name calling, or socially praiseworthy associations.

loose sentence (*§32d*) sentence in which the main idea appears in the beginning, and the remainder of the sentence elaborates on this main idea.

meter (*§69*) rhythmical pattern of stresses typical of poetry.

misplaced modifier (*§9a, Marginal comments*) a modifier that describes the wrong word in the sentence because it is placed incorrectly in the sentence.

mixed metaphor *(§39)* a figure of speech whose parts don't fit together because they refer to contradictory or mutually exclusive frameworks or experiences.

modifier *(§9)* a describing word, phrase, or clause — adjective or adverb.

nominative pronouns *(§4)* pronouns that act as subjects or predicate nominatives.

non-restrictive clause see *incidental clause.*

non sequitur (§42b) an argument whose conclusion does not follow logically from its premise.

non-sexist terminology *(§18e)* gender-neutral nouns and pronouns.

object of a preposition *(§4e)* noun or pronoun that follows a preposition or ends a prepositional phrase.

objective pronouns *(§4d, §4e)* pronouns that act as direct objects, indirect objects, and objects of prepositions.

op. cit. (§52c) in the work cited.

oversimplification *(§45f)* distorts ideas by reinterpreting them in a simplified form.

overstatement *(§45g)* an exaggeration that goes beyond available evidence.

oxymoron *(§37)* a statement or image in which two or more expressions contradict each other, e.g., *a glass anvil.*

paradox *(§48b)* a combination of contradictory propositions both of which are true and point to a truth.

parallel construction *(§26)* keeping related actions or ideas in the same grammatical form.

parenthetical reference *(§65, §72)* in-text citation enclosed in parentheses.

participle *(§8b,§8c,§13)* verbal that acts like an adjective or a verb.

passive construction *(§31)* combination of an inactive subject and a verb that reports indirectly on an action.

perfect tense *(§12a)* indicates an action completed at the time of the statement or at the specific time referred to by the speaker. Uses *time words.* Establishes the completion of one action before the start of another.

periodic sentence (*§32d*) sentence that leads up to the main idea at its end.

phrasal verbs (*§19c*) idiomatic verbs with one or more prepositions attached to the root verb.

phrase group of words without a subject and a verb.

post hoc **fallacy** (*§42c*) an illogical conclusion that because something happened after a fact, it happened because of that fact.

predicate nominative (*§4c, §6b*) a noun or pronoun that follows and completes the meaning of a linking verb.

progressive tense (*§11*) indicates an action or condition continuing over a period of time with no end in sight.

proof by absence (*§41f*) a fallacious argument that assumes the lack of evidence to be a kind of proof.

prose (*§68*) any writing — literature, criticism, history, news, etc. — that is not poetry. Unlike poetry, prose typically does not have rhyme and meter — a rhythmical pattern of stresses.

protasis (*§12f*) the logical cause of an action in a sentence that expresses a contingency.

red herring (*§43d*) a way of diverting attention from a weak argument by sidetracking the discussion.

redundancy (*§36a, §36b*) unnecessary repetition using the same word as different parts of speech to describe one idea.

reflexive pronouns (*§5*) pronouns that end in *-self.*

relative pronouns (*§6, §7, §55e*) *who, whom, whose, which, that, whomever, whoever, whichever.* They take on the person and number of their antecedent.

restrictive clause see *essential clause.*

rhetoric (*preface to Rhetorical figures*) art of finding the most effective way to persuade an audience through speech or writing.

rhetorical argument (*§40–45*) misleading argument.

rhetorical question (*§49b*) a question without a definitive answer that invites the reader into discourse with the writer.

running text reference see *parenthetical reference.*

run-on (*§53a*) two or more complete sentences punctuated as if they were a single sentence.

sic (*§52c,§58a*) thus, so. Indicates that the text has been quoted exactly as written. Points out errors in the quoted text.

simple tense (*§11*) used for habitual and completed actions, and actions being reported as they happen.

situational irony (*§47b*) irony that depends on what people *do* more than on what they *say*.

slang (*§22a*) informal, imprecise, non-standard, transitory expressions specific to particular groups of people.

slippery slope (*§42d*) a logical fallacy that predicts an inevitable chain of consequences from a given act.

split infinitive (*§10a*) an infinitive with a word or phrase between the *to* and the root verb.

squinting modifier see *two-way modifier.*

statistics (*§45h*) numerical interpretations of facts valid if explained in context, but too often misleading because they state only partial truths.

straw man (*§45l*) a fallacious argument that restates an opposing argument in the weakest possible terms so that it can be easily knocked down.

stringy sentence (*§32c*) sentence whose parts are connected by a series of "or's, and's, but's."

subjunctive mood (*§15*) verb form used for hypothetical situations, desires, needs, dreams. Even more uncertain than the conditional.

subordinate clause group of words with a subject and a verb that does *not* express a complete thought.

symmetrical sentence (*§32d*) a sentence in which the main ideas are balanced at the beginning and end.

tautology (*§36d,§36e,§36f,§36g*) unnecessary repetition of an unstated idea rather than of a word — *causal overkill, comparative overkill, additive overkill, conditional overkill.*

telnet (*§74j*) an interface that is text-based. It allows users to log into other computers. Largely supplanted by the web.

time words (*§12e*) *first, second, during, just, never, yet* etc.

two-way modifier (*§9e*) ambiguously placed modifier that could be describing either or two expressions.

understatement (*§47c*) a reverse exaggeration that gives ordinary descriptions of extraordinary qualities.

URL (*§74j*) universal resource locator, a resource address on the web. In citations, it is enclosed in angle brackets (< >).

usage (*§19–§25*) actual way in which words or groups of words are used, sometimes not strictly in accordance with grammatical rules.

verbal a word that looks like a verb but acts like a noun, an adverb, or an adjective.

verb phrase (*§10b*) a main verb and its helpers — *could be, might have known, were given* etc.

verse (*§69*) poetry and song lyrics, often rhymes and typically contains meter.

voice (*§18*) tone of the writer in addressing the reader, choice of narrative person.

viz. (*§52c*) namely.

www (*§74j*) world wide web, is a way of addressing a wide variety of resources on the Internet — text, audio, video etc. Resource addresses are called URLs (universal resource locators).

Index